INDUSTRIAL HYGIENE MANAGEMENT

INDUSTRIAL HYGIENE MANAGEMENT

JACK T. GARRETT
LEWIS J. CRALLEY
LESTER V. CRALLEY
Editors

Contributors

Ralph E. Allan
George H. Andersen
Edward J. Baier
Arthur F. Burk
Howard J. Cohen
Lester V. Cralley
Lewis J. Cralley
Gary N. Crawford
Gerald E. Devitt
Alice C. Farrar

Jack T. Garrett
E. Scott Harter
John L. Henshaw
Joseph L. Holtshouser
Harriotte A. Hurley
Thomas R. Jaeger
Gene X. Kortsha
Michael E. Lichtenstein
Jeremiah R. Lynch
Donald R. McFee

John A. Pendergrass
M. Chain Robbins
James T. Sanderson
Debra H. Schoch
Jennifer C. Silk
Joseph F. Stelluto
James H. Stewart
Neal C. Stout
James K. Sugg

WILEY

A WILEY-INTERSCIENCE PUBLICATION

JOHN WILEY & SONS, New York, Chichester · Brisbane · Toronto · Singapore

Library of Congress Cataloging in Publication Data:

Industrial hygiene management / Jack T. Garrett, Lewis J. Cralley,
  Lester V. Cralley, editors; contributors, Ralph E. Allan . . . [et al.].
  p.   cm.
"A Wiley-Interscience publication."
Includes bibliographies and index.
ISBN 0-471-85128-0
1. Industrial hygiene—Management.   I. Garrett, Jack T.
II. Cralley, Lewis J., 1911–. III. Cralley, Lester V.
HD7261.I47 1988
658.3′82—dc19   87-27032
                                                              CIP

Printed in the United States of America

10 9 8 7 6 5 4

Industrial hygiene is a unique profession that requires an exceptional commitment on the part of the practitioners. Without such commitment no industrial hygienist or industrial hygiene program will ethically survive. Because of this commitment, the organization and management of industrial hygiene programs differ from the management of most other functions within the industrial setting. In a successful program the professional functions of the industrial hygienist and his or her relationship with the workers and their management are fundamentally different than that of line management, regardless of the product or service they are producing.

This book is dedicated to these concerned professional industrial hygienists in the application of their knowledge and experience in the anticipation, recognition, evaluation, and control of health hazards in the workplace.

Contributors

Ralph E. Allan, CIH*, Met-Tox
Associates, Inc., Tustin,
California

George H. Andersen, CIH,
Allied-Signal Inc., Morristown,
New Jersey

**Edward J. Baier, CIH, CSP†,
USDOL/OSHA,** Washington,
D.C.

Arthur F. Burke, E. I. du Pont de
Nemours & Company,
Wilmington, Delaware

Howard J. Cohen, CIH, Olin
Corporation, New Haven,
Connecticut

Lester V. Cralley, Ph.D., CIH,
Fallbrook, California, (formerly,
Aluminum Company of America)

Lewis J. Cralley, Ph.D., CIH,
Cincinnati, Ohio (formerly,
NIOSH)

Gary N. Crawford, CIH, Occusafe
Inc., Wheeling, Illinois

Gerald E. Devitt, CIH, Livonia,
Michigan, (formerly,
Owens-Corning Fiberglas Co.)

Alice C. Farrar, CIH, Clayton
Environmental Consultants, Inc.,
Marrietta, Georgia

Jack T. Garrett, CIH, Kirkwood,
Missouri (formerly, Monsanto
Company)

E. Scott Harter, CIH, Eastman
Kodak Company, Rochester, New
York

John L. Henshaw, CIH,
Monsanto Company, St. Louis,
Missouri

Joseph L. Holtshouser, CIH,
Goodyear Tire and Rubber Co.,
Akron, Ohio

Harriotte A. Hurley, CIH,
CIGNA Loss Control Services,
Inc., Macon, Georgia

Thomas R. Jaeger, CCCA,‡
Eastman Kodak Company,
Rochester, New York

* Certified by the American Board of Industrial Hygiene.
† Certified by the Board of Certified Safety Professionals.
‡ Certificate of Clinical Competence in Audiometry.

Gene X. Kortsha, CIH, GM Technical Center, Warren, Michigan

Michael E. Lichtenstein, CIH, PE, IBM Corporation, San Jose, California

Jeremiah R. Lynch, CIH, Exxon Chemical Company, East Millstone, New Jersey

Donald R. McFee, ScD, CIH, PE,* Occusafe, Inc., Wheeling, Illinois

John A. Pendergrass, CIH, CSP, USDOL/OSHA, Washington, D.C.

M. Chain Robbins, IT Corporation, Torrance, California

James T. Sanderson, CIH, Esso Europe, Inc., London, England

Debra H. Schoch, CIH, Eastman Kodak Company, Rochester, New York

Jennifer C. Silk, USDOL/OSHA, Washington, D.C.

Joseph F. Stelluto, CIH, Holchst Celanese, Somerville, New Jersey

James H. Stewart, CIH, Digital Equipment Corporation, Concord, Massachusetts

Neal C. Stout, CIH, Monsanto Company, St. Louis, Missouri

James K. Sugg, CIH, 3M Company, St. Paul, Minnesota

* Professional Engineer

Foreword

As the profession of industrial hygiene has matured, it has become clear to most of us that we have done the profession a disservice by focusing our attention exclusively on delivering high-quality technical service while neglecting the development of management skills. That we have done this is not surprising given the subjective, sometimes conjectural, nature of management vis-à-vis the scientific nature of industrial hygiene. But we have had to pay a dear price for our neglect—industrial hygienists are too often viewed as being highly skilled in technical matters but not so promising as managers. This is regrettable since most of us, within a few years of entering the profession, find ourselves thrust into a supervisory or managerial position. How well we perform as managers has an effect on the profession in general, not to mention the effect on the quality of our programs and ultimately our own careers. It seems clear that we need help if we are to meet all the challenges of the profession.

The publication of this book represents a milestone in the development of our profession inasmuch as it meets a longstanding need that has been increasingly recognized during the past two decades. As a consequence of that recognition, various elements of the profession have moved swiftly to satisfy the need. Several graduate schools have added management courses to their industrial hygiene curricula. Short courses on management have become standard fare at the American Industrial Hygiene Conference. In 1978 the opening session of that conference was devoted exclusively to the topic of industrial hygiene management. Professional societies, such as ACGIH and AIHA, have established special committees to address program management. In 1982 the American Board of Industrial Hygiene formed a committee to develop a management rubric for the certification examination and to examine the plausibility of a possible certification examination in the management aspect. Management questions will be included in the ABIH certification exams after 1986. In 1982, Ralph Vernon, in a paper to the Joint Conference on Occupational Health, urged industrial hygienists to begin to think of themselves not just as program managers but as potential corporate managers. It is apparent that the need for attention to management has been translated into positive action. That this attention is jusitfied was brought out in the results of a recent poll conducted by ABIH of 200 randomly selected certified industrial hygienists. That poll indicated that certified industrial hygienists are spending 21 percent of their time in management tasks.

Yet, in 1985, when the ABIH Management Committee conducted a literature search for sources from which to draw management questions for the certification exams, a notable text on industrial hygiene management was not found. Moreover, the books that made up the standard body of industrial hygiene literature hardly mentioned the subject. Robert L. Harris, Jr., a member of the ABIH Management Committee, was assigned to contact the Cralley brothers to see if a chapter on management could hurriedly be included in the update of *Patty's Industrial Hygiene and Toxicology,* which was than in preparation under their editorship. Robert spoke with Lewis Cralley by phone and outlined ABIH's need. At once, Lewis recognized both a need and an opportunity. Although the Patty update was already at the printer and could not be revised, he sensed that the professional interest would be great enough to merit an entire book dedicated to the subject. At that point this book was conceived.

Now after much labor, we celebrate its birth. It will not be the last word or the only book on the subject of industrial hygiene management. Nevertheless, it does fulfill a pressing need, and it should be a pathfinder in guiding the profession into a new realm. It will find a welcome space on our bookshelves.

DAVID M. TRAYER

Secretary, American Board of Industrial Hygiene

Preface

In the early study of occupational disease, many health hazards were easily identified due to the high rate of disease and deaths in specific workplaces. Though exposures to specific agents were massive as perceived through sight and other senses, methodologies were not available during this period for quantifying and controlling exposures to suspect toxic agents. Thus, in the very early years of industrial hygiene practice, major attention was given to developing these methodologies for the recognition, evaluation, and control of health hazards in the work environment. The ever-growing experience since this period showed the necessity for backup information through laboratory research and field studies in all aspects of recognition, evaluation, and control if full concept programs were to be developed in assuring a healthful working environment. During the past century this saw industrial hygiene emerge as a science with "prevention" as the major goal.

A tremendous growth has occurred in the profession since the 1950s in the scope and depth of the multidisciplinary professionals needed to carry out these full concept programs as well as backup research. Thus a large number of direct and support programs have come into existence, supported by industry, labor, government, universities, foundations, insurance carriers, and professional associations. To meet specific objectives, these programs became widely divergent in their makeup and in the degree of coordination and management involved.

Experience over the past years has shown that proper organization and management of these direct programs serving industry as well as appropriate participation in support programs are essential to assure they achieve maximal objectives and are as cost effective as the state of the science permits.

In an undertaking of the scope of this book and to keep the book length and time table for preparation manageable, gaps in coverage are inevitable. Also, minor duplication of coverage in some subject areas may occur between chapters, especially when this is needed in the context of specific chapter coverage.

These and other areas of needed change will be addressed in the next book revision.

Chapters 8 and 10 were written by federal government employees and are exempt from copyright.

JACK T. GARRETT
LEWIS J. CRALLEY
LESTER V. CRALLEY

Kirkwood, Missouri
Cincinnati, Ohio
Fallbrook, California
February 1988

Contents

THE AMERICAN ACADEMY OF INDUSTRIAL HYGIENE

CODE OF ETHICS

FOR THE PROFESSIONAL PRACTICE OF INDUSTRIAL HYGIENE

PURPOSE

This code provides standards of ethical conduct to be followed by Industrial Hygienists as they strive for the goals of protecting employees health, improving the work environment, and advancing the quality of the profession. Industrial Hygienists have the responsibility to practice their profession in an objective manner following recognized principles of industrial hygiene, realizing that the lives, health, and welfare of individuals may be dependent upon their professional judgment.

PROFESSIONAL RESPONSIBILITY

1. Maintain the highest level of integrity and professional competence.
2. Be objective in the application of recognized scientific methods and in the interpretation of findings.
3. Promote industrial hygiene as a professional discipline.
4. Disseminate scientific knowledge for the benefit of employees, society, and the profession.
5. Protect confidential information.
6. Avoid circumstances where compromise of professional judgment or conflict of interest may arise.

RESPONSIBILITY TO EMPLOYEES

1. Recognize that the primary responsibility of the Industrial Hygienist is to protect the health of employees.
2. Maintain an objective attitude toward the recognition, evaluation, and control of health hazards regardless of external influences, realizing that the health and welfare of workers and others may depend upon the Industrial Hygienist's professional judgment.
3. Counsel employees regarding health hazards and the necessary precautions to avoid adverse health effects.

RESPONSIBILITY TO EMPLOYERS AND CLIENTS

1. Act responsibly in the application of industrial hygiene principles toward the attainment of healthful working environments.
2. Respect confidences, advise honestly, and report findings and recommendations accurately.
3. Manage and administer professional services to ensure maintenance of accurate records to provide documentation and accountability in support of findings and conclusions.
4. Hold responsibilities to the employer or client subservient to the ultimate responsibility to protect the health of employees.

RESPONSIBILITY TO THE PUBLIC

1. Report factually on industrial hygiene matters of public concern.
2. State professional opinions founded on adequate knowledge and clearly identified as such.

INDUSTRIAL HYGIENE MANAGEMENT

CHAPTER ONE

Introduction

Jack T. Garrett, Lewis J. Cralley, and Lester V. Cralley

In the editors' view industrial hygiene management, or in fact any management of a technical nature, should be broken down into two basic areas: functional management and executive management. A total management program is a meld of these two. This book will point out the difference and what tenents of both must mesh to produce a successful industrial hygiene program.

Functional management is the responsibility of a manager to carry out the professional duties and to respond to the organizational needs within the scope of his or her profession with the aid and advice of usually similar staff professionals.

Executive management, on the other hand, is the responsibility of a manager to conduct business in a sound fiscal and administrative manner with the aid and advice of usually dissimilar staff professionals.

The successful industrial hygiene program has mastered both executive and functional management in the development of a working program for the protection of the workers' short- and long-term health. Often the unsuccessful program is bogged down in the administrative aspects of executive management to the detriment of the workers' health.

The most important single requirement in the development and management of a successful industrial hygiene program is top management support. Without top-level support such a program is not possible. Unfortunately, it often falls to the first, and frequently only, industrial hygienist on a particular company staff to develop this support. Because of the structural location of the industrial hygienist in most companies, the development of support on the part of top management is difficult. Following the old principle that "good works are their own reward" often pays dividends. Top management

1

must see the need for such programs as industrial hygiene before it is willing to fully back their development. Good work on the part of the trail-blazing industrial hygienist will bring this need to the attention of higher and higher management. It is often slow and frustrating, but the need for this support is mandatory for the development of a good industrial hygiene program. Persistance pays off. It is frequently helped by media pressure, the development of new federal and state laws and regulations, and catastrophic incidents. The industrial hygienist must take advantage of any such external influences to advance program goals within the scope of responsible ethics.

A second and extremely important premise to the development of a successful industrial hygiene program is the commitment of the industrial hygiene professional(s). If the industrial hygiene program is a part of a larger occupational health and safety, or broad environmental program, this commitment is better understood. In most other locations within an industrial organization such commitment may be either unpopular, misunderstood, or frowned upon. It is, however, an absolute essential for all industrial hygiene professionals to be committed to the goal of the protection of the health of all workers under their management.

In the early days of occupational medicine, the company physician was often considered part of the labor force by management and a part of the management by labor. This "straddle the fence" pose is still to a certain extent true on the part of management and the industrial hygienist as well. With modern enlightened management, much of this dicotomy has been disspelled, largely through growing social consciousness on the part of industries in general and the development of social responsibility policies and goals by many.

A third foundation block in the development of a successful industrial hygiene program is the necessity to convince management that the production of goods and services and the protection of the health of workers involved are not exclusive goals. This is perhaps the most difficult task for the industrial hygienist, particularly in the lower echelons of production management. It must be understood by any manager in the health and safety field that industrial management, like politics, is populated with short-termers. They are climbing the ladder in the production field, and the successful ones only stay in any specific assignment for a short time. Their perception of how to advance is to produce a good "bottom line." This bottom line is the net profit developed by their process or service after costs are applied against gross profits. Most companies do not apply workman's compensation costs, company health insurance costs, and litigation costs directly against this bottom line. When the industrial hygienist asks, as frequently he or she must, for capital and expense monies to advance the program in protecting the workers' health, the bottom-line concept of production management success is attacked. Unfortunately, some managers are more tempted to see these dollars applied to their successor's bottom line than their own.

Many companies have largely solved this problem by making their intermediate and upper management people meet tough health and safety goals for which they are annually appraised. Lest it seem an exclusively negative issue, the industrial hygienist can and must teach these production managers the advantages of good sound industrial hygiene principles from both the moral and economic point of view. These production managers frequently rise to plant managers, corporate production managers, and corporate executives. It is incumbent upon the industrial hygienist to convince these managers and executives of the need for industrial hygiene programs because their paths will cross again and again in dealing with upper management. If this instillation of young executives with the need for industrial hygiene programs is successful, successors will reap many benefits from an already convinced top management.

The next important issue in the development and retention of a quality industrial hygiene program is the acquisition of qualified subordinates. This is a continuous process in the larger programs and is a far from simple issue. Most of the early people who entered the industrial hygiene field were convertees who were technically trained in another discipline. Today graduates are available from a number of educational institutions offering baccalaureate and graduate degrees in industrial hygiene. There are, unhappily, still a number of industrial managers who feel that a health and safety professional can be made from anyone who has a technical degree. Some even believe that such a person need not be a degree holder and that any good person can fill such a position. Utilizing nondegreed convertees exclusively results in poor industrial practice, and programs under such untrained personnel are invariably shallow and in most cases inadequate. In such programs the trained and committed industrial hygienist in the corporate system must give an incommensurate amount of time to these untrained people, which in essence means that such people are really only technicians who need continuous supervision. Degreed convertees are a different case since they have formal training, usually in one of the science or engineering fields. This latter route for the earlier professionals and many other fine industrial hygienists who came into the field proved effective and established the basis for subsequent growth in the profession. More recently, few such convertees can accept the needed commitment, and in most cases they are continuously seeking employment elsewhere in their own technical field. It is therefore better for a quality industrial hygiene program to seek employees from institutions that train them properly or to seek degreed convertees that have made the needed commitment. Since most industrial hygiene programs are chronically shorthanded and can ill afford laggards on their staffs, it is absolutely necessary to very carefully interview any prospective new employee. Use of the panel interview technique is strongly suggested as well as a careful debriefing of the interview panelists by the industrial hygiene manager before a selection is made. Care in recruiting will pay off in the long run.

Another tenent of a quality industrial hygiene program is the importance of the industrial hygiene analytical program. If one harnesses the field industrial hygienist to the industrial hygiene chemist, a synergism is developed that is rare in any staff function and is particularly rare in the occupational health field where "turf" differences are common. An industrial hygiene quality program is, in fact, a total program that develops the data and ultimately the necessary decisions that can materially affect the workers' health. The committed industrial hygiene chemist is the analytical professional on this team that produces the monitoring results upon which most decisions must ultimately be made. If these professionals are an integral part of the team and report to the industrial hygiene manager, contributions are more timely and concise. When feasible, it may be advantageous to have the industrial hygiene chemist assigned to a specific industrial hygienist and to be responsible for all the needed chemistry functions to lead to successful decisions, which is, of course, the foundation of a quality program. The industrial hygiene chemist in most cases must have pledged laboratory facilities even on a corporate industrial hygiene staff. Such facilities broaden the usefulness of the industrial hygiene team through the development of analytical methods, the developing of monitoring protocols, the development of validation techniques, and the conduct of good laboratory practices. The industrial hygiene chemists' contributions are essential to the production of valid analytical results. The professional, trained in analytical chemistry, that chooses to become an industrial hygiene chemist must also develop the commitment to the health of the workers under the program's jurisdiction. An industrial hygiene program where the analytical function is separately or distantly managed is crippled at the onset. Such an arrangement requires a great deal of "wheel-spinning" or lost motion as the industrial hygiene manager negotiates for analytical services supplied by a different corporate or plant function and managed by a manager who has a vastly different set of priorities. The industrial hygiene manager who has control over the industrial hygiene chemistry function within the industrial organization has a great advantage over those who do not.

In addition to the mainly engineering, chemical, and allied functions of the early industrial hygiene programs covered in this chapter, advanced industrial technology incorporated into industrial production now requires the same input and integration of other specialists, such as physicists, human factors engineering, psychologists, statisticians, toxicologists, physicians, and nurses, serving in the same team style in the anticipation, recognition, evaluation, and control of health hazards in the ever-changing working environment.

This book is a guide to the management of a quality industrial hygiene program. There are many reasons why any such book can only be a guide. Different companies have different management systems or styles. Many executive managers want their people tiered in a specific manner, and health and safety functions are not excused from such requirements regardless of the "poor fit" perceived on the part of health and safety management. The industrial hygiene function reports to different managers in different companies—personnel, labor relations, security, safety, medical, production, research, and maintenance. This book presents the tenents of good industrial hygiene management. It is up to the reader to apply these to a specific management structure in the development of a well-managed industrial hygiene program.

CHAPTER TWO

Ethics

Gene X. Kortsha

1 INTRODUCTION

Several years ago, at an American Industrial Hygiene Conference, I was seated next to a young industrial hygienist. We introduced ourselves, and when she found out that I worked for industry, she addressed me with a look of utmost sincerity tinged with disappointment: "Mr. Kortsha, don't you really think that industrial hygienists should not work for industry?" "Why?" I asked. "As a matter of ethics, of course," she replied.

One can assume that the young lady was not working for industry and, furthermore, that working for industry clearly violated her sense of ethics. Just as clearly, it did not violate mine. In fact, it had not clashed with mine nor had I had any ethical conflict over the years of employment with industry. Here we have two sets of professional ethics, both strongly held, yet both in seeming conflict.

Anyone who has attended Senate confirmation hearings in recent years or has seen them on TV is struck by one or two obvious facts. One, by the discomfort of the nominee as he or she has to look up at the members of the committee towering from the dais. And, two, by the pained look in the eyes of panel members of the Senate minority party as they compare the nominee to the lofty ethical principles they so strongly hold. On the contrary, members of the nominee's party are impressed with the candidate and proudly embrace the same moral values. The picture remains essentially unchanged until—after an election or two—the two parties trade places and confirmation hearings start anew. Except, this time, the roles are reversed, while the posturing remains the same. Again, are we seeing one or two sets of ethics?

As politics has its own rules by which the game is played, maybe the preceding example should not be viewed in isolation. After all, the posturing and maneuvering thus described does not deny a system of ethics; it simply dramatizes, perhaps even exaggerates, the politician's obeisance and respect for such values.

2   HISTORICAL ROOTS

At this point let us focus on some generally accepted ethical values and seek out well-known documents or sources where such values are spelled out.

We may want to begin by addressing the question of when the need for such values must have first arisen. It is likely that when early man started to live and hunt in packs, physical dominance was the prerequisite for leadership and assured all the perks that go with power. As the pack evolved and found within itself the means of satisfying more advanced needs and expectations, talents other than sheer physical strength emerged and were valued. Cunning, intelligence, craftsmanship, the healing arts, religion, and other needs and qualities began to emerge by stages as *Homo sapiens* started the long climb up the ladder of civilization.

In 1935 Carl Becker (1) addressed the problem of human progress by presenting the following timetable to his listeners at a lecture at Stanford University:

> If human progress can be defined at all in objective terms, it must be defined in terms of the increase of man's power. That power has grown directly out of his science and technology: 450,000 years or more in improving his first crude tools; some 50,000 years in acquiring social organization, agriculture, and community life; about 5,000 years since the invention of written records enormously accelerated progress by enabling each generation to pass on to its descendants the fruits of its own achievements and acquisitions; and finally a

mere 350 years of modern science in which the exponential increase of human powers staggers the imagination, and reason itself swoons.

In searching for early documents addressing ethical values, we can follow Becker's timetable and focus on the last 5000 years (2).

King Hammurabi of the first dynasty of Babylon (1792–1750 B.C.) compiled a collection of legal precepts known as the Code of Hammurabi. In it he listed crimes against gods, men, and property and identified proper punishment. The Hammurabi code listed various professions, including physicians, barbers, and builders. In the case of builders, for example, the code required that builders whose constructions collapsed causing the loss of human lives should be put to death. Such an approach was in step with the ethical underpinnings of Hammurabi's code of "an eye for an eye and a tooth for a tooth." No matter how we may feel about such an approach today, it did represent progress inasmuch as it replaced individual revenge with justice administered by the state.

Centuries later, Hippocrates (460–377 B.C.), Greek physician and a prolific writer, formalized what we have come to know as the Hippocratic oath. Because of its importance and the obvious impact it still has on today's healing arts, it bears reproducing the full text:

I swear by Apollo the physician and Aesculapius and health and all-heal and all the gods and goddesses that according to my ability and judgment I will keep this oath and this stipulation—to reckon him who taught me this art equally dear to me as my parents, to share my substance with him and relieve his necessities if required, to look upon his offspring in the same footing as my own brothers and to teach them this art if they shall wish to learn it without fee or stipulation and that by precept, lecture, and every other mode of instruction I will impart a knowledge of the art to my own sons and those of my teachers and to disciples bound by a stipulation and oath according to the law of medicine but to none others. I will follow that system of regimen which, according to my ability and judgment, I consider for the benefit of my patients, and abstain from whatever is deleterious and mischievous. I will give no deadly medicine to anyone if asked nor suggest any such counsel, and in like manner I will not give to a woman a pessary to produce abortion. With purity and with holiness I will pass my life and practice my art. I will not cut persons laboring under the stone but will leave this to be done by men who are practitioners of this work. Into whatever houses I enter, I will go into them for the benefit of the sick and will abstain from every voluntary act of mischief and corruption, and further, from the seduction of females or males, of freemen and slaves. Whatever, in connection with my professional practice, or not in connection with it, I see or hear, in the life of men, which ought not to be spoken of abroad, I will not divulge as reckoning that all such should be kept secret. While I continue to keep this oath unviolated, may it be granted to me to enjoy life and the practice of the art, respected by all men, in all times, but should I trespass and violate this oath, may the reverse be my lot.

What about later documents that have shaped the lives of generations past and will similarly shape those of generations yet to come? What about our Declaration of Independence? What about the Golden Rule?

> We hold these truths to be self-evident, that all men are created equal, that they are endowed by their Creator with certain unalienable Rights, that among these are Life, Liberty and the pursuit of Happiness. That to secure these rights, Governments are instituted among Men, deriving their just powers from the consent of the governed, That whenever any Form of Government becomes destructive of these ends, it is the Right of the People to alter or to abolish it, and to institute new Government, laying its foundation on such principles and organizing its powers in such form, as to them shall seem most likely to effect their Safety and Happiness.

Here is a ringing affirmation of individual and collective rights so sublime that it has defied the challenges of time and of political systems. The values of democracy and of individual and collective freedom are of such vigor and self-renewing strength that even the most blatant dictatorships of our century have felt compelled to pay lip service—if nothing more—to the values expressed in our Declaration of Independence.

In the minds of our Founding Fathers equality, life, liberty, and the pursuit of happiness were strongly held values, intertwined and indivisible. They constituted the ethical substrate of the young nation based on the premise that governments served at the pleasure of the people and that the people retained the sovereign right to give or to withhold political power.

Such ethics were broad and fundamental, fundamental enough to grow with the times and the needs of the young nation. In fact they were so fundamental as to give birth to the Bill of Rights and thus provide room for a broad range of new issues such as the abolition of slavery (1865), the authorization of income taxes (1913), the nationwide suffrage of women (1920), the liquor prohibition amendment (1920), and its repeal (1933). More recently in 1967, triggered by the assassination of President Kennedy, the Ninetieth Congress approved Procedures to be Followed in the Event of the Death or Disability of the President (Article XXV of the Bill of Rights) after 38 of the 50 states had ratified it.

The Bill of Rights and the entire democratic process have been a living testimonial of the evolving needs, the shifting moods, and the tragic realities of our nation. They have inspired many and have been a thorn in the side of the enemies of democracy.

They have also borne witness to the fact that ethical values cannot be separated from a strong sense of justice. Justice is fairness. It is based on uprightness, honor, and integrity. It goes beyond the boundaries of time and geography. Where liberty and equality prevail, justice advances. And vice versa, lack of liberty or equality means the end of justice. We need to remember that justice and legality are not necessarily the same. To wit, what is legal, lawful, may not be ethical or founded on justice. Justice depends on intrinsic values; legality, on the law of the land. Obviously, what is legal in some countries is illegal in others. The persecution of certain ethnic or religious groups is still practiced in some countries while illegal in others. Closer to home, selling liquor was illegal in the United States between 1920 and 1933 but was perfectly legal both before and after those dates. The continuing quest for new laws to promote or protect changing values and objectives bears witness to the difference between justice and legality, with legality often being one or more steps behind justice.

In the Bible, Matthew (7:12) enunciates the Golden Rule: "Treat others the way you would have them treat you: this sums up the law and the prophets" (3).

Some have challenged the validity of this rule by interpreting it in a rather unconventional manner. For example, heeding this rule, a thievish judge would go easy on thieves because, if he were caught, that's what he would want his judge to do unto him. Or, a student deserving a failing grade should receive a good grade instead as he would be willing to grant such a grade to others, irrespective of merit.

Such interpretations miss the moral thrust of the Golden Rule. The Golden Rule must be taken in context with the entire Chapter 7. Matthew begins this chapter by attacking those who judge others harshly while viewing themselves with great leniency. He speaks out against hypocrisy and affirms the mandate to do good to others. Thus, the Golden Rule does anything but justify a lenient but corrupt judge or a student hankering after an underserved good grade.

This concept of caring for the well-being of others has a particular meaning for those laboring in occupational health as it provides a useful yardstick when caught between opposing financial or political interests.

There is one more concept we need to touch on before proceeding to consider the field of ethics in occupational health, namely, the changes that moral values seem to undergo with time. It was not too long ago when women had no political rights, when a double standard was practiced. It was toward the end of the nineteenth century that the children of the needy still had to work at hard labor when they turned five or six years old, even if it caused them to die young. In today's advanced nations women have equal rights and child labor is forbidden by law. Yet, some of these issues are rejected, in part or in their entirety, by other societies and other cultures. Thus, ethical values seem to change with time and location. This further complicates our attempt to identify and agree on moral values acceptable to all—at least in our society in the field of occupational health.

Despite such difficulty, one can attempt to define ethical underpinnings that will lead to a consensus and enable occupational health professionals to function.

3   OCCUPATIONAL HEALTH

First, let us define the term "occupational health" as used in this chapter. I have used this term in a broad sense as encompassing the medical as well as the preventive aspects, thus including occupational medicine and nursing as well as industrial hygiene and its broad scientific components.

By way of a brief historical overview, industrial hygiene and occupational medicine have roots that reach far into history. Pliny the Elder (A.D. 23–79) speaks of slaves using pig's bladders to protect themselves against "vapors" in mines and during melting of ore. Fifteen centuries later, the German mineralogist Georg Bauer (1494–1555), better known by his Latin name of Georgius Agricola, reports widespread lung disease among miners in Silesia. Bernardino Ramazzini (1633–1714), an Italian physician teaching at the University of Padua, associates some diseases with certain trades, thus establishing an early listing of work-related ailments.

While the roots of occupational health may reach into antiquity, its growth as a profession in the United States did not occur till the beginning of this century when the Public Health Service began to focus on work-related diseases. Early on, the American Public Health Association formed a technical committee and began publishing the *Journal of Industrial Hygiene*. In academia, Harvard University established the first curriculum of industrial hygiene in 1922.

Large industries, among them the automotive industry, perceived the need for industrial hygiene services in the thirties. Such early activities led to the founding of the Michigan Industrial Hygiene Society in 1938. Also in 1938, industrial hygienists working for government established the American Conference of Governmental Industrial Hygienists (ACGIH), closely followed by the founding of the American Industrial Hygiene Association (AIHA) in 1939.

4   EARLY LESSONS

Several factors stand out as one examines those early days of occupational health. It was becoming apparent that certain new industrial processes were affecting the health of workers. For example, when the automotive industry switched from wooden car bodies to bodies made of steel, a problem emerged. To mask the joints between body panels, seams were filled with lead solder, and the excess was ground off with power grinders and sanders. As a result, hundreds of automotive workers were hospitalized with lead poisoning. Once the problem was linked to the inhalation of finely divided lead dust, it was promptly corrected. In fact, today's automotive industry has an excellent record of handling lead without causing lead intoxication.

As a rule, and as illustrated by the preceding example, in the early history of industrial hygiene practice, first an undesirable condition had to occur and be recognized before scientists could identify the cause and seek ways to control or eliminate it. This was not a problem of ethics but of the cognitive process itself. Obviously, the greater our knowledge, the better our ability to anticipate and prevent.

As we focus on the history of occupational health in the United States, it is clear that those early efforts laid a solid foundation for what followed. Individuals from a variety of backgrounds—physicians, pharmacists, chemists, chemical engineers, and others—came together, armed with solid technical knowledge and a high level of scientific curiosity. They poured their collective energies into this new field to ensure that factory workers did not pay with their health for greater productivity and progress. This moral tenet of promoting both worker health and industrial progress was their common bond.

The founding fathers of the art and science of industrial hygiene labored unencumbered by a burdensome past and developed innovative thinking. They saw problems that had gone unrecognized by other professions and sought practical solutions, sometimes alone, more often in concert with others. Research groups and industrial hygiene organizations sprang up in several parts of the country. The field of industrial hygiene was on the move; a new profession was born.

5   OCCUPATIONAL HEALTH ETHICS

The ethical underpinnings of such efforts were equally solid. Those laboring in the field brought with them a strong sense of scientific integrity and dedication to the new-born profession. Furthermore, they fully recognized that protecting the health of working men and women was not a problem to be faced by government or industry alone. Instead, it required combining talents and resources to do battle where it would do the most good. They fully understood that tomorrow their knowledge could be found wanting. Nonetheless, they recognized that their knowledge must form a base to build on until replaced by better information. For example, the first permissible limit for exposure to X radiation was set at 3600 roentgen per year only to be cut, step by step, to 5 roentgen per year as better evidence became available. No one challenged the rationale or the ethics of those who had set the initial limit. Likewise, maximum acceptable concentrations, threshold limit values, or whatever the designation for these exposure limits for air contaminants, the concept remained the same: Such values were not necessarily safe for everyone under all circumstances. They might not protect the very old or the very young, the weak or the hypersensitive. They were not absolute limits. Rather, they indicated concentrations to which working men and women could be exposed with relative safety. They were thought to protect most workers against irreversible harm to their health. Such limits represented the best available knowledge despite some shortcomings. Everyone understood this and made good use of such limits in spite of all the caveats involved.

From an ethical point of view, those years represented an era of confidence and trust in the capabilities and integrity of individuals and of the traditional pillars of society, be they government, academia, or industry. Let us consider for a moment the preceding sentence and particularly the words "confidence," "trust," and "integrity." These words were *two-way* concepts. They reflected how individual researchers felt toward themselves and toward others. Such respect and trust had to be earned, for sure, but it was granted on merit, regardless of the other person's employer.

Those years may also have represented a certain self-image characteristic of a successful and optimistic nation. In 1960 *Life* magazine published an issue with a photograph of Pittsburgh on its cover, with tens of stacks belching smoke skyward, and captioned the picture "The Industrial Heart of America." It represented the thinking of a nation proud of its industrial strength and confident of its future. Environmental concerns and self-doubt were still to come.

In retrospect, this cover picture may have marked a turning point, the end of an era.

6   WHAT PRICE PROGRESS?

In 1962, among the heavy din of an industrial society on the march, Rachel Carson was heard like a voice in the wilderness: feeble at first, but with a powerful message. Others followed as they found evidence that nature was not a bottomless sink that could handle any amount of raw waste produced by society. At first a trickle, this evidence swelled into a torrent. Smog was blanketing cities around the world and forests were withering from acid rain. Polluted lakes and rivers could no longer support life. Physicians, epidemiologists, biostatisticians, and many others became concerned and developed new methodologies and ever more sensitive instrumentation to study the effects of chemical and physical stresses on man and the biosphere. Likewise, industrial hygienists and analytical chemists went from measuring contaminants in parts per million to parts per billion and, sometimes, to parts per trillion. For those unfamiliar with such terms, analyzing to one part per million means the ability to find a given marble among one million marbles of different colors. One part in a billion indicates the capability to identify one Canadian penny in $10 million worth of U.S. pennies. Lemonade with one part per trillion lemon juice takes one drop of lemon juice and 500,000 barrels of water. In terms of time, 1 second in 32,000 years is the equivalent of one part per trillion. If we wanted to go back to the first second of these last 32,000 years, we would find ourselves in the year 30,000 B.C.!

Such sophisticated means of investigation literally opened up new horizons. More often than not, the new information appeared alarming. Carbon tetrachloride, for example, had been used extensively in industry, in fire extinguishers, and in many household cleaners. Suddenly, carbon tet, as it was called, was banned by the Food and Drug Administration for household use because of its acute toxic effects and the suspicion that it could cause cancer. And yet, years after carbon tet was banned for home use, a home-maker's magazine recommended that carbon tet be mixed with flour to form a paste to remove stubborn stains. The paste could be rubbed into stains on walls and even on baby cribs. When the paste dried it would come off and so would the stain. And what would happen if the baby ate this paste, people asked? The public became very concerned because it felt it had to stay on top of such news for its own safety.

Another example of a letdown: A diet-conscious nation had switched to beverages containing artificial sweeteners, and now saccharin was being indicted as causing cancer. Canadian scientists reported that saccharin caused cancer in rats and mice, and on that basis the U.S. Food and Drug Administration banned its use in soft drinks and in food products. Others replied that to match the quantities of saccharin fed to rats in Canada people would have to drink 800 cans of pop a day for a lifetime and then, perhaps, one might see an increase in cancer. Furthermore, saccharin was banned in the United States but not in Canada. Whom should one believe?

European physicians, in particular, had given expectant mothers thalido-mide against morning sickness. The results were nothing less than cata-strophic. In the United States tris(2,3-dibromopropyl)phosphate, Tris for short, was identified as an effective flame retardant for children's sleep wear following the tragic death of a youngster who died of burns when the night garment caught fire. A few years later, Tris was being indicted as a supect human carcinogen.

Perhaps worst of all, for years asbestos had been used as a fire retardant in great quantities on ships and in construction. Subsequently, building codes required that it be sprayed on structural beams of schools and public buildings. And now asbestos was being indicted as possibly the worst enemy of all. Because of its carcinogenic potential, it became a veritable nightmare for millions who feared for their health and that of their children, while the asbestos industry found itself mired in court battles threatening its survival.

7 WHAT PRICE INTEGRITY?

The public had trouble sorting and understanding disputes among scientists. Even worse, scientists seemed to cluster according to their self-interests. Scientists whose products were under attack rose to their products' defense, while scientists in the public sector and in academia usually sounded the first alarm. Eventually, the public concluded that scientists knew less than they were given credit for and that some, if not all, fell short of the ethical standards expected of them.

Such voices, by the way, were not limited to the general public. Jaqueline

Feldman, of the prestigious Centre National de la Recherche Scientifique in Paris (4), put it as follows:

> The only guarantee of scientific work of good quality is the deep involvement and devotion of the scientist at work. The handing down of the scientific attitude is possible because of an existing human relationship; that of master and student. This relationship is not given a chance to exist and develop today.
>
> Nowadays a scientist chooses a career. He does not follow a vocation. . . . Showmanship has taken the place of reality. The number of publications is more important than their content. . . . In a sense, science no longer exists. There is only an imperialistic institution of knowledge, based on the scientists ideology.

Pessimistic as this assessment was, it assailed some norms and practices at scientific institutions. It did not deny the existence, nor did it challenge the validity, of ethical standards. It simply deplored their perceived absence.

Even those with an adequate scientific background were often baffled. Information kept pouring in at an ever-increasing pace, testing their ability to fit these new pieces of the puzzle into a meaningful pattern. And so, society stood by in a daze as yesterday's hopes were turning to ashes, as butterflies seemed to revert to caterpillars, as good and bad seemed to trade places without rhyme or reason.

Sometimes individual polluters were identified beyond a reasonable doubt. At other times the picture was less clear. As resentment and anger grew, the population at large began tarring all industry with the same broad brush. Society felt duped by those it had trusted yesteryear. Powerful forces were attacking its very foundations. The war in Vietnam, Watergate, recurring economic recessions, two successive oil crises followed by an oil glut hit in rapid succession. The resulting psychological turmoil seemed to feed on itself. Society became engulfed in a maelstrom of charges and counter-charges as everybody's integrity came under attack. What was happening? What had changed? Where were self-respect and the respect for others that had served us so well for so many years?

8   CHANGING ETHICS

Profound changes were taking place in our society as a large portion of the population began to challenge the wisdom of government, the impartiality of academia, and the integrity of industry. Furthermore, the traditional respect among scientists and scientific organizations gave way to coalitions and alliances. In the heat of battle, each camp fought all others, ceaselessly and without mercy. Respect, trust, integrity were no longer granted to others, not even grudgingly.

Among industrial hygienists, some in government viewed their counterparts in industry as mercenaries who waited to count cadavers before taking action on behalf of those they were supposed to protect. Some of their counterparts in industry retaliated by calling their accusers "checklist Charlies," charging them with ignorance and lack of common sense.

According to these charges, those working in industry lacked ethics, while those in government lacked knowledge. If true, then no industrial hygienist could cross the lines separating government from industry unaided. Take ethics, for example. If ethics were a prerequisite for working with government and lack of ethics if one wished to work for industry, then any industrial hygienist switching from government to industry would have to leave ethics behind, while anyone moving in the opposite direction would need to receive a hefty dose of ethical precepts before starting the new job. Thus, ethics would be something handed out or withdrawn by government, something akin to an ID card to be issued on the first day of work and to be returned on the last. This, of course, is patently absurd. There were plenty of industrial hygienists who moved from government to industry and vice versa without needing either emergency professional training or a preemployment shot of ethics. On either side, mud slinging, even the intellectual kind, said more about the thrower than the intended target.

9 "EARLY FINDINGS," "ZERO RISK"

Additionally, two major developments emerged from all this turmoil and from the ensuing atmosphere of hostility. First, it became increasingly clear that to win in the scientific arena, one had to be first at any cost. All rewards, from monetary awards and contracts to medals and prizes, went to the first individual or research team to go public with new information. The race was on. The literature was being flooded with "initial reports," "early indications," "tentative findings," and the like. And second, one had to cover oneself against future findings as rushing into print increased one's chances of being wrong. Thus, a new philosophy was born. It endorsed "zero exposure" or "zero risk" even though such a concept was long on implication but short on scientific merit. A zero finding did not mean that the substance or the risk in question were not present. It simply meant that they might be there but at a level below our analytical threshold. Tomorrow, with better means of detection, who knows what we might be able to find under those same circumstances. For the time being, the zero-risk concept surrounded the proponent with a golden aura, even if it did little for the worker.

In addition, such hasty information sowed fear among the public and created problems among those charged with translating such findings into action. Was such early information to be given full credence and must the substance be banned at once? Should one look for substitutes and what were their effectiveness and availability? Was it necessary to purge the entire industrial pipeline of the suspected substance immediately or could the existing amounts be used up and replaced gradually? Or, was it safe, for the time being, to do nothing and await further developments? These were not just academic or scientific curiosities. These were real issues affecting real people with real jobs. And the associated ethical dilemmas were just as real.

As was bound to happen, there were times when such early findings could not be confirmed. It became clear that among the torrent of new information, some studies were flawed in design or execution while others presented indeed important information. On what basis, then, were decision makers expected to deal with the emerging issues?

10   COST VERSUS BENEFIT

Things got even more complicated. Beyond the rash of initial findings and the professed desire for zero risk, another consideration arose that allowed neither neglect nor disregard. It was a question of the utmost importance from a practical as well as a moral point of view. The obvious approach to playing it safe, absolutely safe, was to take each new finding at face value and to protect every affected individual to the fullest. Except that, to do so and attack all emerging problems concurrently, one needed unlimited means. Obviously, we were not so blessed. The pace with which information was surfacing clearly strained our ability to react. We lacked laboratories, trained personnel, engineering resources, and funding to do battle on all fronts. Who should decide which studies must be duplicated? Or, in which sequence? Who should target priorities and assign the means? Or should economic considerations be excluded when setting priorities? Right from the beginning, such fundamental considerations put an added strain on our social fabric.

To better visualize such difficulties let us focus on some medical problems where demands exceeded our resources. To quote Steven Rhoads (5):

> In the 1960's when kidney dialysis machines were scarce, a group of hospitals made allocation decisions on the basis of factors such as age, marital status, number of dependents, occupation, past performance, and future potential. . . . Most [hospitals] decided on a first-come, first served basis, although at least one held a lottery.

Which of these approaches was the most ethical? Should beneficiaries of scarce resources be served in the order in which they asked for help, should they be picked at random, or should the most "deserving" be first? And if we chose the last alternative, what selection criteria were acceptable in a democratic society and who was to make the choice?

Next, let us consider cost. In the late seventies, the U.S. Food and Drug Administration (FDA) determined that about 70 deaths per million inhabitants were due annually to diethyl stilbestrol (DES) in cattlefeed. Thus, the

FDA proceeded to ban such use of DES at an annual cost of about $9 billion (6). This is the cost of only one such regulation. If one were to add the many other regulatory costs, the sum total would clearly indicate that the cost of health care is considerable and, whether it is easily identifiable or not, it must be addressed when budget decisions are made—both in government and in industry.

Who should make the decision that funds should go to health care rather than to other competing national needs? Who could tell a bedridden patient suffering in a hospital that funds should go toward better maintaining our national parks or into updating our antiquated railroad system instead of being assigned to medical research or occupational health?

To no one's surprise, the responsibility for such major decisions eventually ended up in the hands of the legislative and executive branches of our government. The government had the technical support, the necessary overview, and the ultimate responsibility to decide how much of our budget should be allocated to the various sectors that, sometimes in concert but mostly in conflict, compete for funding and resources.

Over the years, the governmental machinery of our country has proven rather adept at dealing with complex problems through a decision-making process based on collective input, compromise, and a continuum of checks and balances. Furthermore, the ability of the system to fine tune itself under public scrutiny and pressure has evolved into a rather effective system of government balancing the rights of society with those of its individual citizens. Thus, it was government that found itself called upon to play a bigger role in occupational health.

11 GOVERNMENT AND OCCUPATIONAL HEALTH

Winston Churchill once said that it is easy to choose between good and bad but much more difficult to choose between good and better. At this juncture in our history, government is being called upon to take our society to an ever higher level of industrialization and, in addition, to ensure a work environment free from recognized hazards. It is to do so while maintaining high employment and strong social services. It also needs to improve public education at all levels, foster medical research, rejuvenate our highway and railroad systems, promote good relations with foreign powers, balance the budget, and maintain armed forces capable of protecting us against foreign aggression. Obviously, this is but an incomplete listing of the daily task of our government.

Even within the relatively well-circumscribed field of occupational health and safety, we must consider multiple issues. Some economists, in an attempt to quantify costs and benefits in occupational health and safety, have identified a variety of factors. On the plus side, employment produces both individual and societal benefits. It generates income and fringe benefits for employees and their families, such as life and health insurance. Stockholders who invest in such undertakings deserve a return on their investment, while society benefits from a general strengthening of the economy and the corresponding increase in the gross national product, from the broadened tax base, and from a decrease in welfare costs and other related expenses.

On the cost side, programs to protect and promote occupational health and safety require facilities, funding, and manpower. The facilities and the manpower assigned to these programs will not be available for other projects for the duration, while new funding must be found for other important projects. Furthermore, within the health and safety area, some occupations or working conditions are more hazardous than others. Often, for economic and other needs, the poor and the poorly trained may be forced to accept hazardous jobs at significant risk to themselves and their families. Thus, the argument can be made that certain segments of the population do not have a full and free choice when they accept less desirable jobs. In fact, it has been argued that it behooves the government to step in and protect those who lack a free choice. After all, most people will agree that all workers are entitled to a workplace free from recognized hazards. While employees owe their employer a full day's work for a full day's pay, they must not risk their health or well-being to hold a job.

Among those who share such a belief, there are many who hold that—to be effective and in fairness to all facing occupational hazards—we must weigh costs as well as benefits for the sake of concentrating efforts where they will do the most good. There are many others, however, who believe just as strongly that placing a price on human life is immoral. The latter also believe that any effort—even if it saved but one human life—is worth the cost.

Occupational risk, however, cannot be disposed of that easily. Risk taking is an integral part of life. Besides the daily risks of getting out of bed and crossing a street, some people earn a living as lion tamers, stunt pilots, or construction workers. Others pursue risky hobbies such as hang gliding or deep sea diving. But all such risks are faced voluntarily, at least to some degree, and the benefits accrue to the risk taker.

Those opposed to a cost–benefit approach in safety and health say, however, that in industry it is the workers who risk their health and lives, while the profit goes to the owners and stockholders. Whose risk and whose gain are we comparing? Money spent on making the workplace safe has to come before profits. Such persons are convinced that to wait for industry to make our factories safe of its own volition and at its own expense is akin to daydreaming. Industry, they say, has had enough time to correct things voluntarily. Instead, they urge that strict government regulations be enforced with an iron hand. Time has come, such individuals hold, to hit industry in the pocket book nerve where it is most sensitive.

In line with such reasoning, a massive effort was begun in the late sixties that led to the establishment of numerous governmental agencies, institutes, and other bodies that proceeded to issue regulations, standards for individual chemicals, and other measures intended to protect industrial workers and the public at large. Many such efforts produced good results. A number of hazardous substances were eliminated or brought under stricter control, and worker exposures decreased. In terms of cost, it has been very difficult to come by reliable figures. If one were to guess, actual expenditures lie probably somewhere between the original estimates offered by government and the cost figures projected by the most strenuous opponents of such regulations. Furthermore, it may take several more years before one can determine the actual benefits to society gained through such efforts.

Right or wrong, the resulting approach to the promulgation of health standards was flawed in two respects: (1) It turned out that it took the Occupational Safety and Health Administration (OSHA) several years and $2–8 million to promulgate a single standard. (2) it made it very difficult to update existing standards in light of new information. Furthermore, we still had the fundamental problem of matching expanding occupational health needs with our limited resources. Government had no choice but to establish some system of priorities before assigning resources to one project over another. According to the Office of Management and Budget (OMB): "Without such a comparative, quantitative procedure the government could spend society's resources on efforts that do not reduce risk efficiently" (6).

The values tabulated in Tables 2.1 and 2.2 are taken from this document. In the original, these tables appear as Tables 2 and 3.

Table 2.1. Risks of Various Activities

Activity or Cause[a]	Annual Fatality Risk for Every Million Exposed Individuals
1. Smoking (all causes)	3000
2. Motor vehicle accidents	243
3. Work (all industries)	113
4. Alcohol	50
5. Using unvented space heater[a]	27
6. Working with ethylene oxide[a]	26
7. Swimming	22
8. Servicing single piece wheel rims[a]	14
9. Aflatoxin (corn)	9
10. Football	6
11. Saccharin	5
12. Fuel system in automobiles[a]	5
13. Lightning	0.5
14. DES in cattlefeed[a]	0.3
15. Uranium mill tailings (active sites)[a]	0.002

[a] Indicates that the risk was regulated by the federal government in the last 10 years. For these activities or causes, the risks in the table are estimates of risk prior to federal regulation.

The same source also lists risk–cost trade-offs for selected regulations as well as additional detail (Table 2.2).

Table 2.2. Risk–Cost Trade-offs for Selected Regulations

Regulation	Agency	Year Issued	Cost per Statistical Life Saved ($ Millions)
1. Unvented space heaters	CPSC	1980	0.07
2. Servicing wheel rims	OSHA	1984	0.25
3. Fuel system integrity	NHTSA	1975	0.29
4. Uranium mill tailings (active)	EPA	1983	53.00
5. Ethylene oxide	OSHA	1984	60.00
6. DES ban in cattlefeed	FDA	1979	132.00

Table 3 [2.2] shows that the cost per life saved is over 1,800 times greater for banning the use of DES (a growth stimulant in cattle feed) than for regulating unvented space heaters. (6)

Many occupational health professionals and others actively involved in this field, still consider cost–benefit or cost-effectiveness analyses a shameful, immoral procedure. Others are equally opposed but take a somewhat different tack. Thus, the *Occupational Safety and Health Reporter,* Bureau of National Affairs, carried the following item on page 57 of its June 19, 1986 issue:

A cost-benefit analysis that assigns a monetary value to human life is not an appropriate means for determining the economic feasibility of safety standards developed under the Occupational Safety and Health Act, and should not have been used in the development of proposed revisions to the Occupational Safety and Health Administration's safety standards for concrete and masonry construction, union representatives told the agency at a June 17 hearing.

When Congress passed the act, it determined that the secretary of labor should not perform a cost-benefit analysis in deciding how to achieve the highest degree of occupational safety and health, according to Ruth Ruttenberg, an attorney speaking on behalf of the AFL-CIO Building and Construction Trades Department. . . .

[In] developing the proposal, OSHA assigned a value of $3.5 million to each fatality that would be avoided if the revised rules were adopted. The agency said it was required under Executive Order 12291 to calculate the monetary benefits that a regulation will produce for the public, compared with the cost of compliance by affected industires (*Current Report,* Sept. 19, 1985, p. 325; text, p. 339).

New techniques for performing economic analyses of regulations involving social policy need to be developed, Ruttenberg continued, "It is inappropriate to use conventional cost-benefit analysis" for making decisions involving human lives, she said.

The cost-benefit analysis for the standard has been a controversial issue since 1984 when Rep. David Obey (D-Wis) charged that the Office of Management and Budget wanted to lower the estimate for the value of human life under the proposed standard to $1 million per worker from a higher figure used by OSHA (*Current Report,* Nov. 1, 1984, p. 427).

In a similar vein, Steven Rhoads writes (5):

In 1974, President Nixon urged a reevaluation of the "trade-off" between economic growth and increasing safety, and President Ford later called for an assessment of safety regulations "in terms of cost added and the benefits gained."

Just as the anti-quantifiers always warned, the cost-benefit analysts have tired of valuing dams and are now valuing lives. Their work is not often publicized, but it is affecting government decisions. It is also causing quite a stir. Senator Harrison Williams thought President Nixon's call for trade-offs "unconscionable." A United Steelworkers representative thought it "despicable" when the Council on Wage and Price Stability questioned coke-fume standards costing at least $4.5 million per worker saved.

Can we set priorities without trying to put a dollar value on human life? If we spend money, we need priorities. If we do not spend money, we are saying that the issues were not worth spending money on and again, by our conscious lack of action, we are placing a value on human health and life.

R. C. Schwing of General Motors Research Laboratories (7), has taken the following position:

"Efficiency" [cost-effectiveness] in matters of life and death has often been cast as a symbol of *immorality;* yet . . . , where efficiency is shown to save more lives, it can actually be considered as a criterion for a moral choice; for if information is sufficient to show that within a fixed budget we are actually shortening more lives by implementing an inefficient program, we are confronted with an explicitly immoral situation. The concept that "efficiency" is linked more closely with *morality* than *immorality* is often lost in contemporary debate.

The debate between those who decry the use of economic factors as part of the occupational health regulatory process and their opponents who consider such an inclusion an absolute necessity has not been resolved and may remain in contention for years to come.

In my opinion, we cannot escape the fact that we must find an acceptable scale if we are to rank occupational health problems that await solution. For example, the Environmental Protection Agency concluded in one instance that society is willing to pay between $400,000 and $7 million per statistical life saved (8). Others have stated that a range from $500,000 to $2 million can be used as a yardstick for public policy analysis (9). Obviously, such guidelines may not apply—nor are they followed—in all cases. One has only to look at the values reported in Table 2.2 to see that regulations were promulgated for three of the substances reported, even though their regulatory costs far exceeded these guidelines: uranium mill tailings, $53 million; ethylene oxide, $60 million; and DES ban in cattlefeed, $132 million per life saved.

More recently, John F. Morrall III (10), an economist with OMB, published similar information in an article entitled "A Review of the Record" in the November/December 1986 issue of *Regulation:* "The FDA's proposed ban of the cosmetic coloring Orange 17, for example, would have averted a calculated risk of death of 1 in 10 billion and was projected to save one life in 2,000 years."

In that same article (in Table 4), Morrall also cites figures indicating that the 1967 NHTSA regulation requiring steering column protection was expected to save 1300 lives per year at a cost of $100,000 per life saved. In comparison, the proposed 1985 OSHA standard for formaldehyde would save 0.010 life per year at an anticipated cost of $72 billion per life saved. All costs were calculated in 1984 dollars.

12 CONCLUSIONS

The time has come to draw things together, perhaps to dwell on some earlier points, or introduce new ones as the case may be.

13 PROBLEM SOLVING

Why are we prompt to react to a catastrophe but often do little to prevent one? Let's pause for a moment and recognize some facts. First, there has to be a problem. We just do not apply our minds to solving nonproblems. There has to be a problem that triggers at least curiosity or interest. Isaac Newton could have thought about gravity in many theoretical ways, but it was only after an apple struck him as he was lying under an apple tree that he asked himself why things always fell to the ground instead of flying off in all directions. Eventually, he worked out the theories of gravitation. Or, Leonardo da Vinci, who was fascinated by birds in flight, and who intuitively anticipated that one day man would defy the earth's pull and soar aloft. A few centuries later, other visionaries, undaunted by the experts of the day who held that nothing heavier than air could fly, built machines that had enough power-to-weight ratio to loosen man's shackles and permit powered flight in the atmosphere, to the moon, and beyond.

Developments in the health field proceeded in a similar manner. British scientists during the nineteenth century observed that young chimney sweeps had a high incidence of cancer of the scrotum compared to their contemporaries who were otherwise employed. Thus, these scientists first observed the disease; next, they noted the high incidence and linked it with employment; and, lastly, they sought ways to provent this scourge. Here is another example from the field of medicine. First, there were the deadly smallpox epidemics that swept across Europe for centuries. Next, Edward Jenner, a British physician, observed that few milkmaids contracted smallpox and, of those who did, fewer seemed to die compared to victims among the general population. Furthermore, earlier in his practice he had observed that milkmaids often contracted cowpox, which in many ways behaved like a mild version of smallpox. Then the thought occurred to him. What if one were to inoculate the population at large with cowpox as protection against smallpox? The rest is history. Industrial hygienists should have no problem accepting this gradual progression of knowledge from initial observation to cure or control. After all, "Industrial Hygiene is that science and art devoted to the recognition, evaluation and control of those environmental factors and stresses, arising in or from the work place" (11).

Thus, it is not a matter of ethics if problems generally precede their recognition and solution. More often than not, it is a matter of knowledge, or rather, of lack of knowledge, that delays this evolutionary process. Now that there is more industrial hygiene knowledge to draw from, anticipating problems may be possible. In fact, Ralph Langner, a distinguished industrial hygienist with long years of experience, recently proposed that the definition of industrial hygiene be broadened to include "anticipation." Thus, the new definition would become: "Industrial Hygiene is that science and art devoted to the anticipation, recognition, evaluation and control . . ." The better our ability to anticipate, the sooner prevention.

The time-consuming process for new knowledge to pervade a profession is often ignored. Charges are hurled daily, both in and out of courtrooms, against scientists, governmental agencies, corporations, and other institutions who should have known better sooner and should have . . . and here various claims are made depending on circumstances. There is no question that if the matter is sufficiently grave and if the defendant possessed the necessary knowledge but chose to ignore the threat to life or human health, then seeking recourse in a court of law is appropriate. We must also be realistic and recognize, however, that not all new information has equal merit, that there is a built-in time lag before information matures into knowledge, and that one must use prudence when trying to separate lack of knowledge from malice—particularly in retrospect.

14   IS INDUSTRIAL HYGIENE A PROFESSION?

The time has come to ask: Is industrial hygiene a profession? Much has been said and written about professions and professionalism. According to Webster's *New Universal Unabridged Dictionary,* a profession is "a vocation or occupation requiring advanced training in some liberal art or science, and usually involving mental rather than manual work, as teaching, engineering, writing, etc.; especially, medicine, law, or theology (formerly called the learned professions)." What do such fields and, particularly, medicine, law, and theology have in common? They require that practitioners possess a considerable body of knowledge and that they practice sound judgment on behalf of their client. Moreover, the last three professions in particular deal with weighty matters affecting the physical or spiritual health, the well-being and, at times, the very lives of their clients. One could say then that, the greater the need for knowledge on the part of the practitioner, the graver the nature of problems involved, and the greater the need for trust on the part of the client, the weightier the nature of the profession.

Industrial hygienists, likewise, need a solid and varied scientific background that they must apply with skill on behalf of their clients. They must be able to rise above the fog of professional jargon and make their knowledge available to others. Industrial hygienists must enjoy the confidence and trust of their clients whose life or limb they are called to protect. While privileged information between industrial hygienist and client may be generally less extensive than between, say, physician and patient, industrial hygienists must preserve the confidentiality of such information. By these criteria of educational background, of need for common sense, and of the range of problems falling under its purview, industrial hygiene qualifies as a profession. Like other professions, however, industrial hygiene can also be practiced at the technician's level if one chooses rote over challenge and judgment. Ultimately, how one exercises one's profession is up to the individual practitioner.

15   PREVENTION: AN ETHICAL IMPERATIVE

By definition, physicians treat the sick, lawyers protect the legal rights of their clients, and industrial hygienists and other members of the occupational health team carry the fight against work-related and environmental accidents and illnesses, in and out of the workplace. Industrial hygienists, in particular, are trained to recognize, measure, and control environmental stresses by various techniques. If there is one thing the profession is attuned to, it is prevention. Well-conceived and properly executed, prevention is among the most powerful weapons at the industrial hygienist's disposal. At a minimum, it saves discomfort and aggravation. More likely, it saves human distress and suffering. Properly implemented, prevention earns the respect and support of workers and management and can be cost-effective. In practice, prevention has many faces. It is training against occupational hazards. It is proper posting of work areas and color coding of chemical reaction vessels. It is the mainstay of confined-space entry procedures and the underlying reason for environmental and biological monitoring programs. It permeates industrial hygiene and makes it such an attractive profession. Prevention, as an ethical concept, must occupy a prominent position in the industrial hygienist's professional thinking. It is imperative that industrial hygienists recognize and honor this important precept and do whatever is necessary to promote it for the benefit of those they serve.

It is equally important, though, that industrial hygienists recognize early on that prevention in general is honored more in theory than in practice—in other areas as well as in matters of health. Otherwise, why do so many roofs leak and water faucets drip? Why do so many people avoid seeing a physician or die intestate?

16 SELLING IDEAS

Selling prevention and other valid technical recommendations can be difficult. No one should expect that sound recommendations will always sell on merit alone without proper explanation. Even more importantly, occupational health professionals must never view selling as being beneath their professional dignity. In fact, selling such recommendations deserves the best arguments one can muster. Most people have more problems than money, and there are as many priorities as there are people. Often industrial hygienists outline preventive programs and other recommendations but fail to explain them properly to those who must pay the bill. If rejected, some blame the philistine whose heart beats in sync with the bell on the cash register. Before presenting their recommendations, industrial hygienists should ask themselves: Have they considered the need for, and the full ramifications of, their recommendations? Would they be willing to adopt those corrective actions and pay for them if they were in their client's shoes? Have they offered full documentation and made the strongest possible case to their client? If they can answer those questions in the affirmative, then they have done their best. Even so, they must remember that to make good recommendations is their professional duty but that being able to sell these ideas is ultimately just as important. For, even the best ideas will wither on the vine unless they are bought and implemented.

17 COST–BENEFIT CONSIDERATIONS

One more comment about recommendations aimed at correction or prevention. Any industrial hygienist knows that it is relatively easy to sell recommendations intended to correct an existing violation of an OSHA standard, that it may take more effort to justify preventive or corrective measures when no standard has been violated. Industrial hygienists, however, must remember that the protection of the health and welfare of employees requires more than simple compliance with OSHA standards. To live by standards alone denies the continued quest for improving the workplace based on new information and on the sound application of professional judgment. To do less does an injustice to workers and managers alike. It also violates fundamental principles of the profession.

Industrial hygienists often find it difficult to project and justify anticipated costs. They can take solace in the thought, however, that they are not alone in this struggle. How can one predict with confidence the cost and the impact of new social programs, for example, when it it often well nigh impossible to calculate the benefits of such programs even after they have been in existence for a while? In all such cases, in occupational health and elsewhere, the problem is to find valid scales that weigh the human impact, the good attained, and the pain avoided against the cost in dollars. Some health professionals find it difficult to accept the need for such cost–benefit or cost-effectiveness analyses. And yet, before such programs can be implemented, the basic question is not will they need funding but, rather, how much and why? Failure to answer either or both parts of this question may doom the project from its inception.

18 PRIORITY SETTING

Once occupational health professionals have accepted the concept of weighing funding against expected benefits, they must go on to the task of setting priorities. Industrial hygienists at the policy-making level of OSHA and certain other governmental agencies are called upon to set national or other standards. Sometimes solutions can be so expensive as to endanger the survival of an entire industry. There can be no question that decision making at that level cannot function without ranking such problems or determining the cost to society. It is true that most industrial hygienists do not have to make such decisions. But even in general practice, industrial hygienists must set priorities and rank problems daily. Their decisions may be minor compared to the impact of national standards. Yet, their recommendations may cost a client part or all the profits. Industrial hygienists usually recognize a number of problems at their client's establishment. They must separate the essential from the merely desirable just as OSHA ranks its citations in descending order from willful to *de minimis* and proposes fines ranging from thousands of dollars down to zero. Common sense must prevail at whatever level one practices the profession. Occupational health professionals must not accept, indeed they must firmly reject, the attempts of those who say that cost considerations and hazard ranking have no place in the profession.

To do so is wasteful, at best. And even if wasting resources were the only negative aspect or consequence of such an attitude, it cannot be justified from an ethical point of view when our resources are limited and our needs so great.

19   THE REAL ENEMY

For years, for better or worse, occupational health was deemed management's prerogative. Those who embraced this position justified it in a number of ways. According to them, management had the know-how, the funds, and the responsibility to take care of its workers. In addition, management often felt it could not share the need for, or the findings of, industrial hygiene investigations with the workers for fear of unsettling them. Here is how Frank A. Patty (12), one of the early leaders in the field of industrial hygiene, expressed this concern in 1958:

> It is unpardonable conduct on the part of a surveyor to ask an employee suggestive questions such as: Do you feel all right? Do you get sick often? Does breathing this atmosphere cause you any discomfort or irritation? The psychological effects of such questioning, which is only one step short of suggesting to a workman that he is ill, are obvious and undesirable. To some workmen the mere fact that tests for air-borne toxic materials are being made may indicate that dangerous conditions exist, and careless remarks of the investigator may grow to dire proportions and cause needless alarm among the workers.

In retrospect one might say that such thinking represented a paternalistic attitude that precluded workers from gaining needed insight and information. On the other hand, almost 20 years later, Dr. William G. Fredrick still used to tell his students words to this effect: "If you return to a plant armed with the test results from a previous visit, tell management what it needs to do. Should management ask for the reasons behind the recommendations or for the test results, tell them that you will be glad to discuss those items with someone knowledgeable in the field. Until then, however, all management needs to know is what you tell them." Yet, Dr. Fredrick was another among the founding fathers of our profession in the United States, a distinguished professor and the director of the Detroit Bureau of Industrial Hygiene for many years. It has been my personal privilege to be a long-time member of the General Motors Industrial Hygiene Department that Mr. Patty so ably directed for many years. I feel equally privileged to have studied under Dr. Fredrick at Wayne State University. I view the positions of Patty and Fredrick as a sign of the times. They should not be viewed in a negative sense but as important milestones against which to measure our progress. Lest we misunderstand: We are deeply indebted to both men. They were part of a small group that founded our profession in this country and whose impact reached well beyond our national borders. True, we have progressed beyond those early days. It is equally true, though, that such progress would not have been possible without their personal commitment and their unwavering efforts. Thanks to them, the profession has a solid foundation and an assured future.

Their farsightedness is even more remarkable if one considers that in those early days there was a general lack of awareness and sensitivity toward occupational health. In fact, it was common to give hazard pay if working conditions were substandard. Such practices have practically disappeared in the United States but are still practiced in other countries.

Clearly, times have changed for the better. In progressive enterprises, management has come to recognize that no worker should have to pay with his or her health for holding a job. Progressive labor organizations have acquired health and safety staffs of high caliber. Both management and unions seek advice and counsel from academia and from recognized experts, depending on the organization's need and the expert's fields of expertise. Thus, both management and labor have made significant strides. Both have come to recognize that in occupational health, and particularly in industrial hygiene, what is good for employees is good for management. Here we speak of the true, the best interests of employees in health and safety, not of political pressure points or of short-term expediency. Both sides have come to recognize that in occupational health and safety, the enemy is neither management nor organized labor. The enemy, the common enemy, are injuries and illnesses that hurt and maim. Those are the enemy against whom we must rally. Time has come for both sides to realize that they can do more jointly against such an enemy than in conflict with each other.

20   LESSONS TO BE DRAWN

What lessons can occupational health professionals, and industrial hygienists in particular, draw today?

They must see clearly that their clients are any and all who can benefit from their services. It is their obligation to do their best, to offer solid professional counsel unbent by partisan pressures. They do not serve the workers' best interests by making mountains out of molehills. In so doing they just waste precious resources. Nor do they serve the best interests of management by making molehills out of mountains. If real, the problem will blow up sooner or later—to no one's advantage.

Anyone wanting to see a concise summary of the professional duties of an industrial hygienist toward employees, employers and clients, and toward the public at large should ponder the Code of Ethics formulated by the American Academy of Industrial Hygiene and adopted by both the American Conference of Governmental Industrial Hygienists and the American Industrial Hygiene Association (page xvii).

21 PROFESSIONAL INTEGRITY

The best that occupational health practitioners have to offer is their professional integrity. It can, indeed it must, be offered to those who seek our counsel. But it cannot be for sale. What makes our profession so attractive is that we tell the same story, present the same findings, to management as well as to labor. We do not change the content, most often we use the same words to tell our story. Both workers and management are entitled to a safe and healthful workplace. Both are affected in the same way by health and safety hazards in the environment. Both are entitled to get the most for their hard earned dollar and to see their health at work and their personal and families' future protected. It is the industrial hygienists' good fortune to be called to serve others, to protect their health and to preserve their welfare. As members of the occupational health and safety team, they cooperate closely with other specialties. Beyond that, they serve wherever they can make a contribution, with professional competence, with personal care, and with integrity.

Only through dedicated service can industrial hygienists earn professional respect and thus measure their effectiveness. That will be their moment of truth. For they—and the profession—will grow best when they serve best.

REFERENCES

1. C. Becker, *Progress and Power,* Stanford, CA: Stanford University Press, 1935.
2. *Encyclopedia Americana,* International Edition, Vol. 14, 1985, 218.
3. *The New American Bible,* Cleveland: Collins World Publishers, 1976.
4. J. Feldman, Ethics for Science and Policy, Proceedings of a Nobel Symposium held at Soedergarn, Sweden, 20–25 August 1978.
5. S. E. Rhoads, How Much Should We Spend to Save a Life? *Public Interest* **51,** Spring (1978).
6. Regulatory Program of the United States Government, April 1, 1986–March 31, 1987, Office of Management and Budget, Washington, D.C.
7. R. C. Schwing and W. A. Albers, Societal Risk Assessment—How Safe Is Safe Enough? General Motors Corporation, *Proceedings of an International Symposium held Oct. 8–9,* 1979, New York: Plenum Press, 1980.
8. U.S. Environmental Protection Agency, Guidelines for Performing Regulatory Impact Analysis, December 1963.
9. W. Kip Viscusi, *Risk by Choice: Regulating Health and Safety in the Workplace,* Cambridge, MA: Harvard University Press, 1983, p. 106.
10. J. F. Morrall III, *A Review of the Record, Regulation,* American Enterprise Institute for Public Policy Research, November/December 1986.
11. American Industrial Hygiene Association, Definition of Industrial Hygiene, 1986–1987 Membership Directory, Akron, OH: American Industrial Hygiene Association, 1986, p. 7.
12. F. A. Patty (ed.), *Industrial Hygiene and Toxicology,* Vol. 1, 2nd rev. ed., New York: Interscience, 1958, p. 45.

CHAPTER THREE

General Management Principles

Michael E. Lichtenstein

The management of industrial hygiene and safety programs in industry, government, or academia has many elements in common. It also has some significant differences. The views expressed in this chapter come from my own experiences with the management of industrial hygiene and safety programs in large industrial companies. I have focused on the elements of management that seem to be common regardless of the type of organization and provide some introductory thoughts for subsequent chapters in this book.

1 WHAT IS MANAGEMENT?

1.1 Definitions

man-age 1. To direct or control the use of. **2. a.** To exert control over. **b.** To make submissive to one's authority, discipline or persuasion. **3.** To direct or administer (a business, for example). **4.** To contrive or arrange: managed to wangle a promotion. . . . (1).

Many of the above definitions of the verb "to manage" include connotations of the style of the person who manages. Management textbooks and graduate curricula study the psychological profiles of individuals and how to effectively deal with such styles in the conduct of interpersonal relations. But we do not need to be graduate psychologists in order to be effective managers.

Peter Drucker (2) offers a more pragmatic definition. He says that a manager cannot be defined by style, pay, position, or importance in the organization but rather by one unique function: "The one contribution a manager is uniquely expected to make is to give others vision and ability to perform. It is vision and moral responsibility that, in the last analysis, define the manager."

Simply put, *management* is the accomplishment of predetermined objectives through others. And this accomplishment comes through the leadership ability of the individual who manages.

1.2 Leadership Qualities

What does it take to be a leader in the area of occupational safety and health?

1.2.1 Aptitude and Willingness. The most important factors in being a successful leader relate to personal aptitudes and the willingness to lead. Although technical competence and expertise are important attributes, they will not, by themselves, make a person an effective leader. Anyone having an interest in managing occupational safety and health people and programs should assess his or her own aptitudes and interests. This privately conducted "reality testing" will allow an informed decision about your suitability as a manager.

Larger organizations with formal career development or placement departments can assist in these types of self-appraisal. From their observations of a person in action, a manager or director can often provide a good perspective of one's aptitudes for management. Outside placement or career-counseling services may also be of help. Some self-assessment tools generally available are listed as references (3)–(5).

1.2.2 Technical Competence. Having professional competence in industrial hygiene can help overcome many obstacles in the development, promotion, implementation, and eventual management of occupational safety and health programs. When one's expertise is recognized among those whom you need to influence, the job becomes easier. The need to educate on "basics" will have already been done, and you will be dealing on a peer basis.

Being a technically competent professional, however, does not automatically qualify a person for management. In fact, without the aptitude for leadership, one might find oneself in a very uncomfortable position as a manager.

1.2.3 Commitment: To be an effective leader of one's peers, a person needs to be the spokesperson for occupational health. This commitment must be demonstrable both to the people whose health is being protected and to those whom one chooses to influence. A manager also needs to represent the views of the organization served.

These two commitments need not be in opposition if a manager, and those to whom he reports understand and accept the commitment to the professional code of ethics. Most organization leaders expect occupational safety and health managers to hold organizational responsibilities subservient to "the ultimate responsibility to protect the health of the employees" (6). In fact, most organizations expect the industrial hygiene manager to be a vocal "corporate conscience."

1.2.4 Communication Ability. An important leadership trait is the ability to communicate. As professionals we learn to communicate in the language of industrial hygiene and discuss our business in the shorthand of acronyms (e.g., TLVs, PELs, REMs, dBA). When we communicate with each other, we seem to understand ourselves well enough.

We also need to learn the language of the organization, with its own set of expressions and acronyms. As professionals trying to communicate within our organization, we try to educate those around us to our language to some extent. But as managers who need to communicate on a much broader scale in and out of our organizations, we need to become fluent in the organization's language and style of communicating if we are to be effective. It would be unreasonable to expect everyone else to learn ours. A successful marketing technique is to converse with the customer in the customer's language. As managers, we need to apply the same principle. The art of dealing with contention and escalation is also an important form of communication with which managers need to be comfortable.

1.2.5 Persistence. Another important managerial attribute is persistence. Many technical professionals seem to take the attitude that once a professional recommendation has been presented their job is done. Rarely is this the case in the industrial setting. The problem is not solved until the recommendations are acted upon favorably. This requires diligent tracking of other peoples' progress and escalating issues when progress is not sufficient to resolve the problem.

Closing "open issues" is a key responsibility of management. An industrial hygiene manager must develop the communication skills and problem-tracking tools to "keep other managers honest"—to ensure that others follow through on their commitments to upgrade the safety and health of the workplace.

1.3 Personal Aptitudes

Career placement professionals frequently use self-assessment tools to help people determine potential occupations that match their aptitudes and skills. One such tool is the Self-Directed Search (SDS) (5). The SDS helps to assess activities a person likes to do, competencies one has, occupations of interest, and self-estimates of one's abilities. The assessment looks at the following six categories of traits:

> *Social (S).* People who like to work with people—to inform, enlighten, help, train, develop, or cure them—or are skilled with words.
>
> *Investigative (I).* People who like to observe, learn, investigate, analyze, evaluate, or solve problems.
>
> *Artistic (A).* People who have artistic, innovating, or intuitional abilities and like to work in unstructured situations using their imagination or creativity.
>
> *Enterprising (E).* People who like to work with people—influencing, persuading, leading, or managing for organizational goals or for economic gain.
>
> *Conventional (C).* People who like to work with data, have clerical or numerical ability, can carry things out in detail, and follow through on instructions.
>
> *Realistic (R).* People who have athletic or mechanical ability, prefer to work with objects, machines, tools, plants or animals, or to be outdoors.

People with strong aptitudes in the enterprising (E) and social (S) traits frequently make effective managers and executives. Technical people, such as industrial hygienists, typically have strong aptitudes in the investigative (I), conventional (C), and realistic (R) traits. If a person's aptitudes and skills are strong in the E and S traits, coupled with the I, C, and R traits, and one likes dealing with people and data more than with equipment and other objects, this person probably will do well as a manager of industrial hygiene.

Not every industrial hygienist becomes an effective manager of industrial hygiene. If one's aptitudes, skills, interests, and self-realization lie mostly with sampling and analysis equipment, procedures, data, statistics, design, and the like, this person may have more difficulty with being an effective manager. He or she will need to develop interest and skills in persuading, leading, influencing, and negotiating.

1.4 Management Roles

1.4.1 Line versus Staff Organizations. There is a fundamental question that an industrial hygiene manager must ask of the organization: "Who is responsible for the safety and health of employees?" Most well-managed organizations hold line management accountable.

Line management is typically responsible for directing the conduct of the business of the organization and is responsible for accomplishing agreed-to objectives, reporting variances from plans, developing and implementing corrective actions when needed, and for profit or loss. In forward-thinking companies line management is also held accountable for the safety and health of its employees. If someone is injured or suffers health impairment on the job, line management is responsible for understanding why and developing and implementing appropriate corrective action. Most of these companies recognize the need for having adequately staffed safety and health organizations to develop preventive programs, as well as to provide expertise in dealing with injuries and illnesses.

In most cases the industrial hygiene organization is a staff function. Staff organizations are the supporting elements helping line management run the enterprise. Staff responsibilities typically include advice, counsel, and authoritative opinion on specialized areas; interpreting policies, practices, and regulations; and providing advice on their implementation. Staff organizations play an important role in developing and communicating new knowledge within the organization, providing objective review of methods and procedures, and providing centralized services for different segments of the enterprise. An important staff role, which may seem distasteful to some industrial hygienists, is the independent audit of line management's adherence to plans and commitments.

Although the work of line and staff functions differ, the objectives of the line are the same as those of the staff organizations, that is, to accomplish the business of the enterprise in a safe and healthy manner. Line and staff organizations may have either proactive (preventive) or reactive styles. The style will mirror the style of the parent organization. Staff personnel should not place excessive emphasis on jurisdictional rights but should rely more on the inherent authority that comes from their professional knowledge and competence. A key point to remember is that line managers are responsible for the entire conduct of their organizations. They, therefore, may accept, modify, or reject the advice and counsel received from staff. The staff manager may—and in fact sometimes must—appeal the decision to a higher authority (escalation) and continue doing so until a satisfactory resolution is achieved. (also see chapter 4.)

1.4.2 Levels of Management. Supervisory or first-line managers are closest to the work performed by the organization and have the most influence on the day-to-day work activities. They are frequently motivated by the "crisis of the moment" and have the most demands made on them. They are likely to rely heavily on staff organizations for help and have the tendency to delegate their responsibilities to whoever will take them. In the case of their responsibilities for safety and health, first-line managers may not accept this role willingly, particularly when they don't understand the technical issues. The effective industrial hygiene manager is able to help the first-line manager understand health risks and assist him or her in communicating those risks to employees and higher levels of management. Discussion points that tend to be effective with first- and second-level management relate to employee availability and productivity, for example, time for safety versus time lost. First-level management is likely to respond to safety and health concerns that may affect accomplishing plans that they have committed to their middle managers.

Middle management's primary role is to provide experienced guidance to supervisors or first-level managers and to provide a place for problem solving or resolution. Executive managers look to middle managers to filter out and resolve the less serious matters. The industrial hygiene manager's greatest challenge may be to overcome this natural roadblock to problem escalation. Discussion points that tend to be effective with middle managers relate to bottom-line dollar impact, that is, cost of safety versus cost of carelessness. Middle management is likely to respond to safety and health concerns that may affect accomplishing objectives that executive management expects to be accomplished.

Executive management is responsible to the board of directors, the stockholders, and the public for accomplishing the stated goals of the enterprise, and for the image of the organization. These senior managers are responsible for the bottom-line in all areas of the business. Executives rely heavily on middle managers to raise significant concerns or issues; middle managers, themselves, are expected to resolve the lesser issues. Discussion points that tend to be effective with executives relate to respect for employees as people and to legal exposures. Executive management is likely to respond to safety and health concerns that may affect perceptions of the organization by the stockholders or the public.

1.5 Management Styles

Management styles have been characterized in a number of differing ways by behavioral and organizational scientists. A few examples are briefly discussed. Effective managers usually understand their own style and the styles and methods of operation of those who report to them and those who direct their activity.

1.5.1 Theory X Management. Douglas McGregor coined this descriptive theory, which characterizes one management approach to dealing with people. Theory X assumes that people inherently dislike work and must be driven by management to accomplish everything. It views the average person as wanting to be led, avoiding responsibility, without ambition, and desiring, above all, security. Management, therefore, tends to control and direct every move, uses the carrot-and-stick approach, and resorts to punishment as needed. Theory X could be summed up as "management by control" (7).

1.5.2 Theory Y Management. McGregor's alternative was stated as Theory Y. This theory views people not as passive or resistant to organizational needs but willing to work as naturally as play. Theory Y assumes that people learn to seek responsibility and that real commitment comes from rewards that satisfy a person's sense of self-respect and personal growth. Theory Y could be summed up as "management by objective" (7).

1.5.3 Theory Z Management. Theory Z is sometimes referred to as the Japanese style of management. William Ouchi compares Type A and Type Z management styles in companies. Type A companies tend to have a focus on short-range profitability and use linear planning (see Figure 3.1). Business logic states that "rational decisions" are better than nonrational decisions and that those made using objective facts are better than those using subjective data. The types of decisions usually made can be characterized as "lose–lose" or "win–lose" types as shown in Table 3.1.

Type Z companies, on the other hand, focus on agreed-upon objectives and ways of doing business from a long-term viewpoint and tend to use "accordion planning" (see Figure 3.1). Accordion planning employs multiple input sources and several iterative reviews to attain consensus. Objective data are carefully collected and analyzed, but objective and subjective data are carefully weighed in arriving at a final decision. The types of decisions usually are characterized as "win–win" types as shown in Table 3.1.

Theory Z might be summed up as "participative management by objective" (8). (also see Chapter 4.)

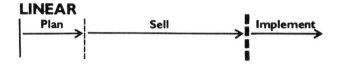

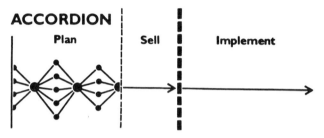

Figure 3.1. Linear versus accordion planning. [Copyright © 1980 by Interaction Associates, Inc. Reprinted with Permission (9).]

Table 3.1. Decision-Making Styles

Lose–Lose	Win–Lose	Win–Win
Stalemate	Majority decision	Negotiation
Protest	Election	Mediation
Strike	Referendum	Facilitation, col-
Riot	Legislative vote	laborative prob-
		lem solving, and
	Individual decision	consensus
	Executive decision	
	Judicial decision	
	Arbitration	

Copyright © 1980 by Interaction Associates, Inc. [reprinted with permission (9)].

2 THE INDUSTRIAL HYGIENIST AS A MANAGER

2.1 Management Aspects of Industrial Hygiene

Management of industrial hygiene work involves much more than supervising the collection of employee exposure samples and making recommendations to management. In subsequent paragraphs we will discuss the three major aspects of effective, preventative industrial hygiene: managing programs, managing people, and managing the "business."

2.1.1 Managing Programs (10)

(a) UNDERSTANDING THE ORGANIZATION'S MANAGEMENT SYSTEM. Successful athletes have a thorough understanding of the rules of their sport, and follow them. The same is true for the successful industrial hygiene manager. We are more likely to be successful when we promote our programs within the rules and context of our organization's system.

Any management system is a complex entity, and no two organizations, companies, or divisions are totally alike. It is important to understand the written and unwritten rules, management styles, and business and technological constraints. Each organization has its own way of doing business: the relaxed, shirt-sleeve approach; the formal, businesslike approach; the customer-is-always-right approach, and so on. Effective industrial hygiene managers understand their own style of operating and the style of those with whom they must deal.

In addition to a thorough understanding of the occupational health risks within an organization, the effective industrial hygiene manager also needs to understand the technology behind the process, current research activities, and technological limitations. When technological constraints are understood, more knowledgeable recommendations can be made, and hence more cooperation can be expected. It is equally important for the manager to understand the business constraints, especially those that may affect the feasibility of a given recommendation.

One of the first things an effective manager of industrial hygiene programs develops is a business awareness. This comes from learning basic management skills and from participating in the mainstream of the organization's activities.

(b) DEFINING THE ORGANIZATION'S INDUSTRIAL HYGIENE NEEDS. Nothing seems to come more naturally to the professional industrial hygienist than defining health risks to workers. If we had the luxury of monitoring every employee and every work operation, we would have a thorough data base upon which to make recommendations to management. But it is neither practical nor desirable to monitor every operation. The demands for activity can never be completely satisfied, and staff organizations (such as the industrial hygiene department) are likely to be under continuing pressure to reduce or contain head count and budget.

When the industrial hygienist becomes the industrial hygiene manager, therefore, he or she must learn how to define what is and is not important to do. Professional judgment must be applied in gathering and sorting information into meaningful segments so that reasonable decisions may be made.

The most important part of defining the organizations's needs is to ensure that there are well thought out programs (not just activities) that deal with major issues.

(c) SETTING PRIORITIES. The organization expects the manager of the industrial hygiene department to provide a rational ranking scheme of issues and recommendations. Logic usually dictates a "worst-first" approach. "Worst" may be expressed in a number of ways: the most severe, the largest number of people exposed, the greatest impact on the operation of the enterprise, the greatest legal risk, and so forth.

The industrial hygiene priority list will most likely be different from other priority lists that senior management is considering. The number one item on the industrial hygiene list will probably be competing with every other department's number one item. The industrial hygiene manager's role is to effectively communicate why industrial hygiene issues merit a high place on the senior manager's issue list, and why he or she should devote time and resources to deal with it. A key part of this process is to define the risks to people and risks to the organization when senior management chooses to disapprove, or only partially implement, recommendations. That is, the decision maker must be given understanding of the full consequences of his or her decision.

(d) COMMUNICATING IN THE ORGANIZATION'S LANGUAGE AND STYLE. Peter Drucker says that managers in the same business enterprise are not automatically driven toward a common goal. Diverse objectives result from such factors as specialization within each managers area of responsibility, the management hierarchy, and differences in vision and priorities [page 61 (2)]. Therefore, many successful companies use the method of management by objective (MBO) to help the organization to focus on a common direction. A number of organizations use participative techniques to arrive at agreed-upon objectives and plans.

The industrial hygiene manager may use MBO techniques to help communicate effectively within the organization. This begins by establishing goals, objectives, and plans for each of the priority issues or programs. Each goal should be based on an understanding of (a) what the current organizational posture is and (b) what the manager's recommended posture is. The following is an example of a department mission statement, goals, objectives, and plans (10):

> *Mission.* A broad description of the organization's purpose or reason for existence.
>
> *Goal.* A broad statement of an end result to be attained in order to satisfy the mission.
>
> *Objective.* A specific, usually measurable element needed to attain a goal.
>
> *Plan.* Individual steps that are specifically assigned to attain an objective by a specific date.

Once goals, objectives, and plans have been established, they need to be sized. That calls for quantifying the resources (people, equipment, and capital) required to implement the goals, objectives, and plans. (See additional discussion in Section 2.1.3.)

Effective managers develop plans with the active participation of those organizations that will be affected by the plans. They first resolve differences of opinion at the lowest level possible. Once agreement is reached at that level, the plans are then reviewed, revised, and approved by succeeding levels of management, beginning with the immediate manager. In this way, consensus can be achieved and given the flavor and style of the organization. If done effectively, by the time plans reach senior management for approval, all necessary lower levels of management will have had a part in and concurred with their development.

The objective of the final presentation to the organization's executive will be to gain approval. This presentation should not be lengthy. It should be a brief synopsis of the major issues, what has been agreed to, and should clearly ask for authorization to implement the plans. [Suggested briefing items are included in Lichtenstein et al. (10).] Some presentations call for executive to sign a policy statement or memorandum that initiates the program or to take some similar action clearly denoting senior management support.

This process is sometimes referred to as "completed staff work."

(e) IMPLEMENTING PROGRAMS IN THE FABRIC OF THE ORGANIZATION. Once programs and plans are approved, the challenge is to have these programs become a normal part of the way the enterprise does business. They need to be "owned" by the organization, not by the industrial hygiene department. If there is a consensus in the development of programs and plans, the industrial hygiene manager becomes a facilitator to ensure the agreed-to steps are taken by those responible. The industrial hygiene manager becomes a technical resource to interpret and answer questions.

If a consensus in the development of plans is not achieved, the task of implementing these programs will become much more difficult. In essence, one must become either a very good salesperson or a "police officer."

(f) MEASURING EFFECTIVENESS AND PROGRESS. In well-managed organizations, senior management establishes measures to judge the effectiveness of important activities. Production quantities and quality performance are the two most common measurements. Every organization has some form of budget performance measurement, as well as limitations on numbers and categories of employees, and employee performance measurements. These measures will apply to the industrial hygiene manager to some extent, who will normally receive training in them.

Effective industrial hygiene managers will also develop a "feedback loop" from which the effectiveness of the industrial hygiene programs may be judged. Examples include Status of Action Plans, Chemical Exposure Statistical Trends, OSHA Injuries and Illnesses, Worker's Compensation Costs, Instrumentation Calibration Records, Proficiency Analytical Testing

(PAT) trends, and Process Hazard Review Summaries [See Lichtenstein et al. (10) for additional examples.]

It is just as important to communicate continuing progress in problem resolution as it is to identify the problem in the first place. An industrial hygiene manager's primary responsibility is to ensure "closure" of open occupational health issues. When issues remain open too long, the manager has an obligation to escalate the unresolved issue to the level of management in the organization capable of resolving it.

(g) UPGRADING EXISTING PROGRAMS. A regular review of program progress will normally highlight areas where improvements are needed. Two questions that a manager should frequently ask are: "Are we doing the right things?," and "Are we doing them right?" It is sometimes useful to employ a technique called "zero-based budgeting" to evaluate the effectiveness of a program that has been in place for some time. According to Drucker [page 355 (2)], zero-based budgeting assumes that each project or activity must rejustify any expenditures (above zero) for each new year, even if the project or activity was justified previously. This technique calls for imagining that the program doesn't exist and assessing what the impact of its absence would be. If significant, it then calls for creating a new program *today* to meet the need.

In assessing what is "right" for today, it is essential that the industrial hygiene manager be in tune not only with industrial hygiene technologies and regulations but also with business technologies and stresses and the social climate.

2.1.2 Managing People. No textbook exists that shows people how to become good "people managers." But if the aptitude and interest are there, many excellent sources of education and training exist that will help. Most large organizations provide some form of management development training for their management teams. There are also many excellent outside firms that provide management development education.

Most effective people managers learn to develop their own strengths in dealing with others.

(a) INTERVIEWING, HIRING, AND STAFF SELECTION (11). The most important investment an industrial hygiene manager will ever make will be in hiring staff members; therefore, the needs, priorities, and strategic directions of the department should be defined beforehand.

The goal, of course, will be to select the best qualified person to meet the department's needs. An objective decision will be made based on the applicant's education, past experience, skills, and personal characteristics. An ideal match will be someone whose personal ambitions, objectives, and attributes closely match the objectives and plans of the organization. The personal interview is the key to effective selection. (Also, see Chapter 19.)

(b) DEFINING RESPONSIBILITIES, SALARIES, AND GRADES. The organization should have an established hierarchy for hiring. If not, the next task will be to determine what payroll classification and salary range will be used for the new position.

Table 3.2 shows the general relationships for the professional industrial hygienist career field (12), from junior to director-level professional. This hierarchy will probably be similar to hierarchies for engineering and other technical disciplines in most organizations. Once a classification system is agreed upon, salaries and grades will normally fall into place, based on how the organization handles those matters. (also, see Chapters 4, 19, 20 and 21.)

(c) APPRAISING PROFESSIONAL'S PERFORMANCE. Once a professional job classification scheme or hierarchy has been established, it is then possible to define expectations for various levels of experience. Table 3.3 provides an example of a responsibility matrix for three levels of industrial hygiene professionals (12). Once professional expectations have been defined, the manager may then measure the industrial hygienist's performance against those expectations using the appropriate criteria established within the organization. (also, see Chapters 4, 19, and 21.)

(d) PROFESSIONAL CAREER DEVELOPMENT. Career development is the process of identifying an individual's unique skills and interests and matching them to the needs of the enterprise (through jobs and assignments) so that both the individual and the organization benefit. Career planning is a shared responsibility of the employee, the organization, and the manager. The employee is responsible for evaluating his or her own interests and aspirations, giving input to management, and making the ultimate career decisions. The organization is responsible for providing an environment for personal growth, training and development opportunities, and information on job availability. The manager acts as a catalyst, counsel, and guide for the employee. A manager should help the employee get needed career information, provide reality testing from time to time, and support the employee's career aspirations wherever possible. For effective career development to occur, all three elements need to be present (12).

According to Burson and Spain, (11) there are differing career development needs as a newly hired industrial hygienist progresses to the expert or director level. New people need to go through a period of orientation and socialization while getting on-the-job training (OJT) from more experienced staff members. A department library of suitable reference material is needed to allow for the self-study that employees need to remain current with the field. Frequently, outside training courses, workshops, or seminars are needed to supplement college education and OJT.

As the industrial hygienist matures in his or her new job, the needs shift toward providing planned experiences and broadening. The employee will begin to make more and more significant contributions to the organization in

Table 3.2. Comparison of Professional Industrial Hygiene Position Relationships

Relative Position	Brief Responsibilities	Titles		
		AIHA	ABIH	Cal-OSHA
Junior professional	Trainee (basic education but no experience)	Industrial Hygienist	(None)	Jr. Industrial Hygienist
Entry–Level professional	Practices IH under direction of more experienced professional (minimal experience)		Certified Industrial Hygienist, in Training	Asst. Industrial Hygienist
Experienced professional	Independent IH practice requiring judgments of moderate difficulty	Professional Industrial Hygienist		Associate Industrial Hygienist
Well-experienced professional	Conducts comprehensive IH practice and makes judgments under general direction; directs others			
Expert professional	Comprehensive IH work requiring independent work and innovation; uses broad judgment and has broad responsibilities; directs broad activities	Industrial Hygiene Director	Certified Industrial Hygienist	Senior Industrial Hygienist (formerly two levels)
Director-level professional	Sets IH policy; exercises broad judgment with broad responsibilities; directs company or major segments of business		(None)	

Reprinted with permission by *American Industrial Hygiene Association Journal* Vol. 44:229–233 (1983).

the process. After the employee has been performing more complex assignments in the organization for a while, improving professional competence, and becoming comfortable with his or her role, the next logical steps will be to prepare for professional certification and to become more involved with professional associations.

Finally, development needs continue for the experienced professional, but in a different way. The expert professional has strong competence in many areas, and additional development may now be found in activities such as publishing, speaking, and teaching (11). (also, see Chapter 15.)

2.1.3 Managing the Business. A key responsibility of an industrial hygiene manager is translating the technical industrial hygiene needs into business terms. Formal education and training will often help in mastering the basics of business management, and many of the larger organizations have internal business education programs that teach the organization's methods in managing the business.

(a) SIZING RESOURCE NEEDS. Once the industrial hygiene needs of the organization are defined and goals, objectives, and implementation plans are established, the next step is to express these needs in understandable terms to higher level management. Lichtenstein et al. (10) include some business estimating ideas for translating objectives into business facts. An example of a business goal and corresponding objectives might be as follows:

> *Goal.* To identify, evaluate, control, and prevent employee exposures to harmful levels of airborne contaminants.
> *Objective 1.* To obtain the required air monitoring pumps, collection media, and calibration equipment within 90 days.
> *Objective 2.* To obtain the required analytical support that meets AIHA/NIOSH criteria for sample analysis in 90 days.
> *Objective 3.* To obtain qualified staffing and to complete industrial hygiene surveys of priority A departments by year's end.
> *Objective 4.* To prepare a report showing the results and recommendations to management in the next 12 months.

From walk-through surveys one can estimate the relative priority of each department, the number of job categories requiring monitoring, and the types of contaminants needing monitoring. A simple work sheet can be devised to tally these data and to estimate quantities of sampling equipment and media, analytical procedures of different types, and the staffing needed to accomplish the objectives. From the detail collected, a summary estimate of broad categories (e.g., sampling equipment, media, calibration equipment, staffing, laboratory services) can be compiled for each level of priority

Table 3.3. Responsibilities by Level of Experience

IH Activity	Entry Level	Levels of Professional Experience	
		Experienced	Well-experienced
Industrial hygiene programs (e.g., ventilation, hearing conservation, radiation safety, etc.)	Recommend goals and objectives Implement action plans Track progress Coordinate program within IH dept. Brief IH manager on status and major problems Coordinate review and approval of outside plans with IH's	Establish program goals for mgr. approval Recommend priorities Coordinate program in/out of IH department Develop and implement action plans Train backup person Sustain quality of established programs	Define specific goals and technical direction for overall site programs Inter-/intra-plant coordination Direct technical effort to broad management guidelines
Health hazard evaluations	Conduct surveys, studies, investigations and tests of the work environment Assist with calibration and analysis Use standard procedures or guidance from higher level IH Evaluate individual survey data and assist with interpretation	Devise survey, study, investigation and test protocols Investigate complaints relating to health hazards Perform or assist with analysis Evaluate own data trends	Devise, plan, conduct and implement studies Prescribe technical criteria and detail Evaluate location trends in data Recommend site priorities

Teaching/training assignments	Assist with course preparation	Assist with course development	Develop and conduct occupational health training
	Conduct basic occupational health training for employees	Conduct education, training and awareness programs on occupational health for employees and management	Assist with development and conduct education programs for IH, medical environment planning, and safety
		Assist with training of IH staff in areas of expertise	

Reprinted with permission by *American Industrial Hygiene Association Journal* Vol. 44:229–233 (1983).

established (i.e., priority A, B, C,). From this data a budget request can be prepared (10).

Other goals and objectives can usually be quantified in a similar way.

(b) BALANCING RESOURCES TO PRIORITIES. Rarely will a budget request be approved without some portions being trimmed. When this happens, the industrial hygiene manager's primary responsibility will be to ensure that responsible management is made aware of the consequences of a budget that is less than fully approved.

For example, assume that the planning and budget called for surveying all priority A departments by year end and all priority B departments by the end of next year, and two additional people would be needed along with a budget of $75,000. If management were to approve only one additional person, and a budget of $50,000, some work would not be done.

The manager would need to decide what changes would have to be made to objectives and planning to accommodate the reduced budget. Once that is done, the manager has an ethical obligation to identify and reevaluate the subsequent risks to employees, the community, and the enterprise resulting from the suboptimal budget, and when justified to escalate that information to the appropriate level of management in the organization.

(c) PRODUCTIVITY TOOLS. All organizations put emphasis on improving productivity and efficiency as a means of cost avoidance or containment. In an industrial hygiene department that might mean many things.

If outside analysis of samples is performed, it might be cost effective to have an internal organization assume this mission or consolidate such a mission with a laboratory already performing similar work (e.g., quality or environmental laboratory). If analyses are done by the staff, costs for large volumes of routine samples might be reduced by installing automated analysis equipment. If there is a long-standing exposure data base, statistical review of such data may show that sampling frequency may be reduced, resulting in cost savings.

Many organizations stymied with a limited staff size or high consultation costs use the services of industrial hygiene college "co-ops" to help with routine tasks. This symbiotic relationship is frequently supported by the organization's personnel or professional recruiting departments.

Quality circles and other facilitated group meeting techniques frequently help to make meetings and work group efforts more productive and meaningful by using the group process to focus on specific topics. The growth of computer hardware and software have helped the industrial hygiene community work more accurately and efficiently in word processing, data management, and data communication.

(d) REGULATORY INSPECTIONS. The industrial hygiene manager is frequently asked to be the contact or focal point for dealings with OSHA, EPA, NIOSH, and other government health agencies, often in an investigatory setting. This activity is usually most effective when a protocol is established prior to the arrival of the official agency at the plant gates. The industrial hygiene manager should work with the organization's safety, medical, and legal organizations to establish an agreed-upon protocol.

A typical protocol would identify who would meet the governmental official, who within the organization would be notified, and what the roles of various people or organizations would be. Many organizations have decided in advance whether they would require a warrant prior to entry, who would chair the opening conference, and what the role of the organizational legal staff would be. Escorting arrangements would be predetermined, and a decision made whether side-by-side monitoring would be performed. Finally, the details of the closing conference would also be defined.

Similar protocols are established in some organizations for proactive review of regulatory or legislative activity related to occupational health issues. (also, see Chapter 10.)

(e) USE OF CONSULTANTS. The manager of an industrial hygiene department may have the occasion to work with outside professional consultants. Consultants are useful in providing specific expertise that may be missing within the organization, as an additional, temporary resource to complete a project or for a second opinion where there may be controversy or disagreement. In all cases, the industrial hygiene manager must be responsible for technical management of the service being provided. This would include drafting, review and approval of the consultant's statement of work, selection of the best consultant, approval of technical protocol in advance of the work, and technical review and approval of the consultant's work product. In some cases, the organization will also ask the industrial hygiene manager to deal with the financial aspects of the consultation contract. (Also, see Chapter 17.)

(f) AUDITS AND PEER REVIEWS. Audits are a common means of testing the integrity of safety programs. Industrial hygienists frequently have an aversion to audits; it is commonly believed that "industrial hygienists do surveys, not audits!" While the industrial hygiene survey focuses on the technical exposure conditions and controls, the industrial hygiene audit examines and verifies that occupational health programs are functioning as designed. An audit can help to build credibility for occupational health programs and bring independent outside opinion to help influence decision makers in their organization.

In large organizations, multidisciplined teams of safety and health professionals are often used. Such audit teams may include a senior safety and health manager, a certified safety professional, a certified industrial hygienist, a fire/life safety expert, a chemical engineer, and a member of line management from the organization. Such team audits should look for positive efforts as well as concerns. (Also, see Chapter 14.) Typical audit goals would be to examine and verify the following (13):

1. To assess the adequacy of location safety and health programs (conceptually).
2. To ensure that those programs are working as intended and not merely on paper.
3. To make creative and constructive recommendations as to how to improve programs.
4. To share program ideas among locations.
5. To strengthen communications between locations and headquarters.
6. To recognize the strengths, as well as the weaknesses, in location safety programs.
7. To provide senior management with an outside assessment of its programs.

In smaller organizations, a simple peer review by fellow professionals or an outside professional consultant might accomplish many of the same goals of audits performed in larger organizations.

2.2 Success: Obstacles and Assets

In 1984, the Northern California Section of the American Industrial Hygiene Association hosted a symposium on Industrial Hygiene and Safety Management. This interactive, 2-day meeting probed key obstacles and assets to achieving success in managing occupational safety and health programs.

2.2.1 Obstacles to Successful Programs. The first question explored was: "What major problems are you facing in implementing your programs?" The six most significant obstacles were:

Management acceptance and support
Poor internal communication
Different attitudes (between management and industrial hygienist).
Time
Understaffing
Keeping up with change

Other obstacles included money, lack of authority to make changes, overlapping responsibilities, lack of public knowledge (of hazards), no one "champion" of the safety and health cause, poor measurability of safety and health, and missing tools or equipment.

The issue of management awareness and support was probed more deeply with this question: "What problems are you having getting management support and awareness?" The following three problem areas were discussed.

(a) COMMUNICATIONS. One of the root problems was related to poor management feedback on safety and health concerns because these matters are difficult to measure and cannot be easily formatted in familiar management terms (such as return on investment). In addition, safety and health people frequently have difficulty communicating in management's "language."

(b) ORGANIZATIONAL REWARD SYSTEMS. Another basic problem arises out of the organizational reward systems. Promotions, bonuses, and other forms of positive recognition in most organizations are given for production, quality, and cost priorities. Rarely are rewards given to management for attaining safety and health goals. Frequently, safety and health efforts are ignored when things are running smoothly, and they have negative consequences when they are not (e.g., disciplining the offender, the manager, or the safety manager).

(c) DIFFERENCES IN STYLE. A final root problem can be found in individual differences between managers and safety and health professionals. Sometimes industrial hygienists are viewed as "super-technicians" with no sensitivity to the organization's mission. Sometimes operating styles are at odds: a Theory Y industrial hygienist may have a fundamental problem in dealing with a Theory X executive; or an industrial hygiene manager who is not able to escalate an issue to senior management may not achieve the desired objectives.

2.2.2 Assets for Successful Programs. Assets were then probed with the following question: "What forces are working in your favor?" The responses fell into three categories. (Some of the assets were also discussed under "obstacles.")

(a) EXTERNAL ASSETS. Historical and current events involving occupational health (such as asbestos workers' mesothelioma, Agent Orange exposures, and the Bhopal tragedy) provide a stimulus to increasing awareness. These events frequently foster public, worker, or union pressure, legislative activities, and potential legal liabilities that are of deep concern to management. Improvements to safety and health educational resources have also improved the quality of research data and industrial hygiene equipment and technology.

(b) INTERNAL ASSETS. Inside the organization, increased awareness of relevant events and basic management integrity foster an open-door policy and willing listeners. Internal history (such as accidents, injuries, litigation, and worker's compensation costs) helps underscore the hard reality of outside events. Other internal activities, such as quality circles and cost-effectiveness programs, may provide allies who also seek to reduce losses and costs to the organization through prevention. The momentum of successful activities and programs is one of the best internal assets.

(c) PERSONAL AND PROFESSIONAL ASSETS. Professional competence and expertise, personal persuasion, and individual concern and commitment to protecting the health of the employee are also very strong assets. They can be further enhanced through professional contacts and associations, sources of advice, and counsel.

2.3 Occupational Safety and Health Leadership

As mentioned at the beginning of this chapter, the manager's main contribution to the enterprise is the vision of objectives and the ability to inspire others to work toward the objectives. An industrial hygiene manager needs to provide leadership both inside and outside of the organization. (Also, see Chapters 11 and 18.)

2.3.1 Leadership inside the Organization

(a) LINE MANAGEMENT. Line management expects the manager of industrial hygiene activities to provide the technical staff resource to understand the legal and moral issues of occupational health, to alert the proper level management of concerns, and, to a large extent, to be the conscience of the organization.

(b) MEDICAL. The medical community looks to the manager of industrial hygiene to be a technical partner in understanding and evaluating the effects of the workplace on employees, to provide intelligence information about workplace risks and controls, and to help effect change in the workplace.

(c) SAFETY AND ENVIRONMENTAL. Safety and environmental professionals also want the industrial hygiene manager to act as a technical partner; although, sometimes they may appear to be in competition or conflict. The industrial hygiene manager must help to define areas of individual and joint responsibility, obtain working agreements, and set the stage for cooperation rather than competition. An effective industrial hygiene manager can become a team leader of joint efforts for the benefit of all.

(d) PERSONNEL. The personnel professional looks to the industrial hygiene manager as an additional resource in dealing with human affairs. The industrial hygiene manager can help with worker job placement issues and provide technical facts to help deal with occupational health concerns. Frequently the competence and reputation of the industrial hygiene organization can be useful in resolving concerns between employees and managers.

(e) DEVELOPMENT, ENGINEERING, AND MANUFACTURING. The professionals who deal with the development, design, and manufacture of products may have mixed expectations of the industrial hygiene manager, depending on the culture of the organization.

In some cases such professionals may view the industrial hygiene organization as an interference to the production of the product. Other professionals may view the industrial hygiene organization as necessary technical resource that will help them develop, engineer, and manufacture the product in a safe and healthful manner.

In the former case the manager of the industrial hygiene organization needs to exert strong leadership in educating these professionals in the benefits of using industrial hygiene expertise as an integral part of the product planning, rather than as a costly afterthought.

2.3.2 Leadership outside the Organization

(a) PROFESSIONAL COMMUNITIES. The manager of industrial hygiene can provide leadership to the profession by assuming leadership roles in professional societies or in industry groups dealing with occupational safety and health. Many organizations recognize the mutual benefit from such a role, especially when the effort being performed can be directly related to an area in which the organization has an interest. The sharing of professional and business experience among peers can be a very important contribution to the body of knowledge of the profession.

(b) ACADEMIA. Academia looks to outside organizations regarding the current state of the art, particularly in the "doing" aspects of industrial hygiene. The industrial hygiene manager can exert leadership by participating in the education process by teaching, sponsoring research projects of mutual benefit, and by hiring college pre-professionals in co-op programs. Some companies encourage the donation of surplus industrial hygiene equipment to universities or conduct in-plant tours to familiarize student industrial hygienists with working occupational health programs.

(c) PUBLIC ARENA. At the public level, the industrial hygiene manager (with the organization's permission) could be a spokesperson on significant occupational health issues of the day for neighborhood or community groups.

(d) REGULATORY AGENCIES. As a technical staff resource, the manager of industrial hygiene (with the organization's permission) could represent the organization's viewpoint at regulatory or legislative hearings pertaining to occupational health issues.

3 THE CHALLENGE OF MANAGING INDUSTRIAL HYGIENE ACTIVITIES

3.1 Personal Change

Many industrial hygienists choose their careers because of personal attraction present in helping others. As they progress from assignment to assignment they have new experiences, find endeavors that enrich their professional stature and personal well-being, and also find activities that they would rather not do. As mentioned earlier, by self-examination they can define a reasonable career plan for themselves. As they gain experience and better self-understanding, their initial goals usually change somewhat, and consequently, their career plans should also change. By understanding the kinds of skills they acquired, they can better plan their direction (12).

3.1.1 Work Content Skills. The education and training industrial hygienists receive early in their careers prepare them for the mechanical chores associated with recognizing, evaluating, and controlling health hazards in the working environment. These might be characterized as work content skills and would be located toward the top portion of a qualifications pyramid (see Table 3.4). These skills change from job to job, and rapid changes cause technology to become outdated quickly. Every time an industrial hygienist moves to a new job he or she needs to learn new work content skills, and these are not always transferable.

3.1.2 Functional Skills. As industrial hygienists learn how to do the job, they acquire process or functional skills, such as writing, organizing, and problem solving. These skills help them apply the work content skills, and they become assets in any job. Functional skills would occupy the middle portion of a qualifications pyramid and increase in importance as a career progresses.

Table 3.4. Types of Skills

Work Content Skills	
Equipment calibration	
Sampling devices	
Analytical equipment	
Statistics	
Ventilation design	
Functional Skills	
Writing	Organizing
Presenting	Persuading
Negotiating	Leading
Listening	Problem solving
Adaptive/Self-Management Skills	
Initiative	Diplomacy
Risk taking	Optimism
Reliability	Enthusiasm
Persistence	Decisiveness

Reprinted with permission by *American Industrial Hygiene Association Journal* Vol. 44:229–233 (1983).

3.1.3 Adaptive/Self-Management Skills. Adaptive and self-management skills would form the broad base of the pyramid and would include initiative, persistence, and diplomacy. These are operational skills that never become outdated and mature as one moves from job to job. If these skills are considered static, they might be characterized as "personality traits." Dynamically, they are the manner in which one deals with life's challenges.

3.1.4 Developing Our Skills. Personal change over time is natural. As one progresses through a career, work content skills decline in importance and functional and adaptive skills increase in importance. By understanding which past activities have been positive experiences and which have not, one can define the kind of activities that are most suitable. If management is the area of pursuit, one can then focus on developing the functional and adaptive skills needed to become an effective manager.

Table 3.5 characterizes the changing demands on industrial hygienists as they mature from starting professional to competent professional to senior manager (14).

3.2 The Changing Profession

During the early years of the profession, the industrial hygienist acted as a one-person consultant, frequently learning as an apprentice of sorts. Effectiveness relied heavily on personal expertise, the "art" of air sampling and ventilation design, and personal integrity and persuasiveness. Growth of the profession was relatively slow, and formal education was available in only a few universities.

With the enactment of the Occupational Safety and Health Act in 1970, the profession grew rapidly, educational resources expanded, and a new breed of industrial hygienist was engendered. There was growth in science and engineering for the professional practice of industrial hygiene, and in its regulatory aspects. The practice expanded both in size and complexity. Today the industrial hygienist is no longer a one-person consultant; now large industrial hygiene organizations exist in industry, academia, government, and professional consulting.

Growth of the profession coupled with a changing society requires industrial hygienists to expand their horizons into nontraditional areas. Several important areas are changing, and the reader is encouraged to explore some additional thoughts on change (15).

3.3 Improving Health and Safety for People

Why become an industrial hygienist? Mostly because industrial hygienists care about people and want to identify and control the health risks people encounter in their occupations. One very important way to improve the health and safety of people is to operate through the management system of

Table 3.5. Industrial Hygienists' Responsibilities with Professional Growth

Responsibilities	ABIH Examination Topics (by importance)*		Typical Senior Manager (%)
	Core (%)	Comprehensive Practice (%)	
Recognizer of health stressors	30	24	10
Anticipate health stressors in plants and operations	7	6	5
Identify potential workplace health stressors	9	6	—
Recognize existing exposures to health stressors	8	6	5
Set priorities by recording/organizing/analyzing data	6	5	
Evaluator of health stressors	42	24	10
Develop data collection plan	10	6	—
Obtain samples/make observations of environmental factors	13	6	—
Analyze biological and environmental specimens	8	4	—
Analyze/interpret results of observations	11	8	10
Controller of health stressors	28	31	20
Educate people about health and environmental stressors	4	4	5
Prescribe appropriate personal protective equipment (PPE)	5	5	—
Design and/or prescribe engineering controls	4	5	—
Design and/or prescribe administrative measures	4	4	—
Communicate recommendations to appropriate people	4	5	5
Verify efficiency of control measures	4	4	5
Develop written rules, standards, and procedures	3	4	5
Manager	0	21	60
Develop a policy for top management	—	7	5
Determine objectives and resources needed to meet policy goals	—	7	20
Plan, implement, and evaluate the industrial hygiene program	—	7	35

* Adapted from Ref. (14).

organizations to provide technical leadership and facilitate change for the better.

Management is not for everyone. But if one cares about people, enjoys a leadership role, and can give others vision and ability to work toward a safe and healthful working environment, then one may choose to seek opportunities as an industrial hygiene manager. The remainder of this book will provide more details on how to attain this goal.

REFERENCES

1. *The American Heritage Dictionary*, Second College Edition, Boston: Houghton Mifflin, 1982, p. 761.

2. P. F. Drucker, *People and Performance: The Best of Peter Drucker on Management*, New York: Harper & Row, 1977, p. 59.

3. R. N. Bolles, *What Color Is Your Parachute?—A Practical Manual for Job-Hunters and Career-Changers*, Berkeley, CA: Ten Speed Press, 1985.

4. D. B. Miller, *Personal Vitality Workbook: A Personal Inventory and Planning Guide*, Menlo Park, CA: Addison-Wesley, 1977.

5. J. L. Holland, *Self-Directed Search—A Guide to Educational and Vocational Planning*, Palo Alto, CA: Consulting Psychologists Press, 1985.

6. American Academy of Industrial Hygiene, Code of Ethics for the Professional Practice of Industrial Hygiene, *Roster of Diplomates of the American Board of Industrial Hygiene and Members of the American Academy of Industrial Hygiene*, American Board of Industrial Hygiene, Akron, OH, 1984, pp. 12–13.

7. D. M. McGregor, The Human Side of Enterprise, *The Management Review*, pp. 22–28; 88–92, November, 1957.

8. W. G. Ouchi, *Theory Z—How American Business Can Meet the Japanese Challenge*, New York: Avon Books, 1982, Chapter 4.

9. Interaction Associates Inc.: *Manage Your Meetings—The Interaction Method*, San Francisco: Interaction Associates Inc., 1980, pp. III-28, IV-3.

10. M. E. Lichtenstein, T. G. Buchanan, and J. C. Nohrden, Developing and Managing an Industrial Hygiene Program, *Am. Ind. Hyg. Assoc. J.* **44**(4) 256–262 (1983).

11. J. L. Burson and W. H. Spain, Safety and Health Management: Professional Development of the Staff, *Prof. Safety* **30**(8): 21–24 (1985).

12. C. A. Bardsley, M. E. Lichtenstein, and V. A. Nusbaum, Industrial Hygiene Career Planning, *Am. Ind. Hyg. Assoc, J.* **44**(3) 229–233 (1983).

13. T. H. Henderson, An Auditing System for Health and Safety, *Prof. Safety* **26**(5): 23–27 (1981).

14. V. E. Rose, G. M. Wilkening, and G. A. Rosen, The Practice of Industrial Hygiene: Role Delineation Analysis, American Board of Industrial Hygiene, *Am. Ind. Hyg. Assoc. J.* **46**(10) A-8–A-10 (1985).

15. M. E. Lichtenstein, Guest Editorial: "Megatrends" and the Occupational Safety and Health Professional, *Am. Ind. Hyg. Assoc. J.* **45**(11) A-17–A-18 (1984).

CHAPTER FOUR

Management Style/System

Joseph F. Stelluto

1 INTRODUCTION

How successful an industrial hygiene program is often depends on the management character or style of the organization. The infrastructure, the cultural mores, the way strategic plans are developed and introduced up the management ladder all influence the successful outcome of any program and are often dependent on the style of the organization.

What is the style of the organization and how does one fit in it? John T. Malloy in *Dress for Success* (1) says, "ideas are often presented in an unacceptable manner and therefore are cast aside for serious considerations." What did Malloy mean by "unacceptable?" A worthwhile project if properly researched and documented should be accepted on its own merit. Why should then a presentation make it unacceptable?

Obviously, in the management way of doing things, there is a proper and improper way: what can be said and not said; how the facts are presented and discussed. This implies a certain style or a certain way of presenting and accepting ideas in an organization. Without the critical knowledge of the organization style, the industrial hygiene professional can run into numerous obstacles to the successful development and implementation of occupational health programs.

To complicate matters further, the different management styles found in today's organizations are also present with the different management systems that drive and steer the organization. The systems have been described by the type of human behavior model practiced (e.g., Theory X, Theory Y) and by the performance measurement model employed (e.g., MBO, MBR). Organization style and system must also be discussed with the life cycle of the organization to acquire a full appreciation of the type of organizational matrix within which the industrial hygienist often works.

The following discussion describes the various organization's systems and styles with a brief comment on the life cycle of business organizations.

2 TYPES OF SYSTEMS/STYLES

2.1 Human Behavior Models

2.1.1 Sensitivity Training. The sensitivity training style is determined by the belief that management's effectiveness is dependent on good interpersonal relationships. As a result, large efforts are expended in training the organization to relate more effectively. This is accomplished with small group sessions whose object is to confront and handle conflicts in a positive relationship.

2.1.2 The Managerial Grid. Blake and Mouton (2) feel that the most effective management style is that of an integrated team operation. Best described as the "managerial grid," the concept implies that management can be measured according to two variables—a concern for people and a concern for production and that the best management is team management. This model can be useful in assessing the behavior preference of the organization's management style.

2.1.3 Situational Leadership. The situational leadership model is described by the relative effectiveness of task-motivated and relationship-motivated leaders in several leadership situations encountered in the organization. The concept suggests that different leaders or styles are necessary according to the needs, development, and maturity levels of the groups encountered.

2.1.4 Management by Exception. In its simplest form the proponents of the management by exception style suggest that management is a technique of identification and communication. It signals the manager when his attention is needed and to remain silent when his attention is not required. The primary objective of this style is to focus on big problems and to avoid those that should be handled by subordinates.

2.1.5 Theory X, Theory Y. McGregor (3) of the Massachusetts Institute of Technology first expounded the theory that management styles vary according to the assumptions made about people. In his Theory X McGregor stated that people are inherently lazy and must be pushed and led to achieve the goals of the organization. In contrast, Theory Y suggests that work is inherently pleasant and satisfying for most people and, given the opportunity to participate in objective setting, employees will perform without needed supervision.

Experience has shown, however, that management cannot be described in such confining theories. In the most part management practices a set of styles that are adapted to the situation, and, if needed, the style may be a combination of Theory X and Theory Y. (For additional information on this subject see Chapter 3.)

2.2 Performance Measurement Styles

2.2.1 Management by Objectives. In its simplicity management by objectives (MBO) is a job performance and achievement style guided by the results to be obtained. It can apply to an entire organization's performance or to an individual. Employees from line management up set objectives for themselves in response to their immediate supervisor's statements of results that the company expects for a satisfactory performance of the job. Both supervisor and subordinate agree on the means to achieve the specified results, and at the end of the measurement period results are compared against objectives. Although MBO has been a difficult system to implement in a number of organizations, it is superior to the previous methods of goal setting and performance measurement. The industrial hygienist will most likely encounter one form or another of MBO in most organizations.

2.2.2 Management by Results. The management by results style focuses on what individuals accomplish as measured against expected results. This style presumes to foster maximum delegation, prevents excessive supervision, motivates subordinates to accept increased responsibilities, and allows time for the supervision of more important matters. Management by results has not enjoyed wide acclaim as intended, for the following reasons:

(a) Subordinates who are measured solely on results may engage in behavior destructive to the organization; the end does not justify the means.
(b) Emphasis on results encourages excessive competition for limited resources.
(c) Looking at results does not help focus on the causes of the problems that lead to poor performance.
(d) Watching for results reduces the advance warning for taking corrective action. Once results are in it's too late to do something about it.
(e) Many staff positions, such as safety and industrial hygiene, are difficult to measure in terms of results.

2.2.3 Management through Quality. Another management style is to piggy-back on a proven method for focusing the organization to achieve outstanding results and expected goals. Crosby (4) proved this and described his approach in *Quality Is Free*. He outlined 14 steps to achieving outstanding commitment, productivity from employees through involvement, and proven tools for problem solving.

Celanese Corporation adopted this approach and made it the "battle cry" to achieving gains in productivity, quality products, and reduced costs. It internalized the concepts so well that Celanese produced its own quality goals and named them "Ten out of Ten." All management levels in Celanese would use the quality program as a vehicle for conducting varied management activities. Anything worth doing well was worth doing through the use of quality principles to achieve it.

An important key ingredient with the quality process is to identify the causes of the problems that lead to poor or undesired results and use team work groups to find solutions to the problems. The amount of participation by all employees has led to a certain style of doing things in Celanese. The industrial hygienist who recognized the importance of the quality process to Celanese quickly interweaved the elements of industrial hygiene into activities that management understands. Given this interaction, support and results are made possible by the existence of a viable management system and style in the organization.

3 QUANTIFYING PERFORMANCE

As we have seen earlier there are several ways that management quantifies individual performance and departmental performance. Many of these methods quantify performance against a predetermined set of objectives. But individual performance, although excellent, may not relate the specific goals of the industrial hygiene function to the long-term objectives of the firm. The reason is the reluctance of hygiene professionals to using criteria and measure of performance consistent with those used by the organization to measure success and failures.

Any benefits achieved by an industrial hygiene program must be stated in terms that allow direct comparison with the competing desires and needs of other business units within the organization.

Some measures of performance successfully used are:

1. Performance standard method
2. Management by objectives
3. Care control
4. Auditing

Let's discuss each one separately.

Performance Standard Method. Mutually agreed-upon standards are set by management, and the individual is held accountable for achieving the desired results, which are compared with a set of standards. Performance can be measured in simple terms: acceptable or not acceptable. However, a more elaborate ranking is often used. For example:

1. Excellent performance
2. Very good performance
3. Good
4. Needs improvement
5. Unacceptable performance

Although these standards are usually applied to the individual, they can also be extended to evaluating the performance of an industrial hygiene program.

A program can be evaluated by assessing activities and resources used to attain objectives when measured against established criteria. The degree of accomplishment of the stated functions may define the success and future viability of the program. Toca (5) described a method for evaluating performance by measuring the extent to which goals have been attained as a result of program activities performed through the expenditure of program resources. The effectiveness of any program, therefore, is the extent to which the program is accomplishing its preestablished objective as a result of fulfillment of the goals.

Management by Objectives. This method is essentially the same as the performance standard method. It is also results oriented with the main difference that MBO requires both quantitative and qualitative measurement and that objectives be set for each level of the organization and be closely interrelated.

The important feature of MBO for the industrial hygienist is that objectives must include those that can be measured (e.g., number of samples taken, amount of equipment purchased, exposures reduced) and those that can only be judged (training programs, diseases prevented, risks averted, etc.). MBO has allowed the industrial hygienist to prepare measurable objectives, to measure quantitatively contributions to his or her organization, to receive proper recognition, and to be viewed as a contributing member of the profit-making team.

The most important advantage of MBO is that it forces the organization to plan for results and not just activities. For the industrial hygienist, MBO helps set objectives that are realistic, but most of all it helps to consider the way in which the desired results will be accomplished. As we all know, the resources that the industrial hygienist needs are often controlled and managed by other departments. MBO serves as a communicating tool to alert those departments whose resources the industrial hygienist needs that their commitment is required to achieve the desired results.

MBO also helps to clarify the roles among the departments competing for resources and elicits commitment for performance. With all its advocates MBO is still unpopular and difficult to use. Some of the reasons for this are due to the weaknesses found with MBO in practice:

1. Learning MBO is still difficult. There are numerous steps that must be mastered by the entire organization before it can work.
2. Goal setters are not given guidelines for setting meaningful goals and objectives.
3. Goals are often not tied to the goals and needs of other interdependent units.
4. Failure to include verifiable objectives often leads to an exercise in wellwishing.
5. The use of inapplicable standards such as those applied to health and safety (unquantifiable and unpredictable) can lead to the ineffective application of MBO.

With all its limitations and unsure success, MBO can be a useful tool for the industrial hygienist who is willing to learn its fundamental techniques. The argument has been made that staff functions like industrial hygiene cannot fit in the MBO world. Not true. MBO can be applied to the staff function if we keep in mind several differences that exist between objectives for the line manager and the staffer. First, the number and length of staff objectives are greater than line management because it is much easier to translate expected results for the line manager in terms of quantitative numbers. Second, staff objectives are often project oriented and deal with a narrower, specific action. Third, staff is usually responsible not only to immediate supervision but also to the people they serve. Objectives, therefore, must be sold and communicated so that concurrence is obtained from immediate supervision and fellow managers. Fourth, staffers do not have the formal authority often accorded to line managers. Therefore, staff has to secure confirmation of its accountability and authority to accomplish its goals.

MBO can and does fit in thinking about managing industrial hygiene issues that are often thought of as unpredictable and unquantifiable. Industrial hygiene problems are often the result of an inefficient and unproductive process and management system. When any of these systems break down, a potential hazard can exist to the employee or the community. Since the process is supposedly managed by a system of objectives, then it can be implied that the same system of objectives can be developed to reduce the risk of an inefficient process that may lead to unnecessary exposures.

Care Control. This concept is built on the premise that employees really believe that their superiors are sincerely interested in them and their welfare. Recently espoused by Blanchard (6), *The One Minute Manager,* supervisors are required to administer routinely positive "strokes" to their subordinates. The frequency and quality of the strokes are measured for each supervisor through the use of attitude surveys of employees. This practice has resulted in improved safety and health and substantial reductions in accidents and costs.

Audits. We have seen how management plans its activities through a setting of objectives, but these plans are only of value insofar as the data on which they are based are reliable. An audit is one way of verifying that the data are based on unbiased information rather than subjective opinion. It is also a useful tool for management checking itself on its performance toward set goals and objectives. Audits are a systematic analysis of objective evidence and present facts rather than value judgments. They also correct, as a result, any preconceived ideas about the status of a company's management system, policies, methods, procedures, and feedback system.

Since there are many layers in a company's communication ladder, an audit report can bypass directly the usual distortion and filtering inherent in any management hierarchy. Audits provide an undistorted picture of company operations and of the effectiveness of these operations within the organization. Audits, however, are often viewed negatively. Most managers view the audits as vehicles of senior management to point fingers at the operations' failures. But if audits are conducted in a positive environment (with management support, team involvement, adequate training, and communication), they can serve as useful feedback on the performance of an operating unit. Any feedback the audit provides can help improve performance, infuse new ideas in the organization, and rally the organization toward a sense of excellence. (see Chapter 14 for more information on this subject.)

4   LIFE CYCLE OF THE ORGANIZATION

Organizations, like people, are born, grow, mature, decline, and ultimately pass on. Few last unchanged for a long time. Business managers can do little to modify these stages, and industrial hygienists may find themselves at the wrong place trying to effect changes in the occupational environment. Knowing the stage of the organization life cycle can assist the hygienist in planning activities to achieve the most desired and effective outcomes. For example, it would be difficult for an organization planning a major product line to accept costly engineering modifications and improvements from the industrial hygiene staff when the product life cycle is short.

The time taken by the life cycle of the organization varies according to the products introduced and market conditions. As the product cycle shortens, planning becomes more important to a successful outcome. The industrial hygienist should time the recommendations for improvements as early in the cycle as possible. Poor timing in this case would hinder an otherwise successful industrial hygiene program. In addition to improving the timing of allocating resources, knowing the life cycle of the organization can also reveal valuable background data about the organization's style.

The style practiced by the organization during specific stages of its life cycle depends on several independent factors:

(a) Its primary objectives
(b) Leader type
(c) Organizational character
(d) Energy focus
(e) Type of planning
(f) Management mode
(g) Organizational model

For example, during the growing years of an organization, the leader is considered an innovator; the character of the organization is struggling and trying to achieve; the planning style is usually catch-as-catch-can; the management is typically one person; and the organization model is set up to maximize profits.

The life cycle of the organization is, therefore, an important tool for the hygienist in planning activities and timing the allocation of resources and impact.

5   WORKING WITH THE SYSTEM

By now it can be seen that the industrial hygienist would be more likely to be successful when working and promoting programs within the rules and context of the management system.

This is easier said than done. The management system is complex, with its unwritten rules, management style, and constraints. But there are certain basic techniques that can help the industrial hygienist navigate through the system. This next section outlines some useful techniques and concepts.

5.1 Getting to Participation

Working within the management system is a key factor in the success of any industrial hygiene program. However, participation in the management system is also one of the most frequent stumbling blocks encountered. This is partly due to the hygienist's lack of management skills and insensitivity of the organization to health issues. In addition, the various goal-setting approaches described generate so much paperwork that they discourage participation. Despite this, the industrial hygienist must learn the management system and performance measurement system and adapt program goals and objectives in this accepted format. Lichtenstein outlined this approach in his example of goal setting (7):

> *Goal.* To identify, evaluate, control, and prevent employee exposures to harmful levels of airborne contaminants.
>
> *Objective 1.* Obtain required air monitoring pumps, collection media, and calibration equipment in the next 90 days.
>
> *Objective 2.* Obtain required analytical support, which meets AIHA/NIOSH criteria for sample analysis in the next 90 days.

These goals and objectives must not be developed without soliciting information and advice from staff and management teams impacted by the industrial hygiene programs. Once the goals and objectives have been outlined, they should be converted to the language that management understands—staffing, budgets, cost control, and return on investment.

5.2 Using Management Language

What line management wants the most from health professionals is proof that the investment made in any health-related activity provides an investment payoff that is both measurable and real. No one likes to spend money without getting some tangible return even if it is for worthy causes. The management game is about the successful use of money, human resources, and economic goods. Production managers minimize their costs per unit by investing in new equipment; the marketing manager invests in advertising with the hope of increasing sales and reducing the per unit cost sold; the safety professional invests in protective equipment and engineering control to reduce both the frequency of personal injuries and the cost of insurance premiums. Professional managers, therefore, spend a good part of their time making investment decisions and proving to management that the results are within the investment risks. Industrial hygienists must do the same to succeed in their organization.

There are three basic concepts that underline much of the management language: (1) cost–benefit analysis, (2) expected value, and (3) present value.

5.2.1 Cost–Benefit Analysis. The underlining basis for this concept is founded on common sense: "Do not do anything unless it is worth doing. It is worth doing if the benefits outweigh the costs." Although not all activities in a profit-making organization can be thought of in this fashion, in general, most activities attempted by the enterprise have passed the cost–benefit analysis. To illustrate this using the example of deciding on noise reduction, the following estimates of yearly cost savings and assumptions can be made:

1. Reduction in energy costs, such as eliminating steam and air leaks.
2. Reducing production downtime as the result of improved maintenance.
3. Increase in production resulting from automation.
4. Increased production resulting from improved work environment.
5. Reduction in insurance premiums resulting from improved risk rating.

Larry Birkner, manager of industrial hygiene for Atlantic Richfield Corp. (8), has successfully used the cost–benefit approach in selling his management on considering alternative control strategies for reducing or eliminating workplace exposures.

An important assumption underlining the use of all cost–benefit analysis is that only factors that can be measured in money are included in the analysis. This assumption places a burden on health professionals in their attempts to convert emotional and aesthetic considerations to dollars and cents. If nonmonetary considerations, such as human life and pain, have a clear value in dollars upon which everyone can agree, then these considerations can be used in the analysis: For example, pain avoided and lives saved become benefit, and costs are those measures used to prevent pain and save lives.

5.2.2 Expected Value. This concept is inherent in any decision management has to make about the future. When projections are made about future sales, managers consider a range of economic conditions such as prosperity, mild recession, and severe depression. Based on this range several probabilities are assigned. The results are a range of expected values given several possible outcomes in the economy. The same approach can be taken in estimating the benefits of any industrial hygiene program by using management language of expected value. This recognizes that each possible future outcome cannot be taken at face value but must be discounted for the probability that it will occur. So used, the expected value concept buys the industrial hygienist considerable credibility with management.

5.2.3 Present Value. Money has time value for management because a dollar invested today can earn more money tomorrow. And a dollar received today is worth more than a dollar received at some future date because of its implicit cost. The higher the rate of interest a company can earn on its funds, the greater the difference between the present and future values of money. For example, at a interest rate of 20 percent, the value of a $1 now becomes $1.20 after one year; conversely, the present value of $1 to be received one year from now, discounted at 20 percent, is approximately 83.3 cents. At 12 percent the discounted value for $1 is 89.3 cents.

Decisions about allocating resources to industrial hygiene are in principle no different than any other activity or asset in which a company decides to invest its resources. All costs and benefits must be reduced to present values to make valid comparisons of present and future costs and benefits. Therefore a company should adopt, from among mutually exclusive strategies, the one that offers the highest ratio of benefits to cost when these values are both reduced to expected present values. In summary: (a) value the problem—state in dollar amounts what it costs the organization now; (b) value the solution—state in dollar terms what the solution/program could save the organization; and (c) value the result—state in dollar terms what the solution actually saved the organization.

The industrial hygiene professional who understands how capital is obtained and why it carries an implicit cost should be able to translate technical concepts to the common language required for management approval. Doing so will compile an enviable record of successfully accepted and implemented programs.

5.3 Introducing Change

Much of the industrial hygienist's success depends on the ability to introduce programs that when successfully implemented lead to removal of hazards from the workplace and the eventual well-being of its employees. This requires extensive skills in negotiating, selling, public speaking, and behavior modification commonly used by change agents.

Change agents are individuals who directly or indirectly affect the change process through direct or indirect interventions in groups or organizations. Their jobs are to develop the climate for planned changes by overcoming resistance and enlisting the necessary resources for positive growth.

The industrial hygienist's primary role is to intervene in the organization with established principles of hazard recognition, evaluation, and control. When applied to the work environment these principles will undoubtedly result in significant organizational changes. The natural process of changing can be made more efficient if not more palatable if the industrial hygienist keeps these basic rules in mind (9):

(a) Seek change when people who are going to have to do the changing are distressed and feel they have a problem. It is easy to convince someone to adopt a solution to a problem if the solution is specific and alleviates the unwanted condition. The difficulty for the industrial hygienist is that many of the work related hazards are not readily recognized as immediate problems to be alleviated or removed. However difficult it might be for the industrial hygienist, his/her role as a change agent and ensuring success will rely on abilities to convert difficult concepts and unrecognized problems into language and realities that management and employees understand.

(b) Get consensus on what kinds of data and what method of collection and assessment the group will accept as valid for evolving a solution to its problem. Enlisting the organization to develop study designs, to isolate problems and to develop measurement criteria helps to remove some of the resistance inherent in most groups when they are asked to change old attitudes and behaviors. The group will then be prepared to change because they will have had a chance to participate in the study and solution to the problem.

(c) Make feedback a critical element; it becomes the catalyst for the people who will have to do the changing, emphasizing the discrepancy between what they believe to be the situation and what is the real truth.

(d) Help people to cope with the change. This is accomplished through training, skills transfer and providing consultations as needed. The trick here is to be omnipresent and readily available to assure smooth transitions.

(e) Repeat the process. First efforts may not always be successful. Many unforeseen problems come up which require new approaches. The change cycle can be repeated as often as necessary to achieve the desired and lasting results.

5.4 Effective Management Style

The misconception that industrial hygienists as staff employees cannot be evaluated in the same way that line managers using measurable objectives can no longer be permitted to exist. Any program that has an impact on the organization can and should be measured in quantifiable terms. This approach characterizes the many styles of management today. Industrial hygiene, if it is to be viewed as an integral part of the organization, must incorporate sound objectives measurement techniques.

The industrial hygienist must give considerable thought to his or her role and mission in the organization before measurable objectives can be prepared. He or she must be clear as to exactly what the primary responsibilities and principal tasks are and how performance will be measured. This may mean stepping out from the usual frame of reference and looking at things from management's point of view: What has the company hired or assigned the hygienist to do? What specific functions and activities does the immediate supervisor need to have the hygienist perform and in what order? What level of performance does the organization expect from the hygienist? What should the results of the hygienist's work be? What does the organization want the hygienist to produce? This kind of thinking is not easy for most hygienists who have been trained in consulting and providing solutions to problems wherever they may occur without thinking about their effectiveness. But to get recognition and rewards in today's organizations, the hygienist's performance must be measured in terms management understands and agrees.

Once mutual agreement is obtained from management, the hygienist should put objectives and priorities in writing—and then actively pursue them. These written guideposts serve to keep the hygienist on track and away from diversions that detract from completing objectives. Objectives should be as specific as possible to allow easy measurement. For staff managers this is not always easy to do. Some guidelines to accomplish this include: (a) Word the objectives in terms of the results to be achieved and not focusing on the activities to be engaged. (b) Make certain that the objective includes a statement of what is to be accomplished. Indicate who, what, where, and when. (c) Avoid general terms such as "sufficient," "adequate," and "reasonable" to avoid quantifying results. Most activities can be measured in costs, time, resources, energy expended, money, and so on. Use these quantifiers where possible. Knowing how well one is doing in accomplishing the objectives is a highly regarded trait by management. It shows proper management style and proper regard for the organization's need to assess its performance along the way. Today's highly computerized organizations make it easier for the hygienist to keep management abreast of impending problems and accomplishments on a timely basis. An important tenet to remember about management is that managers do not like surprises. So, provide as much feedback frequently enough to show management the successes and the progress of what is accomplished. A corollary to this approach is that management must also provide feedback to the hygienist on ways to improve performance and to communicate progress to the entire organization. This active feedback involves the organization in the hygienist's objectives, and as a result it leads to involvement and "buy in" by the entire organization of an industrial hygiene program.

Lastly, an important element in any organization's style is the climate and the way that credit is bestowed to individuals for doing a quality job. Human nature works against us in this respect when we naturally try to take credit for a deserving accomplishment. However, most managers want as much appreciation as the individuals involved do for the results achieved in their organization regardless who was directly responsible—human egos are often blind when it comes to praise and recognition.

Therefore, the hygienist should give credit and recognition to those people in the organization that were involved and assisted in meeting the objectives of the program. Sharing praise with management shows that the hygienist is a team player and deserving of the care and attention often given to loyal employees. So, when a project goes well, the rule is to share the recognition with all those involved.

6 CONCLUSION

The American Society of Safety Engineers' (ASSE) brochure, "Scope of the Safety Professional (10), itemizes four main tasks of safety professionals that I am sure are equally applicable to industrial hygiene:

1. Identify problem areas
2. Develop solutions to these problems
3. Communicate these solutions to management
4. Measure the effectiveness of these solutions

It seems easy enough that by following basic management rules industrial hygienists should succeed with their programs. But we have seen in our discussion that there are many variables to consider before a program can be considered a success. Knowing the style of the organization, how it measures performance, and rewards its management are important considerations for the industrial hygienist. Likewise, the financial language used and its adoption by the hygienist in the organization helps the industrial hygiene program achieve recognition, acquire resources, and involve key managers in its implementation.

The hygienist is not only a problem solver but an important agent of change in any organization. With the knowledge of human behavior, motivation, and communication, the industrial hygienist can improve the way an organization views its occupational health issues and can assist it to cope and progress toward the amelioration of those issues that affect the health of every employee.

Dovetailing the industrial hygiene program with the management structure, style, measurement, and reward system provides the most effective way of accomplishing the objectives of the program.

REFERENCES

1. J. T. Molloy, *Live for Success,* New York: Morrow, 1981.
2. R. R. Blake and J. S. Mouton, *The Managerial Grid,* Houston: Gulf, 1964.
3. D. McGregor, *The Human Side of Enterprise,* New York: McGraw-Hill, 1960.
4. P. B. Crosby, *Quality Is Free,* New York: McGraw-Hill, 1979.
5. F. M. Toca, *Am. Ind. Hyg. Assoc. J.* **44,** 213–216 (1981).
6. K. Blanchard and S. Johnson, *The One Minute Manager,* New York: Berkley, 1985.

7. M. E. Lichtenstein, *Am. Ind. Hyg. Assoc. J.* **44,** 256–262 (1983).

8. L. Birkner, Manager, Industrial Hygiene and Product Safety, Atlantic Richfield Company, Los Angeles.

9. L. R. Sayles, *Leadership, What Effective Managers Really Do . . . And How They Do It,* New York: McGraw-Hill, 1979, pp. 156–158.

10. Scope and Function of the Professional Safety Position, American Society of Safety Engineers, Park Ridge, IL.

CHAPTER FIVE

Line Organization

James K. Sugg

1 INTRODUCTION

There are several major reasons why private firms have taken steps to implement organized health control systems (1). First among these is *initiative*. This is a response to an internally generated concern for protecting employee health and is the primary basis for occupational health programs that existed prior to the regulatory rush of the 1970s. Perhaps the main reason most companies have developed or expanded their programs is response to *governmental regulations.* Undoubtedly the large increase in numbers of industrial hygienists and allied health and safety professionals in the last 15 years is mainly due to the private sector's needs for specialists to organize compliance efforts. Another external factor that has caused corporations to dedicate new resources to preventive programs is *reaction to calamity.* Widely publicized episodes of employee and environmental health problems have probably stimulated many firms to develop or strengthen their own occupational health programs.

The primary purpose of a business in the free enterprise system is to produce goods and services for profit. Therefore, it seems obvious that *economics* must play a most important underlying role in why firms devote resources to programs aimed at preventing occupational health problems. Effective programs can minimize the direct costs of penalties for noncompliance with regulations as well as those associated with workers' compensation claims. In addition, the indirect cost of injuries and illnesses in terms of lost production can be significantly reduced by preventing workplace health and safety problems. Lastly, adverse publicity associated with occupational or environmental health problems presents the potential for decreased sales and profits.

Having briefly explored the whys, it is now appropriate to turn to the methods firms use to respond to the problem. There are a variety of organizational and procedural steps that are necessary to build an acceptable level of public and employee health protection. Following are seven basic elements of programs that are found in both large and small companies that have excellent accident and illness records (2):

1. Management Leadership: assumption of responsibility, declaration of policy.
2. Assignment of Responsibility: to operating officials, safety and health directors, supervisors, committees.
3. Maintenance of Safe Working Conditions: involving safety and health inspections, engineering revisions, purchasing.
4. Safety and Health Training: for management, supervisors, workers.
5. Accident Investigation and Accident and Illness Record System: accident analysis, reports on injuries, measurement of results.
6. Medical and First-Aid Systems: placement exams, treatment of injuries, occupational illnesses, first-aid service, periodic health examinations.
7. Acceptance of Personal Responsibility by Employees: training, maintenance of interest.

Thus, the responsibility for effectively dealing with real and potential hazards tends to be widely distributed throughout many functional areas in companies having excellent accident and illness records. This chapter will concentrate on how such responsibilities may be shared, with special emphasis given to the functions of the line organization.

2 LINE AND STAFF

The process of organization involves establishment of a structure of functional roles that are necessary to carry out the objectives of an enterprise (3). A detailed structure may not be important in a small business; however, as an organization grows, it is difficult to accomplish what needs to be done without dividing work into clear areas of function and responsibility.

Most large organizations are divided into line and staff. Sometimes the terms "operating" and "service" are substituted for line and staff. A line unit is responsible for actually doing the work that is considered the primary function of the larger organization. In a manufacturing firm, for example, products need to be developed, produced, and sold. Therefore, those working in research and development labs, production facilities, and sales units are considered line personnel.

A staff organization is a unit or function that helps the line do its work; it is not actually engaged in the work itself. A line organization needs help from such staff functions as purchasing, payroll, data processing, human resources, and engineering to get the job done. And if the hazards associated with the production and sale of products are to be properly identified and controlled, a number of staff occupational health and safety specialists may need to be involved in helping the firm with its broad mission.

2.1 Centralized and Decentralized Organizations

In addition to the division into line and staff functions, many organizations are divided in other ways. For example, a company may organize itself to serve market sectors or geographic areas. Another common method is to divide by product lines. When executive authority is dispersed throughout the organization, it is usually called decentralization and results in greater autonomy within operating units.

A decentralized line organization often leads to decentralized activity in staff functions as well. Since no hard and fast rules are apparent in this area, many different combinations of centralized and decentralized staff functions exist. Some companies have industrial hygiene units only in corporate staff. Others have industrial hygiene organizations only in decentralized operations. While still others have both. Detailed discussions of the various industrial hygiene organizations may be found in Chapter 6.

2.2 Industrial Hygiene Service Relationships to Line

It is sometimes said that a member of a staff unit cannot tell a manager or a member of a line unit to do anything (4). This may be true in some organizations; however, there is usually some authority that is transferred to a staff unit by top management. For example, a company health and safety policy may define line management's responsibility for implementing corrective action resulting from an industrial hygiene audit.

The relations between industrial hygiene units and operating units are varied. Some examples are covered in this section.

2.2.1 Advisory Service. In the case of advisory service, the industrial hygiene staff unit only offers advice when asked. A line operating manager may or may not avail himself of the service, and he may choose to act or not act on the advice that is provided. This fits the classic definition of a staff function. There are probably elements of this in most organizations, but it is unlikely that many continue to operate in such a rigid structure in today's regulatory and litigious environment.

It is perhaps worth noting that an advisory relationship is essentially what develops when line management obtains the services of an outside industrial hygiene consultant. That is, the consultant waits for an invitation, and there is no obligation for management to follow the consultant's advice, although it is obvious that failure to do so could result in problems with regulatory agencies, increased costs of workers' compensation, legal actions, and possibly criminal charges.

2.2.2 Services Routinely Supplied. Internal industrial hygiene services are usually provided as a routine, rather than by invitation of the operating unit. This is much stronger than a strictly advisory service. And it is typical of organizations in which line operations rely on a central or corporate staff for industrial hygiene assistance. Staff personnel generally operate under a broad policy. There may be several layers of supervisors, managers, and executives on both the staff and operating sides. Staff recommendations have strong force and there is typically a routine flow of communications between staff industrial hygienists and operating personnel at many levels.

2.2.3 Services an Integral Part of Operating Unit. An industrial hygiene unit may report directly to the head of an operating unit such as a plant or division. This typically works very well because day-to-day problems can be handled in a timely, efficient manner. Policies are normally established at the local level. Communications between internal staff and line tend to be very direct and less formal than those in systems covered in Sections 2.2.1 and 2.2.2. Recommendations of the industrial hygienist also have strong force in this arrangement. However, because the industrial hygienists are an integral part of the operating unit, maintaining objectivity may be more difficult than when the staff and operating unit are separated by several organizational layers.

2.2.4 Central Staff and Operating Unit Staff. Some organizations have industrial hygiene units at more than one position in the organization. This combined approach normally means that the industrial hygienists directly attached to operations carry out the day-to-day functions. The corporate industrial hygiene unit establishes broad policies, audits the professional performance of the decentralized units, and serves as a resource.

Many variations exist on what has been discussed in this section. The main point is that the line management must get its information by some method and integrate it into the decision-making process.

3   LINE RESPONSIBILITY

As discussed previously, staff functions are outside the line's chain of command. A staff unit can be closely integrated into an operating unit and its functional responsibility can be broad and highly regarded, but staff personnel are still outside the line decision-making process. Responsibility for executive decisions must be centered in the line of command as a means of clarifying accountability for these decisions (3).

The control of anticipated or actual hazards can be a very complex problem. The industrial hygienist's primary job is to help simplify the problem and propose reasonable and cost-effective systems of controls from an arsenal of tried and true methods: namely, substitution, isolation, ventilation, personal protection, work practices, and employee education and training.

Management must consider the advice of the professional and integrate it into its decision-making process. Decisions to implement a particular control strategy seldom revolve solely around pure health or safety considerations. There are usually confounding issues such as unknown product demand, time pressures, and limited capital that come into play. Often, several ways may be available to minimize the risk of a given operation, and it is management's prerogative to follow the course it deems most appropriate.

Line management can demonstrate its commitment to protecting employee health by routinely authorizing funding for staffing needs and major control systems. However, there is more to management's responsibility than allocation of resources to solve problems. For overall industrial hygiene and safety programs to function smoothly, health and safety need to be made part of the corporate culture. Staff units must play an important role in helping the line create that type of environment, but ultimately it is up to the line organization to foster and maintain the concept. "Motivational controls" (as opposed to engineering controls) is a term used in a recent article (5) to explain the importance of establishing an overall climate of health and safety awareness. Motivational controls "are general, rather than specific in their objectives and are designed to engender and maintain a positive motivation" to the control of risk. These are important for everyone at all levels in the chain of command; however, it is difficult for such a system to flourish unless it starts at the top.

The remainder of this chapter is devoted to how the line executes its industrial hygiene responsibilities. It is possible to discuss this in general terms that apply to any organization that employs industrial hygienists. However, for purposes of illustration, a publicly owned firm that develops and manufactures products is used as a model to explain various responsibilities.

3.1 Board of Directors

The overall legal duty and responsibility of the board of directors is to manage the corporation. The shareholders depend on the board to oversee conduct of the corporate business. In actual practice the board delegates extensive authority to the corporate officers who carry on the day-to-day management of the business. Normally, the board is not directly involved in employee health and safety issues. However, at least one large corporation has made the overall function of environmental, health, and safety answerable to an Environmental Policy Committee of the Board of Directors (1).

3.2 Chief Executive Officer

In every company, someone is responsible for conditions in the workplace that may affect the health and well-being of its employees. In theory, the person in charge of an organization, its president or chief executive officer (CEO), bears that responsibility. But it is typically delegated downward within the line organization to individuals in charge of business units such as subsidiaries, divisions, departments, or manufacturing or research facilities.

The CEO must demonstrate that employee health and safety is indeed important to the health of the corporation. Motivating others is usually accomplished in a number of ways. First, the CEO should sign the corporate policy that describes, at least in a general way, how the company will meet the goal of providing a healthy, safe workplace. The policy should be widely distributed throughout the company so everyone will know that management is committed.

Another method the CEO can use is to communicate to management and supervisory personnel that all potential risks must be properly evaluated. Risk management, whether it is the decision to enter a new marketplace, launch a new product, or modify an unhealthy work environment is, after all, the function of management. Both good risks and bad risks may exist. Failure to act on information that may result in an employee health problem is an example of a bad risk. The CEO should emphasize, in various presentations and internal publications, that bad risks aren't worth taking.

3.3 Top Management

Top management is an imprecise term for a group of people responsible for the overall direction and success of company activities. Top management usually encompasses major staff heads as well as those in charge of operations. The entire group is responsible for developing and carrying out the firm's policies and meeting its primary objectives. Members of top management are held accountable to the CEO for the health- and safety-related concerns, just as they are accountable for meeting the other objectives such as sales, profits, and new product introductions.

A top operations manager, like the CEO, needs to demonstrate to subordinates that occupational health is important. Conducting periodic health-related reviews, authorizing major expenditures for effective industrial hygiene systems, and evaluating health- and safety-related performance of subordinates are methods that top managers commonly use to motivate others in the chain of command.

3.4 Manufacturing Management

Managers in this function are primarily responsible to produce a product of specified quality at a competitive cost and to make it available for delivery to the customer at a time specified by the sales organization. All of this must, of course, be accomplished in a manner that does not pose any undue risk to the health and well-being of the manufacturing unit employees.

The facility manager needs to rely on the information and advice developed by the industrial hygienist, whether the support comes from an outside consultant or a corporate staff member. Specifically, the manager should:

1. Establish a written health and safety policy for the facility that is in concert with the corporate policy. The policy should be posted in a conspicuous place.
2. Develop a written industrial hygiene plan for the facility. This should be done with the direct involvement of the industrial hygiene unit. It should outline goals and objectives, identify those responsible for carrying out the plan, and establish priorities for necessary activities such as process reviews, periodic monitoring, employee training, and equipment maintenance.
3. Hold subordinates accountable for industrial hygiene-related activities. These items should be covered in performance appraisals as well as by direct communications in day-to-day operations.
4. Visit the production areas frequently and show a keen and active interest in employee concerns and the active control of potential hazards.
5. Establish a system that fosters understanding of industrial hygiene and encourages employees at all levels to actively support health and safety activities.

3.5 Manufacturing Supervisors

Supervisors are primarily responsible for directing the activities of the production employees in accordance with the established objectives. It is extremely important to have supervisors well indoctrinated in the fundamental concepts of industrial hygiene and safety.

1. They need to be well informed about regulations, company policies, and guidelines that may affect their own areas of responsibility.
2. They must respond to employee concerns, complaints, or adverse reactions in a prompt manner.
3. They must keep facility management informed about employee occupational health concerns.
4. They must keep employees informed about the potential hazards that may exist in their work area.
5. They must enforce work practice rules pertaining to the use of personal protective clothing, equipment, and other control measures.

Once workers have been trained in safe work procedures, the problem of motivating them to follow those practices is up to the supervisor. Although it is necessary to establish certain rules, it is best to avoid placing undue emphasis on punishing employees who fail to measure up. Fear of punishment may motivate some, but in others it may have a negative effect. That is, employees may learn how to avoid getting caught. Fear can motivate people to avoid unsafe methods, but not necessarily an acceptance of the safe method (6).

Overall, the best way to motivate others to follow safe work practices is to make sure both the supervisor and the supervisor's subordinates understand why the procedures are necessary. The amount of training necessary to bring about the attitudes necessary to create a positive approach to health and safety may be considerable, but is well worth the effort.

3.6 Manufacturing Employees

From top to bottom, the last person in the direct chain of command is the production employee. These individuals are no more or less responsible than others in the organization for doing what they are told to do. From the industrial hygiene perspective, it is important to include that employees are responsible for carrying out their duties in a safe manner. Specific employee responsibilities include:

1. Learning how to operate all equipment in the prescribed manner.
2. Avoiding shortcuts that may compromise health or safety.
3. Understanding the potential hazards associated with the job.
4. Reporting any problems promptly.
5. Using any personal protective equipment and clothing as instructed.

3.7 Product Development Management

Managers in this line function are primarily responsible for developing the information that is needed by the manufacturing unit to produce a new product. Managers in research and development functions have a responsibility to their own employees for making sure occupational health hazards are controlled. But they also have the broader responsibility of choosing materials and methods that will help minimize risks to manufacturing employees, customers and neighbors, and the environment.

Some companies have rigid procedures that involve review at an early stage by toxicologists, industrial hygienists, and safety and environmental engineers. Whether the reviews are mandatory or not, well-informed development managers will utilize the information developed by such professionals to help them in their decisions.

Product development can be broken down into a number of semidistinct phases.

3.7.1 Conceptual Phase. The first phase is the generation of a new product idea and its early exploration. Researchers should be aware of the toxicological and physical properties of experimental materials as well as potential problems associated with various types of process operations. At this very early time it is appropriate to consider health hazard evaluations, including a preliminary check on the regulatory status of possible materials.

3.7.2 Feasibility. In the second phase the technical feasibility of the product is demonstrated. This stage will typically include a successful pilot plant run with the product meeting the critical requirements of the product description. During the refining of the product, health and regulatory assessments of the raw materials, intermediates, and the finished product should be continued. If the product requires licensing or registration, it should be investigated at this time.

The fundamental concept of controlling by substitution works most effectively at this stage because it is often impractical to change once a product has been successfully produced.

3.7.3 Process Development. During the third stage, material specifications and process parameters are established. This is essentially still a laboratory–pilot plant phase; however, there should be an opportunity for the industrial hygienist to observe and evaluate potential problems before scaleup occurs. Any toxicity testing necessary for employee, customer, or environmental considerations should be well underway or finished before this stage is completed.

3.7.4 Scaleup. In this final stage, the lab and pilot plant process is adapted to factory process conditions. When a new process is implemented, it is up to process and industrial engineers to translate the product requirements into an efficient operating procedure that can be readily understood by the production employees.

The process engineer needs to be familiar with equipment and materials and have a good working knowledge of industrial hygiene fundamentals. Manufacturing employees should be trained in the specific potential hazards of the operation and an industrial hygiene evaluation protocol should be established. Safety and environmental evaluations are also completed in this stage. The end result of this phase is the ability to reproducibly manufacture the product to specifications in a manner in which health, safety, and environmental hazards are effectively controlled.

3.8   Engineering

Some engineering functions within a manufacturing organization are outside the direct chain of command from CEO to production employee. These services primarily involve the physical plant rather than the people aspects, but their contributions toward assuring that safe operations are installed and equipment is properly maintained are vital elements of the overall health and safety program.

3.8.1 Design or Project Engineers. Construction of a new manufacturing facility or installation of new equipment or other modifications to existing plants can be an extremely complex process. Health and safety professionals have long professed the need for addressing their respective issues from the beginning of planning. Failure to consider health, safety, and environmental aspects can obviously result in serious threats to employees, neighbors, or the environment. If problems are detected later, correction usually involves expensive retrofitting.

As with other professions, project engineers rely on their education and experience to perform their work. Most engineers probably receive relatively little formal instruction in the health and safety aspects of the design process. But numerous publications have been written to guide the engineer through the difficult task of considering occupational and environmental health and safety issues. A recent publication (7) includes a bibliography of such sources and a comprehensive list of hundreds of points to consider. The list includes items under outside-plant considerations, the plant structure itself, and in-plant physical and organizational considerations.

3.8.2 Plant Engineers. Once the physical plant and its equipment have been installed, there is an obvious need to maintain it in a manner that will minimize the possibility of equipment failure. The vast majority of mechanical, hydraulic, pneumatic, electrical, and electronic equipment that may be classed as critical in the operation of a plant need to receive routine maintenance.

The responsibility for identifying maintenance requirements and implementing a plan of action rests with the plant engineer. In all operations there will be some need for emergency repairs, but the objective of the plant engineer should be to minimize this activity by scheduling general repairs and by performing routine and preventive maintenance.

The major objectives of preventive maintenance are (8):

1. To minimize the number of breakdowns on critical equipment.
2. Reduce loss of production due to equipment failure.
3. Increase equipment life.
4. Protect the safety and health of the workforce.

In many operations, process equipment considerations are essential to the safety of the employees and the community. Measurement and control of explosive mixtures, pressure relief mechanisms, and vessel and piping corrosion are but a few of the process items that need to be closely monitored, evaluated, and maintained to assure employee and community safety. In addition, industrial hygiene controls such as ventilation and noise systems need to be regularly maintained if they are expected to function as designed.

4 SUMMARY

A number of internal and external factors influence how a company responds to potential occupational health-related problems and regulations. As firms establish procedural and technical mechanisms to assure hazards are properly anticipated and controlled, responsibility for industrial hygiene is distributed between line and staff operations in accordance with the overall organizational structure.

Although the staff industrial hygiene unit maintains responsibility for the "technical aspects" of the program, line management is responsible for the overall health and safety of its employees. Starting at the top with the board of directors, there is a downward progression and delegation of responsibility for these aspects among each level of line authority. They tend to be broad and general at upper levels and very specific for first-line supervisors and production employees. Others such as design engineers, product development, and maintenance personnel also play key roles in the health and safety picture.

For the overall system to function effectively, management needs to commit resources and, most importantly, work hard at establishing and maintaining the concept that employee health and safety are part of the corporate culture.

REFERENCES

1. A. Freedman, *Industry Response to Health Risk,* New York: The Conference Board, 1981, p. 6.
2. I. B. Etter, in C. Heyel (ed.), *The Encyclopedia of Management,* 3rd ed., New York: Van Nostrand Reinhold, 1982, p. 1068.
3. M. Zimet, in W. K. Fallon (ed.), *AMA Management Handbook,* 2nd ed., New York: AMACOM, 1983, p. 34.
4. C. Heyel, in C. Heyel (ed.), *The Encyclopedia of Management,* 3rd ed., New York: Van Nostrand Reinhold, 1982, pp. 794–796.
5. S. Dawson, P. Poynter, and D. Stevens, *OMEGA* **11,**(5) (1983); through *Prof. Safety* **32,** 32 (1987).
6. R. L. Burns, in I. R. Vernon (ed.), *Modern Aspects of Manufacturing Management,* Vol. 3, Dearborn: Society of Manufacturing Engineers, 1970, p. 120.
7. L. W. Whitehead, *Appl. Ind. Hyg.* **2,** 79 (1987).
8. B. W. Niebel, *Engineering Maintenance Management,* New York: Marcel Dekker, 1985, p. 146.

CHAPTER SIX

Organization of Industrial Hygiene Management

John L. Henshaw

1 INTRODUCTION

The manager of industrial hygiene programs has the task of creating an organization that, from a productivity standpoint, is larger than the sum of individual efforts. The manager must develop a function that turns out more and is more effective than the sum of the resources assigned to it. This task necessitates that the manager organize an industrial hygiene function, make effective all the strengths there are in his or her resources, especially the professional resources, match these strengths with the existing management style and organizational structure, and negate their weakness.

89

The specific form of industrial hygiene organization used in any company is dependent on the company conditions, policies and purposes, available personnel, scale of operations/diversity, and commitment to health and safety. There is no precise organizational structure for industrial hygiene programs, and it would be unwise to think that because one organization works in one instance it will work for another.

The single most important variable to be contended with in organizing an industrial hygiene program is the people themselves. Second is the management style of the company. It would be impossible to set up an ideal industrial hygiene organization because perfectly adaptable people and companies are never available. Every industrial hygiene organization is therefore a compromise, and the manager must take full advantage of the strong points of each industrial hygiene professional and the company's management style and build into the industrial hygiene organization protective devices against individual and company weaknesses.

In organizing and managing an industrial hygiene program the manager should keep in mind the purpose and elements of the program. The program should be structured to meet the specific needs of a corporation, company, plant, or operation. The overall purpose of an industrial hygiene program is to provide a healthful working environment, that is, adequate control of physical, chemical, psychological, and other stresses in the workplace.

As described by Cralley and Cralley (1):

[industrial hygiene programs] should include all the functions needed in the recognition, evaluation, and control of occupational health hazards associated with production, office, and other work. This requires a comprehensive program designed around the nature of the operations, documented to preserve a sound retrospective record and executed in a professional manner.

The basic components of a comprehensive program include the following:

1. An ongoing data collection system that provides the essential functions for identifying and assessing the level of health hazards in the workplace.
2. Participation in the periodic review of worker exposure and health records to detect the emergence of health stresses in the workplace.
3. Participation in research, including toxicological and epidemiological studies designed to generate useful data in establishing safe levels of exposure.
4. A data storage system that permits appropriate retrieval to study the long term effects of occupational exposures.
5. Assuring the relevancy of the data being collected.
6. An integrated program capable of responding to the need for the establishment of appropriate controls, both current and those resulting from technological advances and associated process changes.

The industrial hygienist at the corporate or equivalent level should have responsibility of reporting to top management. This involves input wherever product, technological, operational, process changes, or other considerations may have an influence on the nature and extent of associated health hazards so that adequate controls can be incorporated at the designing stage.

The industrial hygiene program manager should have cognizance of other related health and safety programs in the organization and have full input with these programs in designing programs for hazardous waste handling, risk assessment, emergency planning, and so on.

2 STRUCTURE

2.1 Classical Organizational Theory

Organizations are designed to simply create or facilitate order out of what could be chaos. From an industrial hygiene program sense, classic organization builds a structure within an existing structure that establishes and delineates essential elements of power, responsibility, division of labor, specialization, and interaction between interdependent parts.

Normally the organizing process is viewed in two ways—construction and analysis. Construction means taking a number of small units and building a much larger whole. The process of analysis considers a particular area and divides it into subgroups such as divisions, departments, or tasks given to specific people. Since industrial hygiene was more than likely an offshoot or additional responsibility given to a group within an organization, such programs were organized through the process of analysis. The objectives of an industrial hygiene organization is to create and manage predictable relationships among professionals, managers, and employees; the health and safety technology; jobs or tasks; and resources so as to join in a common effort to achieve protection of worker health.

The desired result in industrial hygiene, regardless of the size and structure of the existing organization in which we must function, is to ensure all workers have a safe and healthful place in which to work.

2.2 Flat versus Tall Structure

In classical organization theory the basic idea is to establish a workable span of management that is the number of subordinates that should report to one superior. Existing companies and institutions have already established a management style and structure, and whether an industrial hygiene organization has a few or many subordinates per supervisor may be outside of one's control. However, it is important to analyze the strengths and weakness of a broad or narrow span of management so if change is possible it can be made with full understanding of the likely outcome and pitfalls that may need to be accommodated. We all have a finite ability to change our organization, and we should attempt to do so to more effectively achieve our ultimate objective.

As stated previously, the span of management or span of control simply refers to the number of people a manager or supervisor directly manages. A small or narrow span creates a tall structure where each manager or supervisor directly manages only a few individuals (Figure 6.1). This can be an advantage in some functions and a disadvantage in others. The advantages of such a structure are closer coordination or control over the subordinates. In such structures there tends to be less ambiguity and fewer conflicts with roles and responsibilities. However, industrial hygiene is a function comprised of professionals whose responsibilities require them to use their individual experience and knowledge to evaluate unique circumstances and take action. Tight control or close supervision would not be effective in such cases.

In addition, managers in tall organizations have a tendency to lead through expertise that can undermine subordinates' confidence because the manager always knows better and does not hesitate to jump in and prove it. Supervising too closely also reduces the subordinates' growth by removing the challenges of learning and problem solving. Managers in tall structures must be aware of these tendencies that are inherent in the structure and take proper steps to neutralize them.

Tall structures also create longer communication channels, which in turn create a higher probability of misinterpretation as the messages are received and transmitted down the chain. They also tend to be more supervisor-oriented since employees interact with their superior more frequently. The outcome, more often than not, is that the subordinate spends more time trying to please his or her supervisor rather than being creative and productive. Creativity and productivity are hallmarks of industrial hygiene.

A major disadvantage of tall structures regarding perception is that the perceived level of authority decreases as the structure grows taller. The farther away from the top industrial hygiene is as a recognized entity, the less perceived authority or clout the program and its people will have in the overall organization.

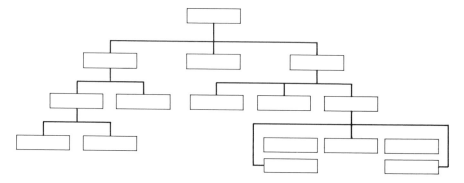

Figure 6.1.   Tall organization.

A flat structure on the other hand represents a broad or large span of management (Figure 6.2). Each manager may have five or more people to supervise. In recent years many corporations have set goals of between 5 and 15 subordinates per manager in an effort to reduce marketing, administrative, and technology (MAT) expenses or staff overhead.

Flat organizations have worked well in many areas of management including industrial hygiene organizations and not so well in others. The reasons will be evident with the following discussion.

Possibly the biggest disadvantage of a flat structure in some functions is the loss of coordination and control over subordinates. Since each manager will have more individuals to communicate with and direct, there will be less time for the supervisor to spend face to face with the subordinate. Some groups within an organization may require close supervision, such as a critical production unit where there may be no allowance for individual judgment and creativity. In such cases a flat structure is not the most effective organization. Industrial hygiene functions in a flat organization are quite effective. Most experienced and certified industrial hygiene professionals work better without close supervision, which is a trademark of tall structures. In fact, depending on the management style of the manager, close supervision in tall organizations is more likely to stifle industrial hygiene creativity and productivity and hamper the exercising of professional judgment.

Flat organization could be considered a disadvantage when an untrained or inexperienced industrial hygienist enters a new function. However, when this happens, arrangements can be made on a temporary basis to provide the needed face-to-face close supervision until the individual gains the necessary experience to function independently.

Flat organizations have a distinct advantage over tall organizations in respect to communication. Communication lines are usually more simple and shorter. A directive or concept that is communicated from the top has less chance for misinterpretation. Flatter structures provide opportunities for allied health groups such as safety, industrial hygiene, toxicology, and medicine to report to the same manager. This kind of structure, whether it be in a corporate or plant organization, is most advantageous since the allied groups can more easily communicate and operate as a united function. Flat organizations minimize the number of steps to the top of the organizational pinnacle. The closer the industrial hygiene function is to the top of the management chain (i.e., chief executive officer or president, plant manager), the more authority and clout the function will carry.

Health professionals, including industrial hygienists, tend to prefer flat organizations since they are not full of hierarchical controls. Like most professionals, industrial hygienists enjoy the freedom to exercise professional judgment without close supervision. This freedom increases job satisfaction and productivity with the least amount of stress.

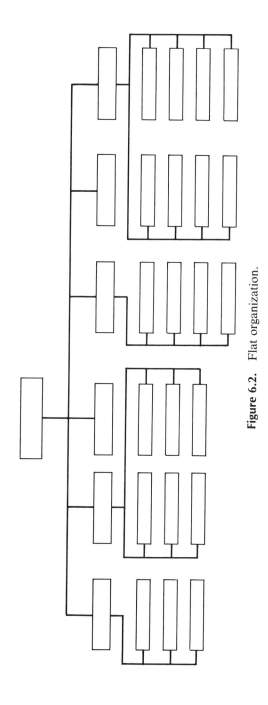

Figure 6.2. Flat organization.

2.3   Centralized versus Decentralized Structure

According to the *AMA Management Handbook* (2), decentralization simply involves dividing the personnel, processes, and functions of an enterprise into subunits or groups. The primary purpose is to distribute authority so that no level becomes overburdened, and the lowest level or division of the organization at which competence can be made available has a greater autonomy in decision making. Centralization is simply the reverse—forcing decision making to more central groups.

In general, companies today have composite structures with degrees of centralization and decentralization. Driven by economies and social pressures, companies cycle between the two, attempting to balance the decentralization of authority and decision making with adequate centralization of controls. The functions that are most often decentralized are those involving operations or manufacturing. With the new concepts of "asset management," whereby all costs associated with a product or service is to be borne by that product or service, decentralization of authority is desirable. Top executives of a company must divest themselves of power to competent subgroups or divisions so that they have the authority to make decisions and can be held accountable for their outcome. Centralization ensures uniformity of action and diminishes the possibility that one subgroup will proceed along lines that are detrimental to the organization as a whole. There are especially cogent reasons for centralizing certain functions. For example, institutional financial policy and administration are primarily a matter for the whole of the organization rather than any one division. These functions are normally centralized in large organizations. Personnel matters and research and development are other areas where a centralized staff is needed to ensure policies are developed and enforced uniformly and that the company's long-term survival is not overlooked.

Health, safety, and environmental issues and the decisions that are made relating to these matters are very critical to the survival of all corporations. Given the social responsibility and litigation environments in which corporations must operate, decisions regarding health and safety made at the lowest level of the organization will impact the entire organization.

Recognition, evaluation, and control of workplace stresses are activities that take place daily in almost every business site in this country. The extent of these activities will vary depending on the size and complexity of the operations. Nonetheless, these activities go on constantly. Because decisions involving industrial hygiene issues will impact the organization as a whole, a centralized function should be established to direct and monitor the activities and decisions of the corporation. Medium to large corporations should have a corporate industrial hygiene function. Comprised of professionals in numbers commensurate with the size and complexity of the business, the function should provide direction, oversight, and assistance to industrial hygiene activities throughout the organization.

2.4   Staff versus Line Structure

Staff–line organizational structure is probably the most common form of organization in today's business world. It is also widely used in governmental agencies and to a great extent in military organizations. Line managers are directly responsible for executing the primary functions of the organizations such as manufacturing, marketing, and sales. In the line organization decisions are centered in the line of command and accountability is clearly established. These same managers have authority commensurate with their responsibility to direct and control the activities of subordinates. In today's complex business environment line organizations cannot keep abreast of all technological changes and advancement made in the field of occupational health and therefore must employ the services of specialists.

Staff groups serve as these specialists that have as their primary function to advise and assist line management in usually highly specialized areas not directly involved in line functions. Staff groups do not normally substitute for the line in decision making. They recommend or expose a different course of action to line managers for their use in decision making. Industrial hygiene organizations, since they are staff, do not and cannot have the same authority as line groups.

All industrial hygiene personnel are staff and are given functional authority because they act from a functional point of view. As specialists they are expected to evaluate the needs of the line and recommend or implement the appropriate actions to ensure worker health is not compromised. Industrial hygiene functions are expected to study the data and come to some defensible recommendation. Functional authority as stated before is strictly advisory, whereas the line authority is the direct line of command, which carries with it the full power of enforcement.

Oftentimes industrial hygiene and other staff groups feel they have been relegated to second-class managers. Many individuals who have worked in the line find it difficult to make their influence recognized when they are transferred to a staff function. Industrial hygienists, because they are staff, must exert their authority through powers of persuasion. This only comes when the data are supportive and presented in an understandable fashion. In addition, the professional must be truly committed to what he or she is doing and to selling the line that what is recommended is the proper action to take.

As defined, there may be several levels of staff industrial hygiene functions in a medium to large corporation. The major difference is simply the relative closeness of the staff function to the lowest level of primary function of the company or "the degree of lineness."

Corporations may have corporate, divisional, and plant staff industrial hygiene functions. Each serves to advise management at the various levels on the implementation and maintenance of industrial hygiene programs. Plant staff industrial hygiene groups have the highest degree of lineness because they are the closest staff industrial hygiene group to the primary function of the organization. Oftentimes divisional and plant industrial hygiene staff groups see themselves as part of the line. The plant staff is closer than the divisional staff and the divisional is closer than the corporate, but they all have the same inherent functional authority. Plant and divisional staff are much closer to the primary function of the line organization and therefore have greater influence over the actions of the primary business function.

To have an effective ongoing program, the staff industrial hygiene function should be located as close as possible to the lowest level of line management. In relatively complex manufacturing facilities (complex in respect to health and safety risks), there should be an industrial hygiene staff group to advise the lowest level of management in the organization and to evaluate and assure proper controls are in place to protect worker health. In addition, this same staff group should function as resources and advisors to all levels of employees.

Good business organizations truly concerned with the preservation of worker health will have industrial hygiene functions at all major levels of management. The level of expertise may vary, but what is important is that all major management levels (i.e., corporate, divisional, and plant) designate a staff group to advise that management level on such issues. This demonstrates a strong commitment to the preservation of worker health and facilitates the proper understanding and integration of industrial hygiene principles in all levels of key decision making.

2.5 Bureaucracy

Organizations are very different from a biological organism, yet they stand under the same laws that govern the structure and size of animals and plants. The surface of most organisms grows with the square of the radius, but the mass grows with the cube. The larger the organism becomes, the more resources must be dedicated to the mass, the inner workings, circulation, and information, and to the nervous system. They become very complex and require greater interaction with other parts of the whole. Large organizations are not necessarily bad, but the larger the organization becomes, the greater the tendency is to be rigid and more bureaucratic.

Bureaucracy is with us in practically every form of organization imaginable. However, the degree of bureaucracy is dependent on the complexity and impersonal detachment of management versus people. Bureaucracy is characterized by a high degree of specialization, a rigid hierarchy of authority, elaborate rules and strict control, and most importantly impersonality. Bureaucracy has a tendency to be more stable and can focus on objectives more directly, but from an industrial hygiene program perspective too much bureaucracy is disastrous and nonproductive. In highly bureaucratic organizations there is a tendency for too much attention to the system for the system's sake. In such instances paperwork and counting boxes becomes the driving force, and whether the actions are truly effective in preserving worker health becomes secondary. Managerial actions in overly bureaucratic organizations are slow to respond to change, and the cost associated with psychological and morale problems contribute to ineffectiveness. According to Dimarco and Norton (3), the findings indicate that job satisfaction decreases as the level of bureaucracy of the organization increases. The only recourse highly bureaucratic organizations have when faced with change is to hire more personnel, which in turn increases the bureaucracy and decreases cost-effectiveness.

Some of the largest bureaucracies in the United States are the military and governmental agencies. Unfortunately, due to the recent increases in litigation and regulation, modern businesses are becoming more and more bureaucratic with increased emphasis on uniformity and documentation. Because we are in a litigious society, all industrial hygiene functions must become more bureaucratic—more specialization, more elaborate rules, tighter controls, and more documentation. Industrial hygienists must document almost every step they take when executing their responsibilities, unlike years past when the outcome was the most important event; today the rationale, procedures, and objective data are the convincing evidence. Unfortunately, the documentation is almost more important than whether the action was effective in protection of worker health. However having the best documented and practiced industrial hygiene program will not prevent wrongful litigation as long as our tort system remains as it is and our legal system permits today's knowledge to judge yesterday's practices. With the proper management style that employs principles of matrix management, industrial hygiene functions can be effective in a more bureaucratic organization. They must, however, overcome the bureaucratic tendencies to resist change and detach people from management, especially those people we are commited to protect.

2.6 Matrix Management Structure

A much talked about organizational structure is the matrix organization. Developed to meet the ever-growing organizational needs of modern business, matrix organizations are a complex organizational form that involves projects and skilled individuals working as a team under one functional supervisor. Matrix structures (Figure 6.3) are created by overlaying one or more organizations on another, which establishes more than one chain of command. Employees who are permanently assigned to one function may be temporarily assigned, with other skilled individuals, to a project team. They may work on a full or part-time basis on the assignment and remain for the life of the project or until their particular specialty is no longer needed. A common example of a matrix organization in modern business is the United Way Campaign. In most cases instead of handling the annual fund drive

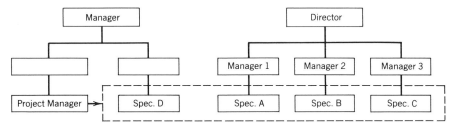

Figure 6.3. Matrix structure.

through the normal hierarchical structures, employees from various parts of an organization are temporarily assigned part-time duties to solicit contributions and manage the campaign. Employees remain with the assignment until the campaign is completed; then the teams are disbanded. When the dual reporting relationships are more permanent, the structure is called a matrix management stucture.

In a matrix organization the old rule of one person, one supervisor is broken. When a person is assigned to a project, he or she may have two or more supervisors simultaneously—a line supervisor representing their permanent assignment and a project or functional supervisor. The two supervisors may report through two different organizational chains. A matrix organization is flexible and better equipped to adapt to change. However, they can be confusing to operate and will require greater coordination and control.

Much of the activity associated with industrial hygiene either at a plant or corporate level can be handled well through a matrix structure. Oftentimes when a problem is identified, a project team will be asked to determine the proper corrective action. In essence, a team comprised of individuals from manufacturing, safety, personnel, the union, and industrial hygiene, which can serve as the team project manager, can be constituted to develop an action plan as shown in Figure 6.4. Each individual has skills in a particular area, all of which may be necessary to effectively institute modified work practices or engineering controls.

There may be other examples where matrix structures can be effective in the industrial hygiene functions. The best industrial hygiene is practiced at the design phase of an operation or plant. Led by the project manager, a project team of experts from safety, industrial hygiene, environmental, research, and various aspects of engineering can be assigned to the design, construction, and successful start-up of the new process. Other situations where matrix structures are used and made effective are in the interpretation and implementation of new health regulations, the evaluation of hearing conservation programs, the investigation of suspected occupational health problems, and so forth. Committees, task forces, or steering committees employ the matrix management philosophy.

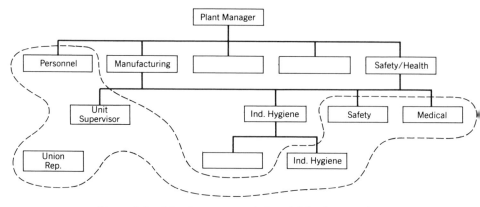

Figure 6.4. Matrix structure industrial hygiene project.

Matrix organizations as a rule will improve personal motivation, especially in technical people, because they can focus more directly on their expertise and the completion of a project. Individuals communicate better because direct contact is encouraged with all ranks in an organization, and the distribution of rank and authority in a matrix organization is more in line with democratic norms, which are held tightly by most technical professionals. In a matrix management structure individuals give more importance to authority of knowledge and how that impacts the project rather than the authority of rank evident in the permanent structures.

2.7   Network Management Structure

As described by DeWine and Casbolt (4), a network is a group of people who maintain contact to communicate and exchange ideas, usually about the same interest. Normally networks center around external interests such as social clubs and recreational sports, but a few organizations have put networking to good use in the industrial hygiene and environmental areas. Because of the rapidly changing events in the industrial hygiene and environmental fields, some companies have established formal industrial hygiene and environmental networks. In these cases individuals in the company who have at least some responsibility in the field have been identified as being a part of a large network of individuals with the same professional interest. Their names, titles, areas of expertise, and phone numbers are printed and distributed to all members of the network. Each member is encouraged to contact any member of the network if they have any questions or concerns.

In general, networks help broaden individual interests and help keep people informed about new developments and who knows what in the area. They can serve as support mechanisms as well, which help employees perform their jobs effectively with less stress. Industrial hygienists, while a necessity for modern business, are not always bearers of good news. Consequently they get their share of negative feedback, and in large organizations plant industrial hygienists may feel isolated, especially when they carry a message that is not well received or have to sell and justify a decision based upon good professional judgment and little objective data. Networks provide them with the needed support as well as the means for airing decisions and judgments among peers. Differences in authority and rank are also provided in networks that allow for nonobstructive communications between ranks. Excellent success has been realized where corporate, divisional, and plant industrial hygiene functions have used principles of network management.

Industrial hygiene functions that have not established or encouraged networking should do so.

2.8   Technology

According to Dobyns (5), we are living in a time of the most rapid technological change the industrial world has ever known. With technology comes new forms of organizations and requirements for specialization, integration, discontinuity, and change.

2.9   Specialization

In the past the principles of industrial hygiene, toxicology, epidemiology, and so on were practiced in the staff capacity by only a select few. At the corporate or the higher levels of institutions, these functions were handled by industrial hygienists, physicians, safety directors, and in some cases personnel or human relations departments. The disciplines were not as developed as they are today and did not require a single individual per area. We now have educated, trained, and certified specialists exclusively in many of these areas. Today many corporations have a certified industrial hygienist, certified toxicologist, physicians certified in occupational medicine, and epidemiologist, each of whom has a segment of what once was handled by one individual.

At lower levels of large corporations, specifically at the plant level, industrial hygiene and other now specialized fields in occupational health were practiced by the safety or personnel department. Thirty years ago industrial hygiene techniques in evaluation and control were less complex than they are today, and with guidance from what few experts existed back then, safety directors at individual sites could handle most of the industrial hygiene issues.

Today, as our industries become more complex, our regulations more detailed, and technology more vast, specialization is further breaking down industrial hygiene, even in the smallest corporation and plant sites. Every business, regardless of the nature of its activities, size, or complexity, must designate an individual or group of individuals as having the responsibility of industrial hygiene or occupational health.

For very simple and relatively nonhazardous operations, the person responsible for industrial hygiene may be a technical person wearing many hats (e.g., safety specialist, laboratory analyst, environmental or building engineer, or personnel manager, site manager). Nonetheless this person is at least the "industrial hygiene contact" responsible for assuring employees are not adversely affected by working conditions. For businesses primarily involved in office activities, ergonomics and indoor air quality most likely are areas of concern. In these and more complex facilities the industrial hygiene contact has the responsibility for interfacing with consultants and executing ongoing surveillance or control programs. As the size and complexity of the operations increase, so too will the responsibilities for site industrial hygiene. Along with the increased responsibility will come the required level of expertise and training in industrial hygiene. Large complex plants must have industrial hygiene staffs, run by certified industrial hygienists who are held responsible for the preservation of worker health.

As a general rule of thumb, we should strive to have one certified industrial hygienist or one working on certification for every 500 employees at a complex manufacturing site. For smaller plants (less than 500 people), industrial hygiene contacts should be assigned to follow the direction set forth by certified divisional, corporate staff, or consultants. These contacts may not have professional training, but they should have, at a minimum, training on the basic principles of industrial hygiene and be able to interact with experts such as those from the divisions or corporate staff when specific help is needed.

The technology of industrial hygiene has grown manyfold over the last 20 years. As an example, personnel monitoring was rarely performed as a routine 15 years ago. In fact, in the early seventies there were only one or two reliable battery-operated pumps that could be used for personal sampling. During the same time period only a few methods were available and routinely used. In contrast, the amount of industrial hygiene equipment available today has increased 20-fold. Methods are being developed daily, and industrial hygiene and chemistry journals are publishing the technical papers by the thousands each year.

2.10 Corporate/Plant Specializations

Because of the rapid technologic advancements, industrial hygienists cannot read and keep abreast of all the new developments in the field. Corporations that have corporate and divisional staffs should assign specific areas or specialities to members of the staff so they can concentrate their study to one or two areas. They then could keep abreast of the technology and advise other industrial hygiene staff members and the corporation on state-of-the-art techniques. In companies that do not have sufficient corporate industrial hygiene staff, areas of specialization have been assigned to divisional and plant professionals. These same professionals can serve on professional or trade association committees that deal with specific areas of specialization. The American Industrial Hygiene Association (AIHA) has over 30 committees dealing with particular areas of specialization in occupational health. In such cases, industrial hygienists devote some of their time maintaining state-of-the-art knowledge in specific areas while carrying out the normal divisional or plant responsibilities. They can serve a dual role, one for the plant site, the other for the corporation or division as a specialist in an aspect of industrial hygiene. From a corporate or divisional standpoint they could be a resource for the entire corporation and critically review or comment on proposed regulatory or legislative action.

The corporations that have tried this approach have found that morale has improved and plant and divisional professionals see they have something to contribute to the total organization. They feel a part of the corporate or divisional group and no longer experience the isolation. Most professionals accept the challenge with enthusiasm and provide a significant contribution to the whole corporation. Areas of specialization for hygienists in corporations that have medical, toxicology, and epidemiology staff may be in statistics, personal sampling, control ventilation, computerized data handling, industrial hygiene analytical chemistry, radiation, hearing conservation, and so on.

To keep most professionals challenged, specializations should be rotated. Many professionals prefer to maintain a comprehensive practice and by rotating specializations, each professional will, over some period, experience most all aspects of industrial hygiene.

2.11 Reporting Relationships

According to Drucker (6), organizations work better when people in it all have something in common and can communicate with each other on some common level. Industrial hygiene and other safety- and health-related disciplines in most locations are highly technical and should have a special commitment to the preservation of worker health and safety. Because of this commitment and the technical nature of the discipline, industrial hygiene functions should report through to a technical manager as high in the organization as possible. A technical manager is an executive in a managerial position who has training and experience in technical details specifically in the area of health and safety. Preferably, to facilitate interaction and communication, allied health and safety professionals, e.g., medicine, industrial hygiene, safety, toxicology, epidemiology, and so on, should report to the same technical manager. Figures 6.5 and 6.6 show examples of technical reporting relationships at the divisional and plant levels, respectively.

In Figure 6.6, plant B's organization is more effective in dealing with industrial hygiene, safety, and environmental issues because these areas

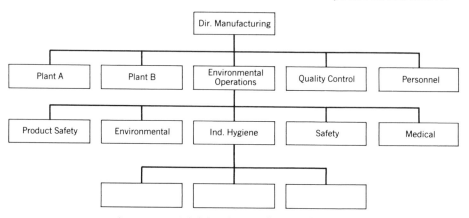

Figure 6.5. Divisional reporting relationships.

report to a manager who understands the technical details and can compete on equal terms with other specialized groups for the scarce resources the plant manager must judiciously hand out. If by chance this manager came from the safety or industrial hygiene function and maintains the same sincere commitment, one could expect the manager to fight for the assurance of health protection with the necessary virosity displayed by his or her subordinates.

If plant organizations are not big enough to support a high-ranking environmental safety and health manager, then industrial hygiene should at a minimum report to another technical manager (i.e., technical services, engineering, manufacturing, laboratory services). All too often plant safety and health sections have reported to personnel or human relations functions.

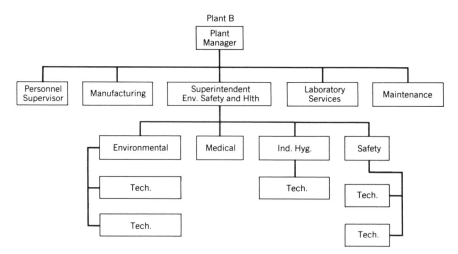

Figure 6.6. Plant reporting relationships.

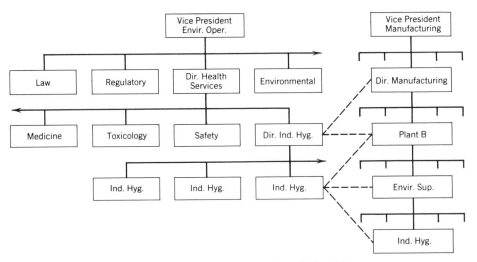

Figure 6.7.   Corporate reporting relationships.

Personnel or human relations functions are not normally technical, and in technical businesses these structures may be ineffective. Problem issues and concepts raised by health and safety professionals are often not understood by nontechnical managers, and therefore they are less able to bring the message forward with conviction to the plant or site manager.

There are of course exceptions to the rule, and depending on the background of the manager and the subordinates' abilities to communicate and motivate their supervisor, nontechnical managers may prove effective executives in health and safety functions.

At the corporate level similar concepts apply. It is desirable in most technical businesses to have all safety, health, and environmental corporate staff within the same organization reporting to a high-level executive who has a technical background. The same advantages as seen at the plant and divisional levels are evident at the corporate level when similar disciplines report through the same technical executive. The type of organization as shown in Figure 6.7 has been tried in numerous organizations, and with the exceptions of only a few they have proven successful and still remain in spite of major restructuring and moves toward further decentralization.

3   CONCLUSION

According to Drucker (7), organizations have three managerial tasks of equal importance, which management must perform before the entity can function and contribute to society. The organization must fulfill a specific purpose, make work productive, and manage social impacts and social responsibilities.

An industrial hygiene organization must traverse all three tasks, making sure, through specific goals and objectives, that workers are productive and workplace conditions are without undue risk.

One of the five basic jobs of an industrial hygiene manager is to organize a function by analyzing the activities, decisions, and relations needed within the framework established by the corporation. To do this one must analyze the pros and cons of the various forms of organizations and operate in such a way as to maximize strengths and minimize weaknesses.

Basic theory states decentralization is the best principle of organization design where it fits. It fits in those functions where it was designed—manufacturing with distinct markets for distinct products or product lines. It does not fit in those areas where decisions are based on highly technical issues and where the consequences impact the organization directly. Industrial hygiene may have a need for decentralized authority at local sites, but this need is to be counterbalanced by maintaining adequate centralization of control at the corporate level. Centralized groups must provide technical direction and corporate oversight to assure all elements of the organization are managing social impacts and social responsibility. Decentralizing local authority without centralized direction and control leads to chaos in our field.

The industrial hygiene structure (plant, division, or corporate) should be flat to maintain relative closeness to top management and good working relationships with peers and other related health professionals. All industrial hygiene functions are staff to the groups that have primary functions of the enterprise. Their job is to ensure that good industrial hygiene practices are employed by the lowest level of the primary operations.

Since bureaucracies are with us, we must recognize their existence and pitfalls, and negate their effects. Bureaucratic red tape will cause us to be more system oriented and document each step on the way, but in the long run it will prove effective in future environments.

Of all the features of organization, reporting relationships and specialization are most important. Both in a centralized and decentralized structure, proper reporting relationships can make or break a function. And without proper specialization—knowledge of the field of industrial hygiene—proper guidance and direction is not forthcoming and preservation of worker health is compromised.

REFERENCES

1. *Patty's Industrial Hygiene and Toxicology,* Vol. 111A, *Theory and Rationale of Industrial Hygiene Practice; The Work Environment,* New York: Wiley, 1985, p. 16.

2. William K. Fallon (ed.), *AMA Management Handbook,* 2nd ed., New York: AMACON American Management Associations, 1983.
3. N. Dimarco and S. Norton, Life Style: Organization, Structure, Congruity, and Job Satisfaction, *Personnel Psychology,* Winter, 489 (1974).
4. S. DeWine and D. Casbolt, Networking: External Communication Systems for Female Organization Members, *J. Business Communication* Spring, 57–67 (1983).
5. L. Dobyns, The Decline of American Productivity: If Japan Can, Why Can't We? *Training Development* J. **8,** 52 (1982).
6. P. F. Drucker, *The Effective Executive,* New York: Harper & Row 1985.
7. P. F. Drucker, *People and Performance: The Best of Peter Drucker on Management,* New York: Harper & Row, 1977.

GENERAL REFERENCES

1 Bradford, David L., and Cohen, Allen R., *Managing for Excellence—The Guide to Developing High Performance in Contemporary Organization,* New York: Wiley, 1984.
2 Daun, Keith, and Newstrom, John W., *Human Behavior at Work: Organizational Behavior,* 7th ed., Company, New York: McGraw-Hill, 1985.
3 Leavitt, Harlod J., *Corporate Pathfinders,* Homewood, IL: Dow Jones-Irwin, 1986.
4 Shapero, Albert, *Managing Professional People,* New York: The Free Press, Collier Macmillan 1985.
5 Tarrant, John J., *Drucker: The Man Who Invented the Corporate Society,* Boston: Cahners Books, 1976.

CHAPTER SEVEN

Corporate Management of Industrial Hygiene Programs at Foreign Locations

Neal C. Stout

1 INTRODUCTION

Managing industrial hygiene programs is a challenging task. Applying management principles to develop an efficient and effective industrial hygiene organization, developing industrial hygiene professionals within the organization and offering these professionals rewarding and satisfying work environments, establishing program goals and evaluating progress toward meeting these goals—these challenges and others can sometimes seem overwhelmingly complex to the industrial hygiene manager. This task is made yet more complex for the corporate industrial hygiene manager responsible for development of industrial hygiene programs at foreign locations.

The objective of this chapter is to assist corporate industrial hygiene staffs to address the task of managing industrial hygiene programs at foreign locations. This objective is accomplished by presenting some of the challenges that must be faced when establishing and maintaining programs at foreign locations and suggesting some approaches that can be used to meet these challenges. Advice given is practical, based on experience and common sense.

The approach is general, using specific situations in identified countries only as examples. Most of the challenges discussed apply to almost all foreign countries. Though the author is employed by an American multinational corporation, an effort will be made not to be provincial. The challenges discussed are much the same no matter what country is home for the corporation.

This chapter does not suggest specific organizational approaches to use for establishment and maintenance of industrial hygiene programs at foreign locations. Organization of industrial hygiene activity is the topic of other chapters of this book (6), (12). The number of organizational structures that could be effectively applied to this task are probably as numerous as the number of multinational corporations. Also, this chapter will not discuss the status of industrial hygiene development in specific countries. To do so in any detail would be exhaustive, and the information presented would undoubtedly be out dated shortly after publication. Rather, common, usually unavoidable challenges of establishing and maintaining industrial hygiene programs in foreign lands are presented, and some suggested approaches to overcome or minimize these challenges are submitted.

2 CHALLENGES

Industrial hygiene should be managed like other business functions rather than being treated as an external entity. As such, the challenges encountered by industrial hygiene managers are similar to the challenges encountered by other staff groups in the organization. The industrial hygiene manager can therefore learn from the successes and failures of other staff groups who also do business at foreign locations. Particularly, the experience of occupational medicine, industrial safety, and environmental protection groups can be very instructive.

Travel to foreign facilities is in most cases more costly than travel to domestic locations. Industrial hygienists with multilocation responsibilities usually depend heavily on routine plant visits to perform walk through surveys, complete audits, provide training to plant contacts, and perhaps perform exposure monitoring. Foreign plants require a similar level of attention. However, in times of budget constraints, travel expense is often a tempting target for budget cutters, and foreign travel, with its higher expense, will frequently become the budget cutters' bull's-eye.

Equipment availability—particularly equipment for sampling and analysis—is sometimes a problem. If the country is a Third World developing country, or an undeveloped one, all sophisticated equipment will probably have to be imported. Trade and economic policies of the host country may make importing somewhat difficult or very difficult. (The author was disallowed by customs agents of two countries to enter carrying sampling equipment that would be used to take samples at a plant and then brought back out of the country.)

Language and communication can be a problem. If English is the native tongue, this is fortunate because English is the international language of business. In most industrialized and developing countries, English is at least a second language spoken by the educated in the country. In short, with English, one can usually communicate with business leaders and technically trained people. If the native language of the host country is different from the native language of the corporation's home country, then there is an additional burden either (1) on the plant, which must generate reports in both languages and hire or train bilingual personnel or (2) on the corporate offices, which must provide for translation of documents. Training materials developed by the corporation, such as safety and health training videotapes, will have to be "dubbed" or redone in other languages to accommodate foreign plants' training needs. Even if the corporate industrial hygiene manager and the foreign plant contacts can communicate in the same language, communication can still be hampered because of (1) expense of overseas telephone calls, (2) time zone differences, and (3) differences in local terminology, expressions, and pronunciation that can lead to misunderstandings.

Keeping track of regulatory developments in one's own country is often difficult enough. The corporate industrial hygienist must also keep track of regulatory development in foreign countries in which the corporation does business. Not only regulatory affairs, but also liability laws, tort actions, workers' compensation laws, and the litigation environment in general must be followed to assess exposure to possible legal action. Usually, the corporate industrial hygiene group will be relied upon to be knowledgeable of specific regulatory developments impacting workplace health, while the corporate law department will be relied upon to assess the broader litigation environment. Nevertheless, the corporate industrial hygiene group should be aware of the general litigation environment to assist corporate management and the law department from a technical viewpoint. The corporate industrial hygiene department should keep track of these broader litigation issues because industrial hygienists have a responsibility to protect their employers from unwarranted legal actions arising from allegation of harm in the workplace. This responsibility goes hand in hand with the industrial hygienist's primary responsibility of preventing harm caused by workplace exposure. It should be noted that, even in cases in which the corporation may own less than controlling interest in a plant, the corporation may still have liability exposure. It is interesting that, in some countries, a foreign corporation cannot by law have controlling interest in a facility. Frequently, a partner may be the foreign government itself.

Customs and attitudes—local, regional, and national—can form very interesting challenges. Examples include:

- Refusal to wear protective equipment, including hard hats, safety eyewear, long-sleeved clothing, long pants, and safety footwear because these protective measures have not gained acceptance among local people. This problem can be as difficult in some industrialized countries as in undeveloped ones. (We should remember that in the United States, where the hard hat has become a proud symbol for the industrial worker, even this simple, effective safety measure had to go through a period of grudging acceptance.)
- The use of hygienic facilities such as wash basins, toilets, and showers may be very strange to some workforces, but very important if handling potentially hazardous contaminants.
- Local plant management may be difficult to convince that an industrial hygiene program is needed in a plant in which the workers come from dirty, dangerous, and diseased living conditions. The plant, even a substandard plant from a corporate perspective, may be perceived to be a safety haven for these workers.

Implementing effective industrial hygiene procedures may be difficult in some locales due as much to resistance from workers as from management. Providing foreign workers "the same health and safety protection" as domestic workers is ethically sound but in practice can be difficult.

Closely related to the challenges of customs and attitudes is the challenge of economic and social conditions in the host country. This is a most complex and difficult challenge for the industrial hygiene manager, involving profound ethical and economic choices. He or she has a primary duty to protect the health of workers in the company's plants. The short-term costs of health protection programs designed to uphold the high standards of a corporation may, in a facility in an undeveloped or developing country, present a heavy economic burden resulting in loss of competitiveness, loss of growth opportunities, and loss of jobs. It is an area in which trade-offs are many; solutions are few.

The level of education and technical training in a workforce can have a profound impact on the level of health and safety protection in the plant. Literacy is certainly required of people who must read standard operating procedures, material safety data sheets, and hazard warning labels to safely operate a production unit. A high level of technical training may be required to operate units that rely on sophisticated, computerized control equipment, which in turn rely on skilled, timely human response in cases of untoward events. When reviewing design specifications of processes to be installed at foreign locations, the industrial hygienist should consider the level of technical training and education in the workforce and the consequences of an accident that may be caused by human error. Governments too should consider the consequences of "industrial policy" that might force complicated and potentially dangerous operations upon an uneducated workforce eager for employment. The following passage from Bidinotto (1) is instructive:

The Indian government had its heavy hand on every aspect of the Bhopal plant, from its design and construction to its eventual operation. Initially, the facility merely imported raw pesticides, such as one called Sevin, and then diluted, packaged, and shipped them. This was a relatively safe and simple operation. But, in accordance with industrial policy, Union Carbide was under constant pressure from the government to cut imports and reduce the loss of foreign exchange. To do this Carbide was required by its state-issued operating license to transfer to the Bhopal facility the capability to manufacture the basic pesticides and, subsequently, even their ingredients. Everything was to be "Indianized." Even the chemical production processes used in Bhopal were developed by Indian researchers. . . .

To produce Sevin, carbon tetrachloride is mixed with alpha-naphthol and a chemical known as methyl isocyanate, or MIC (the chemical that leaked in the accident). Liquid MIC is a highly unstable and volatile chemical, and a deadly toxin. . . . MIC was not required in Bhopal while the factory simply packaged Sevin, its final product. But the logic of "industrial self-sufficiency" and "technology transfer" required the manufacture of Sevin from scratch—and that meant dealing with its hazardous ingredients, including MIC. So in 1971, the Union Carbide factory opened a small plant to manufacture alpha-naphthol, and began to import and store MIC—a chemical which never had to be in India in the first place, except to satisfy the Indian government. . . . In 1977, based upon projections of growing demand, the Bhopal factory began to increase its alpha-naphthol facilities dramatically. A new $2.5 million plant— designed, of course, by an Indian consulting firm—was built. Ten times larger than most similar plants, it at once displayed design problems of scale: equipment would not work or would turn out to be the wrong size. . . .

Ultimately, faced with an inoperable alpha-naphthol facility, the factory's management decided to [open an MIC production facility in 1980]. . . . The parent corporation sent guidelines for the design of the safety systems; but under Indian law, the details had to be determined by an autonomous Indian-staffed consulting firm. . . .

What had begun as a Carbide subsidiary for packaging pesticides was now a government-directed business manufacturing and storing a deadly chemical in a technologically backward culture.

Those were not business decisions. Those were political decisions. . . . One last element of government policy helped lay the groundwork for the pending disaster. The area around the plant had been deserted at the time Carbide moved in. But in 1975 the local government, in a re-zoning scheme, encouraged thousands of Indians to settle near the plant by giving them construction loans and other inducements. In effect, government first helped to make the plant unsafe, and then drew the people into the path of the coming gas cloud.

Karim Ahmed (2) of the Natural Resources Defense Council echoed this concern:

Some countries insist that corporations like Union Carbide, rather than manufacture a product in the U.S. and export it, build a plant in their country and train the local people to run it. So some companies are forced into the double standard in order to sell a product in that market.

3 APPROACHES

The corporation should adopt worldwide internal policies and standards. Recognizing the complexities of economic and social conditions, differences in customs and attitudes, and the general level of education and technical training, these internal, worldwide policies and standards should be performance oriented rather than detailed, specification standards. In this chapter the terms "policy" and "standard" will be defined as follows:

- A *policy* is a broad statement of principle or intent adopted by the corporation on which standards are based. A policy is a statement of required conduct to which all employees must adhere.
- A *standard* is a plan or course of action adopted by the corporation to effect a policy. A standard is a statement of required conduct placed upon certain employees in specified professions or positions within the corporation. Such employees establish goals, objectives, guidelines, and procedures to implement the standard.

A sample set of policy and standards that impact industrial hygiene is shown in Table 7.1.

Exposure limits for dusts, mists, vapors, gases, physical agents, and so on are performance limits. There is flexibility as to how a facility may comply with a given exposure limit. There is frequently a wide selection of engineering controls and administrative procedures from which to choose. There may also be a selection of monitoring methods, from simple detector tubes, through pump and collection media sampling, through passive monitors, to sophisticated, portable direct reading instruments such as gas chromatographs, infrared detectors, atomic absorption units, and the like. Social and economic conditions at some facilities may narrow the selection range. The corporate industrial hygiene manager needs to appreciate that sometimes the "best" monitoring and control technologies may not be feasible or available, and therefore "adequate" technology must be used. Industrial hygiene is a science and an art. In judging adequacy, artistry is required.

As already stated, the issue of social and economic conditions in the host country is a profound and complex issue that the industrial hygiene manager cannot ignore. There is no doubt that establishing high-quality employee health protection programs, including the necessary training, sampling equipment, manpower, analytical resources, protective equipment, and so on is, in the short run, a money spending operation. Local management is rightfully concerned about economic viability and competitiveness of the facility. The wise industrial hygiene manager recognizes this fact and will strive to establish adequate industrial hygiene programs in a cost-effective way. In short, a plant struggling for survival in a poor country may not be able to afford the same high-quality, state-of-the-art industrial hygiene program existing in a plant in a high-technology, wealthy, developed country. The worldwide policies and standards adopted by a multinational corporation should outline minimally acceptable conduct for all plants, while the guidelines, procedures, goals, and objectives designed to meet these minimal codes of conduct should be flexible and adaptable for specific plants and regions.

Recognizing the health benefits of employment to workers, their families, and communities, the industrial hygiene manager must choose the course of action that optimizes the health of workers not just by controlling potentially harmful exposures in the plant but by recognizing the positive health benefits of economic growth. As Wilfred Beckerman (3) said in *Two Cheers for the Affluent Society: A Spirited Defense of Economic Growth:*

> A mistake in a criminal trial might mean imprisonment for one innocent man. A failure to maintain economic growth means continued poverty, deprivation, disease, squalor, degradation and slavery to soul-destroying toil for countless millions of the world's population.

Enlightened regulators recognize the economic burden that health protection programs may place on plants and make adjustment for it. In Japan (4),

> . . . if a violation of labor law is caused by backward social and economic conditions in a region or by the economic plight of a special industry, the violation does not require immediate correction. In such a situation, the inspector informs the firm of the violation and reports his finding to the Chief of the Labor Standard Inspection Office or to the Chief of the Prefectural Labor Standards Office. The decision as to what remedial measures should be taken by the region or the industry is determined on this higher level. In making a decision, these higher officials consider the social and economic problems causing the violations.

Industrial hygiene managers should make the same types of judgments as these "higher officials" when applying corporate policies and standards worldwide. Crutchfield (5) said, "modern safety management theory espouses . . . a goal to control losses in the occupational setting to the greatest possible extent *contingent upon available resources*" [emphasis added].

Quality industrial hygiene programs must be sold to corporate and plant management on the basis of its benefits. John A. Pendergrass (6), appointed in 1986 as the assistant secretary of labor, Occupational Safety and Health Administration (OSHA) in the United States, said it this way:

> To be successful the industrial hygiene manager must understand the goals and needs of the customer. We can learn from the salesman. The effective sales-

Table 7.1 Policy and Standards that Impact Industrial Hygiene

Policy: Workplace Health Protection

The corporation will operate its plants and laboratories in a manner that protects its employees from adverse health effects caused by exposure to chemicals and physical agents such as heat, cold, noise, vibration, and radiation.

Standard: Workplace Exposure Limits	Standard: Workplace Exposure Monitoring and Control	Standard: Safe Handling of Carcinogens	Standard: Fetal Protection
The corporation will comply with the workplace exposure regulations of each nation in which it has facilities.	The corporation will determine and monitor workplace stresses and maintain workplace environmental standards set in accordance with the policy on workplace health protection.	The corporation will comply with all government regulations concerned with exposure to carcinogens.	Women employees of childbearing potential or who are pregnant will not be exposed to work situations that are judged to pose an unacceptable hazard to the human fetus.
Where no such regulations exist or where such regulations are less stringent than deemed prudent by the medical director, the corporation will either (1) comply with the threshold limit values (TLVs) contained in the most recent list published by the American Conference of Governmental Industrial Hygienists or (2) for specific chemical or physical agents lacking TLVs, an internal exposure limit will be established by the medical director when deemed prudent.	Corporate industrial hygiene staff and plant and laboratory industrial hygienists are responsible to: • Conduct routine exposure assessments to determine exposures to workplace stressors and maintain scientifically defensible records of exposure assessments	Where there is any data that suggest that a chemical to which employees are exposed is a carcinogen, and such chemical is not subject to government regulations, we will evaluate that data, and based on that evaluation, take the following action: • Where such data establishes the chemical as a human carcinogen, we will take appropriate action to reduce exposure to the lowest reasonable level, unless exposure is already at such a level.	The medical director will: • Conduct appropriate toxicological tests of raw materials, products, intermediates, and by-products. • Review current literature for information on the hazards of chemicals and physical agents used or produced by the corporation. • Assess safety and health implications and the potential risks posed by these chemicals and physical agents. • Make recommendations to senior management and maintain a record as to work situations judged to pose an unacceptable hazard to the human fetus.

When trends in regulation, early experimental results, or intelligence from industrial, academic, or government sources indicates the need to develop or modify a workplace exposure limit or practice, the medical director shall issue an exposure limit advisory (ELA) for use in facility planning, design, and operation.

- In conjunction with other plant and corporate functions (e.g., engineering, maintenance, personnel, safety, etc.) institute corrective actions where overexposures are detected

- Develop monitoring methods where no adequate methods exist.

- Where such data establish the chemical as an experimental or suspect carcinogen, we will (individually or jointly with others) initiate study to confirm or disprove such designation. During such study, exposure will be controlled at the lowest reasonable level.

- If it is concluded that a potentially carcinogenic material cannot be produced or used without jeopardizing the health of employees, its manufacture or use will be discontinued.

- Management of the site(s) involved will take action so that women employees of childbearing potential or who are pregnant will not be hired into, be allowed to bid into, or continue in job situations that have physical agents or chemical exposure levels that have been identified by the medical director as posing an unacceptable hazard to the human fetus.

- Where rearrangement of the job situation to avoid exposure to the identified hazard cannot be achieved, and an employee has to be transferred out of a job assignment, every effort will be made to protect her job grade level and her seniority.

- In instances where the displacement or exclusion of women of childbearing potential adversely affects equal employment opportunity goals, efforts will be made to hire or place an equivalent number of women in other departments or areas that do not pose unacceptable hazards to the human fetus.

Table 7.1 (Continued)

Policy: Employee Hazard and Exposure Communication

It is the corporation's intent to identify hazards of chemicals and physical agents in the workplace and communicate such hazards to employees who may be exposed.

Standard: Employee Training and Education Concerning Hazards of Chemicals and Physical Agents	Standard: Communication of Exposure Information	Standard: Right of Access to Exposure Records
The corporation will comply with employee hazard communication rules of each nation in which it has facilities.	Employees who participate in individual (personal) industrial hygiene sampling shall be informed of the sampling results.	An employee who requests it will be provided access to his/her exposure records within 15 calendar days after the request is received.
As a minimum, all employees whose work involves potential exposures to a hazardous chemical substance will be informed of the hazards of the substance, will have ready access to reference material, such as a material safety data sheet (MSDS), and will receive training in the nature of the hazards and appropriate work practices, protective measures, and emergency procedures. Such training will be provided to employees when newly assigned to an area with potentially hazardous exposures and annually thereafter.	All employees in an area where ambient air concentrations or physical agents are monitored shall be informed periodically of area concentrations, their relationship to legal and corporate standards and intended corrective action where required.	A designated representative with the appropriate authorization from the employee will be provided access to an employee's exposure records within 15 calendar days of receipt of the authorization. A designated representative is any individual or organization to whom the employee has given written authorization to exercise a right of access to the employee's exposure records. (Note: Some local or national regulations may require that an employee's recognized or certified collective bargaining agent will be treated as a "designated representative" without regard to written employee authorization with respect to access to employee exposure records. Some regulations may also grant right of access to government
Health and safety training of employees is the joint responsibility of site manage-	Though not a corporate requirement, communication of exposure data should be in writing. (Note: some local or national regulations require written notification.) It is the responsibility of the industrial hygiene contact at each facility to ensure that exposure data is communicated to appropriate employees.	

ment, safety and industrial hygiene professionals, personnel departments, and line management.

All employees have the responsibility to obey safety and health rules of the facility.

Any employee inquiry about work exposures must be addressed by site management. The location physician, industrial hygienist or other appropriate management representative(s) should meet with the employee and provide a specific response based on the factual information available.

Corporate industrial hygiene or medical should be consulted in nonroutine situations.

authorities. It is the responsibility of site management to know the regulations impacting the facility and comply with legal requirements.)

Each location shall make such notification of existence, location, and right of access to exposure records a part of its new hire orientation program and shall post or otherwise inform all employees of the information each year.

The appropriate manager, personnel, and environmental counsel in the law department should be advised of requests for access to exposure records from a designated representative.

man knows his product. He knows all the features of the product: what it can do; what limitations might exist; and how it fits into the interests and needs of the customer.

In addition, the salesman must know the advantages his product has that will appeal to the customer. These advantages must be communicated to the customer so that he can recognize or understand the benefits that will be his by purchasing the product. If the price is right, the sale is made. Reorders come when the product has been ordered, delivered on time, and has performed as well as, or better than expected.

Industrial hygiene service is a product. It must meet all the tests of any other product. It must be sold and the customer must be satisfied.

What are the features, advantages and benefits that can make industrial hygiene so attractive to the line organization that it will want to buy what we offer?

Most practicing industrial hygienists entered the profession after OSHA was created. There is no question that OSHA brought attention to our profession. However, what some of us may consider a benefit is not necessarily considered favorably by line management. If industrial hygiene is a profession, and I believe it is, we should neither depend upon federal laws to sell our programs nor to be the authority of good practice. A plant manager does not need a high-priced industrial hygienist to come into the plant, take a few samples during the day, compare the results with OSHA regulations and announce that the plant results are above or below OSHA limits. I believe that every industrial hygiene program should be managed as if OSHA did not exist. Could you operate and would your program survive without OSHA? Did it exist before OSHA?

Industrial hygiene programs that have been sold to corporate management based largely on the fact that we must comply with the law will probably have a difficult time flourishing in world areas lacking such laws.

What are the economic and other benefits of industrial hygiene programs? Why should a plant manager in a struggling plant in a developing country spend money to develop and maintain an industrial hygiene program? There are both tangible and intangible benefits that justify the expense of an industrial hygiene program. Bernard Wyatt (7) enumerated some tangible and intangible returns from industrial health services:

1. Increased production due to improvement of health standards.
2. Increased efficiency and decreased operating costs, due to fewer "occupational incompatibilities."
3. Diminished unjust claims for compensation on the part of malingerers, due to comprehensive records of the physical examinations of all applicants and employees.
4. Improved home and community conditions, due to health education and other measures.

5. Improved relations between employer and employees, due to the factor of community of interests and mutual advantages.

In 1941, the National Association of Manufacturers (8), in an attempt to ascertain the economic benefits of industrial health services, conducted a comprehensive survey of 2064 industrial establishments in the United States. Of the 1625 companies that were asked if they considered the industrial health program a paying proposition, with the exception of five all answered "yes." The greatest improvement reported from the introduction of health programs was in occupational diseases. An average reduction of 62.8 percent was noted in 172 companies, and of 806 groups replying, 92 percent stated that they had experienced reductions. Of the 1388 companies reporting the effect of health programs on accident frequency, 97 percent indicated a reduction, the average reduction in 626 companies being estimated at 44.9 percent. Compensation insurance premiums, absenteeism, and labor turnover were other benefits reported by an overwhelming majority of respondents. Though this survey was done many years ago, it was thorough and the direct economic benefits that it reported undoubtedly remain true today.

If a corporate industrial hygiene program is sold on the basis of ethical principles and long-term economic benefits, then the program will flourish with or without the existence of regulations in the host country. In an analysis of medical services in industry, the American College of Surgeons (9) made this comment:

Humanitarianism has prompted the existence of very few industrial medical services. It has, of course, permeated a number of medical services in varying degree, but as a motivating force it has exerted a negligible influence. The economic factor has been the prime mover in the organization and growth of industrial medical services—and why not? . . . Humanitarianism without its ultimate economic benefits would be futile no matter what its nature or direction.

An adequate budget must be allowed for industrial hygiene activities in foreign lands. These expenses should not become a routine target for budget cutters. If there is a need to cut the industrial hygiene budget, it should be cut across the board in a way that does not place a disproportionate burden upon particular regions or countries. For example, if travel budget is to be cut 20 percent, then cut a proportionate amount out of domestic and foreign travel unless there is a compelling reason to do otherwise. If foreign facilities require more assistance, then perhaps travel to these facilities should not be reduced at all, or even increased, while travel to more "advanced" facilities can be reduced. Some people, both inside the corporation and outside, may view budgetary behavior as an indicator of a corporation's true commitment to development and maintenance of industrial hygiene programs in foreign lands.

When designing a new facility or modifying an existing process, most companies will perform a safety, industrial hygiene, and environmental protection review of the project to ensure that the facility design adequately addresses safety, health, and environmental issues. This kind of review is conducted whether the facility is a domestic or foreign location. Worldwide policies and standards must be applied to each facility design to measure success in addressing these issues. Sometimes the industrial hygienist may have to step back and ask the question: Can this process be operated safely considering the economic and social environment of the country in which it is being installed? In answering this question the industrial hygienist should consider the following:

- Educational level of the workforce
- Technical training available for employees
- Hazards of the materials being handled and the consequences of mishandling
- Experience with other operations in that region or country
- Political stability and consequences of unrest—for example, does this process, because of the kinds of materials being handled, present a tempting target for saboteurs?

These and other issues should be examined to determine the risks posed by the economic and social environments in which the facility will be operated. Additionally, do not be "forced into the double standard" as Karim Ahmed (2) put it. If industrial policy of a given country requires the corporation to install operations in that country due to perceived trade and job creation benefits, and the health and safety professionals of the corporation do not believe that the operations can be run safely in that country, corporate management should be made aware of this judgment and encouraged to seek alternatives. Possible alternatives include redesigning the process to make it acceptable, foregoing the potential market in the given country, and negotiating with the government to grant an exception because of the safety risks.

4 CONCLUSION

The challenges faced by corporate industrial hygiene staffs when establishing and maintaining programs at foreign locations range from the mundane (budgets, travel, customs, language) to the profound (economic, social, and health consequences of industrial hygiene programs). There are no simple answers to questions concerning the proper extent of industrial hygiene efforts in various regions of the world. Judgment based on facts and professional opinion is required of the industrial hygiene artisan. Establishment of corporate, worldwide, performance-oriented policies and standards that declare minimally accepted behavior on the part of management and employees is an important first step in making these difficult judgments. Procedures, guidelines, and practices that are established pursuant to these policies and standards should be flexible and adaptable to meet the diverse needs of facilities throughout the corporation.

REFERENCES

1. R. J. Bidinotto, Bhopal: The Fruit of Industrial Policy, *The Intellectual Activist,* July 19, 1985.
2. *People,* February 11, 1985, p. 81.
3. W. Beckerman, *Two Cheers for the Affluent Society: A Spirited Defense of Economic Growth,* New York: St. Martin, 1976.
4. N. A. Ashford, G. I. Heaton, J. I. Katz, and S. T. Owen, "The Foreign Experience and Its Relevance to the United States," in U.S. Dept. of Labor, *Protecting People at Work: A Reader in Occupational Safety and Health,* Washington, D.C.: U.S. Government Printing Office, 1980, pp. 326–327.
5. C. D. Crutchfield, Managing Occupational Safety and Health Programs—An Overview, *Am. Ind. Hyg. Assoc. J.* **42**(3), 226–228 (1981).
6. J. A. Pendergrass, Interaction and Communication with Management, Am. Ind. Hyg. Assoc. J. **44**(5), 313–315 (1983).
7. C. O. Sappington, *Essentials of Industrial Health,* J. B. Lippincott, Philadelphia: 1943, p. 64.
8. National Association of Manufacturers, "Industrial Health Practices: A Report of a Survey of 2,064 Industrial Establishments, conducted under the direction of Dr. Victor G. Heiser, Consultant," New York, 1941; through C. O. Sappington, *Essentials of Industrial Health,* 1943, pp. 64–67.
9. H. B. Selleck, *Occupational Health in America,* Detroit: Wayne State University Press, 1962, p. 49.

CHAPTER EIGHT

Right-to-Know: Communicating Information About Chemical Hazards

Jennifer C. Silk

Many early practitioners of industrial hygiene subscribed to the theory that knowledge about chemical hazards would overwhelm workers and that such information was best restricted to access by professionals. Today's industrial hygienist is working under a completely different theory—that workers and the public have a right to know the identities and hazards of the materials to which they are potentially exposed. This new climate is the result of both federal and state legislation that mandates these rights. Industrial hygienists are frequently responsible for implementing such legislation.

Right-to-know programs represent both an opportunity and a challenge for the industrial hygienist. The opportunity lies in heightening public awareness of the industrial hygiene profession and its goals. The challenge lies in translating the highly technical information generated and used by the industrial hygienist into comprehensible training programs and written materials. Successful programs will accomplish the goal of right-to-know requirements—reduction in the incidence of chemical source illnesses and injuries.

It should be noted that this chapter is intended to be an overview of the issue and not a specific guide to compliance with existing right-to-know laws. The industrial hygiene manager must obtain copies of the rules applicable to the facilities of concern to ensure such compliance.

It should also be noted that at the time this chapter is being written, the federal right-to-know rules apply to the manufacturing industrial sector, Standard Industrial Classification (SIC) Codes 20 through 39. However, it is anticipated that the scope of the rules will be expanded to the nonmanufacturing sectors in the near future. Industrial hygiene managers for these types of establishments should be prepared to comply with the expanded rule.

1 DEVELOPMENT OF FEDERAL WORKER RIGHT-TO-KNOW REQUIREMENTS

Although occupational safety and health practitioners have long recognized the usefulness of worker training in their arsenal of protective measures, the concept of providing information to workers to help them protect themselves began to be more seriously considered with the passage of the Occupational Safety and Health Act of 1970, Public Law No. 91-596. In the provisions of the act dealing with development of standards for hazardous chemicals, the Congress included the following language in section 6(b)(7):

> Any standard promulgated under this subsection shall prescribe the use of labels or other appropriate forms of warning as are necessary to insure that employees are apprised of all hazards to which they are exposed, relevant symptoms and appropriate emergency treatment, and proper conditions and precautions of safe use or exposure.

The legislative history of the act does not elaborate on the background of this particular provision—it appeared in early working drafts of the document and seemed to incite little controversy or disagreement during the discussions. Thus, by Congressional mandate, every specific health standard promulgated by the Occupational Safety and Health Administration (OSHA) has included provisions for labels and training to ensure "employees are apprised of all hazards to which they are exposed."

The pace of OSHA's rulemaking, however, has not resulted in very many substance-specific health standards. To date, the agency has only completed slightly over 20 such rules. Thus solely pursuing this substance-by-substance approach would not have provided the majority of workers with information about the hazards of the thousands of chemicals in their workplaces. The National Institute for Occupational Safety and Health (NIOSH) has estimated that there are as many as 575,000 hazardous chemical products in American workplaces.

Having available information about all of the hazards in a workplace serves a number of important purposes. First, the employer will have the information necessary to design and implement protective programs. In the past, industrial hygienists and other occupational safety and health professionals have had to devote considerable efforts to trying to find out the contents of the products in use in the workplace, as well as their hazards. Having this information provided with the product will minimize the time spent for this research and thus increase the time available for evaluating the workplace and instituting appropriate control measures. Limited safety and health resources will be put to better use.

The information will also enable workers to participate in these protective programs, thus increasing their effectiveness. A worker who understands why personal protective equipment is being provided is more likely to wear it and wear it properly. Workers who recognize the signs and symptoms of exposure are more likely to report them, enabling the employer to recognize a hazardous situation that needs to be corrected. When both the employer and the employee are operating from the same base of knowledge regarding the hazards of the chemicals in the workplace, protection is a joint process and much more likely to be achieved and thus result in the reduction or elimination of chemically related illnesses and injuries.

This concept of transferring information and thus preventing illnesses and injuries appears, deceptively, to be simple. It is actually a very complex process that involves highly technical information regarding chemicals and behavioral science principles regarding communication of such information in a manner that achieves the desired result. The many difficult issues to be addressed, the lack of clear data upon which to base the decisions to be made, and the differences of opinion regarding the approaches to take resulted in a very lengthy rulemaking process.

OSHA decided to pursue a generic rulemaking to provide information to all workers through one standard, thus implementing Congress' intent in the mandate of section 6(b)(7) of the act in one action, rather than attempting to accomplish this purpose solely through the substance-by-substance approach. To this end, a Standards Advisory Committee was formed in 1974 to provide the head of OSHA with a recommendation as to how this might be accomplished. The committee submitted a report in 1975 and concluded that the agency should promulgate a generic standard to address the issue of warning employees and that a comprehensive approach of labels, material safety data sheets, and training should be included. OSHA also received a criteria document from NIOSH in 1974 that recommended that a generic standard be pursued and that a comprehensive approach similar to that suggested by the advisory committee be incorporated.

OSHA believed at this point that the need for a hazard communication standard was clear, but the agency did not have enough information to proceed with a rulemaking at that time. The general content of what the standard should contain had been suggested by the recommendations of the advisory committee and NIOSH, but OSHA still had to deal with some very difficult issues before regulatory provisions could be developed. These included evaluating hazards, dealing with chronic hazards, and addressing trade secret protection.

Work continued on the project, and on January 28, 1977, an advance notice of proposed rulemaking (ANPR) was published in the *Federal Register* (42 FR 5372). The ANPR alerted the public to the agency's intent to publish a proposed rule and solicited public input on the issues of concern. The responses received generally supported the conclusion that transmittal of hazard information is useful, but viewpoints on the specific approach that OSHA should take varied significantly. Many companies had already implemented hazard communication programs but had done surprisingly little to evaluate those programs to determine the most effective means of communication.

Over the next 4 years, staff work continued in various areas. One part of the original project—providing employees access to records employers had generated of their hazardous exposures and results of medical surveillance—was published as a separate rulemaking action. Since that particular effort dealt with records that employers had chosen to generate of their own assessments of exposure and medical status, many of the difficult questions, such as those concerning hazard definitions, did not need to be addressed in the same fashion as would be necessary in a hazard communication standard. Through implementation of the records access rule, employees would have immediate access to currently available information concerning their exposures to hazardous chemicals and to results of medical surveillance programs, while work continued to determine the appropriate means to address hazard communication. The two rules would be complementary in that they would provide different types of protection in related areas. The final rule for "Access to Employee Exposure and Medical Records" was published on May 23, 1980, and is codified at 29 CFR Part 1910.20. It is important for the industrial hygiene manager to be aware of, and in compliance with, this regulation as part of the right-to-know program.

The Toxic Substances Control Act was adopted during this time period, and the Environmental Protection Agency (EPA) acquired labeling authority under that law. OSHA and EPA considered doing a joint rulemaking to address the issue, with OSHA covering workplace labeling and EPA addressing products in commerce. Differences in statutory mandates and staff opinions regarding content and approach of such a standard developed, and both agencies subsequently agreed that EPA would withdraw from the project.

On January 16, 1981, OSHA published a notice of proposed rulemaking entitled "Hazards Identification" (46 FR 4412). This proposal was withdrawn by the new administration on February 12, 1981, for further consideration of regulatory alternatives (46 FR 12214). The 1981 proposal was a labeling standard, rather than a standard that comprehensively addressed the issue of hazard communication. No provisions were included for the development and distribution of material safety data sheets or for training programs.

Following withdrawal of the 1981 proposal, the agency formed a standards development team to develop and consider regulatory alternatives to the approach taken in that proposed standard. As a result of that reconsideration, the agency published a new proposal on March 19, 1982, entitled "Hazard Communication" (47 (FR 12092). This proposal returned to the comprehensive approach of labels, material safety data sheets, and training that had been considered by the agency prior to the January 1981 proposal. The difference in titles—"Hazards Identification" versus "Hazard Communication"—represented a significant difference in the approach taken. The new proposal recognized that simply requiring labels to be placed on containers gives no assurance that employees will understand or act on that information. To effectively communicate the information, and thus accomplish the goals of right to know, a more active, comprehensive program must be undertaken. The standard proceeded through all the steps required for an OSHA rulemaking, and the final standard was published on November 25, 1983. It is codified at 29 CFR Part 1910.1200.

Public participation in this rulemaking indicated that the interest in this subject is great. OSHA received over 200 written comments during the comment period that followed publication of the proposal. Public hearings were convened in 4 cities, and over 4000 pages of testimony were recorded during the 19 days of hearings. The agency also received 62 posthearing exhibits. The public rulemaking record was thus quite extensive and provided considerable information upon which to base the final rule.

It should be noted, however, that the type of information presented during this rulemaking tended to be quite different from that which is usually collected during an OSHA proceeding on a health standard. There have been few studies conducted on the effectiveness of the various means of communicating hazards, and the information available tends to be anecdotal, rather than quantitative, in nature. Therefore, although there were a number of decisions to be made that had technical implications, many of the problems to be resolved simply involved choosing between different opinions expressed regarding the available scientific data.

One area where there was virtually universal agreement, however, was on the need for the standard. Although particular reasons for supporting the need varied among the interested parties, there were very few participants who did not recognize that employees in the manufacturing sector must be apprised of the hazards in their work areas. Thus, support for proceeding with the rulemaking and developing a final standard was strong, although opinions as to approach and the appropriate contents of the standard continued to vary considerably.

These differences of opinion have continued into the implementation of the rule, and a number of court actions on the standard or issues related to the standard are being pursued. These actions generally concern the policy and legal aspects of the rule, rather than the technical approach.

It should be noted that although this discussion has focused on the development of federal worker right-to-know legislation, there was also concurrent activity in the states. In fact, a number of states had adopted right-to-know legislation prior to promulgation of the federal standard. Industrial hygiene managers who are responsible for facilities that operate in OSHA-approved state plan states should consult the state governments for the right-to-know rules applicable in that state. Although such rules are largely consistent with the federal standard, there are some differences specific to certain states.

2 PROVISIONS OF THE FEDERAL WORKER RIGHT-TO-KNOW STANDARD

The following is a brief overview of the requirements of the federal Hazard Communication Standard (HCS). In reviewing these requirements, the industrial hygiene manager should be aware that the HCS is unique among OSHA health standards in two major respects. First, as already described, it is a generic rule and thus departs from the usual substance-by-substance approach pursued by OSHA. Second, it is the first major rule promulgated by OSHA that is largely performance oriented, that is, the provisions are flexible enough to allow employers to use different means to accomplish the desired goals. Thus the provisions are not as specific as those in other safety and health standards, and employers can devise a compliance plan that best suits their particular facilities rather than follow a "cookbook" approach to compliance.

2.1 Purpose

The initial paragraphs of the final standard establish the purposes of the rule. The primary purpose is to ensure that all chemicals are evaluated to determine their hazards.

One alternative to this broad approach would have been to incorporate a list of chemicals as the scope of coverage for the rule. OSHA decided that limiting coverage to a particular list would result in a much narrower scope than would be appropriate for a right-to-know standard. If a single, comprehensive list of hazardous chemicals existed, developed on the basis of thorough, professional evaluations of hazard information, then incorporation of such a list would obviously be a viable alternative. Unfortunately, no such list exists. The most protective approach, therefore, is to ensure that every chemical is evaluated to determine its hazards. It should be noted that the term "chemical" is used in the broadest sense in the standard, being defined as any element, compound, or mixture of elements or compounds. Thus it goes far beyond a liquid in a 55-gallon drum, including, for example, asbestos, welding fumes, and wood dust.

Once the chemical has been evaluated, and hazard information has been compiled, the standard requires that this information be transmitted to employers and employees. This is to be accomplished by means of labels on containers, material safety data sheets, and training programs.

Another purpose of the standard is to establish uniform national requirements by preempting state laws in states without OSHA-approved state plans, and by requiring rules in state plan states to go through the normal approval process for such rules. When federal OSHA promulgates a standard, state plan states must also adopt a rule that is at least as effective as the federal standard. If a state rule is applicable to products in interstate commerce—for example, if it requires labels to accompany chemicals in commerce—the state plan state will have to show a compelling local need for a different standard and demonstrate that such a standard will not unduly burden interstate commerce. The authority to preempt non-state-plan state standards with a federal standard is provided by section 18 of the act.

2.2 Scope and Application

The standard applies to chemical manufacturers, importers, distributors, and employers with employees exposed to hazardous chemicals as a part of their employment.

The HCS applies to hazardous chemicals that are known to be present in the workplace. Only those substances that are found to be hazardous are covered by an employer's hazard communication program, but the definition of hazard in the standard is broad enough to include most chemicals.

Laboratories are covered by the standard in a limited fashion. Customarily, when OSHA promulgates a health standard, laboratory professionals request exemptions on the basis of their expertise in handling chemicals and the special feasibility concerns of laboratories when applying standards written for general industry. In the final standard, OSHA has recognized these feasibility concerns, but did not think it appropriate to exempt such laboratories completely since their work involves chemicals, and some members of their staffs may not have received extensive training in handling hazardous materials. Thus the HCS requires laboratories to keep labels on containers that arrive in the lab with labels attached, to keep and give employees access to material safety data sheets that are received, and to train employees.

A number of other federal agencies have labeling authority and have enacted labeling regulations. OSHA has recognized the potential for duplicate regulations by exempting containers that are labeled in accordance with the requirements of certain other federal agencies from the standard's requirements for shipped containers. The standard, however, does not exempt such substances completely. For example, employees involved in the manufacture of pharmaceuticals will be protected by the standard, although the final products their establishments produce will be labeled in accordance with the requirements of the Food and Drug Administration rather than those of OSHA.

A number of items are completely exempted from the standard, such as hazardous waste when regulated by EPA, tobacco and tobacco products, wood and wood products, articles, and food, drugs, or cosmetics brought into the workplace for employee consumption.

2.3 Definitions

Detailed definitions are provided in the standard, and OSHA encourages anyone reading the rule to consult these definitions since they are essential to comprehending the provisions.

The most important definitions in determining the coverage of the rule are the definitions of hazards. The standard has divided hazards into physical and health categories. Physical hazards—such as flammability, combustibility, and reactivity—are specifically defined using test methods and other precise measures for determinations. These definitions are consistent with OSHA's existing rules for such hazards. The full range of health hazards cannot be defined as specifically, and a broad approach is incorporated in the definition, which in effect requires that any type of health effect that has been identified must be reported. The definitions are supplemented by an appendix to the rule that discusses in detail the problems of defining and identifying health hazards (Appendix A).

2.4 Hazard Determination

It is essential to the standard that the evaluation of the hazards of each chemical be thorough and accurate. Hazard evaluation is a complex and somewhat controversial process, which relies heavily on the professional judgment of the evaluator. The rule places the primary duty for evaluation on the employers responsible for introducing the chemical into the workplace—the chemical manufacturers and importers. Although downstream users may choose to evaluate the chemicals they purchase, they are permitted under the standard to rely on the information provided by their suppliers. During the rulemaking, it was emphasized repeatedly that the downstream users are generally unable to develop hazard information on products because they are not familiar with the contents or properties of the chemicals. Since many of them are small concerns, without professional safety and health staffs, they want to be assured that hazard information is provided to them with purchased products so they can properly protect their employees.

OSHA agrees that chemical manufacturers and importers are in the best position to adequately evaluate their products and has required that they do so and provide such information to their own employees, as well as to their customers.

Employers who generate hazardous chemicals in their workplaces, rather than purchase them, become "chemical manufacturers" for purposes of this standard. Thus intermediates or by-products of processes are covered by the rule since the employer will be required to do hazard evaluations for any chemical that is known to be present in the workplace in such a way that employees may be exposed under normal conditions of use or in foreseeable emergencies, and for which no information has been received from a supplier.

It was clear during the rulemaking that there are no generally agreed-upon, specific procedures available for the process of hazard evaluation. Some chemicals have well-known hazards, have been used for many years, and have been studied extensively. For others, data are not readily available. The extent of the literature search and professional evaluation necessary for the latter will be much greater than for well-known chemicals. Therefore, OSHA determined that the requirements must be performance oriented, with appropriate definitions of hazards and general guidelines provided. The primary guideline in terms of health hazards is that one good study is the threshold for a finding of hazard. The evaluator must report the results of any studies that are designed and conducted according to established scientific principles and that have statistically significant conclusions regarding the health effects of the chemical.

The only areas of general agreement in the record with respect to hazard evaluation are that professionals consider a chemical to be hazardous if it is regulated by OSHA or if the American Conference of Governmental Industrial Hygienists (ACGIH) has published a threshold limit value (TLV) for it. OSHA incorporated these principles into the standard by stating that chemicals that are regulated by OSHA or appear on the TLV list are to be considered hazardous in all situations. It should be recognized that these chemicals vary in both degree of hazard and extent of the data used to determine their hazard potential. Nonetheless, since there was agreement on consulting these sources, OSHA decided to incorporate these lists by reference into the standard.

The record also indicated that the health effect that excites the most controversy is carcinogenicity. As OSHA has discovered during many years of rulemaking, there is considerable diversity in opinion among professionals as to the level of proof required to substantiate that a substance may pose a carcinogenic hazard to employees.

Since this rule deals with disclosure of information, not specific control measures, OSHA believes that it is necessary to establish the sources of information that conclusively determine carcinogenicity for purposes of disclosure. The agency decided that if either the National Toxicology Program

(NTP) or the International Agency for Research on Cancer (IARC), both well-recognized authorities in hazard evaluation, find that a substance is a potential or confirmed carcinogen, then that information must be reported on the material safety data sheet for the substance. The evaluator may not agree with the findings of NTP or IARC, but the information must nevertheless be reported. In addition to these sources, an evaluator must still review any other available toxicological studies regarding carcinogenicity to determine if they must be reported as well.

Another difficult issue to deal with in promulgating the Hazard Communication Standard was the treatment of mixtures of hazardous chemicals. Most toxicological evaluation is done on discrete chemicals, while most workplace exposures are to mixtures of such chemicals. It is very difficult to determine if a chemical poses the same hazard in the mixture as it does in its essentially pure form. This determination is particularly difficult in the case of health hazards.

The standard allows evaluators to make a determination as to whether a mixture with a component that poses a physical hazard will have the same hazard as the substance itself. While scientifically valid information must of course be used to make that determination, calculations and other such information may also be used in making an appropriate determination about the potential physical hazards of chemical mixtures.

It is not possible, in OSHA's judgment, to allow a similar evaluation approach in the case of health hazards. Thus the standard requires that unless a mixture has been tested to determine its health hazards, the assumption must be that the mixture has the same hazards as any of its components comprising one percent or more of the total composition and that the mixture poses a carcinogenic hazard if it contains a carcinogen in concentrations of 0.1 percent or greater.

2.5   Hazard Communication Program

Once the hazardous chemicals in the workplace have been identified, the employer is required to establish and implement a hazard communication program. This is to be a written plan that describes how the requirements of the Hazard Communication Standard will be met in the workplace.

The written program is to include a list of the hazardous chemicals known to be present. The list will serve as an index of the material safety data sheets so that the employer and employees will know which chemicals have been determined to be hazardous, and thus for which chemicals information must be generated and made available.

In addition, the hazard communication program is to include the methods the employer will use to inform employees of the hazards of nonroutine tasks and the hazards of chemicals in unlabeled pipes. Although the employer is required to train employees about the hazards of their jobs, employees must sometimes perform unusual tasks such as cleaning out reactor vessels. In these situations, the employer must make arrangements to provide employees with the information necessary about the hazards of the new task. The standard does not mandate that employers label all pipes but requires them to have a means of conveying to employees the hazards of any operations with pipes containing hazardous chemicals.

The standard also requires employers to include in their program the methods they will use to inform on-site contractors of the hazards to which their employees may be exposed. A number of employers hire contractors for the jobs at their work sites that involve the greatest exposures to hazardous chemicals. In these situations, OSHA believes it is appropriate to at least ensure that these contractors are provided with information about the hazards of the chemicals so they can protect their employees.

2.6 Labels

Labels on containers are the first of the three major means, or components, included in the standard to transmit hazard information. The labels required under the HCS are to be put on shipped containers, as well as on containers within the workplace. Their purpose is threefold: to serve as an immediate visual warning that the chemicals in the container are hazardous, to remind employees of what they have been taught about handling these chemicals, and to advise that more detailed information is available on the material safety data sheets. The labeling requirements are performance oriented—that is, kept to an essential minimum, while the format of the presentation is left to the preparer of the label. This was done to accommodate the many different and effective labeling formats that are currently in use.

On shipped containers, the label is to include an identity, appropriate hazard warnings, and the name and address of the chemical manufacturer, importer, or other responsible party. On in-plant containers, the label is to include an identity and appropriate hazard warnings.

The HCS recognizes that there are some feasibility problems with labeling in-plant containers, particularly when the operations are batch processes and the chemicals change frequently. Alternatives to labeling stationary process containers are permitted, as long as the information is available in written form in the work area so that employees have ready access to it.

2.7 Material Safety Data Sheets

The focus of detailed hazard information under the standard is the material safety data sheet (MSDS). These are written documents that provide extensive information on the chemical identification of components, as well as other useful information such as the hazards of the chemicals and protective measures. Material safety data sheets are required for each hazardous chemical in the workplace.

Many manufacturers produced and distributed such sheets for their products prior to the promulgation of the HCS, but with significant variation in content and quality. This was largely because these sheets, except in the maritime industries, were provided voluntarily and did not have to conform to any particular information requirements. The standard establishes the minimum information that must be included on the data sheets and requires that the sheets be provided automatically at the time of initial shipment of a hazardous chemical, and that new sheets be provided whenever the information has to be updated. Furthermore, MSDSs are to be made readily available to employees and to their designated representatives. Thus employees will always have access to detailed information on the identities and hazards of the substances they are exposed to in their work areas.

Although the information to be included on the MSDS is specified, the format of the presentation is to be determined by the preparer of the sheet. OSHA has developed a nonmandatory format, OSHA Form 174, to assist those who do not wish to develop their own forms.

2.8 Training

The third major communication component of the standard is training. This is regarded by many as the most important aspect of the hazard communication program—the provision that makes the program effective. It is the training requirement that ties together the various other components in a forum that can most readily ensure that employees understand the information being provided to them. Training is required for all employees exposed to hazardous chemicals before their initial assignment to such work and whenever the hazard changes. The training is to include a discussion of labels and MSDSs, so that the employee will understand the material on these documents and how it can be used. Beyond that, the HCS also requires employees to be trained regarding the hazards of the chemicals they are exposed to, ways to detect the presence of these hazards, and measures employees can take to protect themselves. In addition, they are to be informed of the operations in their work areas where hazardous chemicals are present, and the location and availability of the written hazard communication program and material safety data sheets.

OSHA's Training Institute has developed voluntary training guidelines that outline the elements that should be considered in developing and conducting a training program. These guidelines were published in the *Federal Register* on July 27, 1984 (49 FR 30290).

2.9 Trade Secrets

As mentioned previously, the standard requires that detailed information on the chemical identity of the hazardous chemicals be included on the MSDS for the substance. The only exception would be when the specific chemical identity is a bona fide trade secret. In that case, the chemical manufacturer, importer, or employer can withhold the specific chemical identity, as long as all other information about the chemical is disclosed and it is noted on the MSDS that the specific chemical identity is being withheld because it is a trade secret. It is important to emphasize that all hazard and protective measure information must be generated and disclosed regardless of the trade secret status of the chemical.

The standard requires disclosure of the trade secrets to health professionals, employees, or designated representatives who provide medical or other occupational health services to exposed employees. In medical emergencies, the information is to be disclosed immediately to a treating physician or nurse. The holder of the trade secret may require the professional to sign a confidentiality agreement after the emergency is abated, but the professional's judgment as to the emergency nature of the situation is to be the determining factor with regard to disclosure.

In nonemergency situations, the process of disclosure is somewhat different. A physician, industrial hygienist, toxicologist, epidemiologist, occupational health nurse, employee, or designated representative needing the information must submit a written request to the holder of the trade secret, substantiating the need for the information, stating why other information would not satisfy that need, and describing the means that will be used to keep the information confidential. The holder of the trade secret must disclose the information if these requirements are met. If the holder denies the request, the denial must be in writing and provided within 30 days of the request. The denial must include evidence that the specific chemical identity is a trade secret, state why the request is being denied, and explain how alternative information may satisfy the health need.

If the requester does not agree with the alternatives and still needs the information, the matter is to be referred to OSHA for enforcement purposes. The standard specifies the steps that OSHA will take in reviewing the situation and determining a subsequent course of action.

Disclosure of trade secrets involved the most controversial and difficult policy considerations in the rule. OSHA's aim was to ensure that necessary information was provided to protect employees, while means were also provided for employers to preserve the confidentiality of bona fide trade secrets. OSHA believes that such trade secrets are not common, but that in instances where they do exist, the holder must be able to provide adequate substantiation of the need for confidentiality for it to be granted. Most importantly, by allowing professional access to specific chemical identities if they can substantiate the need for such access, employees should be adequately protected.

2.10 Recordkeeping

The rule requires that written plans of compliance and material safety data sheets be kept current. Outdated sheets need not be kept unless they are subject to the requirements of OSHA's Access to Employee Exposure and Medical Records regulation, 29 CFR Part 1910.20. Under that rule, if an employer has no other record of exposure the data sheets may have to be retained for 30 years.

2.11   Documents Available

In addition to the MSDS form and voluntary training guidelines mentioned previously, the industrial hygiene manager may wish to obtain from OSHA the inspection procedures used by the agency to enforce the rule (CPL 2-2.38A). These procedures provide insight into agency interpretations of provisions in the HCS and may help an employer in developing an appropriate program.

3   COMMUNITY RIGHT TO KNOW

The industrial hygiene manager should also be aware of existing requirements for public disclosure of hazard and identity information regarding chemicals. On a federal level, such requirements are included under Title III of the Superfund Amendments and Reauthorization Act of 1986 (SARA). The EPA is implementing this legislation. The two community right-to-know reporting requirements under SARA are found in Sections 311 and 312 of Title III.

Section 311 requires that facilities that must prepare or have available material safety data sheets under OSHA regulations submit either copies of the MSDS or a list of MSDS chemicals to the local emergency planning committee, the state emergency response commission, and the local fire department. Section 312 requires submission of inventory forms to those same organizations. As this is being written, EPA is in the process of finalizing the regulations implementing SARA. Managers should follow developments in this area and ensure that state and local requirements are met.

4   CONCLUSION

Right-to-know legislation represents an important step forward in ensuring that everyone is provided necessary information about potentially hazardous exposures. A commitment must be made to meet the intent of the laws, as well as the specific legal requirements. Industrial hygiene managers are in an excellent position to ensure this commitment is made by their firms and thus ensure that their program is effective.

CHAPTER NINE

Managing Process Safety to Prevent Catastrophes

Arthur F. Burk

1 INTRODUCTION

An analysis of the worldwide chemical and petroleum industry safety performance over the past 30 years quickly leads one to the conclusion that there is a need for a concerted and dedicated effort to improve the methods, approaches, and techniques used to handle toxic materials. Figure 9.1 summarizes an analysis of the 100 largest losses in the past 30 years by Marsh and

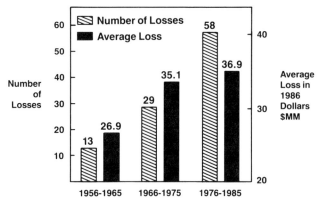

Figure 9.1. One hundred largest losses. A 30-year review of property damage losses in hydrocarbon chemical industries. (From M and M Protection Consultants, *One Hundred Largest Losses,* 9th ed., April 1986.)

McClennan and clearly illustrates the magnitude of the problem. Most of these incidents involved fires and explosions; many resulted in serious injury and loss of life and sometimes affected the surrounding community.

More significantly, there have been a number of major chemical or chemical-related incidents in the past 14 years that have had a major effect on the surrounding community. These are summarized in the following list:

Some Key Incidents	Impact
Flixborough (1974)	$232 million damage; 28 fatalities on-site; damages to homes off-site
Seveso (7/76)	Widespread contamination on- and off-site
Mexico City LPG (11/84)	$20,040,000 damage; 300 fatalities, mostly off-site
Bhopal (12/84)	2,800 fatalities off-site; 200,000 persons affected off-site
Chernobyl nuclear plant (4/86)	300 square miles evacuated with 31 fatalities
Sandoz Warehouse Fire (11/86)	Rhine River—major effect upon ecology of the river

Not one of these incidents had to occur! Not one of these incidents should have occurred! In each case there was a breakdown of established controls, some procedural, some training, some engineering, and in all cases managerial controls.

The subsequent sections of this chapter discuss the principles and key features of a process safety management system that, if practiced and implemented, will prevent industrial catastrophes! The importance of the "corporate mission/philosophy" and of "operating discipline" are also discussed. The corporate mission/philosophy provides the leadership and foundation for a process safety management system. Operating discipline is the glue that holds the individual elements of process safety management together. The corporate mission/philosophy in turn is an important ingredient of the glue.

2   ROLE OF THE CORPORATE MISSION/PHILOSOPHY

The corporate mission/philosophy regarding the issues of safety, health, and the environment is extremely important in that it provides the foundation for a process safety management system.

In every business operation, there are conflicting and competing priorities. Managers, supervisors, operators, and mechanics must continually make decisions regarding conflicting priorities in areas such as production, quality, cost, personnel, and security as well as safety, health, and the environment. Without leadership and guidance from the top of the corporation, it is possible to have production priorities placed ahead of safety, for example. This is a highly undesirable situation and will lead to increased frequency of process incidents.

The corporate mission/philosophy must clearly state what the corporation's position is regarding the safety and health of its employees and members of the surrounding communities, as well as protection of the environment. It must provide guidance regarding the handling of conflicting priorities. There must be no question where the corporation stands on the issues of safety, health, and the environment.

3   PROCESS SAFETY MANAGEMENT: WHAT IS IT?

Process safety management is the application of management controls in a way that process hazards are identified, understood, and controlled so that process-related injuries and incidents can be eliminated.

The elements of process safety management address technology, personnel, facilities, and emergencies, and focus on hazard identification, risk analysis and assessment, risk mitigation, hazard management and control, and emergency response.

There are a number of very important words in the definition of process safety management. The first is *management*. We are not talking about the traditional concept of management, that is, managers and supervisors. Rather, we are talking about everyone involved in the management of process safety. When one thinks about management in that sense, one quickly realizes that it includes everyone from the operator and mechanic up to and including the plant manager of a given site. The operator, in fact, is a key member of the process safety management team—often the only manager immediately available.

The next three words—*identify, understand,* and *control,* involve a very methodical process in gaining solid control of process hazards. Before one can even hope to control process hazards, one must begin with a comprehensive effort to identify the hazards. This effort to identify must continue until a thorough understanding of the hazards is achieved—an understanding of the interrelationships of the different individual hazards and the mechanisms by which they can go out of control. Once the identification and understanding is achieved, then and only then can you proceed to develop appropriate controls.

4 THE KEY ELEMENTS OF PROCESS SAFETY MANAGEMENT

The 12 elements of process safety management may be broken down into 4 areas as follows:

Technology

1. Process safety information
2. Process hazards analysis
3. Management of change (technology)
4. Operating procedures

Personnel

5. Personnel training and performance
6. Incident investigation
7. Auditing

Facilities

8. Equipment tests and inspections
9. Prestart-up safety review
10. Management of change (facilities)
11. Quality assurance

Emergency Response

12. Emergency response and control plan

These 12 elements, in turn, focus on the following areas of activity:

Hazard identification
Risk analysis and assessment

Risk mitigation
Hazard management and control
Emergency response

Table 9.1 illustrates how the individual elements are related to these areas of activity. To strengthen the reader's understanding of the elements of process safety management, each element is further discussed from three different viewpoints:

1. What is the principle involved, that is, why is this element important?
2. What are the essential features of each element in an overall process safety management program?
3. Supporting discussion.

Each of the 12 elements of process safety management will be presented through an outline of their principles and essential features and followed by appropriate discussion.

4.1   Process Safety Information

PRINCIPLE. The safety information package provides a description of the hazards of the chemical process or operation. It provides the foundation for achieving an identification and understanding of the hazards involved—the first steps in the process safety management effort. The process safety information package generally consists of three parts: hazards of materials, equipment design information, and process document (technical basis for manufacturing processes).

ESSENTIAL FEATURES OF SAFETY INFORMATION PACKAGE

I. Hazards of materials: Provides a listing of all pertinent data from a hazard point of view for each chemical:
   Boiling points, freezing points
   Vapor pressure
   Flash points, combusion limits
   Ignition temperatures
   Thermal stability
   Reaction kinetics
   Toxicity information
   (a) Chronic and acute toxicity data: oral, inhalation, and skin
   (b) Permissible exposure limits
II. Equipment design information: Provides description of key equipment design data:
   Vessel sizes
   Materials of construction
   Pump specs and characteristics

Table 9.1. Process Safety Management

Elements of Process Safety Management	Hazard Identification	Risk Analysis and Assessment
Technology		
Process safety informa-tion	Process safety information →	
Process hazards analysis	Process hazards analysis →	→ Process hazards analysis —
Management of change	Management of change →	
Operating procedures		
Personnel		
Personnel training and performance		
Incident investigation		
Auditing (PSM compli-ance)		
Facilities		
Equipment tests and inspections		
Prestart-up review		
Management of change	Management of change →	
Quality assurance		
Emergency response		
Emergency response and control plan		

Material and energy balances
Piping and instrument diagrams
Agitation requirements
Maximum allowable working pressure
Vent sizing—basis and calculations
Ventilation requirements
Electrical classification
Electrical diagrams

III. Process document (technical basis): The process document is a technical document that describes the path to "safe operation":
Process chemistry—clear description and understanding
Process steps and limits—provided for each step

Normal operation	Temperatures
Maximum	Pressures
Minimum	Flows
	Compositions

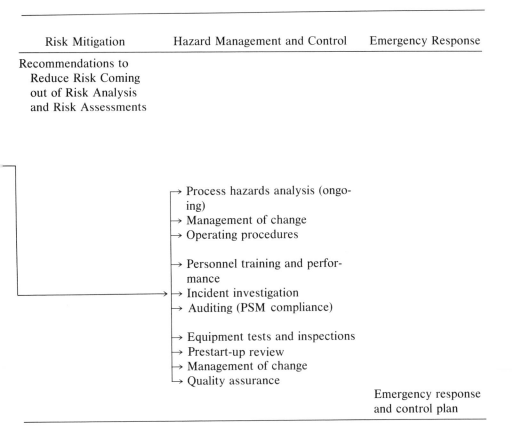

Risk Mitigation	Hazard Management and Control	Emergency Response
Recommendations to Reduce Risk Coming out of Risk Analysis and Risk Assessments		
	→ Process hazards analysis (ongoing)	
	→ Management of change	
	→ Operating procedures	
	→ Personnel training and performance	
	→ Incident investigation	
	→ Auditing (PSM compliance)	
	→ Equipment tests and inspections	
	→ Prestart-up review	
	→ Management of change	
	→ Quality assurance	
		Emergency response and control plan

Consequences of deviation (described for each step): above maximum, below minimum

Maintained "evergreen": changes closely scrutinized (See management of change)

DISCUSSION. The first part of the process safety information package (i.e., the hazards of materials) is a collection and development of all pertinent data from a hazard point of view for each chemical involved. It includes both physical and chemical properties such as flammability and thermal stability data, reaction data, and any other property relevant to a particular hazard. Toxicity data is an important part of the package. Hazards of materials focuses on the identification of hazards.

Whether it be a manufacturing, storage, or handling operation, the equipment design package is an important part of the safety information package. During design of each facility, the *design basis* is developed and documented. It is extremely important that the design basis be preserved and passed on to those who operate the facility. Without a sound understanding of the design basis, it is unlikely that proper decisions will be made subsequently during the routine operation of the equipment or during times where changes to the operation are proposed. The design basis for a pressure-relief device on a storage tank containing a toxic material is a good example. It is important to know and understand the design basis for the storage tank pressure-relief device. Is it sized for fire conditions?—or—Is it sized for the maximum pressure that can be developed in the tank if the feed pump is operated in a deadhead condition with the tank full or if the nitrogen regulator fails and full nitrogen pressure is applied to the tank? If the design basis is the latter, then the personnel responsible for the operation of the tank must preserve the design basis and ensure that under no circumstances is the tank to be exposed to the presence of flammable or combustible materials. Without an understanding of the design basis, it (the design basis) is susceptible to being compromised by subsequent changes.

The process document for a manufacturing facility describes the path to safe operation. There are two key parts of this document. The first is a clear understanding of the process chemistry, including the potential for undesirable side or runaway reactions. The second is the process steps and limits section, which defines the boundaries for safe operation. An essential feature is the development and description of the consequences of operation outside the boundaries. It is that thorough understanding of the consequences of operation outside the maximum and minimum boundaries that provides the basis for development of appropriate process controls to ensure safe operation. Without this understanding it will be difficult to (1) develop suitable process controls during the design stage and (2) maintain them during routine operation.

4.2   Process Hazards Analysis

PRINCIPLE. Process hazards analysis effectively identifies, evaluates, and controls hazards associated with process facilities in a way that utilizes an orderly, organized, methodical approach and documents results for future use in follow-up and training of personnel so that injuries and incidents are prevented. A description of four of the more commonly used methods of process hazards analysis (reviews) can be found in Table 9.2.

ESSENTIAL FEATURES OF A PROCESS HAZARDS ANALYSIS PROGRAM

New Facilities

Series of process hazards reviews (PHR) held at basic data, preauthorization, design, and prestart-up stages of a project.

Table 9.2. Formal Hazard Assessment Techniques

A. What-If/Checklist

The what-if/checklist is a broadly based hazard assessment technique that combines the creative thinking of a selected team of specialists with the methodical focus of a pre-prepared checklist. The result is a comprehensive process hazard analysis with excellent utility in training operating personnel on the hazards of the particular operation.

The review team is selected to represent a wide range of disciplines—production, mechanical, technical, safety, exempt, and nonexempt. Each person is given a basic information package regarding the process to be studied. This package typically includes information regarding hazards of materials, process technology, procedures, equipment design, instrumentation control, incident experience, previous hazard reviews, and so on. A field tour of the process is also conducted at this point.

At the second (and subsequent) meeting(s), the review team methodically goes through the process from receipt of raw materials to delivery of the finished product to the customer's site. At each step the group collectively generates a listing of what-if questions regarding the hazards and safety of the operation. When the review team completes the generation of the questions, it systematically goes through a prepared checklist to stimulate additional questions.

At the next series of meetings, answers are developed for each question. A key concept during this series of meetings is achieving consensus by the broad range of disciplines.

A listing of recommendations is developed out of those answers specifying additional action or study. The recommendations along with the listing of questions and answers become the key elements of the hazard assessment report.

B. HAZOP: Hazard and Operability Study

A HAZOP study consists of a detailed review of a piping and instrument diagram by a selected team of specialists, who critically analyze the effects of problems arising in *each* pipeline and vessel involved in the operation. A list of key words is selected for investigation, for example, more of, less of, none of, part of, and these, are used to lead the study.

Pertinent parameters are selected, for example, flow, temperature, pressure, and time and the effect of *each* is looked at for a potential hazardous situation. For each deviation, consequences of *failure* of all protection are examined.

The system is evaluated as designed and with deviations noted. All causes of failure are identified. Existing safeguards and protection are identified. Assessment is made weighing the consequences, causes, and protection requirements involved.

C. Failure Mode and Effect (FMEA)

The failure mode and effect method is a methodical study of component failures. This review starts with a diagram of the process that includes all components that could fail and conceivably affect the safety of the process. Typical

Table 9.2. (*Continued*)

examples are instrument transmitters, controllers, valves, pumps, rotometers, and so on. These components are listed on a data tabulation sheet and *individually analyzed* for the following:

Potential mode of failure, i.e., fails open, shut, on, off
Consequence of failure
    Effect on other components
    Effect on whole system
Hazard class, i.e., high, moderate, low
Probability of failure
Detection methods
Compensating provision/remarks

Multiple concurrent failures are also included in the analysis. The last step in the analysis is to analyze the data for each component or multiple component failure and develop a series of recommendations appropriate to risk management.

D. Fault Tree Analysis

A fault tree analysis is a quantitative assessment of the probability of occurrence of an undesired top event, such as a toxic gas release or explosion. It begins with a graphical representation (using logic symbols) of all possible sequences of events that could result in this event. The resulting diagram looks like a tree with many multiple branches—each branch listing the sequential events (failures) for different independent paths to the top event. Probabilities (using failure rate data) are assigned to each event and then used to calculate the probability of occurrence of the undesired event.

This technique is particularly useful in evaluating the effect of alternative actions on reducing the probability of occurrence of the undesired event.

Existing Facilities

Review schedule developed for all hazardous processes to include one or more of the following types of reviews:

    1. What-if/checklist
    2. Failure mode and effect (FM&E)
    3. Hazard and operability study (HAZOP)
    4. Fault tree analysis

at a frequency not to exceed 3–5 years

Committee makeup to achieve interaction between manufacturing, technical, maintenance, and others as appropriate.

Subsequent reviews need not duplicate original or previous review; in fact certain advantages can be found in changing the periodic review method.

Follow-up established to achieve completion of PHR recommendations.

ESSENTIAL FEATURES OF PROCESS HAZARDS REVIEW

Provides clear understanding of hazard(s).

Provides clear understanding of the lines of defense (i.e., engineering and administrative controls).

Provides understanding of consequences of breaching the lines of defense.

Recommends features to safely control hazard(s).

ESSENTIAL FEATURES OF PROCESS HAZARDS REVIEW REPORT

Defines scope of review and summarizes hazards.

Documents all questions and answers (what-if/checklist).

Lists recommendations along with responsibility and timing for follow-up.

Multidisciplined consensus achieved; committee concludes whether or not process is safe to operate.

DISCUSSION. Process hazards analysis builds upon the identification of hazards developed in the safety information package and strives to achieve a complete understanding of the hazards at hand. It extends beyond the understanding stage and moves into control of hazards through recommendations coming out of the process hazards reviews.

TYPES OF PROCESS HAZARDS ANALYSIS. Four of the more commonly used methods of process hazards analysis currently used: what-if/checklist, failure mode and effect (FM&E), hazard and operability study (HAZOP), and fault tree analysis (FTA) are briefly described in Table 9.2. It is beyond the scope of this chapter to get into a more detailed description of the methods and how to use them. Additional information along these lines can be found in the list of references.

PROCESS HAZARDS ANALYSIS FOR NEW FACILITIES. For new facilities the key question is not "which method of process hazards analysis to use?" Rather, the key question is "which methods of process hazards analysis should be used and when in the life of a project should they be applied?" Generally, process hazards reviews should be conducted at the following stages during the life of a project for a new facility:

1. *Basic Data*. Generally, the first process hazards review should be conducted during the basic data stage of a project. In this stage the proposed

process and equipment are still in the conceptual stage and thus it is quite appropriate to challenge why a particular hazardous material is being used and why other less hazardous alternatives are not being considered.

2. Preauthorization (Scope of Work). During this stage of a project, design is approximately 20–40 percent complete and conceptually things are starting to gel. Since the project has not been authorized yet, it is an appropriate time to conduct a comprehensive process hazards analysis to flush out any unknown hazards and to crystallize one's understanding of the hazards at hand. A key objective of this particular review is to ensure that appropriate control features are included in the design and in the project estimate. Typically this review will not get into the finite detail of the detailed design review. It must address, however, those hazards that could have a significant effect on the project cost, such as size and location of storage facilities for hazardous materials.

3. Design. Once a project is authorized, the conceptual features in the basic data report gel pretty quickly, and it becomes very costly to make major changes—thus emphasizing and underlying the importance of the two previously discussed process hazard reviews. At this stage of the project a third process hazards review is conducted to further refine one's understanding of the hazards relative to the particular process. This review usually focuses on the design being developed and on the design decisions to be made. Accordingly, the design process hazards reviews typically focus on the piping and instrument diagrams and on the detailed equipment design drawings. Also, at this stage, in those processes where the potential for a catastrophic incident is present, it may be appropriate to conduct a risk assessment consisting of the following analyses:

> Definition of the potential catastrophic incident
> Downwind dispersion analysis (for toxic gas releases)
> Community impact analysis
> Quantification or probability analysis for incident occurrence

4. Prestart-up. The prestart-up stage is really an inappropriate time in the life of a project to begin a process hazards review. It is too late to effect significant changes. It is appropriate to go over the existing process hazards reviews that have been conducted and to update them to include changes made in the latter part of the design stage. The prestart-up stage is more appropriately a checkpoint stage where all of the safety, health, and hazard analysis efforts are checked for accuracy, thoroughness, completeness, and follow-up of open recommendations.

5. Which Method To Use? There is no definitive answer to this question. Different organizations quite effectively use different methods at different

Table 9.3. Applicability of Method to Project Stage

Method	Basic Data	Preauthorization (Scope of Work)	Design	Prestart-up
What-if/checklist	X	X	X	[a]
Failure mode and effect			X	[a]
HAZOP			X	[a]
Fault tree analysis		X	X	[a]

[a] See comments regarding prestart-up reviews.

stages in the life of a project. Nevertheless, some general guidance is given in Table 9.3 for methods that can be appropriately used at each stage.

One additional comment. Oftentimes there are advantages to using different methods of process hazards analysis on the same process or project. Each method addresses or focuses on the hazards using a different approach. When used together, they complement each other and strengthen the overall process hazards analysis.

PROCESS HAZARDS ANALYSIS FOR EXISTING FACILITIES. The same methods described for new facilities are also used to analyze process hazards for existing facilities. The essential features of a process hazards review program are pretty straightforward. They include setting up a process review schedule that lists for each process (1) type review to be conducted and (2) frequency or when the review is to be held. In addition a system to ensure follow-up of open recommendations should be established. The essential features of a process hazards review listed previously provide a good basis upon which to judge the quality of a review. To be effective a process hazards review must effectively communicate the criteria listed to operating personnel, that is, those who operate the facility.

4.3   Management of Change (Technology)

PRINCIPLE. Process changes potentially invalidate prior hazard assessments; accordingly, all process changes beyond safe limits as defined in appropriate process technology must be subjected to the same rigorous review that is applied to new processes.

ESSENTIAL FEATURES OF MANAGEMENT-OF-CHANGE SYSTEM

Document to Authorize Change
   Technical basis for change is clearly described, that is, what experiments were run, what data was developed?
   Proposed modification to process technology; contains sections on

Safety (including fire protection), health, and environment
Effect on and changes in equipment
Process steps and limits
Process hazard review
Need (?) acknowledged
Approved review attached (if required)
Approved operating instructions attached (if changes required)
Documents plans to provide appropriate training
Authorized for specific time limit (suggested maximum 1 year)
Appropriate authorization levels established

Document To Provide Closure

Summarizes results and recommendations (where tests were conducted)
Document can only recommend change within limits originally authorized
Process hazards review closure required
Approved operating instructions must be attached (if changes required)

DISCUSSION. As stated in the principle, whenever changes are proposed to the established technology as defined in the safety information package, it is imperative that such changes receive appropriate review to ensure protection of the safety and health of personnel as well as protection of the environment. To accomplish this, the proposed change must be clearly documented beginning with the technical basis for the proposed change. The technical basis is needed to assess potential hazards introduced by scaleup. The documentation should update all appropriate elements of the process safety management program:

Process safety information package
Hazards of materials
Equipment and process design package
Process document
Operating procedures
Equipment test and inspection schedules
Quality assurance, maintenance program
Plans to provide Training
Emergency Response & Control Plan

In addition to providing the proposed updated documentation, the changes proposed should be clearly evident to those approving and authorizing the document.

Another important part of the authorization document is a thorough discussion of the safety, health, and environmental considerations. If potential adverse safety, health, and environmental considerations are present, the proposed changes should be subjected to a process hazards review that then becomes part of the authorization document.

It is only after all appropriate parts of the process safety management program have been acknowledged and documented that those who approve and authorize change are in a position to assess and judge the adequacy of the proposal. They must proceed only after ensuring that all elements of process safety management have been adequately addressed.

4.4   Operating Procedures

PRINCIPLE. The operating procedure provides a clear vision of the path to safe operation for those who are operating the process. Likewise, where appropriate, it also provides a clear vision of the consequences of straying from the documented path.

ESSENTIAL FEATURES OF AN OPERATING PROCEDURE

Clear, straightforward organizational format

Comprehensive safety (including fire protection), occupational health, and environmental control section

(a) Properties and hazards of materials
(b) Special precautions to prevent exposure
(c) Spill and fume control measures
(d) Description of special/unique hazards
(e) Emergency shutdown precedures

Clear definition of safe path from raw material to finished product

(a) Typical format: Batch: Steps A—Z
                         Continuous: Start-up/Stand-by/Normal
                                         Stand-by/Shutdown
(b) Process limits listed, including:

Consequences of deviation (where adverse safety (including fire protection), health, and environmental considerations are present)
Steps to avoid deviations
Actions to correct deviations

(c) Language: Understandable to reader

Use of equipment sketches, tabulations, and graphs (where appropriate) to clarify and aid understanding

Evergreen and up-to-date—always current:

Conforms with process technology

Procedure and field practice are mutually consistent with each other

Input from people who have experience in operating the process equipment

DISCUSSION. The purpose of an operating procedure is to clearly communicate to operating personnel the path to safe operation. It is based on and reflects information in the safety information package, that is, hazards of materials, equipment and process design information, and process technology (process steps and limits).

The operating procedure goes beyond the above information and summarizes pertinent data and information from the process hazards reviews. In short it must contain all of the relevant safety, health, and environmental information to provide a comprehensive understanding of the hazards (present and potential) to the operating personnel. This understanding must include a knowledge of the consequences of deviation from process limits (where safety, health, and environmental considerations are present) and the controls in place to prevent or correct deviations.

Recognizing how important the operating procedure is, it is no surprise to realize that the operating procedure provides the foundation for operator training. The procedure and training go hand in hand. The close relationship between the operating procedure and operator training is further discussed under "How it all ties together!"

One final point worthy of discussion is what is meant by "evergreen and up-to-date." Very simply, to be effective an operating procedure must always be current. Once an operating procedure is firmly established as the path to safe operation, complete with personnel training to the point that the procedure and field practice are consistent with each other, then no change in technology, facilities, or procedural steps can be permitted until the operating procedure is properly updated and authorized and until personnel have been trained in the proposed change(s).

4.5 Training and Performance

PRINCIPLE. Properly trained personnel are not only a key feature but an absolute requirement to keeping complex process equipment and machinery on the documented path to safe operation.

All other key elements of process hazards management can be in place—without properly trained personnel, the chances of safe process operation are greatly diminished.

ESSENTIAL FEATURES OF A TRAINING AND PERFORMANCE PROGRAM

Management commitment in place: personnel are forecast (budgeted) to "conduct" the training and to "receive" the training

The *key elements* of training are

1. Conceptual training: explains how and why
2. Field training: complements conceptual—"shows"
3. Hands-on: student demonstrates understanding or lack of understanding
4. Qualification testing versus defined minimal requirements
5. Refresher training: an on-going process

Qualified instructors: Instructors selected based on previously developed criteria to ensure excellence. Criteria to include items such as knowledge and communication skills.

DISCUSSION. Properly trained and qualified personnel are an essential requirement for the safe operation of a manufacturing process. Inappropriate operator actions have been important factors in many major process incidents. Examples include attempted continued operation after process variables exceed safe limits, delaying emergency shutdown or evacuation, or ignoring indications of differences in materials, reaction characteristics, or labeling. These problems can usually be traced to inadequate procedures or training, and in some instances are abetted by inadequate supervisory direction. The principle of properly trained and qualified personnel is basic and fundamental, applying to highly automated complex processes as well as labor-intensive operator-controlled processes. For those processes that are highly automated or computer controlled, the operator must have a thorough understanding of the control instrumentation including:

Location and methods of measurement
Measurement principles (dp, pressure switch, etc.)
Method of signal transmission
Control limits
Alarm points
Interlock provisions
Location and method of interlock action

To assess the significance of nonstandard or alarm conditions, the operator must have a thorough knowledge and understanding of the potential causes or circumstances that could lead to the alarm condition. This knowledge and understanding is a prerequisite for the next basic responsibility: If the alarm condition is not brought under control by the automatic instrumentation provided, the operator must quickly assess whether the appropriate interlock devices have properly functioned and if not what intervening manual steps must be taken to correct the abnormal condition and bring the process back within normal control limits.

It is only when knowledgeable, skilled, and qualified operators are in place to complement the hardware, software, and procedural features of a process that one achieves the necessary and required level of process safety management. To operate a facility with inadequately trained personnel, thereby solely relying on hardware control features, is directly comparable to skating on thin ice. It becomes no longer a question of *if* the ice will break, rather a question of *when* the ice will break. In the case of labor-intensive operator-controlled processes, the need for training is equally important and readily apparent.

The essential features listed are the basic elements that are necessary to achieve the quality of training commensurate with the many hazards present in today's process and handling facilities. As one can see, personnel training and performance are an ongoing challenge and responsibility. Once all personnel are properly trained and qualified, then performance must be assessed periodically to ensure compliance with established standards. This may be done through interviews and observations or more systematically in combination with a formal job knowledge review procedure.

4.6   Incident Investigation

PRINCIPLE. Serious and potentially serious incidents are likely to reoccur unless positive steps are taken to prevent recurrence. Aggressive and persistent investigation of all serious and potentially serious incidents is necessary to continually improve safety performance. A serious or potentially serious incident is an incident that either results or could reasonably have resulted in one of the following:

An injury or illness involving lost or restricted work activity
A significant spill or release of chemicals or products
Significant damage to buildings or equipment
Significant damage to the environment
Off-plant impact or reporting

ESSENTIAL FEATURES OF AN INCIDENT INVESTIGATION

1. Preplanning: Investigation and communication procedure established and in place

2. Prompt establishment of investigation team organization:
   (a) Essential to capture information before it evaporates
   (b) Team should be multidisciplined and should include representatives from outside the area in which the incident occurred

3. Investigation includes:
   (a) Preservation and collection of physical evidence
   (b) Prompt interview of eyewitnesses and other appropriate personnel
   (c) Determination of cause(s)—consists of a systematic approach to focus in on the cause(s)—an "example" of one of many approaches is summarized below:
      (1) Develop chronology
      (2) List conditions that deviated from normal
      (3) Jointly list all hypotheses that could account for incident occurrence
      (4) Test hypotheses versus all available evidence
      (5) List in order of likelihood
   (d) Statement of causes, contributing causes, or other significant factors
   (e) Recommendations: Actions needed to prevent reoccurrence include (1) responsibility and (2) timing
   (f) Communication to other appropriate groups
   (g) Follow-up to ensure closure

DISCUSSION. Incidents present a unique opportunity to an organization—the opportunity to define areas of one's process safety management program that need improvement. Failure to capitalize on this opportunity will surely result in additional incidents and with potential for more serious consequences.

Before an organization can establish an effective incident investigation program, some pretty important groundwork has to be laid in the area of reporting incidents. It is a plain, simple fact—one cannot investigate incidents if they're not reported! A common reason incidents are not reported is that in some organizations the incident investigation tends to focus on a "search for the guilty" rather than a "search for the facts" coupled with a fair and firm handling of any employee relations aspects of the incident." Certainly where negligence is involved some form of disciplinary action is appropriate and welcomed by all members of the organization. Keep in mind also that where human error is involved, there is often a managerial deficiency involved either procedural, training, or in staffing levels provided. Nevertheless, when the incident is handled in a positive, open manner, the entire organization will work together to (1) report incidents and (2) correct deficiencies, be they procedural, training, human error, managerial, or whatever. One must realize that when this approach is taken, there will be an increase in the number of incidents reported—and that is good! The key objective here is to get the "cards on the table" so the entire organization can work to correct deficiencies and prevent recurrence. With time what one would expect is not necessarily a reduction in the frequency of incidents but certainly a reduction in the frequency of serious incidents. For reporting purposes an incident should be viewed as "anything that occurs that is unusual or out of the ordinary." Initially, the information to be reported should be limited to what happened (date, time, description, size, impact, etc.) and the action(s) taken.

The problem with limiting initial reporting to serious or potentially serious incidents is that the seriousness cannot always be assessed at the time of occurrence. Those that are indeed serious or potentially serious can then be selected for further investigation.

Another important point to ensure an effective incident investigation effort is "preplanning." People will often ask: When should the incident investigation begin? Many will respond with "within a short period" or "immediately, as soon as possible" or "within one second after the incident occurs." The proper response is that the incident investigation should have started before the incident occurred with the establishment of a well-thought-out incident investigation procedure. The importance of preplanning is clearly evident when one realizes that relevant information begins to evaporate immediately following the incident either through cleanup efforts or possible corroboration of people's recollections where human error is involved. By carefully thinking through, preplanning, and documenting the essential stages in an incident investigation ahead of time, the evaporation of relevant information can be minimized or eliminated.

An important part of the incident investigation procedure is prompt establishment of the incident investigation team organization. This is extremely important for those incidents that are obviously serious right up front. For example, a serious incident that occurs on saturday night at 11 p.m. should be brought under control and secured by the preestablished emergency response organization(s). The investigation team members should be assembled from shift personnel and other relevant site and nonsite personnel as designated by site or corporate management as soon as the area is secure. Shift personnel must be held over to ensure capturing thoughts, recollections, and so forth while they are fresh. No one should be allowed to enter the area to begin cleanup until all relevant records and evidence has been inspected and preserved. Prompt establishment of incident investigation leadership with priority over operation, maintenance, and reconstruction is vital at this stage.

The remaining elements of an incident investigation shown under "essential features" are pretty straightforward and common among the chemical and petroleum industry companies. The follow-up of open recommendations and communication to other appropriate groups are necessary elements of the effort to prevent recurrence.

The individual parts of an incident investigation effort are closely interrelated. Aggressive investigation, follow-up, and inclusion of operators/mechanics as part of the investigation team all help foster a positive healthy attitude toward incident investigation that in turn encourages and facilitates prompt reporting of all incidents as they occur. With this approach and attitude in place an organization will most assuredly see a continual improvement in the frequency and severity of serious incidents.

4.7   Auditing

PRINCIPLE. The only way one can know and understand "how one is really doing" is by observing (in the field) and comparing performance versus established standards. Proper auditing includes positive feedback on significant strengths as well as corrective feedback on areas needing improvement.

ESSENTIAL FEATURES OF PROCESS SAFETY MANAGEMENT AUDITING SYSTEM

> Audits established for each key element of process safety management on a periodic frequency
>
> Results documented, analyzed, and reported to appropriate management
>
> Auditors have relevant experience

DISCUSSION. It is not enough to establish and implement a process safety management program and assume that it will continue to function as implemented. The best intentions and most comprehensive program will erode with time if left unattended. The causes of such erosion are many fold; some of the more common ones include changes in management, changes in personnel, preoccupation by management with other priorities, and confusion over priorities.

The auditing function provides a measurement or sampling of the health of one's process safety management efforts. When conducted frequently, the audits will pinpoint deficiencies while the corrective efforts required are still small.

To be effective there should be a two-prong auditing approach: (1) by the line organization and (2) by an outside group, independent from the line organization. The primary auditing responsibility should rest with the line organization. The corrective process resulting from self-analysis is always easier to implement. Also the self-audit (1) reinforces understanding of priorities and of the corporate mission–philosophy and (2) lays the groundwork for an excellent outside, independent audit. Taken in the above context, the outside independent audit will be a positive report to site and corporate management for a job well done! One final point, the two-pronged auditing function is an ongoing process.

4.8 Equipment Tests and Inspections

PRINCIPLE. Periodic inspection and testing of important equipment is necessary to ensure reliable and incident-free operation. Such programs help prevent premature failure and ensure operability of systems required for emergency control.

ESSENTIAL FEATURES OF INSPECTION AND TEST PROGRAM

>   Application listing developed; some examples:
>   Pressure vessels
>   Pressure-relief devices
>   Key interlocks/alarm/instruments
>   Emergency devices
>   Fire protection equipment
>   Piping in critical service
>   Key process to service tie-ins
>   Electrical grounding
>   Emergency alarm/communication system
>
>   Inspection objectives defined
>   Inspection methods developed
>   Inspection frequency established
>   Acceptable performance limits provided
>   Exception list for follow-up
>   Recordkeeping: Suitable to facilitate review and analysis of results

DISCUSSION. All mechanical equipment and devices are subject to failure. The purpose of the equipment test and inspection program is to

>   Predict failure in advance where possible (such as wall thickness) and to schedule replacement prior to failure
>   Ensure operability of systems required for emergency control

This particular element of process safety management focuses on maintaining reliability of emergency control equipment and of process equipment. The program itself involves a lot of data collection, documentation, and analysis of results to be used as a basis for (1) making equipment modifications (improvements) or (2) altering test frequencies.

The inspection method for each test must be clearly spelled out or the owner/operator is likely to operate under a false sense of security. The classical example is the periodic test of a temperature alarm/interlock function. There are many ways to test this function. One is to introduce a false signal behind the panel board and see if the high-temperature alarm light and bell sounds and if the respective automatic valve (cooling water) opens wide in the field. But what about the thermocouple in the field, the temperature transmitter, and the transmission signal lines to the control panel? They were not included in the above test but are a vital part of the control loop. A better method to test the temperature alarm/interlock function is to test the thermocouple in the field and expose it to the alarm point temperature (via hot oil bath) and test the entire loop. Unless each inspection method is clearly spelled out, one may be getting the *easier* method of testing rather than the *best* method of testing.

The inspection frequency chosen depends on a number of factors: (1) failure rate data, (2) criticality of the control device, (3) consequences of failure, and (4) redundant devices present. Taking these factors into account, some inspection frequencies may be annually or longer; others may be semiannually, quarterly, monthly, weekly, or even more frequent.

Like incident investigation, equipment tests and inspections provide an opportunity to correct deficiencies and to improve the process safety management effort by improving the reliability of one's process and emergency control equipment. To capitalize on this opportunity requires a methodical and comprehensive system for documenting results and the subsequent analysis of results to pinpoint areas where corrective action is warranted.

4.9 Prestart-up Safety Review

PRINCIPLE. The prestart-up safety review is used to confirm the following:

Safety information package documentation is complete and readily available

Construction is in accordance with specifications

Safety, operating, maintenance, and emergency procedures are in place and adequate

Process hazard review recommendations required for startup have been completed

Operator training has been completed and has been effective

Equipment test and inspection schedules are complete and in place

All elements of process safety management system have been completed and are in place

Process is safe to operate

ESSENTIAL FEATURES OF PRESTART-UP SAFETY REVIEW

> Development and use of appropriate prestart-up checklist(s) relevant to particular process
>
> Responsibilities assigned to appropriate personnel for execution and follow-up

DISCUSSION. The prestart-up safety review is not used to trigger the beginning of any of the elements of a process safety management system. Development of each of the elements of process safety management should have started long before the prestart-up safety review.

The primary purpose of the prestart-up checklist is to make sure that all of the requirements of the process safety management system are completed and that none fall through the crack. Ideally it works best if a member of the startup team prepares a checklist of all of the items that need to be checked (by element of process safety management) prior to startup. The checklist should include accountability for the review of each item (i.e., who did the review and when) and responsibility for execution and follow-up.

4.10 Management of Change (Facilities)

PRINCIPLE. Physical changes in the field must be consistent with the established process technology in order to avoid serious process incidents. The process safety management requirements for all field modifications must be established up front (and documented) prior to authorization. Process safety management requirements must be completed prior to implementation of the modification.

ESSENTIAL FEATURES OF A MANAGEMENT-OF-CHANGE SYSTEM. Facility modifications as a result of problem request/project and field changes are controlled by use of a management approval system that defines requirements for

> Authorization-of-change document
> Process hazard reviews
> Operating procedures
> Safety checklist
> Field inspection

DISCUSSION. Subtle changes in the field can and have led to catastrophic events. Changing materials of construction of a valve, nipple, or plug; modifying major piping without analyzing stresses; increasing system pressure by "inches" of water are examples of subtle changes that have resulted in major fires and explosions. In each case the change was made without prudent review and without authorization by multidisciplines and levels of management.

The key part of a management-of-change system (facilities) is to have a mechanism in place to trigger plant personnel to direct any proposed change that is not a "replacement in kind" to special authorization via the management-of-change (facilities) system. Stated another way: No changes are to be made to process equipment and instrumentation that is not a replacement in kind unless authorized under a management-of-change system. Let's take a look at three examples:

1. Replacement of a valve and piping with a new and different material of construction would appropriately be covered via authorization-of-change document (technology), process hazards review, field inspection, communication/training of personnel, and perhaps an update of the operating procedure.
2. Receipt of a raw material via top-unloading tank trucks (normally received in bottom-unloading tank trucks) would appropriately be covered via process hazards review, modified operating procedure, and training of personnel.
3. Installation of an access platform to difficult to reach valving would appropriately be covered by safety checklist, field inspection, and communication/training of personnel.

Note: The safety checklist is simply a site-developed checklist to cover new installations. It would stimulate the mind to make sure certain items were covered in the design and installation. It would include such items as pinch points, tripping hazards, electrical grounding required, equipment guarding required, and so on.

With the management-of-change system (facilities) it is important that the requirements for implementing the change be documented up front as the proposal is conceived and expenditures authorized. Implementation of the modification is then contingent upon completion of the process safety management requirements. The bottom line in using a management-of-change system is that all modifications (1) get prudent review, (2) are appropriately documented, and (3) are authorized by appropriate levels of management.

4.11   Quality Assurance

PRINCIPLE. Quality assurance efforts focus on ensuring that process equipment is fabricated in accordance with design specifications, assembled and installed properly, and maintained to original level of integrity. All three efforts are important in ensuring safe operation. The last item becomes an ongoing responsibility of the maintenance organization.

ESSENTIAL FEATURES OF QUALITY ASSURANCE PROGRAM

 Design bases and criteria are documented and communicated to operating and maintenance personnel as part of the equipment design package (see process safety information element)

 Inspections of critical service equipment and components carried out in vendor's shop during fabrication

 Maintenance procedures and training in place to ensure mechanical integrity is maintained during (1) assembly, (2) installation, and (3) on an ongoing basis

 Equipment inspection and test program is an important element of the quality assurance effort

 Site makes appropriate use of consultants when problems are encountered to ensure that mechanical integrity is maintained and often enhanced

DISCUSSION. Quality assurance addresses the maintenance portion of process safety management from all aspects starting with the original design bases and proceeding through inspection of critical service equipment during fabrication in the vendors shops, installation and assembly, on through to maintenance on an ongoing basis. Preventive and predictive type maintenance activities are included in the equipment test and inspection program. There are areas of overlap between the essential features of a quality assurance program and the other elements of process safety management. The overlap is intentional to provide a "complete overview" of a quality assurance effort. In actual practice, there is no duplication of effort; different organizations will address and organize the elements of process safety management in different ways.

Like the group responsible for operating the facility, the maintenance people also need to have a thorough knowledge of the design bases and specifications for each piece of equipment. Included with the information in the original design package are the detailed equipment design drawings, assembly and disassembly instructions, and lubrication and maintenance instructions. All of this information accumulated in the design of the original facility and subsequent procurement of equipment must be carefully documented, collected, and communicated to the organization responsible for ongoing maintenance. If some of the above information is left solely in the design engineers files, a potentially serious gap in knowledge occurs.

The quality assurance effort continues right into the vendor's facility if critical service equipment is involved. Inspections (as specified in purchase agreement) can and should be used to confirm such things as (1) proper materials of construction, (2) proper welding techniques are being used, (3) qualified welders are being used, (4) dimensions are correct, and (5) appropriate quality control procedures are in place. It is analogous to the auditing element of process safety management. If the vendor knows what is expected and required, and knows he or she will be audited for results, the quality of the work will in most cases meet specifications. In those cases where it does not, the deviation will be picked up early in the game. Another way to appreciate the importance of this effort is to recognize that when highly toxic materials are being handled or processed in specially designed equipment, the ultimate responsibility to protect the safety, health, and environment rests with the proprietor—the "buck stops with the facility owner."

Like operating procedures and training, the need for procedures and training for maintenance personnel is equally important. The safety of a facility is dependent on mechanics using (1) proper materials of construction, (2) the right kind of gaskets, (3) proper bolting techniques, and so on. Like the operator, the mechanic is an important "manager" of process safety. His strength as a manager of process safety is dependent on his being trained and qualified, with the training being based on documented procedures, codes, and regulations.

The equipment test and inspection program has been discussed earlier. Typically this is where the traditional preventive maintenance and predictive maintenance activities are located.

The last item listed under the quality assurance essential features, that is, use of consultants, again provides an opportunity for an organization to improve or enhance its process safety management in the area of mechanical integrity. One of the outputs of the equipment test and inspection program will be the definition of areas needing improvement, that is, areas where repetitive deficiencies are observed. The use of consultants specializing in a particular field helps ensure that a wide range of possible solutions including most recent technology is considered.

4.12   Emergency Response and Control Plan

PRINCIPLE. Development and execution of emergency control procedures are essential and necessary to (1) minimize the impact of process incidents and (2) to bring the emergency under prompt control.

ESSENTIAL FEATURES OF AN EMERGENCY RESPONSE AND CONTROL PLAN

Each site establishes and develops a link with local emergency response organizations. Link to include:

1. Notification of hazardous chemicals handled

2. Notification of safety and health data for hazardous chemical inventories
3. Participation in developing community emergency response plans consistent with Title III (SARA, 1986)

Each site develops and has in place an emergency response and control procedure. Procedure to address:

1. Methods of determining release and the probable affected area and population
2. Notification and coordination of emergency response with public officials or public emergency response organizations, including law enforcement, fire fighting, regulatory bodies, hospitals, and local government.
3. Prompt notification and alerting of affected personnel
4. Evacuation planning
5. Actions to take to minimize the effect of the emergency and to bring the emergency under prompt control

Description and schedules of training program for emergency response personnel

Designated emergency control center and an alternate location established. Both control center locations equipped with

1. Plant layout and community maps
2. Utility drawings, including fire water
3. Meteorological conditions (input)
4. Emergency lighting
5. Emergency phones with separate power supply
6. Emergency radios
7. Appropriate reference materials
   a. Government agency notification list
   b. Company personnel phone list
   c. Technical materials (e.g., MSDS, procedures)
8. Listing (including location) of emergency response equipment and mutual aid information

Emergency drills are held to test an organization's knowledge, understanding, and implementation of emergency control procedures:

1. No less than once per year
2. Public officials and organizations to be involved in the emergency response are invited to participate as appropriate

DISCUSSION. The 11 previous key elements of process safety management deal with managing process safety to prevent incidents. The twelfth key element focuses on dealing with emergencies in such a way as (1) to minimize the impact and (2) to bring the emergency under prompt control. There are a number of examples in the chemical and process industries where a well-thought-out and executed emergency response plan would have significantly reduced the extent of personnel injuries and death.

Since most sites handling hazardous materials have the potential to affect the surrounding community, emergency response plans cannot be developed in a vacuum, that is, within a particular site. They must be developed in close cooperation with local emergency response organizations (local officials, fire departments, police, hospitals). The emergency planning and community right-to-know act portion of Title III (SARA, 1986) addresses the first two essential features in great detail.

Once the emergency response plans are developed, the remaining elements of an effective emergency control program include (1) training of personnel, (2) facilities (i.e., emergency control centers and emergency response equipment), and (3) auditing—conducting drills on a periodic basis to test effectiveness of personnel training efforts. Conducting the drills on a community wide basis provides the opportunity for all participating organizations to practice their response skills as a closely coordinated team. Drill frequency should be adjusted to ensure that response skills are maintained at a high level of proficiency.

5   IMPORTANCE OF OPERATING DISCIPLINE (5)

All of the principles and essential features discussed thus far mean nothing when it comes to operating a facility safely and preventing catastrophes—if the principles, procedures, and practices established and set in place are not followed! Stated another way, the most technologically advanced plant in the world will not have a safe operating track record unless the individuals managing and working there are dedicated and committed to keeping it free from accidents—by following the established safe path to manufacture, handling, processing, or storage.

There are a number of chemical plant accidents—catastrophes—that have occurred not because the technology was lacking but rather because the discipline required to follow procedures was lacking. In the following three examples lack of operating discipline was a major contributing factor to either the cause or to the extent of the incident:

Flixborough: Fire and Explosion   1974   28 fatalities

This accident occurred when the plant bypassed a disabled reactor. The bypass assembly, a piece of 20-inch pipe, was not properly analyzed for stress nor properly supported. The bypass assembly failed and released a large vapor cloud of cyclohexane that subsequently ignited.

Seveso: Dioxin release   1976   Widespread contami-
                                                          nation

This accident occurred when an exothermic decomposition reaction caused the rupture disc on the reactor to fail, venting dioxin into the atmosphere and contaminating the surrounding community. In this case the production run in question ended at 6:00 a.m. Saturday morning, a time that coincided with the closing of the plant for the weekend. A number of procedural violations occurred in order to terminate the production run by Saturday 6:00 a.m.:

> Only 15 percent of the solvent was distilled off at the end of the batch versus 50 percent as specified by the operating procedure
> No water was added to cool the reaction to 50–60°C versus 3000 liters specified
> Stirring stopped after 15 minutes instead of stirring until fully cooled as specified by the operating procedure
> Operators left at 6:00 a.m. instead of remaining with the unit cooling to 50–60°C as specified by the operating procedure

The release from the exothermic reaction took place some 6.5 hours later.

Bhopal: Methyl isocyanate release   1984   2800 fatalities

This accident is believed to have occurred when water entered a storage tank containing methyl isocyanate. At the time of the incident the following emergency control equipment either was not in commission or not in full working order:

> Vent gas scrubber designed to scrub vapor discharged from the MIC storage tank relief valves
> Flare system designed to burn any vapor that gets through the vent gas scrubber
> Cooling system for the storage tank

Just what is this concept of operating discipline and who is responsible for establishing the proper level of operating discipline? These are two commonly asked questions. Operating discipline is a dedication and commitment to "doing the job the right way the first time." And if there is not sufficient time available to do the job the right way, then the job must be stopped until there is sufficient time! It means following established principles, procedures, and practices as documented in the site's process safety management program. It means production is not placed ahead of safety and health of personnel or of the environment!

An effective and lasting sense of operating discipline is only established through leadership by example throughout the line organization from the site's manager on down. People hear the words; they believe and follow the actions! As with the key elements of process safety management, the corporate mission philosophy also provide the foundation for operating discipline.

6   SAFETY MANAGEMENT OF HAZARDOUS MATERIALS: "HOW IT ALL TIES TOGETHER"

Figure 9.2 provides an illustration of safety management of a facility handling hazardous materials and how it all ties together. The illustration depicts a series of important building blocks. The foundation begins as discussed earlier with the corporate mission/philosophy. From there the foundation continues with the procedural elements of a process safety management program, for example, process technology, process hazard reviews, operating procedures, equipment test and inspection programs, and

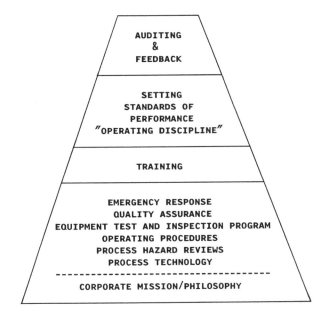

COMMUNICATION "UP & DOWN" TIES IT ALL TOGETHER

Figure 9.2.   Safety management of hazardous materials—how it all ties together.

quality assurance programs. The foundation contains all of the documented perceptions of how things are to be. It reflects current codes, regulations, laws, and the company's process safety management program. It describes the safe path for handling, storing, processing, and manufacturing hazardous and highly toxic materials.

Once the foundation is in proper position, the next building block is training of personnel. In the case of operating procedures, it would consist of training operators on the procedural content to ensure that they had a thorough understanding not only of the "whats" and "hows" but also the "whys."

The mortar that holds these blocks together is communication, as illustrated by the solid lines in Figure 9.2. The communication to be effective must be two way. In the case of operating procedures, the trainer will communicate what is in the procedures, why it is there, and how to properly follow them. Operators will often communicate back (1) problem areas in following the procedure as written and (2) suggestions for improvement. Out of this two-way communication will grow an improved procedure.

The next building block is an important supervisory responsibility—setting standards of performance. This includes standards of performance for every aspect of safety management, such as housekeeping, filling out log sheets and checksheets, keeping operating procedures up-to-date. Once again the importance of two-way communication is critical. The standards of performance need to be clearly communicated to site personnel. In return, site employees will communicate back any problems they foresee in meeting or exceeding the desired standards of performance. Out of this two-way communication will grow a mutually agreed-upon standard of performance.

It quickly becomes apparent that good communication is vital; it is what holds the building blocks together. Communication is the combined circulatory and muscular systems of the process safety management effort. It carries and transmits information; and, as a result of that flow of information, it solidifies understanding thereby tying things together in an overall coordinated safety effort!

The final building block is auditing and feedback. If we have done a good job on the other building blocks, the feedback will be positive encouragement for a job well done! And the bottom line will be a safe operating facility and the prevention of catastrophes!

ACKNOWLEDGMENTS

The author wishes to acknowledge the excellent efforts and input of V. E. Boyen, Monsanto Corporation, and R. L. Brandes and A. W. Burns, ICI Americas, in developing the twelve key elements of Process Safety Management. The author also wishes to thank R. E. Munson and L. C. Schaller, E. I. Du Pont, for their professional review and critique of the document.

GENERAL REFERENCES

A.I.Ch.E., *Guidelines for Hazard Evaluation Procedures,* New York: American Institute of Chemical Engineers, 1985.

Boyen, V. E., R. L. Brandes, A. F. Burk, and A. W. Burns, *Document on Process Hazards Management,* Washington, D.C.: Organization Resources Counselors, Inc., February 1987.

DuPont Management Consulting Services, Course material on "Process Safety Management," Wilmington, Delaware: E. I. Dupont de Nemours & Co., Inc., 1987.

Marsh & McLennan Protection Consultants, *One Hundred Largest Losses,* 9th ed., Chicago, April (1986).

Rausch, D. A., Operating Discipline: A Key to Safety, *Chem. Eng. Prog.,* Vol. 82, No. 6, pp. 13–15, June (1986). Excerpts reproduced by permission of the American Institute of Chemical Engineers.

Union Carbide, *Bhopal Methyl Isocyanate Incident Investigation Team Report,* Danbury, CONN: Union Carbide Corp., March, 1985.

CHAPTER TEN

Regulatory Compliance

Edward J. Baier and John A. Pendergrass

The benefits and hence the importance of a safer and more healthful workplace have long been recognized by responsible and forward-thinking employers. In addition to the obvious benefit of workers who are whole and healthy, the safe workplace is positively correlated to high production and quality, good morale, and low absenteeism. These motivating forces make job safety and health good business.

Compliance, by definition, is to act in accordance with rules, regulations, guidelines, and standards. When these coincide with business objectives, compliance is assured. When governmental requirements or objectives are counter to those who are being governed, compliance will not be voluntary nor will enforcement be easily attained. In a democracy it is essential that regulations can be shown to be necessary, reasonable, and easily understood. Occupational health and safety regulations also must be technologically and economically feasible. These criteria can best be achieved if regulations are promulgated in an open forum that can serve to convince concerned parties that the benefits of the rule are real. All regulatory action assumes that enforcement will be required to assure compliance and hence the benefits accrued to the action.

The Occupational Safety and Health Act was signed into law in December 1970 because Congress had perceived that work in the United States was hazardous and that not enough was being done to control risks. As with public health, worker protection was regulated by the individual states and territories. At the time five states (California, Michigan, New Jersey, New York, and Pennsylvania) dominated the field in occupational health. These states employed as many health and safety professionals as did all of the other states and territories. Many states had no occupational health and safety programs.

History shows that regulation of health and safety conditions in the workplace accompanied the industrial revolution in England. In the United States serious efforts by the states to regulate began just prior to World War I. It was at this time that workers compensation laws were being enacted. Massachusetts, New York, and Pennsylvania established state programs because of public demand following plant and mine disasters. Federal action was initiated in 1914 when an air hygiene (industrial hygiene and sanitation) unit was created in the United States Public Health Service. The first office was located in Pittsburgh. This inaugural federal effort was and continues to be oriented toward research rather than toward regulatory enforcement.

The federal effort in worker health and safety has involved the Public Health Service, Bureau of Mines, the Department of Interior, Department of Commerce and Labor, and the Department of Labor. A Bureau of Labor was created in the Department of Interior in 1884. In 1903 Congress established a Department of Commerce and Labor and in 1913 the Department of Labor achieved cabinet status.

At about this time the Bureau of Mines was investigating the health of coal miners. Much of the coal was used in the production of steel. It was logical that the Public Health Service Air Hygiene Unit in Pittsburgh join forces with the Bureau of Mines to study plant sanitation and working conditions along with the health of workers in the mills and mines.

By the mid 1930s states that had occupational health and safety programs were developing and enforcing standards. Standards and enforcement varied widely and became increasingly important to employers with operations in more than one state. At a meeting convened by the surgeon general of the Public Health Service the standards of the various states were compared and an effort was made to standardize worker exposure levels. To achieve uniformity the group decided to meet annually to review the exposure limit lists. The group called themselves the National Conference of Governmental Industrial Hygienists, which later became the American Conference of Governmental Industrial Hygienists (ACGIH). The annual publication of the ACGIH threshold limits values (TLV) became and remains the most authoritative guidelines for worker exposure in the world.

On the federal scene enforcement of standards began when the Division of Labor Standards was created in 1934. The division compliance activity was strengthened with the 1936 passage of the Walsh–Healey Public Contracts Act. This law made it mandatory for anyone contracting with the federal government for more than $10,000 of service or supplies to maintain a safe and healthful work environment. The legislation was not effective at the time, but the World War II production effort gave it increased meaning. The realization by management that protecting the health and safety of employees was essential during a period of high production and limited labor supply was probably more effective than the broad provisions of Walsh–Healey.

No major occupational health and safety legislation was passed between

1936 and 1970. During this period industry efforts in health and safety were voluntary plus compliance with the various state requirements. Industrial hygienists looked to the ACGIH Threshold Limits Values Committee for guidance. The American National Standards Institute (ANSI) (then known as American Standards Association) produced exposure standards that were much more complete than the TLVs. Rather than a single number, the ANSI documents provided an 8-hour time-weighted average exposure limit, a ceiling limit, a maximum exposure limit, and a discussion of potential health and safety hazards with a section on occupational medical considerations. These were complete documents and of much greater value than TLVs. The number of chemicals that were subjects of ANSI standards was limited.

The practice of industrial hygiene and safety was to change dramatically following the signing of the Occupational Safety and Health Act of 1970 by President Nixon. Compliance with legally enforceable regulations replaced what had been primarily a voluntary responsibility of employers. During the first 16 years of existence the Occupational Safety and Health Administration (OSHA) has gone through dramatically different approaches to enforcement. The enforcement pattern has gone from heavy-handed confrontation by inspectors, many of whom were not technically competent, to a staff which, for the most part, is well-educated professionals who provide a service to employers, issuing citations where appropriate, but working with the employer to obtain abatement of conditions that may result in injuries or illnesses.

An obligation of the regulatory agency is to describe what is required to be in compliance. This is done by publishing rules, regulations, guidelines, instructions, brochures, and so forth. The OSHA act specifies that in developing compliance standards the secretary of labor (via delegation of authority to the assistant secretary of labor for occupational safety and health)

> . . . shall set the standard which most adequately assures, to the extent feasible, on the basis of the best available evidence, that no employee will suffer material impairment of health or functional capacity even if such employee has regular exposure to the hazard dealt with by such standard for the period of his working life. . . . Whenever practical, the standard promulgated shall be expressed in terms of objective criteria and of the performance desired.

The health and safety hazards in the United States are legion, while the number of standards that have been promulgated to address them are few. Under the act and requirements of the Administrative Procedures Act, Paperwork Reduction Act, various presidential orders, and Court decisions, standards development and promulgation has been a deliberate but painfully slow process. Consequently standards, particularly health standards, are frequently outdated. New health standards have been added at a rate of one per year. The problem of inadequate and outdated health standards has been solved by the Hazard Communication Standard. The provisions of the standard were in effect for manufacturing (SIC Codes 20 through 39) in May 1986 and for all workplaces in 1987.

The Hazard Communication Standard follows the requirements of the act: "The standard promulgated shall be expressed in terms of objective criteria and of the performance desired." The standard specifies that vendors of hazardous chemicals shall inform users as to the hazards that can be expected. Further, as new information becomes available, that too shall be promptly passed on. Hence this regulation is a dynamic document that will maintain its effectiveness.

The older, traditional chemical standards are specific in requirements: The concentration of chemical X in the air shall not exceed Y parts per million. In order to determine if compliance has been attained, the agency has spelled out in detail how compliance officers will sample the air, conduct the analysis, and evaluate the results. This has created a cookbook compliance/enforcement genre. If the workplace contaminants are regulated, that is, have been assigned permissible exposure limits (PEL) and the OSHA methods as published in the Field Operations Manual are followed and the results are less than the specified limits, citations can be avoided. Regulatory compliance has been achieved but possibly without worker health protection.

Even if the minimum effort just described were satisfactory, compliance with the general duty clause of the act would not have been evaluated. It states that the employer must provide employment and a place of employment that is safe and healthful. The employer's responsibility extends beyond the confines of the PEL lists and the few expanded standards currently on the books. The employer must provide a safe and healthful workplace regardless of materials, processes, procedures, or equipment used. Compliance by the employer and enforcement by the compliance officer are both more difficult when the general duty provision is applicable. Now, science, judgment, and professionalism are required. Neither hazard recognition nor techniques for evaluation are obvious. Good industrial hygiene principles and practices must be used:

1. An exposure limit that will not impair a worker who may be exposed 8 hours per day, 40 hours a week for a working lifetime.
2. Determination of worker exposure in the workplace.
3. Controls that assure that exposures do not exceed the acceptable level.
4. Appropriate medical surveillance.
5. Accurate records.
6. Worker training and education pertaining to materials used, hazards attendant, and precaution needed to avoid harmful exposure.

Regulatory compliance is a management responsibility that requires employee cooperation. The OSHA act provides that the employer can be penalized for violation of regulations. However, an employee who disregards precautions or who refuses to use personal protective equipment cannot be penalized by the agency. The employer can discipline a wayward worker but in doing so cannot discriminate. Neither can an employer discriminate against nor discipline an employee who exercises a right to report to the agency violations or suspected violations of OSHA standards.

Where and when an inspection is to occur is the prerogative of the agency. These details must be kept confidential to ensure that no employer is given preinspection notification. The extent of an inspection is also the choice of OSHA. To be sure that enforcement is fair and balanced, a list of plant sites to be inspected is prepared in a random procedure. All workplaces on the list must be inspected before a new list is prepared. These procedures were developed to avoid making repeat visits to one location, while others in the area were not inspected.

Finite resources make it imperative for OSHA to direct inspectors to those workplaces that are most likely to have more serious problems. This is accomplished by selecting high-hazard industries for the randomized inspection list. At the time of the inspection a decision may be made to limit the investigation to records and required written programs. This has been mistakenly referred to exemption of certain workplaces from inspection. A limited inspection permits OSHA to concentrate the enforcement effort where it will most effectively reduce workplace hazards. One of every 10 scheduled inspections will result in a full-scale investigation regardless of the results of the examination of the records.

The right of the OSHA compliance officer to enter a place of employment for the purpose of inspection is provided for in the act. This provision has been repeatedly upheld by the courts. Normally the compliance officer presents official credentials to the responsible person at the workplace. Following an opening conference the inspection is conducted. If entry is refused the compliance officer seeks a warrant from a federal court. If necessary, protection of a federal marshall can be obtained.

During the investigation samples of raw materials and air may be collected. When appropriate, still pictures or video tapes may be taken. These are used to demonstrate conditions at the time of the inspection. It is incumbent upon the inspector and the plant management to protect trade secrets, remembering that all reports are public records and are open to scrutiny by anyone.

In addition to good common sense, compliance with OSHA regulations requires knowledge of the regulations and how the agency determines that a violation exists. Two publications have been developed to provide the detailed information needed. The regulations have been codified in the Code of Federal Regulations 29 Parts 1900 to 1910. The OSHA *Field Operations Manual* details how compliance officers will conduct inspections and interpret the regulations. The act itself also spells out the broad responsibilities of management to provide a safe and healthful place to work.

CHAPTER ELEVEN

Liability

Ralph E. Allan

1 INTRODUCTION

Since the Occupational Safety and Health Act of 1970 was passed by Congress, the law has become an intricate part of the industrial hygienist's life. From its inception, the act has established a framework from which health and safety regulations flow where an employer–employee relationship exists. For an industrial hygienist devoted to recognition, evaluation, and control of health hazards in industry, initial responsibility lies in assuring that the legal requirements are met, as a basis for industrial hygiene involvement in industrial operations.

The 1970 act provided the structure for implementation of health and safety regulations relating to all employers in this country. For the first time in history, along came other vital environmental health-related legislation: Toxic Substances Act, Noise Control Act, Clean Air Act, Safe Drinking Water Act, to name a few. In fact, there were many pieces of legislation enacted on the federal level in the 1960s and 1970s relating to environmental health and safety protection. States followed suit with their own environment-related legislation.

Concurrent with the regulatory changes is the development of tort action related to toxic substances. This is a reflection of society's interest in safe and healthy work and community environments. In the seventies, the term "toxic tort" was coined. Environmental law is one of the newest evolving fields of law practice. The creation of new regulations have occupied large numbers of attorneys across the nation, and these new regulations reflecting society's intent are the basis for the developing litigation explosion.

During the seventies society developed and continues to present a questioning posture: Is our environment safe and healthful? Laws are promulgated reflecting that concern. The law, as such, is confronting technology with responsibilities that have never been so direct and searching.

There is a constant tug between law and technology and science in general. Society demands that laws protect the health and safety of the citizens. In most instances, however, the necessary clear and concise scientific answers to health-related questions are not available; therefore, the law does what it can with the information available. Allowable toxic substances exposure levels are, indeed, examples of uncertainty in knowledge.

The importance relegated to a healthy and safe environment is also reflected by the developing criminal liability associated with intentional disregard for provision of a safe and healthy environment.

The industrial hygienist with the background and capability for recognizing, evaluating, and controlling health hazards in industry and the community is a key to assisting society in unraveling the mystery of dealing with toxic substances. With this responsibility comes liability if the responsibility is not performed appropriately.

The trend toward increased liability has been experienced by all professionals (i.e., doctors, lawyers, accountants, and engineers). It is only a matter of time before industrial hygienists are included in the group.

2   CIVIL LIABILITY

When one is involved with the rendering of services related to toxic substance production or handling, the risk arises that such activity will present a potential liability for the participant. For example, if an industrial hygienist is doing an industrial hygiene study, an inadequate offering of such services can result in this person becoming a defendant or liable in a case arising out of the inadequate provision of such services.

More traditionally, architects and engineers are vulnerable to such disposition due to their more formulated recognition and history as identified professional groups providing such services. This history is important as industrial hygienists and related professionals consider their legal liability (1).

Cases such as *Balagna* v. *Shawnee County* (2) relate specifically to an architect/engineer's involvement as a responsible party in litigation concerning the cause of a worker's death when that architect/engineer had actual knowledge of a safety violation that resulted in injury. Industrial hygienists and associated professionals have not at this writing found themselves to be a significant principal focus of toxic tort liability; however, greater expectation of such involvement is anticipated as the legal emphasis continues.

The most likely legal concept for industrial hygienists' concern is that of negligence. Negligence is "conduct which falls below the standard established by law for the protection of others against unreasonable risk" (3). The cause of action for negligence is established by the plaintiff proving that the defendant was under a duty to conform to a standard of conduct, that the duty was breached, that there was a casual connection between the breach and the injury, and that the conduct was the proximate cause of injury (4).

This particular basic legal concept of negligence impinged upon the toxic tort claim provides the basis for significant industrial hygiene liability exposure potential.

A toxic tort claim involves a number of characteristics not all of which are present in a single tort case. The main characteristics include (5):

1. The injuries involved allegedly arose from exposure to a harmful substance.
2. The nature of the exposure was such that there is a significant risk that a large number of people suffered comparable injuries (i.e., drinking from a contaminated aquifer as opposed to being hit by a truck).
3. The full consequences of the exposure may not be immediately apparent (e.g., diseases with long latency periods may be triggered).
4. The connection between the exposure and the injuries suffered is open to reasonable dispute, either because of questions about the nature of the substance (was it harmful?), the nature of the exposure (was it significant?), or the nature of the affliction (was it one that can derive from multiple causes?).
5. The identity of the particular party responsible for the agent allegedly causing injuries is an open question (e.g., who manufactured the particular generic drug taken by the claimant?).
6. The evidence used to establish causation is on the frontiers of medical science.
7. The injuries suffered are so serious or the claimant's situation so sympathetic that traditional legal defenses such as contributory negligence and statue of limitations are evaluated extremely critically by the court.
8. The actions that have been or will be brought raise serious administrative and legislative problems for the judiciary, and these problems are capable of being resolved in a manner that provides tactical advantages to either claimants or defendants.
9. Insurance coverage disputes are or will be present.

10. The facts involved give rise to additional potential liability exposure such as possible application of the criminal law or imposition of individual responsibility upon corporate officials.

The toxic tort claim is based on the presence of a chemical substance that, of course, is a major constituent of the involvement of an industrial hygienist in the performance of recognition, evaluation, and control of potential health hazards in industry or in the community. Therefore, the potential for industrial hygienist involvement in the legal arena either as an expert or a defendant is significantly increased since the implementation of governmental regulations for environmental and occupational health and safety.

The liability of an industrial hygienist in a toxic tort action for negligence relates to the industrial hygienist's specific business arrangement with the user of services. If the industrial hygienist is an employee in a private company, the co-worker exemption of liability under the worker's compensation system may isolate the industrial hygienist from the toxic tort action, although there is some erosion of this protective concept occurring. A recent trend provides for workers to bypass the worker's compensation system and bring a civil action against an employer and co-employee. This would expose co-worker industrial hygienists to vulnerability as defendants if such a trend were to continue. The likelihood of such occurrence is perhaps minimized or reduced in that a plaintiff worker would be more guaranteed of a recovery by suing the employer or some other third party with greater financial support than would occur if a co-worker industrial hygienist were the defendant.

The innovative theories of law that have transcended the traditional exclusive remedy theory of worker's compensation have generally been difficult to sustain.

In addition to the worker's compensation exception, an employee may become vulnerable to civil system actions where there may be a nonemployee involved in the area of responsibility of the industrial hygienists scope of work activity. A visitor to the facilities or a contractor, for example, could bring a civil claim against an industrial hygienist if they are damaged due to the industrial hygienist's negligence.

A negligence action against an industrial hygienist also may result where insurance companies provide industrial hygiene services for their clients.

The insurance company, however, may be protected from such allegations if it furnishes industrial hygiene services for its own benefit in order to "reduce risk for liability in the policy" (6).

Claims against Occupational Safety and Health Administration (OSHA) inspectors have generally been disallowed. Upon enactment of the Occupational Safety and Health Act, Congress clearly allocated responsibility upon the employer to enforce health and safety standards (7) and, therefore, the law is not the basis for a specific cause of action by private and individuals against OSHA inspections. On occasion, some attempts have been made, however.

As a private consultant, an industrial hygienist is most vulnerable to civil claims. A private consultant is, by the nature of the business, not a co-employee but an independent contractor. The legal tests involved in delineating an employer–employee relationship from an independent contractor relationship include the (1) indicia test and (2) control test. Such elements as salary, routine hours of work, and employee benefit coverage are elements that relate to the indicia test, whereas the control test relates to the right of the employer to control the acts and judgment of the industrial hygienist (8). These tests become very important at times in determining protection from civil liability under the worker's compensation exclusive remedy doctrine or vulnerability to a civil law suit as an independent contractor where an industrial hygienist may be a defendant or proposed defendant in a lawsuit.

3 CRIMINAL LIABILITY

The current administration of the U.S. Environmental Protection Agency (EPA) and the U.S. Department of Justice have publicly declared that the criminal enforcement of environmental laws is a high-priority action. Action, in reference to this declaration, has already begun. In 1986, there were nearly 400 cases referred to the Department of Justice by the EPA. Between 1982 and 1986, there were 118 management-level employee indictments filed against individuals. The recent reauthorization of the "superfund" staffs is being increased and more active investigative activity will be expected in the future.

In the early days of the Reagan Administration, there was an effort to defuse the regulations relating to hazardous waste. During the later part of 1986, Congress passed a hazardous waste law tougher than President Reagan's target of earlier years and in early 1987 approved a clean-water bill that provides for more enhanced government authority to reduce the dumping of toxic chemicals. Currently, there is a regulatory revival that will carry forth further regulatory emphasis in the matters associated with toxic substances (9).

As with civil liability, where the traditional criminal system interacts with toxic substances, the vulnerability for industrial hygiene interaction increases. A very specific example (the Golab case) of a specific criminal interaction with occupational health (industrial hygiene) matters occurred in reference to a 1985 murder conviction (currently undergoing appeal) of corporate officials at a plant located in Cook County, Illinois.

Although not the first criminal action in this area of interest; indeed, in past history a rare occurrence, the case highlighted a renewed criminal law concern for all who are involved and have responsibility in occupational safety and health affairs.

In the Golab case, the prosecution set out to prove that Mr. Golab died of exposure to hydrogen cyanide emitted from the vats of chemicals used in film processing at Film Recovery Systems, Inc. The prosecution alleged that the executives knew about the hazardous conditions, failed to take appropriate action to warn the employees, and tolerated generally unsafe conditions. The defendants claimed that Mr. Golab died of a heart attack. Cook County Circuit Judge Ronald J. Banks returned guilty verdicts against the executives after a 2-month trial (10).

There has been a gradually increasing public acceptance of legal action where forbidden acts are done deliberately and with knowledge or where they show complete disregard for the safety and health of others. Local district attorney offices throughout the nation are developing increasing interest in more thorough investigation and indictment for those responsible for criminal conduct.

The primary interest of the prosecution is to bring to trial those parties that are truly responsible for the flagrant violations of their own duty such that a criminal action will lie. Owners and officers of corporations, for example, are primary targets where such irresponsibility is found (11). Unless an industrial hygienist holds such a position, a criminal indictment of an industrial hygienist would be unlikely; not impossible, but unlikely.

Consider the following situation: Damage has resulted as a result of a toxic chemical exposure that was easily preventable; the media creates intense public interest in the situation; the government officials involved are seeking favorable publicity because of interest in a higher official capacity. Could an unprepared industrial hygienist become entangled in the web of indictments that could spin out of this scenario? Still improbable, but not impossible.

4   LIABILITY INSURANCE

There are two major types of liability insurance coverage available to the industrial hygienist. In earlier years, before the toxic substance tort era, the most common form of insurance coverage available was the occurrence-type policy. This policy provided for a right to extended discovery or an unlimited tail. With this provision, the insured was covered even after termination of the policy for acts, errors, or omissions committed prior to the termination of the policy but not discovered until after the termination of the policy. In other words, if an industrial hygienist changed insurance companies or retired or left industrial hygiene for another career or business venture, any service rendered during the period of the policy would be covered even if the claim was made against the industrial hygienist when the circumstance surrounding the claim was discovered some years later than the time of the policy.

With the increased litigation developing in the 1970s, the occurrence-type policy began to become extremely burdensome to insurance companies.

With the increasing number of claims, this type of policy is difficult to obtain.

An alternative to the occurrence policy is the claims-made policy. Coverage, in this case, is similar to the ordinary automobile insurance policy in that there is no prior acts coverage or tails attached. Coverage under this policy extends only to those liabilities incurred and asserted during the policy period. For the industrial hygienist, this type of coverage has very limited effectiveness since any adverse health effect or damage that could occur usually occurs many years after the time of the incident alleged to have been at fault in failing to protect the damaged party.

It is evident that the occurrence-type policy is the most helpful for the industrial hygienist. Because of the remarkable increase in liability, where there is insurance available, insurers are beginning to practice careful review before insuring industrial hygienists against professional liability. In fact, presently any work relationship to toxic chemicals is a discouragement to insurance considerations. It is to be hoped that there will be a change in the future in reference to liability insurance for the practicing industrial hygienist.

5 SUMMARY

Whether for a civil or criminal liability, it is important to develop a liability prevention practice that would reduce such possibility of liability arising. If you can answer "yes" to all of the following questions, you are well on the way toward having such a program:

1. Are all health and safety regulations complied with?
2. Do you know your scope of work performance?
3. Do you know your responsibility and authority in reference to your scope of work performance?
4. Do you carry out your responsibilities and use your authority?
5. Have you conveyed all pertinent, current health and safety information to individuals for whom you are responsible?
6. Do you maintain current knowledge in your area of responsibility?
7. Do you maintain detailed appropriate records?
8. Do you have a detailed policy and implementation plan for your health and safety program?
9. Is the plan followed faithfully?

In the end, the sound practice of industrial hygiene by a competent certified industrial hygienist (12) is the best defense against any allegation whether civil or criminal.

REFERENCES

1. D. Hirst and A. Karpowitz, *Liability of Architects and Engineers,* Springfield, VA: Defense Research Institute, 1982.

2. 233 Kan. 1068, 668 P 2d 157 (1983).

3. Restatement (Second) of Torts, Section 282 (1977).

4. W. Prosser, *Handbook of the Law of Torts,* Section 33, 37, 4th ed., St. Paul, MN: West Publishing Co., 1971.

5. M. Dore, *Law of Toxic Torts,* New York: Clark Boardman Company, 1987.

6. *Brown* v. *Michigan Millus Mutual Insurance Company,* 665 S.W. 2d 630 (Mo. App. 1983).

7. Occupational Safety and Health Act, 29 U.S. CA, Section 653 (b) (4), 1970.

8. *Gigax* v. *Ralston Purina Company,* 136 Cal App. 3rd 591 (1982).

9. *Wall Street Journal,* Western Edition, page 1, April 21, 1987.

10. *Editorial,* (R. Allan) *AIHAJ,* 1986.

11. Personal Communication, Brown, Jan Chattan, District Attorneys Office, Los Angeles County.

12. American Board of Industrial Hygiene Certification.

CHAPTER TWELVE

Industrial Hygiene Laboratory

Alice C. Farrar and Harriotte A. Hurley

1 INTRODUCTION

The industrial hygiene laboratory is an integral part of every industrial hygiene program. Although principles of general management are applicable to management of any functional area, including the industrial hygiene laboratory, there are management areas unique to the laboratory worthy of separate discussion. The scope of laboratory management is so broad that an entire text, or several texts, could be dedicated to the subject. This chapter will focus on management aspects of the role of the laboratory within the industrial hygiene program and will provide an overview of the practical aspects of daily laboratory management. Readers are encouraged to consult references listed at the end of the chapter for a more in-depth discussion.

2 ROLE OF THE INDUSTRIAL HYGIENE LABORATORY

According to Wilcox et al. (1),

> the purpose of a laboratory is to obtain answers to questions. More specifically, the laboratory gives information, based on analysis of materials, that enables the consumer of laboratory services to make decisions for action. The person framing the question may or may not be aware of the resources or limitations of the laboratory. He may or may not realize the need for care in sample selection or handling and, in some cases, may need help with interpretation.

This statement could not be truer than in the case of the industrial hygiene laboratory. The laboratory is the primary resource in the evaluation of environmental stresses arising in or from the workplace or the community. In order to assure that the answers given are helpful, the industrial hygiene laboratory must concern itself with all phases of activity, from the asking of the initial question to the interpretation of the answer.

2.1 Importance of Industrial Hygiene Sampling and Analysis Data

Industrial hygiene samples to be analyzed by the laboratory may include samples of airborne contaminants collected on varied sampling media, such as solvent vapors on activated charcoal tubes; bulk materials, such as asbestos-containing sprayed-on fireproofing or insulation; body fluids for biological monitoring, such as lead in blood; or microbiological samples, such as microorganisms sampled to assess indoor air quality. For most analyses, results are expected to be qualitative as well as quantitative.

The "answers" produced in the form of analytical data by industrial hygiene laboratories provide the basis for making important and costly decisions. For example, laboratory analytical results for analysis of sprayed-on fireproofing may be the basis for a decision to spend millions of dollars to remove asbestos-containing materials from a high-rise office building. Laboratory results of an employee's blood lead level may be the basis for a decision to remove that employee from the current work environment. Laboratory results for analysis of free silica in airborne dust may be the basis for a decision to install expensive engineering controls, or to eliminate the manufacture of a certain product because the cost of engineering controls will eliminate any profit from the product.

These decisions, and others like them, are important. They affect people's health, people's lives, and the assets of individuals and business entities. Since the laboratory is ultimately responsible for the answers on which these decisions are based, it must insist on involvement in all aspects of sampling, analysis, and data interpretation. The wise and experienced consumer of laboratory services will insist on a high degree of laboratory involvement.

2.2   Functions of the Industrial Hygiene Laboratory

2.2.1 Interface between Field and Laboratory. The field industrial hygienist cannot successfully operate independently of the industrial hygiene laboratory. As shown in Table 12.1, the laboratory is involved directly or indirectly in every step of the sampling and analysis sequence. The proper completion of all steps is necessary to accurately evaluate exposures to harmful materials. Teamwork is called for between the industrial hygiene field manager and the industrial hygiene laboratory manager, as well as between the field industrial hygienists and laboratory staff, to ensure that sampling and analysis data are meaningful. Constant communication is essential.

2.2.2 Establishing Criteria for Sampling Methodology. The method of analysis to be used by the laboratory generally dictates the sampling methodology. Therefore, in preparing to sample for a certain material, the industrial hygienist should contact the laboratory to determine the appropriate sampling technique. The variety of sampling and analytical methods is surprisingly broad, and growing every day. There are possibly several methods available for sampling and analyzing a given analyte. The choice of sampling and analytical method will depend on the analytical instrumentation available in the laboratory, interferences that might be present in the environment with the analyte of interest, and the detection limit required for the analyte in order to make a decision from the data. For example, sampling for iodine on a specially treated charcoal tube is inappropriate unless the laboratory to perform the analysis has an ion chromatograph (IC) and has validated the method required for analysis. Analysis of crystalline free silica will be of little value by the colorimetric method when differentiation between the polymorphs of quartz, cristobalite, and trydimite is required. X-ray diffraction is required to allow differentiation and quantitation. A 120-liter air sample for analysis of lead is of little value if a 960-liter sample is required to determine exposure levels at the OSHA Lead Standard action level because of the detection limit of the laboratory atomic absorption instrument.

Because of the many variables in sampling and analysis, the laboratory

Table 12.1. Sampling and Analysis Sequence

Responsibilities of the Industrial Hygienist

1. Determine what to sample: Determine each specific contaminant to be sampled and any interferences that may be present. The laboratory may serve as an information resource.
2. Prepare for sampling: Obtain information and advice on sampling and analysis methodology, limitations, and special requirements from the laboratory that is going to perform the analysis. Obtain sampling media and instructions for shipping and handling from the same laboratory.
3. Take the samples: Conduct sampling according to instructions obtained from the laboratory.
4. Transport samples to the laboratory: Ship or transport samples according to instructions received from the laboratory. Notify the laboratory well ahead of time to anticipate perishable or rush samples.

Responsibilities of the Laboratory

5. Receive the samples: Log samples in with identifiable, traceable numbers. Anticipate and handle appropriately perishable or rush samples.
6. Store the samples: Store the samples appropriately at room temperature, in the refrigerator, or in the freezer until analysis can be performed.
7. Analyze the samples: Analyze the samples after performing quality assurance analyses that are in control.
8. Report results: Report the results to the industrial hygienist or laboratory user.

Joint Responsibility

9. Interpret the data: Upon receipt of laboratory analytical results the industrial hygienist interprets what they mean. If there is any question about the way results are reported, or unusual findings, the industrial hygienist should consult the laboratory.

---

must establish the criteria for sampling methodology based on the limitations of its analytical methodology and on input from the field industrial hygienist on the contaminants to be sampled and analyzed. In-house or consulting labs should be able to provide this information in a sampling manual or routinely on a daily basis over the phone.

2.2.3 Provision of Sampling Media. Along with establishing the criteria for sampling methodology, the laboratory must have control over the sampling media that is utilized. Many inexperienced industrial hygienists have had their consciousness level raised with regard to the need for laboratory-provided sampling media when, having traveled many miles and having spent many hours sampling, they are advised by the laboratory that their samples are invalid because inappropriate sampling media or outdated sampling media was used. The variety of sampling media is extensive. As methodology is developed for solid-sorbents or specially treated filter sampling to take the place of impinger sampling, sampling media is becoming more specific to the particular analyte. Many types of media have limited shelf lives. Others require special handling such as refrigeration before or after sampling and protection from sunlight.

Blanks or unused portions of the sampling media are required by laboratories in order to correct for background levels of contaminant contained in the sampling media. Blanks are critical to the production of accurate sampling and analytical data. Laboratories have the right to refuse and should refuse to analyze samples that have not been sampled in the appropriate media or for which blanks are not provided. The analytical data are only as good as the samples that are taken.

2.2.4 Analysis of Samples. The primary function of the laboratory remains the analysis of materials submitted to it. Laboratories should provide to users forms for capture of sampling data required by the laboratory for calculation of analytical results in appropriate units, such as milligrams per cubic meter, parts per million, or micrograms per milliliter. The laboratory user should consult with the laboratory if special needs are anticipated, including less than average turn-around times for sample analysis. Most laboratories operate under standards of performance for throughput time for samples, such as "90 percent of samples to be completed within 10 working days." The laboratory user should be familiar with the operating parameters of the laboratory and advise the laboratory manager if special requirements are anticipated. Analytical results are normally provided to users in the form of a typewritten or computer-generated report. Problems with analysis, interferences noted, or sample oddities should be reported by the laboratory.

2.2.5 Equipment Calibration. A function of many in-house laboratories is to provide calibration of field instrumentation including sampling pumps, sound level meters, organic vapor analyzers, and other direct reading instruments. By having a fixed source, such as a laboratory, for calibration, records and documentation on instrument use and calibration can be well maintained. Also, calibration procedures can be consistently applied.

Industrial hygienists at locations remote from the laboratory must be prepared to calibrate their own equipment. Calibration is not valid if equipment is shipped.

2.2.6 Information Resource. Internal and consulting laboratories serve as excellent informational resources to laboratory users in the field. Labs normally have their own technical libraries or have immediate access to a company's technical library. They also may subscribe to chemical and environmental data bases such as CHEMLINE, TOXLINE, and MEDLARS. Such informational resources are invaluable to the field industrial hygienist who, while in the field, encounters the need for information such as the chemical name for a trade name product, what types of air contaminants are generated from a certain type of operation, or the toxicity of a certain chemical. While that industrial hygienist may have all the resources needed at one's fingertips in the office, when out in the field, it is comforting to know that a call to the laboratory may save the day.

3   DECIDING ON AN INTERNAL OR EXTERNAL LABORATORY

Every industrial hygiene program with a responsibility for assessing the workplace environment will require the services of an industrial hygiene analytical laboratory. Services may be provided by a company's in-house laboratory or may be purchased from external consulting laboratories. Where there is an existing in-house laboratory with limited capabilities, services may be augmented by external laboratories with specific capabilities. There are pros and cons to both internal and external laboratories. Many factors must be considered in deciding on the most reliable yet cost-effective source of laboratory services.

3.1   Cost of Service

In any business, cost of operation is a primary consideration. Laboratories are inherently labor-intensive, expensive operations. Building or continuing to operate an in-house industrial hygiene laboratory requires a major capital investment and ongoing operational expenses. In order to wall-in a laboratory in existing space and equip it with benches, hoods, fixtures, and a minimum of instrumentation, a capital investment of at least $350,000 (1987 U.S. dollars) will be required. In order to justify operation of an in-house laboratory purely on a cost basis, the laboratory annual operating expenses would have to be less than total annual consulting laboratory fees that would be required to perform the company's industrial hygiene analytical work. A volume of at least 10,000 analyses per year or a volume of work equivalent to approximately $250,000 per year would be required to break even. Establishing and operating an industrial hygiene laboratory can be an expensive venture, but, if the size of the industrial hygiene program is quite large, an in-house laboratory may be cost effective.

In-house laboratories may be justified on factors other than cost. For example, services may be provided by an in-house laboratory that cannot be obtained from an external laboratory. The in-house laboratory may serve as the internal technical data center, may provide equipment calibration, may provide training to new staff, and may serve as the focal point of the industrial hygiene program for a company.

3.2 Company Image

There is prestige within an industry associated with operating one's own industrial hygiene laboratory. Corporate objectives regarding image within the industry must be considered.

3.3 Convenience of Use

If all company industrial hygienists work out of the same location as the in-house laboratory, information exchange as well as receipt of sampling materials and delivery of the samples to the lab would be facilitated. However, if industrial hygienists work out of plants or manufacturing facilities located regionally, it may be more convenient to work with a consulting laboratory near the manufacturing facility. Organizational structure and geographic location of laboratory users is a factor.

3.4 Control and Credibility of Data

With an in-house laboratory, an industrial hygiene manager should have control over the quality assurance program of the laboratory and have increased confidence in the reliability of results produced. At the same time, while the accuracy of analytical results from an in-house lab may be as good or better as that from a consulting lab, the consulting lab results may be more credible in a court of law because they are determined by what is deemed to be an unbiased source. A reasonable solution might be a combination of internal and external laboratory services with criteria established for when to use each.

3.5 Choosing a Consulting Laboratory

If it is determined that analytical support from an external source is best, a consulting laboratory or several laboratories must be chosen. Cost should not be the only factor considered in making the choice. The following guidelines may be useful.

- Consider several laboratories whose analytical capabilities match the needs of the industrial hygiene program. While a laboratory might have an excellent reputation, if it does not have high-performance liquid chromatography (HPLC), it would not be a good choice for an industry whose primary industrial hygiene concern is employee exposure to polynuclear aromatic hydrocarbons (PNAs).
- If face-to-face contact with laboratory staff is important, consider laboratories that are geographically close to the industrial hygiene program manager or staff.
- Consider only laboratories accredited by the American Industrial Hy-

giene Association if comprehensive industrial hygiene analytical services are being sought.

- Consider only laboratories proficient in the Proficiency Analytical Testing (PAT) Program of the National Institute for Occupational Safety and Health (NIOSH). Ask to see NIOSH PAT results for the past 12 months.
- Ask laboratories for a copy of their written quality assurance program.
- Ask laboratories for user references. Contact the references to obtain their assessment of services provided.
- Visit each laboratory and make an assessment of the competence of the staff, the management commitment to quality, and the service orientation of the staff. (also, see Chapter 17.)

3.6   Managing Services Provided by a Consulting Laboratory

If an external consulting laboratory is chosen to be the source of laboratory services for an industrial hygiene program, the activity must be coordinated and managed in order to run satisfactorily. It is desirable that one member of the laboratory user's staff serve as the focal point for laboratory contact. Where sample flow to the laboratory is anticipated on a regular basis, service instructions should be established clearly delineating the responsibilities of the laboratory and the laboratory user. Fees, expected turn-around times, provisions for reporting format, supply of sampling materials, and other items important to either party should be agreed upon prior to initiation of service. If the laboratory is to serve as a source of technical information to laboratory user staff, clarity should exist on how much informational service is to be provided as part of the analysis fee and at what point additional charges would be necessary to cover the laboratory staff's time for informational service.

It is prudent for laboratory users to conduct quality assurance activities on purchased laboratory services. This can be done by submitting spiked samples along with field samples for analysis. Percent recovery of spikes should be monitored. Feedback should be provided to the laboratory on its performance. The laboratory user may also ask for copies of raw data from analyses in order to evaluate documentation of analyses and to verify analytical calculations. Where the volume of analyses performed for a user is extremely large, the user may wish to conduct an annual audit of the laboratory operation. However, where laboratories have many large users, annual audits by each of them would be considered extremely burdensome. If an audit is conducted on an annual basis, consideration should be given to reimbursing the laboratory for staff time expended in conducting the audit.

If possible, the coordinator chosen by the laboratory user should be the focal point for submission of samples to the laboratory. This focal point will enable the coordinator to ensure that forms have been properly completed and all data required provided for submission to the laboratory. The coordinator can also track dates samples are submitted, dates analytical results are received, and match invoices against services received. Likewise, in the laboratory, a focal point should be established for handling requests from a large-volume user to ensure that service instructions are followed.

4 STAFFING

The size and complexity of industrial hygiene laboratories may vary from one with a single person, such as a private consultant performing phase-contrast microscopy for asbestos, to one employing several hundred people, such as the comprehensive U.S. Department of Labor Laboratory in Salt Lake City. Regardless of the size of the laboratory, people are its primary resource. Staffing needs are determined by first setting the objectives for the laboratory. Setting laboratory objectives includes determining what work the laboratory will do, how it is to be accomplished, and the standards that will be set for the work. And of course, laboratory objectives must be set within the framework of company objectives and administrative and financial constraints. (also, see Chapters 15, 19, and 20.)

4.1 Organizational Structure

Industrial hygiene laboratories currently exist as functional groups in major manufacturing corporations, property and casualty insurance groups, universities, government agencies, and as private consulting laboratories. Obviously, the reporting relationships of the laboratories in each of these scenarios may be different. Hopefully, laboratories will report to functional groups who understand the staffing and funding needs of laboratories in relation to scope of services, user service needs, and quality of work.

4.2 Key Positions and Responsibilities

Operation of an industrial hygiene laboratory requires the positions of laboratory director, laboratory supervisor, chemist, technician, and clerical staff. In the one-person laboratory, that one person may wear the hats for all of these positions, performing all duties from washing of glassware, to analysis of samples, to setting policies and purchasing major equipment. In the large laboratory, there might be one director, several supervisors, and many chemists, technicians, and clerical staff. Key responsibilities for these various positions are as follows:

1. *Laboratory Director.* The laboratory director performs the true management functions of the laboratory. The director must set the objectives for the laboratory within the framework of objectives of the parent organization or the stockholders. He or she must ensure that there is sufficient qualified

staff to perform the work; that the staff have the facilities, equipment, and materials necessary for them to do their work; that budgets are not exceeded; that lab users are satisfied with quality, timeliness, and scope of analyses; that hazards are reduced to the absolute minimum; and that the whole organization runs as smoothly as possible. He or she must measure success in achieving objectives and be able to resolve problems. The director must be able to respond upwardly, downwardly, and laterally, to superiors, to users, and to staff.

2. *Laboratory Supervisor.* The major function of the supervisor is to see that the various work objectives are met on a daily basis. Duties might include assigning work, determining what methods will be used, ensuring that operational and technical procedures are followed, communicating with laboratory users on technical matters, and ensuring that timeliness standards are met.

3. *Industrial Hygiene Chemist.* The industrial hygiene chemist is responsible for the actual analysis of materials submitted to the laboratory. There may be various levels of chemists from entry level to senior or supervising chemist. Specific tasks and complexity of work performed will depend on the position and level of experience.

4. *Quality Control Coordinator.* There should be one person in every laboratory assigned the responsibility of coordinating quality control activities. In a small laboratory, this may be a chemist or supervisor. In large laboratories, there may be one or several people whose sole responsibility is quality control.

5. *Industrial Hygiene Laboratory Technician.* There may be several levels of technician depending on level of education and experience. Duties and responsibilities may range from washing of glassware to preparation of sampling media to performing low-complexity analyses. Technicians may be responsible for sample log-in and tracking or this responsibility may be assigned to appropriately trained clerical staff.

6. *Clerical Staff.* Clerical staff are required for typing of reports, data entry, communications with users, and other clerical duties related to the operation of the laboratory.

4.3 Qualifications

Most laboratories that are serious about industrial hygiene analytical work will pursue accreditation by the American Industrial Hygiene Association (AIHA). The AIHA Laboratory Accreditation Program is very specific about qualifications required for laboratory personnel. Qualifications desired for the various positions are as follows:

1. *Laboratory Director.* The laboratory director must be on-site and actively involved in laboratory administration. Qualifications include either an earned degree in a basic science and a minimum of 5 years

industrial hygiene experience or full certification by the American Board of Industrial Hygiene.

2. *Laboratory Supervisor.* Qualifications include either an earned degree in a basic science and a minimum of 5 years experience in industrial hygiene chemistry or related procedures or full certification by the American Board of Industrial Hygiene in the chemical aspects of industrial hygiene.

3. *Quality Control Coordinator.* The quality control coordinator must have a minimum of a baccalaureate degree in the basic sciences and must be knowledgeable about statistics and quality control procedures. He or she should be independent of the analysts and be capable of effectively running a quality control program.

4. *Laboratory Personnel.* Laboratory analysts shall be qualified by education and/or experience to produce reliable analytical results.

While technical education and experience qualifications are important, not every outstanding chemist or scientist makes a good laboratory manager. The laboratory director or manager must be able to build teamwork among laboratory staff and be able to motivate people to be productive and to perform accurate work in the laboratory.

If the laboratory has a specific analytical need where expertise is required, an individual with that particular expertise may be sought. For example, expertise in electron microscopy or mass spectrometry may be required.

4.4   Sources of Qualified Staff

Recruiting staff for an industrial hygiene laboratory is not an easy task. There are only approximately 300 industrial hygiene laboratories in the United States, so there are not very many laboratory directors or chemists specially trained in the industrial hygiene field. The following sections discuss sources of qualified staff.

4.4.1 AIHA-Accredited Laboratories. There are currently 296 industrial hygiene laboratories accredited by the American Industrial Hygiene Association. The staff of these laboratories should meet the qualifications for AIHA Laboratory Accreditation. A listing of accredited laboratories is published in the *American Industrial Hygiene Association Journal* (2) four times a year, in March, June, September, and December issues. In addition, a listing of accedited laboratories is available from the American Industrial Hygiene Association (3).

4.4.2 Roster of Diplomates of American Board of Industrial Hygiene. Individuals who are technically well-qualified to be laboratory directors may be certified by the American Board of Industrial Hygiene (ABIH) in the Chemical Aspects of Industrial Hygiene. A roster of ABIH diplomates indicating their names, addresses, and areas of certification is available from the American Board of Industrial Hygiene (4).

4.4.3 AIHA Employment Service. The AIHA operates an employment service for individual members and member companies, as well as nonmembers. Information on this service, designed to place qualified industrial hygiene personnel with companies having a specific need, may be obtained from the headquarters of AIHA (3).

4.4.4 American Industrial Hygiene Conference Employment Service. A free employment service is operated annually during the American Industrial Hygiene Conference. This conference is a joint conference of the American Industrial Hygiene Association and the American Conference of Governmental Industrial Hygienists. The conference is normally held during the latter part of May. Companies are able to post open positions, industrial hygiene staff can post their resumes, and interviews can actually be conducted on site. Information on this service may be obtained from the headquarters of AIHA (3).

4.4.5 Universities. There are very few baccalaureate programs in chemistry offering training specifically in industrial hygiene chemistry. Therefore, most industrial hygiene labs seeking entry-level chemists will recruit from local universities and train their own staff in industrial hygiene laboratory techniques and methodology.

4.5 Staff Development

Planned training and staff development for all laboratory staff, from the new recruit to the seasoned veteran, is critical to the success of the operation. Regardless of their prior experience, all new employees should be given adequate training so they perform work in the manner desired by the director and supervisor. Training is equally important for existing employees. As industrial hygiene analytical methodology is continuously changing, training of staff is required to keep up to date. Professional development in the form of participation in professional associations and pursuit of ABIH certification enhances the value of laboratory staff to an organization. The following sections will provide an overview of internal and external staff training and development.

4.5.1 Internal Training. A critical area of internal training that is often treated too lightly is orientation of the new employee. The laboratory director should have some type of structured orientation program for every new employee. It should be designed to provide the new employee with information about the organization, its policies, procedures, and regulations, and to instruct the new employee in the specific job requirements, so the standards for quality, productivity, and timeliness can be met as soon as possible. Large companies may have a human resources department to assist with orienting the employee with information about the organization's policies and procedures. However, the laboratory orientation must be conducted by laboratory staff.

Although the laboratory director will make every attempt to recruit adequately educated staff, the laboratory director cannot assume that new graduates or experienced analysts from other organizations are skilled in any or all of the techniques used in the industrial hygiene laboratory. A training manual, covering techniques and individual analyses, is of tremendous value in providing step-by-step training and documentation of completed training for newly hired analysts.

Laboratory personnel should be not only qualified and adequately trained in chemical analysis but should be knowledgeable in industrial hygiene to facilitate communication with laboratory users and to be able to establish criteria for sampling methodology. For this reason, training in industrial hygiene as well as laboratory analysis is more than necessary. Having the laboratory staff accompany industrial hygienists on field surveys is an excellent means of training. Seeing where industrial hygiene samples come from helps an analyst appreciate the difficulties in sampling and understand the interferences that might be present.

4.5.2 External Training. Many larger companies offer tuition aid programs for employees who wish to pursue attainment of a baccalaureate or graduate degree at a local university. Where such opportunities are available to laboratory staff, laboratory directors should encourage staff to take advantage of this benefit. Particularly where high-potential employees without college degrees are identified, attainment of a degree would provide opportunities for advancement and enhance successor planning for the laboratory.

Successor planning in the laboratory is a critical concern. An organization will be wise to annually review potential successor candidates for key positions such as laboratory director, laboratory supervisor, quality control coordinator, and senior chemist. Candidates should be identified who could be developing to step into a key position, should it become vacant. This procedure will ensure that the work flow and services to users provided by the laboratory will not be disrupted if a key staff vacancy occurs.

When potential candidates for key positions are identified, deficiencies in skill or knowledge that might improve their ability to assume the next position should be identified and a training plan developed to eliminate those deficiencies. External training courses in management or technical areas may be required.

As new methodology and new instrumentation is introduced, external training courses may be needed for technical staff. External training is cost effective when the expertise is not contained within the laboratory or when the in-house staff time necessary for delivering training is as costly as the external training tuition. External training courses are available from universities, instrument manufacturers, professional associations, and private consultants.

Certification by the American Board of Industrial Hygiene is a worthwhile pursuit. An individual who is certified in the chemical aspects of industrial hygiene has passed an 8-hour exam in general industrial hygiene as well as an 8-hour exam in industrial hygiene chemistry. Information on certification can be obtained from the American Board of Industrial Hygiene (4).

Participation in the activities of organizations such as the American Conference of Governmental Industrial Hygienists and the American Industrial Hygiene Association provides an opportunity for laboratory staff to communicate with industrial hygiene professionals from all types of industries and organizations. This forum for exchange is a valuable part of continuing education. It also allows the laboratory staff to meet other individuals and expand their information network.

5   ADMINISTRATION

Administration of the laboratory is similar to that of any small business and can be divided into three major areas: personnel, work accounting and control, and financial accounting and control. In some cases these basic administrative policies and practices must be translated into the technical language of a laboratory environment. This section outlines basic administration and covers some of the special needs of the laboratory.

All laboratory policies and procedures should be written, organized, and available to all staff members. Areas that should be well covered include general laboratory operations (i.e., working hours, vacation and holiday policies, staff reporting relationships, and purchasing and accounts receivables practices), quality assurance procedures, safety and health precautions, analytical methods, and personnel policies and procedures.

5.1   Personnel

5.1.1 Personnel File. As with any business, personnel records must be maintained to retain a history of employment. Employee information that should be documented accurately in a continuously updated personnel file includes full name, social security number, birth date, employment date, home address and phone number, office address (for larger companies), current and past salary history, current and previous position titles and promotion dates, and work performance information.

5.1.2 Payroll and Tax Records. Records of wages paid to employees must be retained. Government regulations require recordkeeping and payment of income and social security taxes on a periodic basis. Laboratories that are divisions of larger companies can usually obtain these services from the company's financial department. Managers of other laboratories may be able to handle these functions without assistance; however, it is recommended that the services of a capable and qualified bookkeeper or CPA be retained. Employee withholding information and payroll records should be maintained in a central computerized or paper file. Duplicate protected records storage is recommended in the event of a catastrophe.

5.1.3 Benefits Records. Most employers offer employee benefits programs that may include vacations, holidays, insurance, pension plans, investment programs, educational support, and compensated or noncompensated leaves. Records of available benefits and options selected by each employee should be retained for payroll deduction and informational purposes. Employees should retain records of their benefits also.

5.1.4 Employee Performance Management System. An effective employee performance management system ensures that employees know what is expected of them, that their work is monitored in a manner that truly represents their performance, and that they are informed of their results and progress.

Each position in the laboratory should have a written position description that lists the official name, the laboratory or company name, the date the job description was written or approved (larger companies may require approval of position descriptions by the personnel or employee relations department), an indication of the reporting relationship and the level of the position in relation to other positions in the laboratory or company (this level is usually referred to as a position code, position grade, or position level), a brief statement of the major objective of the position (e.g., "perform industrial hygiene analyses"), the key responsibilities of the position, an authority statement (e.g., "authorization to quote prices," "authorization to approve purchases"), and the qualifications required and desired for the position.

In addition to a written position description, each position should have written performance standards that consist of a list of measurable responsibilities and objectives. An indication of the expected performance for each responsibility or objective should be given (e.g., "complete required training courses"). The standards and the means by which they will be measured should be provided to each employee. Optimally, employees should have the opportunity to input into their performance standards.

Performance standards are somewhat difficult to develop for laboratory analysts because of the seemingly intangible nature of laboratory work. However, opportunities do exist for objective, numerical measurement of productivity, timeliness, and quality. By maintaining the information mentioned in the work accounting and control section (5.2), accurate records on individual analyst performance can be generated.

Productivity can be monitored as hours produced versus hours available. The "average analysis times" produced from time studies, which are discussed in Section 5.2, can be multiplied by the number of completed analyses to obtain a total number of hours produced for a given time period. The available working time is calculated by subtracting vacation, holiday, training, and special project time from the total gross working hours for the same time period. Productivity can now be calculated by dividing the hours produced by the available hours. This value expressed as a percentage should result in approximately 100 percent if the employee is producing work at an acceptable level.

Timeliness measurements are based on the successful attainment of laboratory throughput times. If individual analysts meet their turn-around targets, then overall laboratory throughput targets will be met. By monitoring the sample batches that do not meet target, individual analyst problems can be documented.

Quality can be measured in several ways. The number of careless errors made by an analyst can be documented during the peer review process. Comparing this number of errors to the total number of analyses performed produces an error rate. Analyst performance can be measured versus an overall lab average error rate. Similarly, successful completion of internal quality control spikes or, conversely, the number of outliers, can be compared to the number of analyses performed. Tracking outliers obtained on external quality control program samples, such as NIOSH PAT's or Environmental Protection Agency (EPA) bulk samples for asbestos identification, can also provide a numerical quality assessment tool.

Using these and other measurement tools to evaluate an analyst's performance will assist the laboratory manager in correcting deficiencies, assessing promotional potential, and determining salary increases. A performance appraisal should be conducted with the employee at least once a year. Comparing performance standards with the employee's results is generally a good way to begin an appraisal. It is recommended that the employee be allowed and encouraged to input into the performance appraisal by completing a self-appraisal that the manager takes into consideration when conducting the performance appraisal meeting.

5.2 Work Accounting and Control

As with any business, the laboratory work input and output should be monitored in order to maintain control of the operation. A successful work management program can assist the laboratory manager in determining the appropriate staffing level and equipment needs. The laboratory work management system can easily be compared to a normal business inventory method. Monitoring the sample "inventory" and maintaining records of work quantities produced form the basis for an effective laboratory work management program. A laboratory system can be broken into two parts: sample tracking and workload monitoring.

5.2.1 Sample Tracking. A good laboratory sample tracking system allows for sample log-in, determination of analysis progress, sample log-out, and records and sample storage. The quality-related aspects of this system are discussed briefly in the quality assurance section (9.3).

Upon arrival at the laboratory, samples to be analyzed are recorded in a format that allows retention of the following information: laboratory sample identification number; date received; submitting company, division, or department; and type of analysis to be conducted. Small labs can function with manual paper systems; however, a computer will be required for larger volume labs or labs with multiple users.

Analysis progress is monitored by analyst sign-off on worksheets, in notebooks, or on computer files, depending on the particular laboratory system. When analyses are completed, the date is recorded and the data are compiled for the work accounting system. If required, samples are stored in a retrievable fashion. All records pertaining to the samples are maintained in paper or computerized files so that they can be retrieved for future inspection if necessary.

5.2.2 Workload Monitoring. Information likely to be helpful in a lab workload monitoring system includes the number of sample batches, number of samples, number and type of analyses, number of quality control samples analyzed, number of hours required per analyst, sample fees (for revenue or allocation purposes), and throughput time for each sample batch. This information is easily documented by having the analyst(s) complete a sample batch form for every batch of samples. A completely computerized sample tracking system would eliminate the necessity of generating paper documents.

To avoid the tedious process of each analyst maintaining minute-by-minute records in order to generate the ''hours'' information, average analysis times can be used. These average times should be based on time studies where several analysts record exact times required to perform specific types of analyses (e.g., two-component solvent analyses, three-component metals analysis by graphite furnace). The average of the times of several time study tests performed on a specific analysis can be multiplied by the number of analyses completed to obtain a fair estimate of the amount of time required for the analyst to complete the work. Thus, the total number of hours required to complete a batch of samples is easily obtained on a batch-by-batch basis.

In addition to providing productivity and work output information, this hourly information can be used to determine the average cost per hour that is needed to determine analytical costs for pricing or allocation purposes. When using this information for setting allocations or fees, it is important to consider nonanalytical time requirements also (e.g., vacation, special projects, methods development, training, management and clerical overhead).

When the data are totaled from the sample batch data forms for every sample batch completed during a certain time period (usually monthly and yearly), the work accounting process is completed and a good picture of the progress of the laboratory is obtained. Informed planning and controlling can then take place.

5.3 Financial Accounting and Control

Financial documentation and control are a critical part of most laboratory operations. Procurement, budgets, and accounts receivable or allocations are elements of the financial control process. (also, see Chapter 21.)

5.3.1 Procurement. The procurement of supplies and equipment requires an effective purchasing and supply inventory control system. Laboratory items that should be inventoried include chemicals, gases, sampling materials, labware, office supplies, and forms. The use of numbered purchase orders facilitates the retention of information on each item ordered. Received items can be checked off on the purchase order and then added to the list of inventoried items. Items are subtracted from the list when they are used up or discarded. Computerized inventory control software programs are readily available. Maintaining this system will help ensure that the lab does not run out of critical items. Another useful method for controlling critical supplies is a well-enforced laboratory policy requiring that the responsibility of requesting a re-order lies with the analyst who opens the last bottle of a critical chemical (e.g., carbon disulfide), opens the last box of a frequently used supply (e.g., autosampler vials), or begins using the last gas cylinder.

Capital furniture and equipment are easier to inventory, but, for most laboratories, more difficult to purchase. Appropriate planning for instrument selection and financial justification must be completed. Usually, a needs assessment or return-on-investment study must be completed before the equipment is purchased.

Procurement necessitates an accounts payable system. Invoices for purchases that have been received are approved for payment; the payment is made, and records of purchase orders, invoices, and checks are maintained for at least one year. Capital equipment payment records are usually maintained for a longer period of time. For tax purposes, these items are usually depreciated over the expected life of the equipment.

It is advisable to maintain a central source of information for supplier addresses and discount agreements. Also helpful are records indicating the least expensive sources for specific supplies and the quality of equipment and service.

5.3.2 Budgets. Depending on the size of the laboratory and its position within the corporate structure, the budgeting process will vary in complexity. Annual expense budgets should be prepared a minimum of six months before the beginning of the new fiscal year. The budget is usually broken down by the type of expense (e.g., salary, benefits, supplies, phone, photocopy, freight, capital equipment, travel, rent). Budget projections are based on the current year-end expense projection and an estimation of expense increases or decreases based on anticipated growth, changing user needs, inflation, and major laboratory equipment, facility, or staffing changes. As the year progresses, expenses are compared with the budget to control variances. (Also, see Chapter 21.)

5.3.3 Accounts Receivable/Allocations. If the laboratory is a profit center, an accounts receivable system must be in place. Invoices should include complete pricing information, customer purchase order numbers, a return address, and an indication of the payment due date (e.g., "due upon receipt"). Overdue receivables should be closely monitored with periodic resubmittal of the overdue invoice. A proper accounting system should be in place to record, credit, and deposit received checks. Copies of all checks should be maintained. If possible, the person recording and handling the received checks should be someone other than the person who performs the invoicing. Accounts receivable records should be maintained for a minimum of one year.

If the laboratory is not a profit center, a system for allocating services is probably needed. Depending on the company, this may simply be a paper process with a report of services performed for specific divisions, or it might be a system of expense allocations to divisions based on the percent of services performed for each division. Regardless of the allocation system, the laboratory manager should maintain this information so that he or she knows who the laboratory users are.

6   FACILITY MANAGEMENT

6.1   Building a Laboratory

Building a laboratory is an awesome but exciting task for the laboratory director. For those having worked in less than ideal facilities, it is exciting to be able to provide input into the planning for location, space considerations, and design of a new laboratory.

6.1.1 Location. Most independent consulting laboratories are housed in one- or two-story buildings specially designed for the consulting firm. Therefore, geographical location is a matter of choice of the owners of the facility. However, industrial hygiene laboratories with parent organizations are usually located within a major office complex. Location of the laboratory within the office complex buildings is a major consideration because of special ventilation, plumbing, electrical, storage, and access needs of the laboratory. In choosing a location within an existing building, the following factors should be considered:

1. The need to exhaust fume hoods to the external environment.
2. The need to install water lines and acid-resistant drains.
3. The need for special electrical installations.
4. Convenient access for laboratory users.
5. Convenient access for delivery of gases and supplies.
6. Fire and safety considerations for laboratory staff and other occupants of the building.

6.1.2 Space. In planning for space requirements for a laboratory, future as well as current needs must be considered. Experience has shown that by the time most laboratories are built, space needs have already exceeded the space allowed. Where space must be limited and optimal utilization of resources is a major consideration, scheduling staff for longer periods during the day, for example, a 4-day work week with 10-hour days or even having more than one 8-hour shift, may be the best approach to handling the workload in a timely manner.

6.1.3 Design. Planning for the design of a laboratory starts with the selection of an architect. This is a critical step in the process, as very few architects are experienced in the design of analytical laboratories. Design considerations for a doctor's office or a clinical laboratory are significantly different from those for an analytical laboratory. Architects of industrial hygiene laboratories that have been properly designed should be identified. It will be worthwhile to actually visit laboratories that have been designed by the architect being considered. Also, in planning for input to the architect, discussions with other laboratory directors on the pluses and minuses of their current facilities will be helpful.

Once an architect is chosen, the laboratory director must be able to provide clear information to the architect on the current requirements of the laboratory and on the need to plan for future growth, flexibility, and adaptability. Within the design, adequate consideration must be given to not only analytical bench space and space for special instrumentation, but also space for offices, computer operations, storage, sample receiving, materials preparation, technical library, and staff lunch rooms and restrooms.

6.1.4 Special Needs

6.1.4.1 FUME HOODS. Because of the wide variety of chemicals used in an industrial hygiene laboratory, significant thought needs to be given to the selection of fume hoods. If perchloric acid is used, a perchloric acid hood must be installed. For the acid ashing of metals on filters, a hood that is resistant to corrosion by acids should be chosen. For handling of asbestos-containing materials, a hood with a HEPA filter may be required. Discussion with other industrial hygiene laboratory directors will be an excellent source of recommendations for types and makes of hoods for individual uses.

For all fume hoods, space is critical. The number of hoods and the size of hoods should be matched to the current and anticipated workload. Fan motor noise and vibration should be taken into consideration when planning the laboratory. Delicate lab instrumentation should not be placed where fan motor vibration might affect it.

Ventilation engineers experienced in hood design can be contracted to design fume hood systems for laboratories. The services of such an engineer can be quite worthwhile in achieving proper system balance, achieving desired exhaust rates, and considering energy saving design ideas.

6.1.4.2 PLUMBING. Water supply systems that may be needed include cold, hot, chilled, and distilled or demineralized water systems. Locations of instruments and operations requiring certain types of water supplies should be considered in the planning stage so that an adequate supply will be provided at the immediate site.

Drainage systems must be considered for sinks, areas where water is used as a coolant, and for the eyewashes and safety showers. Because of the wide variety of chemicals used in the industrial hygiene laboratory, the composition of drainage pipe must be acid and organic resistant. Pyrex glass pipe can be used but is expensive and easily broken. Numerous plastic pipe materials are available today that have good corrosion resistance to the various chemicals occurring in laboratory wastes. The type of plastic should be carefully investigated in order to ensure optimum resistance to the chemicals used in the laboratory.

6.1.4.3 ELECTRICAL. Because of the wide variety of instrumentation used in today's industrial hygiene laboratory, electrical needs are varied and complex. The needs of current instrumentation and possible future instrumentation should be considered in planning for electrical installations and in planning for the overall electrical load of the laboratory. Irregularly fluctuating surges of power supply require voltage regulators or constant-voltage transformers connected between analytical instrumentation and outlets.

6.1.4.4 GASES. Most laboratories traditionally have air and natural gas piped to bench locations. In the industrial hygiene laboratory, additional gases are used for atomic absorption, gas chromatography, and other instrumentation. If laboratories are small, these specialty gas needs may be best handled by the use of gas cylinders at the location. However, if the laboratory is large or its needs extensive, a central piping system may be required or desirable. Gases may be provided from banks of high-pressure cylinders located in a convenient and safe place from which gas is piped through reducing valves to desired locations. This type of system is also an asset to laboratory housekeeping and safety, as gas cylinders are removed from the immediate work area.

6.1.4.5 STORAGE. In the industrial hygiene lab, storage must be available for chemicals, gas cylinders, sampling materials such as filters and charcoal tubes, glassware and supplies, packaging materials for shipping sampling supplies, insulated coolers for shipping samples under regrigeration, forms and office supplies, files, incoming samples, samples in progress, and residuals of samples that have been analyzed. Storage needs are extensive and flexibility and growth should be considered in planning for laboratory space.

6.1.4.6 BENCHES. In planning for laboratory benches, consideration should be given to bench space required per analyst and per instrument, composition of benches in order to be compatible with chemicals and materials used, height of benches in order to be compatible with need, and whether open space or cabinet storage is best underneath each bench area. While bench space in a new laboratory may look expansive, once instruments are set in place, space rapidly dwindles leaving very little work area for the analyst. Each type of analysis should be critically analyzed to determine bench space needs for the instrument, for the analyst, and also hood space required. Sinks also take up a great deal of space and should be strategically placed for optimum use.

The height of benches should be compatible with the operation for which they are planned. For example, low benches with cut-outs may be preferable for microscope work. Gas chromatographs with top-mounted autosamplers or top-mounted injectors may be more convenient for use if placed on a bench at approximately 3-foot height rather than normal bench height in order to facilitate easy injection or manipulation of the autosampler by the analyst. Thought should be given to each type of operation and the movements required by the analyst in planning for bench height.

6.2 Maintaining a Laboratory

6.2.1 Housekeeping. Cleanliness and orderliness in a laboratory are necessary for consistently good performance. Housekeeping is the responsibility not only of the custodial staff but also of laboratory staff on a daily basis.

Usually, the custodial staff is not under the direct control of the laboratory director and will provide housekeeping during a period of time when the laboratory is not occupied. In order to prevent this staff from disturbing equipment and work that might be damaged, and to protect them from laboratory hazards they may not understand, they should understand what portions of the laboratory they are to clean and what portions not to disturb.

Laboratory staff should understand that housekeeping is one of their responsibilities and that a certain standard of housekeeping is expected. Technical staff members should have definite assignments to keep certain portions of the laboratory clean and orderly, such as bench tops and chemical and supply storage areas. Supplies and reagent containers must be placed in their proper storage areas when not in use. Work areas, including analysts' desks, should be left clear at the end of the day. Space should be provided for hanging laboratory coats and smocks, and the analysts should hang their lab coats there when not in use.

6.2.2 Maintenance of Environment. It is the responsibility of the laboratory director and the organization to provide a workplace that is not only free of health and safety hazards but that is comfortable and conducive to good employee morale and productivity. Control of lighting, temperature, and humidity is necessary to keep both the employees and many of the instruments working well. Instruments produce a good deal of heat and contribute to the temperature of the laboratory environment. A separate thermostat control for areas with analytical instrumentation is desirable. Also, air exhausted by hoods and air contributed in make-up air affect the temperature. All of these factors should be considered in planning for laboratory comfort and temperature control.

As mentioned, the laboratory environment is critical not only to the employees but to proper performance of instrumentation. Many instruments are temperature and humidity sensitive. Also, dust control is important, especially in an industrial hygiene laboratory where microscopy is conducted.

The laboratory director must maintain a good working relationship with the maintenance staff. In a small facility, it may be possible that laboratory staff perform some maintenance functions. Maintenance staff should be made aware of the needs of the laboratory and of things that could happen requiring immediate assistance, such as a broken water pipe. Maintenance staff should be aware that interruption of a service such as electicity may have disastrous effects upon the work in progress. The laboratory needs to be notified of any planned interruptions of services such as electricity so that proper precautions can be taken or work planned accordingly.

6.2.3 Security. Laboratory security is important in protecting the safety of employees, the safety of those who might enter the laboratory, and the protection of laboratory work and capital assets. The laboratory should be in an area that has limited access. All individuals entering the laboratory should come through a reception area requiring identification and sign-in. During hours when the laboratory is not staffed, areas housing equipment, samples, or laboratory records should be locked. Only laboratory, custodial, and maintenance staff should have access to the laboratory during nonoffice hours.

7 ANALYTICAL EQUIPMENT

Other than personnel, analytical equipment is the most important laboratory resource. The appropriate use of labware and analytical instrumentation is essential to the successful operation of the industrial hygiene laboratory.

7.1 Labware and Miscellaneous Equipment

Labware must be both accurate and appropriate for the analytical method. Its selection requires forethought and planning. For example, glass vials are acceptable for solvent work, but polyethylene ware should be employed for work on free silica. Low-density polyethylene bottles are required for formaldehyde samples because other types of bottles may give off interfering contaminants. At least one analyst in every laboratory has made the foolish mistake of selecting a syringe with a metal needle for measuring microliter quantities of metals samples. Stainless steel tweezers and stirrers must be avoided when working on hexavalent chromium analyses.

Measuring devices must be accurate, and time-saving devices are available that do not adversely affect accuracy. Automatic pipettes that measure ± 0.05 percent can be purchased. Multisample shakers and multisample, manually dispensing syringes are available. Vortex mixers can help improve both efficiency and accuracy for samples that are difficult to mix. Automated pipette bulbs can speed up the use of transfer pipettes.

7.2 Instrumentation

Instrument selection and maintenance are key areas of concern for the industrial hygiene laboratory.

7.2.1 Selection of Analytical Instrumentation. The first question to be asked when selecting an instrument is, ''What do I want it to do?'' If all one desires to analyze is lead, inductively coupled plasma would probably not be the instrument of choice. Similarly, it would be an unfortunate circumstance if a packed-column gas chromatograph with flame ionization detector were selected, and later it was discovered that the primary client need was the analysis of polychlorinated biphenyls. The decision on which compounds will be analyzed (currently and in the future) must be made before the instrument is selected. Once this decision is made, the selection of instrument attachments (i.e., detectors, columns, lamps) is also facilitated.

The extent of automation desired and the ease of use must be considered. If the lab is staffed with less-experienced individuals, an instrument that is easy to use should be selected. Generally, the more automated the equipment, the less complicated it will be to use successfully. Autosamplers, integrators, and computer-controlled systems are more the rule today than the exception. In addition to being easier to use, automated instruments can improve productivity for routine work, improve documentation, and in many cases, improve accuracy. On the other hand, automated instruments require more maintenance than simple instruments, they experience longer periods of downtime, they can lull analysts into increased errors because of the decreased necessity for constant attention, and they usually require higher associated costs because of the necessity for expendables such as autosampler vials and syringes.

Quality and cost are the next considerations. The instrument manufacturer should be reputable and should be able to provide quality and timely instrument maintenance service. It is highly recommended that a demonstration of the instrument be secured and that contact is made with current users of the same instrument. Instrument manufacturers can sometimes arrange trial periods of the equipment in the laboratory. Once the choice is narrowed down to several quality instruments, then price negotiations can begin with the various manufacturers or distributors.

7.2.2 Maintenance. Regardless of the quality of the instrument or the reputation of the manufacturer, Murphy's law does apply to laboratories, and the instrument is going to break down. Preventive maintenance, which is part of any good quality assurance program, can postpone and lessen the severity of breakdowns, but they will happen occasionally. Most instrument manufacturers offer maintenance contracts, and the laboratory must decide whether it is more cost effective to pay for a maintenance contract from the manufacturer (or independent service organization) or to use staff time and perform the maintenance in-house. Most instrument manufacturers offer training courses on maintenance, technical assistance over the phone, and direct sale of instrument parts. Instrument contracts are generally offered in several options, from annual preventive maintenance visits to full-service, all parts-and-labor contracts. These maintenance decisions should be part of the instrument selection process.

8 ANALYTICAL METHODS AND REPORTS

Analytical procedures and reports of analytical results are integral parts of the successful laboratory operation. They must be well-documented and accurate. This section details the development and content of methods and reports.

8.1 Methods

When selecting an analytical method, one must ensure that the sampling method is compatible and that the laboratory has the equipment and chemicals necessary to perform the analysis. Analytical methods can be obtained from several sources. The NIOSH *Manual of Analytical Methods* (5) is the most available and most often referenced source. The *OSHA Analytical Methods Manual* (6) can be purchased from the American Conference of Governmental Industrial Hygienists (ACGIH) (7). The *American Industrial Hygiene Association Journal* (2) is an excellent source of new procedures. Existing industrial hygiene laboratories will often share methods with other labs. Standard analytical texts, instrument manufacturer manuals and technical literature, and analytical chemistry periodicals can also be used as sources of industrial hygiene analytical methods. If the appropriate resources are available, the laboratory can develop and validate its own methods. Regardless of its source, before the analytical method is accepted and employed in routine sample analysis, it should be proven in the laboratory by successful analysis of a series of quality control samples. Analysts should complete a comprehensive training program in the use of the analytical method before they begin working on unknown samples.

The procedures utilized by the laboratory should be documented in writing and should indicate exactly how the procedure is performed in-house. The methods should include exact details of the analytical procedure, quality control procedures, sampling methods, interferences, reagents, standard curve information, equipment, accuracy and precision information, range, calculation instructions, and indications of potential problems. The method should be approved and signed by the laboratory director. A system for accomplishing and documenting method changes and updates should be in place. A suggestion for documenting revisions is showing the revised date and revision approval on the updated method and storing superseded methods in a "Superseded Methods Manual." Current and superseded analytical methods should be available to laboratory users.

8.2 Reports

An analytical results report should be issued following completion of sample analysis. This report may be as simple as results recorded on a sample information form or as complicated as a typed report with statistical information and recommendations. Completeness and accuracy are the key concerns and any report should contain, at a minimum, the following information: the unique laboratory sample batch number, lab name, sample submitter's name, correctly labeled results by sample number and analyte name, signature, date, analytical method utilized, and comments concerning the results (e.g., results corrected for blank).

For maximum efficiency, computerized reports should be considered. If computer reports are generated or if results are typed by a clerical staff, the report should be carefully reviewed and proofed by the analyst who performed the work. It is recommended that the analyst sign the report and that it be reviewed by the laboratory director (or a technical supervisor) prior to release. A laboratory policy of result confidentiality should be considered for all laboratories and should be mandatory for consulting labs.

9   QUALITY ASSURANCE

Detailed laboratory quality control recommendations are readily available
from several sources. Several references are listed under General References on page 218. This section will deal more with the overall laboratory
picture as it relates to quality assurance and quality control. To be successful, a laboratory quality assurance (QA) program should incorporate a written quality assurance plan, staff qualifications and training, chain of custody,
and, perhaps most importantly, management commitment. To ensure that
the program is appropriately monitored, it is suggested that one senior staff
member be assigned the responsibility of maintaining the quality control
(QC) program.

9.1   Written Quality Assurance Plan

The QA plan should include and document both internal and external quality
assurance and control policies and procedures. The exact procedures to be
followed should be carefully spelled out along with staff responsibilities for
accomplishing the procedures. The written QA plan should document procedures for all the areas listed in this section: quality control, training, chain of
custody, and management involvement. Some specific areas for documentation of internal and external QC programs follow.

9.1.1 External Quality Control.   The written external QC plan should list all
the external programs in which the laboratory participates. Available programs include the NIOSH Proficiency Analytical Testing (PAT) Program,
the AIHA Asbestos Analysis Registry, the EPA Bulk Asbestos Quality Assurance Program administered by Research Triangle Institute, the West Allis
Memorial Blood Lead Program, and various state programs. The documentation should indicate the frequency of the sample rounds and addresses and
phone numbers for questions and results submission. All results and the
documentation for work done on the external QC samples should be retained
in an organized file.

9.1.2 Internal Quality Control and Documentation.   A detailed, written
quality control plan for each analytical method should be developed. The
plan should cover such areas as the preparation and number of standard
curve points, the preparation techniques for and number of QC spikes, procedures for and frequency of replicate analyses, preparation and frequency
of blind spikes, instrument calibration procedures and frequencies, and the
use of standard reference materials. Actions to be taken for out-of-control
points should be included in the written plan. It is recommended that these
QC procedures be an integral part of the written analytical method.

 All QC results should be recorded on QC logs and plotted so that compliance with control limits can be easily monitored. Any actions taken regarding out-of-control points should be documented. The control limit calcula-

tion procedures should be carefully spelled out. QC records should be maintained indefinitely. It is suggested that old logs and charts be maintained in a "Superseded QC Log" so that the current logs will not become too unwieldy.

Instrument "Use and Maintenance Logs" should be maintained. Any preventive maintenance (PM) procedures should be documented in detail and exact records kept whenever the PM procedures are carried out. Instrument service records and service contracts should be maintained.

9.2 Staff Qualifications and Training

Staffing issues have been covered previously in Section 4.5. However, no quality assurance discussion would be complete if the issue of staff qualifications and training were excluded. Regardless of the extent of instrument automation, the completeness of procedural instructions, or the complexity of the quality control program, an experienced and capable staff is needed to assure that accurate results are produced by the laboratory.

New analysts should be assigned to work with experienced analysts in a given technique or method and should be adequately trained in an analytical method before being allowed to perform analyses using that method. It is recommended that a training program be developed for each analytical method or instrument. The training plan should specify QC procedures, exact analytical procedures and equipment, calibration, preventive maintenance, potential problems and solutions, interferences, sampling methods, important time considerations, chemical stabilities, and instrument set-up, usage, and trouble shooting. The training plan should spell out how the training is initiated and what factors determine its completion (e.g., successful completion of 10 blind QC spikes). It is suggested that a system be set up to allow for training completion sign-off by the analyst and the trainer.

9.3 Chain of Custody

Accurate chain of custody procedures should be followed and documented to ensure a traceable and secure sample storage and transfer process. When samples are received, the package should be carefully searched so that any discrepancies with the sample submission paperwork can be documented. The name of the person who checks the samples and the date should be recorded on the sample submission forms. Samples should be stored in a locked area. The sample records should indicate the changes in possession of the samples until the analytical work is completed. If possible, sample storage is recommended for a 3-month period after report release in the event that questions arise and reanalysis is required. Longer storage periods may be required by the government (e.g., asbestos) or for legal evidence maintenance reasons. Some companies have policies forbidding sample storage after analysis for liability reasons.

9.4 Management Commitment

Management commitment and involvement is essential if a high-quality operation is to be maintained. The laboratory manager must insist on quality work. He or she must provide the leadership to motivate the staff to perform ethically and professionally.

A significant financial commitment is also required. Quality assurance procedures are time consuming and, therefore, costly. Approximately 10–20 percent of the work should be dedicated to quality control standard curves, spikes, and external QC sample analysis. In addition, time must be made available for peer reviewing of analytical work and monitoring the quality assurance program. Equipment must be maintained to ensure accurate results, and expensive standard chemicals must be purchased. Experienced, qualified staff members demand higher salaries than less well-educated employees, and appropriate training is an expensive, on-going necessity.

10 SAFETY AND HEALTH

Safety and health are important issues in any laboratory. Because protection of workers is its main purpose, the industrial hygiene laboratory should be the exemplary safe and healthful workplace. This section will briefly address laboratory safety and health issues. It is not intended to be a comprehensive reference, but rather a short overview of the various issues that are involved in the management of safety and health in the industrial hygiene laboratory. Additional details should be obtained from the references listed under General References on page 218.

10.1 Staff Training

Establishing a safe and healthful environment requires management commitment and the active participation of the laboratory staff. The employees must be informed of the hazards and the necessary safety precautions. A training program that complies with the OSHA hazard communication regulations should be instituted. Employees should be informed of the safety hazards and the adverse health effects, both acute and chronic, of the chemicals to which they may be exposed. They should know what safety and personal protective equipment is available, when to use it, and where it is stored. The correct uses and limitations of the equipment should be carefully explained. It is suggested that all lab staff members be trained in first aid techniques.

10.2 Equipment

The following types of equipment should be available and maintained in working order.

10.2.1 Worker Protection Equipment. Protection of laboratory analysts will require, at a minimum, appropriate ventilation hoods, protective eyewear, various types of protective gloves (for chemical resistance and temperature extremes), aprons, protective clothing, face shields, respirators, and biological/radiological waste disposal equipment.

10.2.2 Accident Prevention Equipment. The laboratory has very specialized needs because of the variety of potential catastrophes. The accident prevention equipment might include the following items: explosion-proof refrigerators, perchloric acid hoods, adequate glassware, appropriate plumbing for gases and liquid wastes, grounded equipment, proper lighting, gas cylinder storage facility with blowout walls, gas leak detection equipment, and flammable solvent storage cabinets.

10.2.3 Accident Control Equipment. To lessen the severity of accidents, various types of equipment are needed: sprinklers (or other fire dampening system), fire extinguishers, eyewash, shower, spill control/cleanup equipment, mercury cleanup equipment, and first aid equipment.

10.2.4 Monitoring Equipment. Necessary monitoring equipment includes personal sampling pumps, calibration devices, sampling media and equipment, shower/eyewash/sprinkler test equipment, velometer, thermometer, and radiation testing equipment.

10.3 Emergencies

As with any operation where the potential for catastrophe exists, the laboratory should be prepared to address any emergency. Written plans should cover emergencies caused by fire, explosions, worker protection from chemical releases and their cleanup, evacuation, and injuries. Occasional practice of planned protective, control, cleanup, and evacuation measures should be undertaken. It is advisable to communicate with the local fire department, the landlord, and other building inhabitants, to ensure that they are aware of the potential for explosions and toxic chemical releases. Appropriate fire, ambulance, hospital, and poison control numbers should be listed on every telephone in the laboratory. It is suggested that contact is made with the nearest emergency care facility to ensure that the physicians are familiar with the treatment of chemical burns, especially that of hydrofluoric acid.

10.4 Monitoring Programs

In the industrial hygiene laboratory, the safety and health program should go beyond the maintenance of protective equipment and the development of emergency plans. Programs should be developed and implemented for monitoring and documenting safety and health practices and protection.

10.4.1 Safety Monitoring. A complete safety program should require periodic inspection of equipment to check for availability and proper operation. Management must continually observe the lab staff to check for the proper use of personal protective equipment and the utilization of safe and healthful work practices. The safety checks should be documented along with any continuing staff noncompliance with the established laboratory safety and health practices. Continued abuse of safety and health guidelines should be grounds for employee termination.

10.4.2 Industrial Hygiene Monitoring. An on-going industrial hygiene monitoring program should be established. Personnel should be periodically monitored to document exposure to routinely used chemicals, such as carbon disulfide and benzene. The ventilation hoods should be checked for proper and adequate air flow. Noise measurements should be obtained if a problem is suspected or if a new piece of noise-producing equipment is installed. Gas chromatograph electron capture detectors should be monitored for radioactive emissions.

The requirements of the industrial hygiene monitoring program should be in writing and the results of the testing should be documented. If significant exposure levels are encountered, they should be addressed according to standard industrial hygiene practices.

REFERENCES

1. K. R. Wilcox et al., "Laboratory Management," in S. Inhorn (ed.), *Quality Assurance Practices for Health Laboratories,* Washington, D.C.: American Public Health Association, 1978, p. 6.
2. *American Industrial Hygiene Association Journal,* American Industrial Hygiene Association, Akron, OH.
3. American Industrial Hygiene Association, Akron, OH.
4. American Board of Industrial Hygiene, Lansing, MI.
5. P. M. Eller (ed.), *NIOSH Manual of Analytical Methods,* 3rd ed., U.S. Dept. of Health and Human Services, Cincinnati, OH 1984.
6. *OSHA Analytical Methods Manual,* OSHA Analytical Laboratory, Salt Lake City, UT, 1985.
7. American Conference of Governmental Industrial Hygienists, Cincinnati, OH.

GENERAL REFERENCES

The information presented in this chapter provides only a brief introduction to industrial hygiene laboratory management. For this reason, the following general source references are included.

Eller, P. M. *NIOSH Manual of Analytical Methods,* 3rd ed., Cincinnati: U.S. Department of Health and Human Services, 1984.

Grover, F., and P. Wallace, *Laboratory Organization and Management,* London: Butterworth, 1979.

Inhorn, S. (ed.), *Quality Assurance Practices for Health Laboratories,* Washington, D.C.: American Public Health Association, 1978.

Laboratory Quality Assurance Program for Industrial Hygiene Chemistry, Analytical Chemistry Committee, American Industrial Hygiene Association, Akron, OH, 1987.

Lewis, H., (ed.), *Laboratory Planning for Chemistry and Chemical Engineering,* New York: Reinhold Publishing, 1962.

OSHA Analytical Methods Manual, OSHA Analytical Laboratory, Salt Lake City, Utah, 1985.

Prudent Practices for Handling Hazardous Chemicals in Laboratories, National Research Council Committee on Hazardous Substances in the Laboratory, Washington, D.C.: National Academy Press, 1981.

Prudent Practices for Disposal of Chemicals from Laboratories, National Research Council Committee on Hazardous Substances in the Laboratory, Washington, D.C.: National Academy Press, 1983.

Steere, N. V. (ed.), *Handbook of Laboratory Safety,* 2nd ed., Cleveland: Chemical Rubber Co., 1971.

CHAPTER THIRTEEN

Data Management

Debra H. Schoch, E. Scott Harter, and
Thomas R. Jaeger

1 INTRODUCTION

Industrial hygienists collect and analyze large quantities of data relating to the employee and the workplace. They may also be responsible for maintaining inventories of specific regulated materials (pesticides and radiation sources), environmental control equipment (ventilation systems), and personal protective devices (respirators). In addition, recordkeeping is required

221

for various employee training programs, including hearing conservation, respiratory protection, and hazards communication.

Such activities, which represent a significant component of an industrial hygiene department's operations, require programs for efficient data management. Staff professionals must be able to retrieve and analyze information in order to respond to questions, identify study needs, and monitor trends in employee exposure.

Several companies (1–5) have published information on their computer-based systems for handling industrial hygiene data. In this chapter, we describe three applications that have been developed by the Industrial Hygiene Section of the Eastman Kodak Company Health and Environment Laboratories in Rochester, New York. These are (1) a system for retrieving industrial hygiene reports, (2) an equipment inventory control application, and (3) an occupational noise system. Sample reports have been created for illustrative purposes.

2 WORKPLACE

Approximately 45,000 men and women are employed at the Eastman Kodak Company corporate headquarters and manufacturing facilities in Rochester, New York. Major industrial products include sensitized goods (photographic film and paper) and electronic equipment (imaging devices, blood analyzers, copiers, etc.). The company also maintains such support functions as power generation, construction, transportation, and waste disposal. In addition, it manages a large laboratory complex responsible for both basic and applied research in the physical and biological sciences.

The industrial hygiene unit, established in 1954, is responsible for providing services to all Rochester-based plants as well as Kodak photographic processing laboratories, distribution and service centers, and subsidiaries throughout the United States.

3 REPORT RETRIEVAL SYSTEM

3.1 Introduction

During the past three decades, the industrial hygiene department's information-handling requirements have expanded remarkably as the scope and diversity of the program have grown. The need to access industrial hygiene information in an efficient and timely manner has prompted the development of a computerized information retrieval system.

3.2 Description of System

Industrial hygiene documents are prepared on terminals connected to the laboratory's minicomputer. After entering the information listed below to create a search file, the hygienist writes the report using word processing software:

1. Building number(s)
2. Last name of author
3. Plant(s) identification
4. Report number, including year of study
5. Department number(s)
6. Abstract (maximum 189 characters organized by subject, summary of data, and conclusions)

On-line search requests may include any combination of the above data elements or textual material from the report itself submitted as Boolean constructs (and/or conditions) in the form of characters or character strings. An example of a hypothetical search is shown in Table 13.1.

The purpose of this inquiry was to retrieve all industrial hygiene reports in which noise was evaluated during film processing, other than movie or microfilm processing, in a specific plant (PP) and building (No. 9). The first output screen identifies all reports satisfying the above criteria, whereas the second presents more detailed information about the specific document selected (No. 003R), including an abstract of the report. A copy of the entire report may also be displayed or printed.

Reports prepared before 1987 are stored as microfilm images accessible through the use of an optical scanning (bar code) device. A computerized permuted index containing report number, agent, date of study, abstract, and so forth was implemented in 1978. Cumulative listings of this data base, sorted by (1) agent, (2) building number, and (3) keyword are used for manual retrieval.

3.3 Discussion

On-line access offers substantial improvements in search capability (speed, accuracy, complexity, etc.) compared with use of the cumulative indices. It also is more efficient since a number of manual procedures have been eliminated, including reviewing printouts, recording pertinent report numbers, searching microfilm, and copying documents. Implemented with minimal training, the system uses commercially available software, is user friendly, and requires no extensive software support.

4 EQUIPMENT INVENTORY CONTROL SYSTEM

4.1 Introduction

As a large industrial user of ionizing radiation, the Eastman Kodak Company has recognized the need to develop a system for managing its inventory

Table 13.1. Industrial Hygiene Report Retrieval System Screens

Search Request

Retrieve all studies that have "noise, film, and processing" as key words but not "movie or microfilm," at Pine Plant, Bldg. 9.

Input Screen

Building	9
Author	
Plant	PP
Report No.	
Dept. No.	
Abstract	
Words in text	noise and film and processing
But not	movie
But not	microfilm

Output Screen

Building	Author	Document ID
9	Smith	003R
9	Smith	0017R
9	Jones	2222R
9	Eastman	1122R
9	Davis	0300R

Output Screen 2 (Selection of Document 003R)

Doc ID	003R
Building	9
Author	Smith
Plant	PP
Report No.	87010
Dept No.	152

Abstract: Personal dosimetry of slide film processing operation (No. 6 and 7 machines) indicated 8-hour equivalent exposure of 83 dBA, range = 82–85 dBA, $n = 6$. Recommend machine lubrication.

of X-ray equipment and other radiation devices. Information was first keypunched from handwritten forms as early as 1970. The system was upgraded in 1984 to facilitate on-line data entry by industrial hygiene personnel and to permit limited retrieval. Additional improvements, including increased security against loss of information, enhanced query capability, and greater ease of operation, were implemented in 1986.

4.2 Description of System

The system was designed to generate lists for periodic equipment inspection and employee training, provide reports for regulatory agencies, and respond to questions. At present (1987), information for more than 2000 sources of ionizing radiation is stored in the data base. Also included are the names of approximately 100 "radiation safety supervisors" responsible for ensuring the safe use of the X-ray equipment and other devices containing radioactive material (static eliminators, instruments, etc.) in their respective organizations.

The following information is recorded for each radiation source:

1. Identification number.
2. Employee number of department safety supervisor.
3. Location (plant, building and room numbers, department number and name).
4. Isotope and activity (radioactive material only).
5. "Wipe test" required?
6. Tube voltage and current (X-ray equipment only).
7. Description of equipment.
8. Name of manufacturer.
9. Model and serial numbers.
10. Registration and license numbers (if applicable).
11. Dates of acquisition and disposal.

Based on our experience during the past decade, a number of enhancements have recently been introduced: (1) calculation of decay correction for radioactive material, (2) linkage with the company personnel data base to update information about plant safety supervisors (name, telephone numbers, mailing addresses, etc.), (3) on-line audits (alpha/numeric format, field size, etc.), (4) data translation (plant abbreviation changed to regulatory agency registration number), (5) design of menus for selection of common entries (license numbers and manufacturers' names) to avoid redundant data entry, (6) maintenance of equipment disposal records in accordance with regulatory requirements, (7) automatic assignment of identification numbers for new sources, and (8) preparation of initial and follow-up inventory forms. It is also important to note that state and federal agencies responsible for regulating sources of ionizing radiation have accepted our standard report format for registration renewals.

The procedures used to conduct the semiannual inventory are as follows:

1. Source documents (Table 13.2) are computer generated for distribution to the plant safety supervisors.

Table 13.2. Example of Ionizing Radiation Inventory Control System Report

Radiation Safety Supervisor: Thomas X. Jones (Bldg. 200, PP)

Instructions

1. Perform in-person inspection of each source shown below.
2. Note any corrections on printout.
3. Refer to sources by acquisition number (ACQ NO).
4. Keep one copy for your records.
5. Sign and return second copy (with corrections) within 2 weeks to: Company Radiation Safety Officer, Industrial Hygiene Section. Bldg. 311, 1st. floor, PP.

Bldg No	Room No	Dept No	Acq No	Manufacturer	Model No	Serial No	Isotope	Curies	Use	Description	Date Acquired
200	107	549	99	Oak Ridge NA	Custom	None	AM241	0.100	Meter Calib	Dwg No 2339A	05–09–61
201	115	640	2399	New England		NES-136T	AM241	0.000410	Ref Stand	Lucite Tube Fits GMA	08–27–84
201	229	640	2401	Tech/Ops	773	S-498	CS137	0.145	Meter Calib		09–20–84

2. After performing an on-site inspection, the supervisor updates the information and mails the form to the industrial hygienist designated as the company radiation safety officer.

3. The report is edited and, where appropriate, changes are made to the data base.

4. If a document has not been received within a designated time frame, follow-up notices are automatically prepared.

5. Operational statistics (percent of inventory completed) and related data (identification of nonresponding supervisors) are also generated.

4.3 Discussion

In addition to assisting in the collection of information from the plant safety supervisors, the system provides data for the industrial hygiene section, specifically, lists of sealed radiation sources for semiannual wipe (leakage) tests, and of X-ray devices for an annual inspection survey. It has been used to identify personnel for radiation safety training. For example, company transportation specialists have requested a listing of employees responsible for shipping leased static eliminators, and industrial hygiene personnel have retrieved the names of individuals with knowledge about certain types of equipment (X-ray diffractometers, beta thickness gauges, etc.). We have also responded to inquiries from governmental agencies concerning the annual disposition of radioactive materials. Finally, it should be mentioned that this program has served as a model for similar applications that have been developed for lasers and local exhaust ventilation systems.

5 OCCUPATIONAL NOISE SYSTEM

5.1 Introduction

Efficient administration of a noise program, including project planning and evaluation, requires the collection of and access to comprehensive noise monitoring data for both individuals and groups of employees. The hearing conservation program at Kodak, which has evolved during the past four decades, represents such an effort.

The Occupational Noise System, an essential component of this program, identifies noise areas and records information about employee exposure. It also provides a mechanism for identifying needs for annual audiometric examinations and employee training.

Implemented in 1982, the system was designed to (1) identify employees working in noise environments; (2) generate input to the medical department recall system for scheduling annual hearing tests; (3) monitor departmental response to industrial hygiene recommendations concerning the need for engineering consultations, personal protective devices, employee training, and so forth; and (4) assess the effectiveness of Kodak's hearing protection program.

5.2 Description of System

5.2.1 Noise Zone (NZ). The zone concept for grouping employees by similarity of exposure has been discussed by other contributors (4, 5). The NZ, the basic unit of the system, may represent a physical location (building), an occupational title (welder), or a production operation (metal fabrication). NZs are defined as areas/processes of similar employee exposure. They are established by the industrial hygienist after consultation with the area physician, unit supervisor, and department safety coordinator. Yearly updates are performed.

5.2.2 Hearing Conservation Program. Two of the major components of the company's hearing conservation program are annual audiometric testing and employee education. Once a NZ is created, a registry of noise-exposed employees is produced, hearing protection is mandated, signs are posted in the work area, engineering consultation is provided, and a training program is initiated. The medical department is also notified so that employees' annual audiometric examinations may be scheduled.

5.2.3 Computer Data Base. NZs are identified by a unique, seven-character field that includes the plant designation, department number, and sequence of noise zones within the department. The date the NZ was created is also recorded.

NZ records are comprised of a zone description, noise characterization, and names of personnel in the zone. The description segment identifies the NZ according to its location and company organization. The noise characterization segment describes the zone according to the type of noise (continuous and/or impact), the number of employees in the zone, the frequency of the operation, and the measured intensity of the noise. To assist the hygienist in re-evaluating the zone, the report number of the most recent noise survey is included. Additional descriptive information, such as the type of hearing protection and noise control measures used, may also be entered. The final segment identifies employees in the zone.

5.3 Administrative Reports and Analyses

5.3.1 Noise Zone Report. A printout summarizing the status of each NZ is prepared annually to aid the hygienists in updating information about the zones in their respective areas of responsibility. Table 13.3 shows an example of a typical report.

Table 13.3. Example of Noise Zone Report

| Dept. No. 399 | Occupational Noise System | January 7, 1987 |
| Zone P399010 | | |

Industrial Hygienist Ruth J. Smith (Bldg. 320. KP)

1. Noise Zone

Date	Plant	Organization	Division	Department	Bldg	Floor	Room	Last Update
03-01-81	KP	Product X Manufacturing	A	399	4230	2		11-20-85

Description: Machine tenders; wet end of X-machine. B-4230 personnel on 7 days, off 2 days, 21 days per month; annual 5-week shutdown. Contact: J. Duncan, X884.

2. Usual Personal Exposure

Noise Type	Estimated No. Workers /Shift	/Yr	Est. Avg. Yearly Shifts	Est. Avg. Daily Hours	Approx. Exposure Level (dBA)[a]	Dose (%)	Peak Sound Level (dBA)	Exposure Control Codes	I.H. Report No.	Last Update
Continuous	1	6	240	8.0	85.0	50.0	93	Disposable plugs	85042	11-17-86

3. Personnel

Employee Number	Last Name	First Initial	Last Education Year	Last Audiogram Year	Date of Last Update
11223	Smith	T	1985	1986	11-07-86
14006	Jones	R	1985	1985	11-07-86
15229	Jackson	I	1985	1986	11-07-86
29876	Sims	J	1986	1986	11-07-86
38576	Abel	L	1986	1986	11-07-86
63891	Robinson	H	1986	1986	11-07-86

[a] Representative value based on industrial hygiene measurements.

229

5.3.2 Annual Hearing Conservation Summary Report. An administrative report is produced for evaluating the effectiveness of the company's hearing conservation effort. The results are summarized yearly according to four organizational levels as well as NZs. As Table 13.4 indicates, the program is assessed in terms of (1) noise exposure (number of employees at or greater than a specified 8-hour equivalent noise intensity), (2) percent receiving education/audiogram, (3) ear protection usage, and (4) audiogram results.

5.3.3 Special Analyses. In addition to routine reports, special statistical analyses may be prepared, as needed, in order to evaluate noise exposure and audiometric data, and associations with other information. Figure 13.1 shows an example of a cumulative distribution (with 95 percent confidence limits) of 8-hour noise exposures among employees of a particular occupation. The number of days in a year (right axis) in which employees would be expected to receive a given exposure has been inferred from the frequency of sampling results (left axis). This type of information is useful in recommending hearing protection, evaluating hearing loss potential, establishing priorities for engineering assessment, and monitoring trends in a particular job/department.

5.4   Discussion

One of the major benefits associated with the system is that it allows one to assess the quality of the hearing conservation program in terms of its effectiveness in (1) controlling noise exposures and (2) preventing hearing loss or threshold shifts.

By monitoring departmental response to recommendations concerning the need for engineering evaluations in noise areas, industrial hygienists play an active role in implementing required workplace modifications. With respect to audiometric analyses, it has been possible to identify specific areas where more preventive efforts are necessary. In addition, program effectiveness is evaluated by reviewing statistical reports comparing the total number of employees working in noise versus the number participating in various aspects of the program (receiving annual audiometric examinations, wearing hearing protection, attending educational sessions, etc.). The system also provides information about the status of the program. At the departmental level, for example, review of the data with the safety supervisor may be useful in addressing specific problems and making recommendations for improving the program.

From an operational standpoint, maintaining a current file of employees in NZs represents the system's most difficult challenge. To improve this process, which previously involved manual transcription, lists of employees, prepared from the company's personnel system, are merged with the NZ data base to create departmental rosters. As a result of this change, the number of data entry errors relating to inaccurate employee identification

Table 13.4. Example of Hearing Conservation Summary Report

Plant Organization Division Department Noise Zone	Noise Exposure (TWA)		Education (%)		Audiogram (%)		Ear Protection Usage (%)			Audiogram Analysis (%)	
	Number ≥ 85 dBA	Percent ≥ 90 dBA	1 Yr	3 Yr	1 Yr	3 Yr	Always	Some	Never	Threshold Hearing Shift[a]	Hearing Loss[b]
Plant A	2230	0	85	91	90	98	58	26	15	6	6
Organization A	118	0	87	83	83	94	55	31	14	8	7
Division A	68	0	83	87	89	95	52	34	13	9	9
Department 1	16	0	50	75	63	81	30	38	32	0	0
P001010	16	0	50	75	63	81	30	38	32	0	0
Department 2	15	0	87	80	93	100	87	0	13	0	7
P002010	15	0	87	80	93	100	87	0	13	0	7
Department 3	37	0	97	97	100	100	42	48	9	11	11
P003010	22	0	95	95	100	100	50	45	5	9	9
P003020	7	0	100	100	100	100	43	43	14	14	14
P003030	8	0	100	100	100	100	25	75	25	13	0

[a] Average change in hearing level ≥ 10 dB at 2000, 3000 and 4000 Hz for either ear. From (OSHA–STS) (6).
[b] Threshold average > 25 dB for 500, 1000, 2000, and 3000 Hz in either ear.

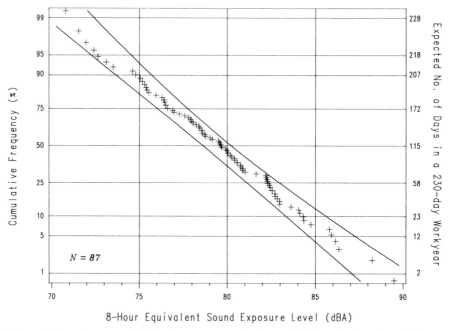

Figure 13.1.   An example of an inverse cumulative probability distribution of 8-hour sound exposures.

has been greatly reduced. Communications between industrial hygiene and the operating units, which assist in the data collection effort, have also improved.

6 SUMMARY

The data management applications described have provided a mechanism for evaluating and improving industrial hygiene programs. Systems such as these are dynamic in nature and require periodic modification in order to respond to changes in technology, client needs, and regulatory demands.

ACKNOWLEDGMENTS

The authors wish to acknowledge the contribution of Richard F. Scherberger, CIH, who designed the original radiation, laser, and industrial hygiene report systems, and assisted in the development of the Occupational Noise System. Frederick Grose, CIH, provided the data and analysis in Figure 13.1.

REFERENCES

1. G. E. Socha, R. R. Langner, R. D. Olson, and G. L. Story, *Am. Ind. Hyg. Assoc. J.* **40,** 553 (1979).

2. F. W. Lichtenberg and G. E. Devitt, *Am. Ind. Hyg. Assoc. J.* **41,** 103 (1980).

3. R. A. Greenberg and C. H. Tamburro, *J. Occup. Med.* **23,** 353 (1981).

4. E. R. Verminski, C. Protopapas, and F. M. Toca, *Am. Ind. Hyg. Assoc. J.* **42,** 437 (1981).

5. D. A. Rossi, J. D. Cox, and M. J. Seger, *Am. Ind. Hyg. Assoc. J.* **43,** 444 (1982).

6. OSHA (1983), 29 CFR Part 1910.95, Occupational Noise Exposure; Hearing Conservation Amendment; Final Rule, *Federal Register* **48** (46), Tuesday, March 8, 1983, pg. 9777, par. (g)(10).

CHAPTER FOURTEEN

Program Evaluation and Audit

Jeremiah R. Lynch and James T. Sanderson

How do we know if we are doing it right? This question should be asked often by each industrial hygienist and by every level of management. Program evaluations and audits are the tools we use to answer this important question.

1 DEFINITIONS

Program evaluation has been defined as "a part of the decision making process in which actions and their results are assessed against norms and criteria in order to measure accomplishments" (1). This definition puts program evaluation in the context of the management decision-making process that seeks continuous improvement by comparing accomplishments with goals. As Drucher has said, "only performance can be appraised" (2). Program evaluation is a general management tool used continuously by industrial hygiene managers and by the managers responsible for industrial hygiene activities. An audit, on the other hand, is defined as "a methodical examination, involving analyses, tests and confirmations of local procedures and practices leading to a verification of compliance with legal requirements, internal policies and practices" (3, 4). Thus, while program evaluation is a general continuous process, audit is a discreet, specific testing action. Another difference is that those who are operating a program will also be evaluating the program. While self-audits are useful, the external look at a program provided by most audits is a key characteristic. Program evaluation and audits are complementary. The unevaluated program is probably not auditable. The criteria by which the program is evaluated are the same as those by which it is audited. At the same time the results of an audit are fed back into the program evaluation process to serve the goal of continuous improvement.

2 PURPOSE OF AUDITS

A wide variety of specific purposes can be served by various types of audits, all within the general purpose of program improvement. Depending on regulatory pressure and internal management concern, an audit can be focused to serve one or more purposes or can be conducted broadly enough to deal with a wide variety of needs.

2.1 Determine and Document Compliance Status

Increasingly, industrial hygiene and environmental health programs in industry are driven by regulations. Also, history has shown that management performance and legal responsibility for past acts may be judged by future regulations and standards. In this environment it is necessary to work diligently to remain in compliance and to observe management policies that anticipate, to the extent possible, the requirements of the future. Even with the best of programs there still remains some risk of an exceptional event that will attract a great deal of public, regulatory, and legal attention to the company. In this event it is very helpful to be able to demonstrate that "due diligence" has been applied in the execution of all of the actions taken to prevent harm to employees, the public, and the environment. The fact that an audit has been conducted and that the findings have been acted on is a demonstration that management has exercised due diligence.

2.2 Improve Performance

All programs suffer from the tyranny of the urgent. The audit, in addition to providing a structure for evaluation, provides a specific occasion to stand back from the program to see if the things that are being done are really what are most needed and that they are being done effectively. This new look at tasks and detailed consideration of work practices will usually result in an improvement in individual performance.

2.3 Assist Facility Management

While some facility managers resist audits, most recognize them as a way to obtain information and insight not otherwise available. The external view and multilevel testing that the audit provides is a valuable tool to the site manager in local efforts to achieve an optimum program.

2.4 Increase Level of Awareness

Essentially all companies seek to improve efficiency by eliminating waste, and this often leads to the reduction of manpower. There is insufficient time to do all that should be done, and it is necessary to set priorities so as to identify and accomplish the most important tasks. Since health and environmental activities are not directly related to the business, they are not always seen as strategically valuable company assets (5). Where there is a suspicion that these activities have slipped to a less than optimum position on the priority list, an audit can determine if this is indeed the case and can provide the evidence of management emphasis that will stimulate a review of health and environmental priorities.

2.5 Accelerate Development of Management Control Systems

Management confidence that laws, regulations, and company policies are being complied with depends on the existence of management systems that continuously ensure that intended actions do in fact occur. The systems are characterized by such elements as organization, personnel development, planning, quality control, and accountability. The rapidly increasing burden of new regulation, the increasing cost of tort liability, and the personal liability of chief executives have made it necessary that these control systems be more effective than ever before. Therefore, their development needs to be accelerated beyond the normal rate of growth and improvement. Program evaluation and its tool, the audit, enable an assessment of the quality of current control systems in the light of an exponential growth in operating constraints and is a rapid way of ensuring the systems fulfill future needs.

2.6 Reduce Risks

Direct action to reduce risks is accomplished by technical industrial hygiene surveys and the control and precautionary measures taken as a result of the recommendations generated by these surveys. Program evaluations and audits are aimed more at the secondary task of ensuring that surveys are carried out and appropriate follow-up actions occur in regard to recommended remedial measures. While audits do not include a detailed evaluation of the present status of health hazard control, they can provide a snapshot of the situation by evaluating a sample of hazards. This may help uncover situations where prompt action is required. Correction of such situations, which may not have been locally recognized or on which action may have been deferred for one reason or another, will mitigate many risks.

2.7 Reduce Liability

Toxic tort liability usually hinges on perceived negligence on the part of the employer. The allegation is frequently made that an employer was ignorant of conditions, health hazards ignored and employees not warned. To be able to document that effective systems were in place to recognize and control potential health hazards can provide a vital defense against accusations of negligence.

2.8. Optimize Resources

Initial optimization of resources is provided by the planning process and reviewed by the accountability process, which compares accomplishments against plan. This process depends, however, on the accurate setting of planning goals and measurement of accomplishments. If goals are set too high or too low or if achievement of goals is not accurately measured, the planning process, by itself, cannot correct improper resource allocation. The audit supplements the planning and accountability process by providing fresh data and judgment on program status and needs.

3 AUDIT SCOPE AND APPLICATION

Audits are specific, discreet program evaluations and as such are distinct from technical industrial hygiene surveys and other elements of the industrial hygiene program. The object of an industrial hygiene audit is to assess the overall adequacy of programs in place and the system used to develop and manage such programs, including measures used for quality assurance rather than to directly determine if health hazards are under control. Still, within that concept there is considerable range for variation in industrial hygiene audits in terms of what is audited and when. The following are some of the choices that must be made in designing a specific audit.

3.1 Functional versus Management Audit

The first question to be addressed must be "who should be audited by whom?" The auditors typically consist of experts drawn from several parts of the company and carry out the audit under the authority delegated to them by senior management to whom they will subsequently report their findings. Thus the scope, content, and focus of the audit will depend on the scope and responsibility of the management sponsoring the audit. From the industrial hygiene perspective the question of who is auditing whom is simple: Either functional management is auditing the internal performance of industrial hygiene or business management is auditing health hazard control.

3.1.1 Functional Audits. The American Industrial Hygiene Association has for some years provided an audit instrument, "Standards, Interpretations and Audit Criteria for Performance of Occupational Health Programs" (6). This comprehensive document provides a basis for self-auditing of occupational health programs including industrial hygiene. Audits of this kind are typically used by management with responsibility for the occupational health or industrial hygiene programs throughout a company or in a region of a company. The audit looks at the internal operation of the function in terms of policy, staff, facilities, equipment, education, practice, records, and emergency planning. It does not consider management aspects of the function, the interface with the business organization, or management programs and action taken to control health hazards.

3.1.2 Management Audits. Most companies regard health hazard control, like safety, as a management responsibility. The line manager, in this mode of organization, has complete responsibility and the necessary authority to protect the health of employees. Industrial hygiene is the professional resource used by line management to achieve this goal. The industrial hygiene function should be responsible for managing itself and for maintaining a standard of excellence in the performance of its role. In this mode of operation, for health hazard control to be effective, industrial hygiene must interact with other staff functions and business management to obtain the information to anticipate, identify, and evaluate health hazards. It must also rely on external groups, such as engineering or first-line supervision, to select, design, and implement effective control measures. An audit of health hazard control must therefore be an audit of all activities at a site to see if management systems are in place to control health hazards on a continuing basis. This type of approach involves an audit of site management by regional or headquarters management in which industrial hygiene both participates in the audit team and is one of the elements examined.

3.2 Functional Core and Overlap Areas

Although it is possible to audit the industrial hygiene functional core area of employee health hazard control, it is usually desirable to broaden the audit to include overlap areas or to include other functional core areas (see Table 14.1). If each function is audited separately, there will be an almost continuous series of audit teams arriving at a plant, upsetting normal operations and plant management. Also, many of these functions are closely related and, while clear distinctions can be made by those closely involved, they merge into a single responsibility in the eyes of senior management. Also, many regulations, such as recent US EPA regulations under the Toxic Substances Control Act overlap functional areas.

A disadvantage in the combined audit of all health, safety, and environmental functions together is that it places heavy demands on the time of a few people, especially at small facilities where one person may have many duties. Also, combining many functions in a single audit may lead to an excessively large team required to include all the necessary experts. These factors must be weighed against the advantages of multiple function audits to arrive at an optimum mix of components.

3.3 Regulatory Compliance versus Good Practice

Some audit instruments focus on compliance in the sense of ensuring conformity with a set of existing regulations (7). Audits of this type are certainly essential and the need for them is obvious to management. Less obvious to some, however, is the need to broaden audits to include compliance with the company policy or the general duty to observe good practice and operate in a socially responsible manner. This need was referred to earlier in connection with the need to demonstrate due diligence and the absence of negligence. In industrial hygiene, in particular, broad audits that cover all aspects of health hazard control are to be preferred over strictly regulatory audits because only a few hazards are regulated and regulations change frequently, and simple compliance does not adequately protect employees and the company. A good program should go beyond the minimum required by regulation and

Table 14.1. Health, Safety, and
                Environmental
                Functions

Industrial hygiene
Occupational medicine
Safety
   Personnel safety
   Engineering safety
Environmental conservation
Product safety
Emergency prevention and response

should be audited as a whole to ensure that the management responsibility to protect the health of employees is being accomplished.

3.4 When to Audit

The major consideration in the timing of the first audit is that the target organization should feel a need and be receptive. If an audit is performed on an organization that is unfamiliar with the standards being applied or is very far from achieving them, then an external audit will prove to be a very frustrating and threatening event likely to produce hostility. A better approach is to acquaint the site with the audit criteria well in advance of the actual visit. Where possible, the criteria could be negotiated with the site, particularly if there are national differences involved. Given the audit criteria, the site could conduct preliminary self-audits and begin an action program to correct the deficiencies.

After the initial audit, the timing of subsequent ones depends on how long it will take to act on the recommendations of the first report and the urgency created by its findings. As will be explained, the output of recommendations of the audit may be integrated into the established planning system and action on these items accounted for in the usual way. Serious items requiring urgent action during an audit should be corrected immediately, perhaps before the audit is complete. For other items more time may be required, and there is little point in doing a subsequent audit until action has been taken on the results of the first one. Also, if the first audit failed to identify any significant weaknesses, there may be no urgency to implement a second audit. As audit programs progress, fewer deficiencies should emerge, and the interval between audits can be extended or the focus of the audit shifted to other areas where continuous improvement is more likely.

4 AUDIT PROCEDURE

The procedure has almost as much to do with success as the substance of what is examined. Auditing in general is a long established practice, and health and environmental audits have been common for at least 10 years. In all this time considerable experience has been gained on the procedural approach, and it is wise to take advantage of the lessons learned before embarking on a series of audits.

4.1 Management Commitment

Although it is very hard to sell the idea that "I'm an auditor and I'm here to help you," it is both possible and necessary to convince management that the audit will provide a net benefit. The positive aspects, such as the opportunity for everyone to improve the way they are doing their job and the endorsement of external experts that they are doing it right, should be emphasized. A frequently perceived threat by those being audited is the public disclosure of weaknesses that could adversely affect their careers. Distribution of audit results, which is discussed later, is clearly a sensitive matter and requires very careful forethought. Although it is true that the quality of a program will be a factor in evaluating the performance of those responsible, no reasonable manager expects any complex program to be fault free and will be positively impressed by willing acceptance of identified problems coupled with incisive action to correct the weaknesses.

4.2 External Audit versus Self-Audit

Self-audit is almost a contradiction in terms since an essential element of a true audit is the need for an unbiased review. Furthermore, internal program evaluation is a normal tool used by management. However, an internal simulation of an external audit remains very useful. It is an exercise that familiarizes managers and staff with the audit standards and criteria, identifies some deficiencies, and gives personnel confidence so that they can be at ease and helpful during a true external audit. Self-audits should be carried out in the same manner as for an external audit, including a specially selected audit team reporting to top management and an intensive schedule to complete the work over a few days. However, it must be recognized that internal or self-audits cannot compete with external audits in terms of real insight and in meeting all of the objectives of an audit.

4.3 Testing

The degree and methods of testing are fundamental characteristics of any audit. A usual audit finding is that procedures that were thought by top management to be followed had in fact been modified or lapsed in practice. For this reason it is necessary for the auditor to test procedures at several levels within the organization and compare answers. Discrepancies are not a question of honesty but of misunderstanding and failure to communicate. The object of testing is to see if the complete system is working, not to detect each individual deviation. Consequently, an audit can sample procedures rather than examine every detail. The same sampling error considerations apply as in any other sampling scheme, so it is necessary to take more samples when compliance is more critical.

4.4 Audit Team

The audit team should be external to the organization being audited and should not include those managers whose usual job it is to oversee the organization being reviewed. In other words no member of the audit team should have a stake in the outcome of the audit except to be seen as having done a fair and accurate job. The team will usually need experts in the program areas audited. The seniority and degree of expertise needed by these specialists is inversely proportional to the detail and exactness of the audit standards and criteria. When criteria are vague and general, the auditor needs better judgment and credibility. In addition to experts, it has been found useful to include a senior business manager where the audit focuses on the system being used to manage industrial hygiene or environmental health. These executives can rapidly identify failures in management systems and can better appreciate the perspective of the management being audited. In health and environmental audits, the presence of this individual on the team helps increase management awareness of functional issues and problems.

A final consideration in selection of the audit team is size. A successful audit is time intensive. Even for the smallest facility, a minimum of two people is an advantage and three or four may be needed for a medium size facility (about 1000 employees). Care should be taken to keep the team number small so that the facility does not feel that they have been invaded.

4.5 Audit Steps

All audits should begin by meeting with the manager of the organization under review so that the team can receive any special advice, instruction, or concern. Following this meeting the team should be introduced to key members of staff to explain the auditing procedure and be advised of logistic arrangements.

The conduct of the audit consists of a series of data collection steps (interviews, document reviews, site inspections) mixed with data analysis followed by more data collection. Interspersed with this process are meetings of the audit team to review results, look for overlaps, and assign work.

When the audit is complete the team should prepare a first draft report for discussion with management. A copy is usually left with them. Discussing the findings with the senior management at a closing session permits correction of misconceptions and other mistakes in the report. Also, by leaving the draft report, it is possible for the management to take action to correct some of the weaknesses even ahead of receiving the final report.

After the audit visit a final report should be submitted within a reasonable period, for example one month, and this document should identify the strength as well as the weaknesses of the organization reviewed. The organization then needs to define an action plan to consider and respond to the weaknesses found.

4.6 Interviews

Audit interviews should be entirely open, professional, and straightforward (8). The auditor should ask specific questions and insist on specific answers. Where the answer given in a particular interview differs from the information obtained elsewhere, the auditor should point that out and ask for an explanation. In such cases recalling personnel for further interview may be necessary. The basic technique of constructive confrontation is to confront the facts not the person. The whole focus should be on getting an accurate assessment of the facts and not on evaluating the performance of interviewees. To be effective the audit team needs to interview a complete spectrum of personnel, including typically the chief executive, medical and industrial hygiene managers, legal advisor, public affairs manager, environmental affairs coordinator, safety advisor, marketing manager, nurse, salesman, and a small number of blue-collar workers.

Site inspections are also useful audit tools. It is necessary, however, for the industrial hygienist on the audit team to remember that this is an audit and not an industrial hygiene survey. Thus the purpose of the site visit is to detect examples of discrepancies that may be indicative of problems with management control systems rather than to evaluate the status of health hazard control or get into excessive detail on technicalities.

5 AUDIT CRITERIA AND STANDARDS

Generally industrial hygiene programs are developed based on judgment and experience adapted to a particular situation and are not codified to any significant degree. Exceptions are programs done in strict compliance with a particular regulation. Thus auditing, aside from the regulatory part of the program, is a judgmental process involving an estimation of the degree to which program elements meet the need.

5.1 Program Elements

There are many possible lists of program elements, but most would include certain core items common to all programs.

5.1.1 Legal Aspects. What constraints exist? Are they monitored? Is the legal department aware of developing legislation in the health, safety, and environment related areas?

5.1.2 Policies. Are there appropriate policies? How widely are they disseminated? Are they complied with? Are they only "motherhood" statements?

5.1.3 Plans. Is there a plan for the occupational and environmental health function? Is it developed with support from the business lines? How is it developed? How is it stewarded? Who determines priorities when work has to be dropped?

5.1.4 Organization. What are the reporting routes, committees, and interfaces? Is there a clear description of roles/jobs?

5.1.5 Staff. How many will be needed? What training in professional/management skills do they have? What support staff is available? Are other resources such as external consultant services employed?

5.1.6 Support. Is equipment adequate? What is level of quality control? Are information needs fulfilled?

5.1.7 Risk Assessment Surveys. When were the last industrial hygiene and environmental control surveys carried out? Are there routine monitoring programs? Is there a rational basis behind exposure monitoring? What follow-up action is taken? Who sets priorities? Will data be shared with employees?

5.1.8 Training. What training do employees receive? Are contractors treated identically? How effective is the training? Do employees know the hazards of the substances they are handling? Are employees aware of company resources, problems, and achievements in occupational and environmental health?

5.1.9 Engineering Projects. What is the system for reviewing design documents? Are health aspects reviewed? Is there a sign-off procedure for functional specialists? Is functional expertise adequate for input? Will there automatically be a pre- and post-startup industrial hygiene survey of the new facility?

5.1.10 Hazard Inventory/Data Base. Does the location have an inventory of all substances and potential hazards? How is routine exposure surveillance data recorded? Can rapid reviews be carried out? How are new chemicals screened? How is compliance handled?

5.1.11 Specific Programs. Are there adequate programs on specific higher risk topics such as noise control, hearing conservation, effluent/emission control, personal protection, confined space work, product safety and liability, hazard data sheets for customers, and labeling?

5.1.12 Emergency/Disaster Planning. Do emergency plans exist? Is there a specific medical plan? How are external queries regarding poisoning incidents from products handled? What is the system for handling on-site or off-site emergency situations? Are rehearsals used? Is there 24-hour coverage for emergencies of all types? What involvement by industrial hygiene function in emergency response situation?

5.1.13 Interactions. Are communications satisfactory between the medical and industrial hygiene manager and their staffs and with other key functions (safety, industrial hygiene, toxicology, environmental conservation, legal, public affairs), including the operating management? Is there adequate input to trade association and professional bodies particularly in regard to common problems, such as developing legislation and emerging health concerns? Does everyone have a clear understanding of respective roles in the organization?

5.1.14 External Relations. Is there appropriate support and adequate communication to customers? How are contractors handled? If the community has a query or concern, what system handles the item? Are we sharing new health information with academia, authorities as well as with our own staff? What system is used to handle public affairs problems in the health area.

5.2 Audit Instruments

A written document detailing how and why the audit is to be conducted and what standards and criteria will be applied is an essential tool for a successful audit. An example of such an audit guide is given in Appendix A. Such an audit instrument is needed not only by the audit team but also as a means of communicating with the management and staff of the site to be audited. The guide informs each team member of the procedures to be followed so they can work together in harmony. At the same time it advises site personnel of what to expect. The audit is much less threatening if there is no mystery involved. Also, the process of development of the audit guide is a mechanism for negotiation with the auditee leading to understanding and agreement on what is to be done. Such a guide should be prepared for each cycle of audits and broadly communicated in advance of the site visit.

6 CONCLUSION

The benefits of audits are manifold and the deficits few. If it is organized and conducted with appropriate forethought recognizing the potential sensitivities involved, the activity will not be perceived as threatening but as highly supportive for all concerned. Follow-up or repeat surveys are essential when major weaknesses have been identified and usually these can be carried out on a miniscale compared with the original audit. In the absence of major weaknesses repeat audits need only be scheduled on an infrequent basis; for example, in a timeframe of every 5–7 years. Audits present the occupational and environmental health function and business management with an extremely powerful and valuable tool that must be used more widely in industry than appears to be the case today.

APPENDIX A: INDUSTRIAL HYGIENE AUDIT GUIDE

Introduction

An industrial hygiene audit is an objective assessment of the management systems that ensure that the policies, regulations, and procedures that protect health are implemented. This guide provides a basis and procedure for evaluating measures taken to reduce health risks on a continuing basis. It describes the elements needed in a comprehensive industrial hygiene program and provides questions to aid in collecting information to be used in deciding if these elements are in place and working.

An industrial hygiene audit does not have the same purpose or methods as the traditional industrial hygiene survey. In a survey, information on existing conditions is used to determine the present status of health hazard control. An industrial hygiene survey is part of the program that controls health hazards. An audit, on the other hand, assumes that a program is in place and uses a range of observations, records, and interviews, including examples of health hazard control, to determine if the program is adequate to maintain control over health hazards in the long run.

Why Audit?

Audits are helpful to the people who work at health hazard control, to site management, and to the company as a whole.

Audits provide functional staff at a site an independent, outside view of their activities.

Site management receives verification that essential systems are in place and working.

Management at all levels can document that they exerted due diligence in protecting the health of employees.

Opportunities to improve program balance and efficiency are identified.

Scope and Application

This guide covers all industrial hygiene activities to protect health. In practice, management responsibility for health protection may be divided differently between industrial hygiene, medical, safety, environmental conservation, and other functions in different plants and regions. This guide strives to be inclusive and thus covers not only the core areas of industrial hygiene but also the overlap areas where industrial hygiene interaction with other functions is necessary for complete and efficient coverage. The object is not to promote any particular position on where the functional interface should be but to ensure that adequate interaction is preventing gaps.

Management may have occasion to use other available audit, survey, and evaluation tools. Hazard and operability surveys, safety risk management reviews, and safety and loss prevention surveys are aimed primarily at high-consequence, low-probability events, such as explosions or major toxic releases, which significantly impact both the plant and the nearby community. Industrial hygiene audits, on the other hand, are aimed primarily at insidious hazards that may impact health over the long run.

This audit guide lists the program elements that should be present at a site to a greater or lesser degree depending on the circumstances. For example, all sites need an inventory, but for a small, single-product-line plant, the inventory may be just a several page list, while for a large plant, it may be a sizable computer data base. Similarly, each of the special programs (hearing conservation, respiratory protection, etc.) would only be present and evaluated if it was needed. Further, laws and regulations may create specific requirements at some plants but not others.

For each program element in the guide there is a general, explanatory statement of the requirement. However, aside from strictly regulatory requirements, there are no audit criteria to determine when these general standards are met. Instead, the joint judgment of the audit team and the site management is used to decide if a program element meets the need at a site.

The questions that follow each standard should not be expected to have the same answers at different facilities. Although the questions might seem to imply that there is a "right" answer, in fact, the answer will depend on what is needed given the circumstances. Also, there is no single right way to run an industrial hygiene program, and it is to be expected that good programs will differ from site to site.

Audit Procedure

An audit involves the collection and analysis of information to form the basis for a judgment of whether each program element and the overall program is adequate to meet the need. The data collected comes from existing documents (reports, plans, role descriptions, organization charts, etc.), interviews with managers, first-line supervisors, employees, and observations of physical conditions. Some depth of looking is needed to find causes and not merely conditions, but it is not necessary to gather enough data to establish the status of control of every potential health hazard in the plant. Typically, in all but the largest plants, the on-site phase of the evaluation can be done in less than a week by a team of two or three evaluators. Very small facilities, that is, marketing terminals, may only require a single evaluator for a day. Whether the evaluation is done internally or externally, it is better to devote full time to it over a short period rather than spread it out due to the time demands of the data gathering and the contrast between the evaluation role and the usual problem-solving role.

Testing, in program evaluation, means to determine if the procedures and practices actually followed are those expected by management. Are all the steps of a standard procedure being followed? Where respirators are being relied on for protection, are they actually used? Do workers retain enough from training to take proper precautions? Most program deficiencies found in audits result from misunderstandings as to who does what and what is expected. To test the relation between expectations and performance, interviews and records are examined to confirm that things are done the way they are thought and expected to be done.

The object of testing is to find out if things are the way they should be; the object of analysis is to find out, if not, why not. A variety of reasons may be found. A common cause is that the "piece of paper" establishing a procedure, policy, or practice was issued long ago and has since been lost in a file or elsewhere and is no longer governing behavior. It might also be that an individual who used to ensure observance of a requirement has left. At a deeper level, it may be that prescribed procedures are not practical or workable or may no longer fit the situation. Finally, organizational barriers may block implementation.

Industrial hygiene audits cannot be done mechanically. The auditors and the site management must jointly use their judgment to determine the degree to which the standards apply and what constitutes an acceptable program given the conditions at each individual site. An audit is most successful when plant management and the audit team can reach agreement, by the end of the closing conference, on the facts developed in the audit, the main strengths and weaknesses of the program, and the need for action. Site management then has what it needs to develop an action plan to correct any program deficiencies.

Audit Steps

1. Initiation. An audit may be initiated by site management or by other levels of management, usually with the advice of functional staff. At the time of initiation, it should be decided what facilities are to be covered, what reporting procedures will be used, and who will be on the audit team. Also at this time, this audit guide is transmitted to the site to be audited so that they can do a preliminary evaluation and propose any additions or changes in the audit procedure or content.

2. Audit Information. The site should assemble the following information so that it will be readily available to the audit team when they are at the site. Copies of the items marked with an asterisk should be sent to the audit team members between 1 and 2 months before the audit.

*Plant health, medical, safety, and environmental policies.

*Organization charts that delineate line and staff responsibilities for the area being audited and related areas.

*Organization, charge, and membership of relevant committees (safety, environmental affairs, etc.) and minutes of recent meetings.

*Role statements of industrial hygiene and related functional staff.

*List of regulations that apply to the site.

Inventory of substances present at the site.

Records of air contaminant measurement results.

Industrial hygiene equipment procurement, maintenance, and calibration records.

List of new investments and plant modifications made over the last 2 years or presently in process.

Industrial hygiene, safety, and environmental conservation plans and stewardships and segments of product line plans related to industrial hygiene.

Manuals and operating procedures in the areas covered by the audit.

Emergency plans and procedures, including critiques of recent drills.

Correspondence files of internal industrial hygiene reports and external correspondence with government agencies, trade associations, and so forth.

Reports of investigations of incidents involving overexposure to chemical or physical agents. Reports of employee or public complaints about alleged health hazards and their resolution.

Copies of laws and regulations that apply to potential health hazards at the site.

3. Conduct Audit. At the start of the on-site phase of the audit, the audit team usually meets with the plant manager privately to hear his or her concerns and special instructions. They then generally meet with all of the site management and staff involved in the audit and related areas. This larger meeting serves to introduce participants and allows the audit team to explain the audit scope and procedures. Following these meetings, the team will begin to gather data, working either individually or as a group, by means of observation, record review, and interviews. It is not intended to conduct a comprehensive survey but rather, to the extent that deficiencies are found, to use them to search for the possible weaknesses in control systems intended to prevent them. Some fact-gathering techniques are as follows:

WORKED PROBLEMS. Where a significant risk has been found, such as a measurement of an overexposure, is there a series of documents leading to resolution? Perhaps there were further measurements that showed that the initial measurement was spurious. If the overexposure was real, is there a recommended corrective action followed by a reply or other evidence that action was taken?

EMPLOYEE AWARENESS. Although employees are not expected to have detailed recall of everything presented in training, they should have learned enough to be able to discriminate between hazards and to know why and what to do to protect themselves. Employees might be asked to name and rank the major hazards in their workplace, to describe the controls that are used, and the precaution they need to take.

MANAGEMENT EXPECTATIONS. Interviews with department and product line managers, especially at mid and operator levels, might focus on their interaction with industrial hygiene. What contact have they had, what have they asked industrial hygiene to do, what recommendations has industrial hygiene made, how is industrial hygiene planning for them done?

4. Data Analysis. Data gathering and data analysis overlap throughout the audit. Early in the audit it is usually possible to identify the areas it would be most useful to develop. Key facts are confirmed and contradictions resolved. Analysis is the step that generalizes from the specific situations to the underlying program characteristics. This is an iterative process since more data is often needed to determine if an observed irregularity is an exception or a sign of a program defect.

5. Closing Conference. The results of the audit are presented to site management at a closing meeting before the audit team leaves the site. One purpose of immediate reporting is to make possible rapid corrective action, if needed. Another purpose of the closeout meeting is to examine and resolve any disagreements on facts or conclusions. If the auditors and site managers can agree on the findings, then there will be no blocks in getting on with corrective action even before the written report is received.

6. Reporting. After the closing conference, the audit team prepares its report and submits it to the site management for response with no further distribution at this time. The audit report will describe both the strengths and weaknesses of the program. The site will usually prepare an action plan in response to the audit (or a statement of action already taken) and may also include the site view on differences that were unresolved at the time of the audit. The audit and response are then forwarded to affiliate or regional management. Continuing progress on the action plan is stewarded by the site as part of its overall planning and stewardship process.

Industrial Hygiene Program Elements

For audit purposes, it is convenient to divide the function into a set of elements and to evaluate the overall program based on evaluation of each element. The following set of industrial hygiene program elements corresponds to the usual way in which industrial hygiene is done and covers essential core activities. For each element, there is a general standard and a set of questions to help gather the information needed to evaluate that element of industrial hygiene. As already discussed, there are no fixed audit criteria; the degree to which a site meets the standard is judged based on site needs and circumstances.

Policy. A clear, specific statement of where management stands on the legal, business, ethical, and moral issues of health and the environment is needed as a guide to decision making where economic, legal, and ethical factors are involved.

> Does the plant have written policies on health and related matters?
>
> Are these policies consistent with regional and corporate policies? Are they periodically reviewed and updated?
>
> Are the policies definite and specific enough to be useful in decision making?
>
> How are the policies communicated? Do managers, supervisors, and employees know and understand the policies?
>
> Are policies followed, particularly in cases where economics alone would lead to other decisions?
>
> What internal and external management systems, program evaluations, and audits are used to verify adherence to policy?
>
> What laws and regulations impact the industrial hygiene program? How is current awareness of regulatory activity maintained? How is compliance with regulations determined? Are actions taken to influence regulations?

Planning and Stewardship. The industrial hygiene plan should be specific, reflect priorities, and maximize planned use of time as opposed to unscheduled activities. It should be developed in cooperation with the plant departments and product lines served, coordinated with adjacent functions, and approved by and stewarded to management.

> Is there an industrial hygiene plan? How was it developed? Were plant departments involved? Is the plan approved by management?

Are there designated contacts in each department? Are they aware of the plan? Was the plan coordinated with environmental conservation and safety.

Is the plan specific in terms of priorities and who will do what by when? Are the priorities accurate? Is the plan followed?

Do the groups served know what to expect? Do they monitor delivery of industrial hygiene services?

Do the groups served steward performance of their health protection responsibilities as a part of their overall stewardship? Do they plan and steward their action on industrial hygiene recommendations?

Hazard Recognition. The starting point for a health protection effort is to become aware of all potential hazards present. An essentially complete inventory of all materials in manufacturing, off sites, and maintenance should be collected and the hazard of each material assessed. Other hazards that are brought into the plant (e.g., cleaning chemicals used by contractors) or which occur as a result of work done (welding fumes) should also be included. Physical agents such as noise or ionizing radiation should also be listed. The objective is to be as comprehensive as possible so that all the information needed for subsequent hazard assessment stages will be available.

Is there an inventory of all chemical substances present in the plant? Of all physical hazards? Are they updated periodically?

What system is used to ensure that new materials (purchased) are added to the inventory?

Have hazard data sheets been obtained on all supplied materials, products, key intermediates, and wastes?

Has this information been reviewed for completeness and adequacy? Have gaps been filled? What external resources are used?

Have the substances present been sorted into risk groups based on toxicity, amount present, opportunity for exposure, and so forth?

Is there an established and understood procedure by which industrial hygiene is notified when changes are planned that may alter the potential chemical and physical hazards present?

Is there an established system for ensuring that new toxicological and regulatory information is received and analyzed? Are hazard assessments reevaluated when new information is received?

Does the hazard recognition procedure cover all facilities—process units, off sites, labs, terminals, waste sites, toll processors?

Hazard Evaluation. The hazard evaluation step ranks substances and agents that present an exposure risk based on toxicity, quantity, and exposure opportunity. Suspected exposures to hazards should be evaluated by exposure measurements that consider ambient exposure, task-related exposure, and exposure episodes resulting from scheduled and unscheduled events. The results of the measurements should be evaluated against established exposure limits using appropriate statistical techniques. Where these evaluations reveal actual significant exposure, routine monitoring should be undertaken to ensure that overexposure does not occur or to establish the need for and effectiveness of control measures.

Has there been an exposure potential analysis that relates tasks, locations, and inventories so as to rank exposure potential?

What exposure measurements have been made? What substances are monitored routinely? How are exposure measurement priorities decided?

Does exposure measurement include task-related exposure and exposure episodes for both operators and mechanics? Are short-period samples collected?

What exposure limits are applied? How are exposure limits kept current? How are decisions regarding the acceptability of exposure made?

Are measurements made to determine the source of air contaminants? To evaluate control effectiveness?

What sampling methods are used? How is sampling equipment calibrated? Where are samples analyzed? What analytical methods are used? Is the laboratory qualified? What quality assurance is conducted? What is the turnaround time?

How are monitoring results recorded? How and to whom are they communicated? What are the results used for?

How is monitoring data analyzed? Is it used to determine if exposure reduction measures are needed? Is it used to manage the industrial hygiene program?

Hazard Control. Where hazard evaluation has defined exposure circumstances that are unacceptable, measures to reduce exposure should be taken. These measures may be engineering or process changes, work practices, or personal protection. However control is to be achieved, there should be a definable process from initial recommendations through control action to control effectiveness verification in order to ensure that the intended level of protection has been achieved.

Is the need for exposure reduction communicated to the proper people? Are specific recommendations made? Is there a system for tracking what happens to recommendations? Is there feedback to industrial hygiene on whatever is decided on recommendations?

How are control programs initiated? What process is used to make control decisions? Does industrial hygiene participate in task groups set up to work hazard control problems?

Are all new processes and projects reviewed by industrial hygiene? Is there feedback on actions taken resulting from this review? Which engineering plans are reviewed locally and which are sent to an external industrial hygiene reviewer?

Is the continuing effectiveness of control equipment and procedures periodically evaluated?

Are any specific hazard control programs, such as respiratory protection, hearing conservation, personal protection, or confined space entry, required?

Are there written, standard procedures for each specific program? Do these procedures cover application, responsibilities, controls, equipment, training, and so forth? How are specific program procedures developed, coordinated, changed, evaluated?

Are specific program procedures followed? How is this determined?

Training. Health protection depends on management and worker attitudes and behavior. Training should convey an appreciation of hazards, the measures taken to control them, and the precautions to be followed. The ultimate test of the effectiveness of training is safe behavior, that is, good work practices, proper use of equipment, and adherence to accepted procedures.

Is there a training plan that describes who should be trained in what and when? Are there records of who has been trained? Is the training on schedule?

What mechanisms are used for training? Are there training guides, outlines, aids, and so forth? Are they accurate, appropriate, and effective?

Is the training conducted in an effective manner? Short enough sessions to retain attention? Qualified and interesting instructors? Freedom from distractions?

Is management emphasis on training apparent? What managers participate in training?

How is the effectiveness of training evaluated? What are the results of these evaluations?

Are the lessons learned in training reinforced by job supervision and by example?

Does the training cover the hazardous properties and precautions to be followed for the hazards to which each employee is exposed?

Have hazard communications, such as safety data sheets, been assembled and made available to employees? Have employees been trained and encouraged to use this information?

Awareness. To be effective the industrial hygiene staff must be aware of conditions, practices, behavior and attitudes in the plant. To create and maintain this awareness the industrial hygiene staff should actively familiarize themselves with the broad range of plant activities and be receptive to information regarding potential health hazards.

How frequent are industrial hygiene walk-through surveys of the plant?

What department and product line meetings does industrial hygiene attend? How often?

Does industrial hygiene receive information on medical findings that could be related to occupational exposure?

How are employees complaints of health hazards handled?

Do operations and maintenance personnel inform industrial hygiene of potentially hazardous exposure events?

Organization. Industrial hygiene reporting relationships should provide the access and status needed to surface and solve problems and should ensure constructive interaction between related functions so that they support one another and avoid gaps.

Does industrial hygiene report at a high enough level to facilitate the solution of problems? Is top management routinely apprised of the status of health issues?

Are there committees that bring together industrial hygiene, medicine, safety, environmental conservation, management, and so forth? Is there good communication between the functions? What access to information does industrial hygiene have?

Does industrial hygiene participate in the safety committee?

Is the organization of industrial hygiene shown on a chart available to and understood by those concerned?

Are role statements complete, accurate, and up to date? Are they generally understood and followed?

Is the division of responsibility between functions clear and appropriate?

Staff. The professional and technical staff should be adequate in quantity and quality to develop and implement the industrial hygiene program. Some plants may have professional industrial hygienists assigned, while others may have an industrial hygiene contact supported by off-site industrial hygienists. Either way the time spent should meet the need, and the people involved should be qualified for their roles and work closely together to provide an integrated program.

Who provides industrial hygiene services?

Does the staff have enough time to do the job—both assigned and actual?

Is the staff adequately qualified? Is time allowed to maintain/upgrade qualifications?

Are appropriate career plans in place for the staff and replacements?

Where the local resource is an industrial hygiene contact, is there adequate backup? Is communication sufficiently open and frequent?

Are support personnel adequate? Are they under the control of the industrial hygiene staff for the part of the time they spend on health work? Are they qualified? Is there a program of training and career development for support personnel.

Resources. Certain resources and support services are needed for an effective health hazard control program.

How are industrial hygiene costs planned and budgeted? Is the budget appropriate? Are resources procured in a timely and responsive manner?

Is the equipment used by industrial hygiene appropriate and in good working order? Is there adequate space to store, calibrate, assemble, and repair equipment.

Are there adequate information sources available? Does industrial hygiene use local or national sources?

Conclusion

The result of the audit will be to identify elements that are needed and in place and working well, elements that are not needed, and elements that are needed but are not working well. The audit report should cover both strengths and weaknesses. The strengths of the program should be described both to give credit to those who have done the work and to document that the company has diligently managed risk. Where needs are seen that are not met by existing program elements, the report should discuss the result to be achieved by any corrective action and should suggest criteria by which to judge the effectiveness of change.

REFERENCES

1. R. K. Hewstone, Management Systems Surveys in the Field of Environmental Health, 9.7-01-15, Handbook of Occupational Hygiene, London: Kluwer Harrop, 1987.

2. P. F. Drucker, *The Changing World of the Executive,* New York: Times Books, 1982.

3. M. Corn and P. S. J. Lees, The Industrial Hygiene Audit: Purposes and Implementation, *Am. Ind. Hyg. Assoc. J.* **44**(2): 135–141 (1983).

4. J. T. Sanderson, An Approach to Auditing Functional Effectiveness in a Multi-National Company. Proceedings of an "Audit" Symposium, Royal Army Medical College, London, 1986, Research Panel of the UK Society of Occupational Medicine, 1986.

5. L. B. Tepper, The Strategic Dimensions of Occupational Medicine, *J. Occ. Med.* **29**(4): 325–329 (1987).

6. B. H. Hass, Industrial Hygiene Audits, *Am. Ind. Hyg. Assoc. J.* **43**(8): 562–568 (1982).

7. American Industrial Hygiene Association publication, Standards Interpretation and Audit Criteria for Performance of Occupational Health Programs, 1977.

8. Arthur D. Little Inc., Current Practices in Environment Auditing, Report to US Environmental Protection Agency 1984, Report EPA-230-09-83-006 (EPA Contract 68-01-6160).

CHAPTER FIFTEEN

Professional Development

Gerald E. Devitt

1 INTRODUCTION

The development of one's staff, with all the various personnel-related aspects that this infers, should be one of the primary responsibilities of the department's leader. Included in these responsibilities is that of advising and assisting subordinates along a career path, an integral part of which is the professional development of that individual. Although the path chosen should coincide with the requirements of the organization, it is also of concern that the desires and needs of the individual be considered.

In a field as dynamic as industrial hygiene, it is almost trite to say that to remain where one is with regard to knowledge is actually to fall behind. As professionals we have a real obligation to keep up to date, for only by doing this can we remain proficient in the practice of our profession.

The subject of this chapter is the why and how of keeping current with ongoing developments in our field, which appears to expand and broaden on almost a daily basis. We need to keep a broad view so that we have some

259

familiarity with the whole field, and we must also remain proficient in the specific areas particular to our own job responsibilities.

The very broadness of our field is also a factor that causes some of the difficulties in keeping up with the practice. As with any profession, both the education and the experience of its practitioners cover an almost infinite range of abilities. This means that we have newly minted hygienists who have an undergraduate degree and essentially no experience. At the other extreme is the senior practitioner whose academic training may include graduate training through the doctoral level and also many years of practical experience, covering a multitude of aspects or exposure evaluations. Thus it is self-evident that the subject of professional development is a complex one, which, when realistically faced, is not prone to a simple answer. With these comments as a frame of reference, it soon becomes apparent that any professional development program, to be of maximum benefit to the recipient, needs to be customized for the individual. Therefore, it behooves the reader to become familiar with the opportunities available to increase the professionalism of one's staff.

1.1 Education Opportunities

The educational process must be both dynamic and ongoing. One of the primary goals is to eliminate obsolescense. But an even more laudable goal is to prevent obsolescence in the first place. Such a preventive program requires that one plan and carry out such activities over a professional lifetime. Such a program, starting with a level suitable to the new practitioner with a minimum level of formal education and then progressing by increments of advancement and complexity until suitable for the experienced graduate-level hygienists, would be a practical way to go. Then, dependent on the various levels of the staff, employees could be plugged into such a plan, with adjustments made as needed to meet the needs of each individual.

In general, several courses of action are basic to all development programs. The first is keeping up to date with the technical literature. As an absolute minimum, the journals of the American Industrial Hygiene Association (AIHA) and the American Conference of Governmental Industrial Hygienists (ACGIH) should be reviewed, and articles of interest should be read. There are also several abstracting services that provide summaries of articles and papers of interest to industrial hygienists in publications that might not be normally read by such professionals. The problem with such sources is that they are far from complete, and the papers that are commented upon depend on the judgment of the editors.

1.2 Association Membership

Second, as the AIHA continues to grow, more and more local sections are being formed, and there are few parts of the United States where membership in such a section is not available. Most of these groups have periodic meetings, and in most cases, attendance is a worthwhile means of improving and updating one's knowledge. Further, such meetings permit interaction with other industrial hygienists, which in turn can lead to the interchange of ideas. It has been my experience, after many years of such contacts, that one of the characteristics of most hygienists is a willingness to share experiences and knowledge with their fellow professionals, including those with national and even international reputations in this field. These local section meetings are usually smaller in size and number of attendees, which, in turn, permits closer contact with those attending. The building of a network of fellow professionals who may be contacted for information is, in one sense, another means of developing one self.

These activities should be instituted and continued as long as one is practicing industrial hygiene, for as stated earlier, professional development must be a continuing action, and one should never "rest on one's laurels."

2   GENERALIST VERSUS SPECIALIST

As one's career progresses, the industrial hygienist should begin to "customize" his or her own program. One way is to become more of a technical expert in one or more of the various aspects of the practice, such as engineering or chemistry. Even these disciplines are becoming too broad, and it is entirely possible for one to have a fulfilling career, specializing even further within a discipline. By contrast, one can also remain a generalist, being involved in the overall practice of industrial hygiene. This choice will be dependent not only on the aims and desires of the individual but also the requirements of the organization for whom the hygienist is working. Possibilities for specialization are probably more likely in larger organizations that have a number of professionals on the staff. Likewise, if the organization is involved in specialized processes, or a particular line of products, then these needs may be the driving force for the direction of the staff's capabilities and development.

In contrast, one could choose to remain a generalist for several reasons. Many practitioners of industrial hygiene came to this field for the variety of assignments and responsibilities with which one can be involved, and remaining a generalist is one means of continuing this practice. Also, in organizations with smaller professional staffs, or a broad range of products and processes, the staff may be required to handle assignments in the vast array of possibilities open to the industrial hygienist. A second reason for remaining a generalist is the possibility of advancing one's career, not as a technical specialist, but into the broader field of management. These skills as a manager are needed whether one is an industrial hygiene manager or becomes involved in the broader areas of general management. There is a general, unwritten rule of management that early in one's career the job is probably

90–95 percent skill oriented and 5–10 percent people oriented. However, as one begins to move up the organizational ladder, these ratios begin to reverse, and in the upper levels of most organizations, the manager is faced with job responsibilities needing skills that are primarily people oriented. Thus, in most cases, the future manager does not want to develop either the skills or the reputation of being a technical (read narrow) specialist. Again, depending on the individual and the circumstances, it is entirely possible to combine these approaches. However, it would appear likely that if this path is chosen, it would most likely be to go from specialist to generalist, rather than vice versa, as one begins to move up the ladder of promotion and opportunity.

2.1 Meetings and Conferences

Another means of professional development is attendance at national professional meetings and conferences. In the spring an annual $4\frac{1}{2}$-day Industrial Hygiene Conference is held, co-sponsored by ACGIH and AIHA. Each year it is held in a different location in the United States. In addition to the technical sessions held, arranged by particular topics of interest to the profession, short courses are also presented on a variety of subjects and at levels of technical competence that range from very basic to advanced. Such courses are an ideal way of acquiring further knowledge in particular fields or becoming better acquainted with an area where one's knowledge is weak. Another informative conference is the Professional Conference on Industrial Hygiene, sponsored by the American Academy of Industrial Hygiene, a group made up of certified industrial hygienists. Attendance at this conference is not limited to those who are certified but is open to all with an interest in the field. This conference, usually $2\frac{1}{2}$ days in length, is also preceded by short courses.

2.2 Short Courses

As mentioned, short courses are a definite advantage in the development of the professional hygienist. Such continuing education, or noncredit courses, is a definite asset toward improvement. The journals of AIHA and ACGIH both carry lists of announcements of such courses in every issue, and there is usually a relatively large choice of courses, especially for the industrial hygienist. Obviously, such listings are far from complete, and therein lies part of the problem. There is really no centralized source of where or when such courses are presented. In addition to the journals, both the Occupational Safety and Health Administration (OSHA) and the National Institute for Occupational Safety and Health (NIOSH) have training institutes that regularly present courses of interest to hygienists, many of which the public is permitted to attend, usually for a nominal fee. Thus, contact with these groups would provide excellent information. There are also a number of

Educational Resource Centers (ERC) scattered throughout the country, affiliated with various universities and consortiums, which have such educational offerings.

If there is a weakness in such courses, it is that the subject content rarely satisfies the needs of the more experienced hygienist. Thus, the more experienced hygienist has difficulty finding short courses that enhance his or her professional development. This is probably not the case if one needs a review or refresher course, but advanced courses are not available in many areas outside of formal academic programs. In many cases, such an academic commitment is beyond the availability of the working hygienist because of job responsibilities. However, several academic institutions appear aware of this difficulty and have instituted programs under various names (a common one being "on job, on campus") to meet this need. In such a program, the majority of courses may be given for one long weekend (3 days) per month, and an individual can obtain advanced degrees in the field. Although such programs obviously require the cooperation of one's employer, they are a definite means of improving one's competence. Several schools are also giving graduate-level courses as part of a late afternoon or evening program. While these are far more convenient for the practicing hygienist, job location and travel responsibilities can severely curtail the opportunities to take advantage of these courses. However, many companies, especially in the larger organizations, will not only encourage such educational work but will also financially support it, which is not an insignificant item. But this requires a definite commitment on the part of the hygienist, for such a program should not, and cannot, be undertaken in a light-hearted manner, for it will have an impact on the total life-style of the individual.

2.3 Other Opportunities

Some organizations, especially governmental agencies and the armed forces, often can receive duty assignments that permit full-time attendance in graduate school, with full pay, and living allowances or salary paid while obtaining graduate degrees. Part of the individual's obligation is often fulfilled by committing to some extended period of service with the sponsoring group to help pay back the support received. For example, if one is in school for a period of 2 years receiving a degree, the hygienist promises to work three times as long after receiving the degree (6 years) for the organization. The availability of such programs is not an inconsequential item, and this possible choice, as a means of professional development, is not an unrealistic one.

2.4 Management Training

However, if one wishes to develop professionally in the area of management or administration, rather than as a technical specialist, the options for development, especially in areas of formal academic training, are much more widespread. The availability of MBA-type programs, given in evening sessions of graduate schools of business administration, are far more easily available than are graduate industrial hygiene courses. Almost any university in the United States that has such programs will also offer them in the evenings for the working professional. Likewise, weekend-type programs, adjusted for the working professional, are very common, and it is also quite usual to have extension classes that can be taken for credit either through closed-circuit TV classrooms or attendance at branches of major universities. Many of the larger corporations in America will also have training departments within them that give such training, although without formal academic credit, as part of the on-the-job development of their own staff. It belabors the point to note that in many cases the academic training and desires of the scientist are not conducive to good managerial performance. People relations and the handling of personnel performance are not always compatible to the scientific, factual form of analysis used by the practicing scientist. Organizations with professional and forward-looking human resources departments recognized this fact many years ago, with the result that highly technical groups, such as research, often have "parallel ladders" of performance. One of the primary reasons for this is to circumvent the situation of making a "poor manager" out of a "good scientist" simply in order for one to be promoted. The rewards and perks of upper management become available to the scientist without the professional having to stop practicing science. The availability of MBA-type academic programs is much greater than for the hygienist who wishes to pursue a technical academic schedule. (also, see Chapters 3 and 16.)

3   CERTIFICATION

Certification, and its maintenance, strictly speaking are not a means of professional development but rather an indication of accomplishment. Although these were originally set up as voluntary programs to indicate peer evaluation of one's technical ability as an industrial hygienist, this is not the situation anymore. When a position at a higher level becomes open, many organizations, will often require certification as one of the qualifications for promotion. This certainly takes certification from the voluntary mode and essentially makes it mandatory if one wishes to advance in the field of industrial hygiene. Although fulfilling the requirements for certification on a professional level and then maintaining them is an indication that the hygienist has proven his or her qualifications, this really is not a sign of continuing professional development. However, it should be difficult to say or prove that one has continued to develop as a professional without going through, and successfully accomplishing, the status of a Certified Industrial Hygienist (CIH). As the certification program itself has developed and matured over the years, adjustments have been made that reflect the evolution of the industrial hygiene field itself; thus obtaining and maintaining certification is an indirect indication of the continuing professional development of the hygienist. Activities that provide credit for maintenance of certification are becoming more strict with the passage of time, although this is a subtlety most people do not appreciate.

Organizations that have industrial hygiene staffs made up of many members can, and often do, have internal meetings that can add to the professional development of the staff itself. While in most cases the driving force for such meetings is the obligation of the staff to its own sponsoring organization and its responsibilities, enlightened companies will usually schedule part of such meetings for the technical aspects of the profession itself. As stated earlier, the field is in a continual state of flux and alteration, and a comprehensive occupational health program mandates that professionals remain current, for only then can they do the best job for employers. In fact, the ABIH encourages this type of internal meeting by awarding certification maintenance credits for time spent on technical matters pertaining to industrial hygiene. Likewise, it is extremely difficult to evaluate the contribution to development of the day-to-day communications among the staff itself, discussing problems or situations of common interest. This is especially true if the staff is professional with varying interests and amounts of experience; thus the junior staff members can learn and develop with the aid of more senior staff. This type of interplay should be strongly encouraged by the management of the group as a most valuable tool for staff development.

3.1 Performance Review

Most organizations have some type of formal performance review as part of the company's standard operating procedures. These reviews are normally set up in as nonconfrontational an environment as is possible between two individuals. These sessions can and should be used in great part as a communication and counseling session. These sessions can be used to determine the desires of the professional, and at the same time, they permit the manager to impart his or her own experience in professional development and to suggest possible courses for action for the subordinate staff member. This type of dialogue should prove to be most valuable for both parties and also permit the superior to guide the staff in a manner that will result in maximum benefit for all in the setting of goals for the short and long term.

3.2 Future Trends

For the future, the availability of advanced formal training in the industrial hygiene field appears to be on the increase. As the number of professional industrial hygienists continues to increase, the market and its demands for such training will increase, and various academic institutions and training organizations should respond to this demand. Also, the fields of interest and subjects of concern for the hygienist continue to expand into new areas of varying modifications. Thus, subjects like indoor air quality and hazardous waste site and disposal, which were almost unheard of a few years ago, are becoming an ever-widening field of interest. The subject of hazard communication has almost become a field in itself with which the hygienist is becoming involved. More and more short courses, given under the auspices of both academic and private-for-profit training groups, are becoming available. Furthermore, these organizations appear to be more cognizant of the needs of the working professional who has commitments that normally have to take priority over educational and developmental desires. Although the availability of technical industrial hygiene courses appears to becoming more widespread, it is highly unlikely that it will ever approach the availability of management and business school courses.

4   ACADEMIC CONCERNS IN PROFESSIONAL DEVELOPMENT

The place of academia in a program for the professional industrial hygienist is a complex one. There are any number of suitable graduate programs for the hygienists that require full-time attendance, and thus are not a viable alternative for the practicing professional. Likewise, there are a number of short courses presented in continuing education programs, but many of these are basic or introductory in their content. Thus, there are two areas in which there appears to be a real need, which academia is in a position to fulfill.

The first area, which can probably be responded to more quickly, is the need for short courses or noncredit courses at an advanced level for the professional who is already in the field and needs a greater depth of knowledge in a particular aspect of industrial hygiene. Several academic institutions have, for a number of years, been giving periodic courses in advanced ventilation, and there has been no shortage of enrollees. While this is only a limited sampling, nonetheless it is our opinion that a real market for advanced courses of a technical nature exists. For the working professional, an area of concern is the length of such courses. In most cases, the hygienist does not wish to spend more than one full week at a time on such training.

The second area of need is the availability of graduate courses for credit for the employed professional. This is an area where it is difficult to determine the market. As more and more baccalaureate-level degree programs in industrial hygiene are instituted, their graduates start work in this field at the entry level. As their jobs progress, many see the advantage of a graduate-level degree, but often, for personal or financial reasons, cannot return to school on a full-time basis. Thus, classes that could be attended on a part-time basis would fulfill a real need. As stated earlier, such programs are readily available for the business school enrollee, but are few and far between for the prospective industrial hygiene student.

Academia also needs to look at the curriculum with respect to changes in the field of industrial hygiene and occupational health. The technical content of master's-level programs is becoming more and more complex as the field itself continues to expand. This appears to be a mixed blessing. A number of professional hygienists have bemoaned the fact that they are looked upon by their employers as purely a technologist in training and interest. Thus as their careers begin to evolve and as general management and administrative jobs become available, the hygienist is rarely considered for such jobs. It is my opinion that some minimal knowledge needs be given to the hygienist so that he or she has at least a basic understanding of the viewpoint of the businessman. Although the primary trust of the professional hygienist is to protect the health of the working population, this usually cannot be accomplished in a vacuum. In many instances, considerations of cost and benefit must be considered when a course of action is to be undertaken. The career success of many hygienists is accomplished to a large extent when the professional has an appreciation of the total impact of a proposed plan, of which health is one factor only. If the health problem is a serious and real one, this may be the overriding factor. However, in many of the situations with which the professional has to deal, health is one of several factors, including economics, and the hygienist must have an appreciation for the viewpoints of other interested parties. Only with this appreciation can one tailor the recommendations to get maximum support from others. Certainly professional standards and ethics should never be compromised, but this does not mean that emphasis and appreciation of other viewpoints can be ignored. Several graduate schools have suggested that electives for their industrial hygiene students include fundamental courses in principles of business management and organization. While obviously only a beginning, hopefully it will develop some understanding of how and why organizations exist as they do. With this background and understanding, the developing professional should find that his or her effectiveness becomes greater. It is almost self-evident that, at times, good proposals were never properly implemented because they were not effectively "sold" to management, and this can be partially attributed to a lack of understanding or appreciation for management's viewpoint. Also, as the professional's career advances and develops, this becomes a greater and greater factor toward ultimate success, both as a professional and an individual. As the problems become more complex so do the solutions, and the higher in the organization the wider the effect of such actions.

Thus we feel that academia needs to look at the programs available in the field of industrial hygiene and occupational health in two ways. It needs to make sure that the professionals that they train are first, technically qualified to practice the profession of industrial hygiene. As stated earlier, the field continues to expand, but the professional must be equipped to deal with it. Then, as the professionals develop, they should have available the means to mature in either of two ways: as a technologist or as a manager. To do either, courses and opportunities to further expand must be made available, and it is the academic institution that must take a leading role. They cannot nor should they be expected to do it alone, but they certainly should take a leading role. Part of this must be directed toward the advancement of the working professional, and this is a change in direction for many parts of academia, but it is definitely needed.

5 SUMMATION

In summation, the driving force for professional development must come from the individual. It requires both an understanding and essentially a permanent commitment in order that it be properly established and organized. Regardless of whether one wishes to remain in the technical practice of this complex and ever-changing field or to advance into the area of management and supervision, the need to avoid obsolescence and remain proficient is an absolute necessity. The individual needs to seek and obtain the counsel and consent of supervisors and the business organization, for this commitment is not to be undertaken lightly. The path used to develop professionally is a multifaceted one, and there is no single best way for an individual to accomplish this goal. The industrial hygiene manager should act as a resource person and a guide to assist the staff to mature and expand its knowledge in order to provide maximum service for the goals of the profession and the organization it serves.

CHAPTER SIXTEEN

Administrative Education and Training

James H. Stewart

1 INTRODUCTION

Knowledgeable and competent industrial hygienists—a timely topic and one that managers today must face if they are to have the quality of people needed to handle today's complex health and safety problems. Training of industrial hygiene professionals should be required in the same way that we require training of employees. Each industrial hygiene professional should have available all the training needed to reach his or her full potential. We should strive to meet this goal because it is more than just training we are offering; it is career development. If career development is done correctly, we shall also satisfy the organization's needs. This chapter covers a practical means of assessing *what* training needs to be done, *who* should be trained, and *what* types of training are available.

To be effective and productive is to be well informed; it's true in the manufacturing area and it's true in the health and safety office.

One of the most important issues facing a manager of professional industrial hygienists today is the challenge of keeping the industrial hygienists current with the explosive growth of knowledge. The challenge for the manager is to identify the learning conditions that will produce the change in behavior desired. The resulting change in behavior must satisfy both the organizations' and the employees' needs. The ultimate goal is to have competent industrial hygienists. What is a competent industrial hygienist? *Competency* is one of those characteristics we all find necessary and appealing yet very difficult to define and especially evaluate (6). Evaluating an industrial hygienist's competency based on his or her responses to questions on a multiple-choice test may or may not reflect a measure of competency. Similarly would we go to physicians who have been qualified by examination yet have never seen or talked to a patient. The results of the test are meaningful but may not reflect the total competency of the individual. One must keep in mind this desire for competency when planning the career development of the industrial hygienist and realize that competency may be the goal but it may be very difficult to evaluate when one has actually reached it.

Is competency not achieved through learning? What is learning?

Learning is a process resulting in some modification, relatively permanent, of the way of thinking, feeling, doing of the learner (1).

Learning is an individual activity that can be facilitated by an appropriate teacher. Learning is also a cooperative process, usually the result of some experience. The experience could be of a practical nature or abstract, as in a classroom setting. Using this definition, we would expect to see some change in a specific behavior in an industrial hygienist after returning from training. After all that is why he or she was sent to the training course, wasn't it?

How is it determined which employees go to which training courses? Are assignments made after assessing the company needs, the individuals career needs, and in some cases regulatory needs? This process is called *needs assessment*. It involves taking a structured look at the needs of the organization and the individual. On the basis of this assessment one can then formulate an efficient, cost-effective training plan.

The remainder of this chapter will be directed at the practical aspects of implementing an effective industrial hygiene training/professional development program. The sections are arranged in the following sequence: performing a needs assessment, defining educational objectives, planning and implementing a program, and evaluating the effectiveness.

The simple and straightforward appearance of these steps belies the complexity involved with implementation. The sections include a theoretical discussion along with a practical example taken from the field of industrial hygiene.

2   PERFORMING A NEEDS ASSESSMENT

Before one can define educational objectives one must evaluate the tasks that must be undertaken for satisfactory performance in the current position, the tasks that will be needed to be undertaken by the employee in the next position, or finally what new duties will be required of the employee for continued satisfactory performance in the future due to organizational/manufacturing changes. In short, what does the employee need to know?

Steps in Performing a Needs Assessment (2)
1. Develop a model of the skills required for current and future jobs.
2. Identify current levels of performance.
3. Specify desired level of performance.
4. Differentiate administrative and technical needs.
5. Assign priorities to the educational needs.

All these steps can be accomplished in one sitting, interactively with the employee.

For example, an employee is currently required to perform air sampling for organic solvents, heavy metals, and respirable silica dust at various operations for a foundry/metal casting company. To perform well in the current position the industrial hygienist must have knowledge of

air-sampling techniques,
calibration techniques,
methods of documenting exposures,
knowledge of metal casting operations,
understanding of basic principles of toxicology,
ability to write effective reports,
good people skills to deal with managers and employees in a nonalarming manner, and so forth.

In short, the industrial hygienist, to be effective, must know the equipment being used, the operation being evaluated, and be able to communicate the findings of the survey in a clear and concise manner. The specific skills, however, will be different in each setting. The challenge to the manager is to be able to identify those requisite skills and then compare those to the inventory of skills of the industrial hygienist.

This needs assessment is representative of current tasks and does nothing to assess the skills that will be needed for future jobs.

This process of looking at an employee's current job and developing a training program is often the way training resources are allocated. A more complete needs assessment would include career development planning, evaluation of manufacturing changes over the foreseeable future, and potential impacts of new regulations. If the various aspects are not assessed, then either the employee or the company is not going to have their needs met.

One practical means of performing a needs assessment is conducting an annual or semiannual career development session with each employee. This session should be separate from the performance review the employee will receive as part of evaluating suitability for a raise in pay. This emphasizes to the employee the importance the manager places on his or her career development. The session should last 1–2 hours and involve an assessment of the level of performance of the employee as well as a discussion of how the employee sees his or her career developing. Discussion should take place around current activities and performance against goals as well as discussion of how the person's career is developing. It is a two-way discussion and involves an assessment by the employee of how well the manager has satisfied the employee's expectations. The reason for these discussions is to allow mid-course corrections to be made in the employee's development plan (if the employee makes changes to the long-term career goals).

For example, at the initial career development session the person may state that a long-term goal is to be an individual contributor with a high degree of expertise in one area. In a later session the career plans are now changed from the technical individual contributor role to a managerial role. Knowing that this new career goal is desired allows one to make these mid-course corrections and include activities such as budgeting and strategic planning into the employee's activities. Because it involves the employee, the needs assessment process will be supported by the employee and should therefore be more effective. The cooperative nature of this activity is essential to its success (1–3).

3   DEFINING EDUCATIONAL OBJECTIVES

The educational objectives obtained from the needs assessment activity fall into three categories:

Practical, that is, manual skills
Communicative, that is, writing and verbal skills
Intellectual, that is, the ability to synthesize or analyze data and information

In the example given it can be seen that all the duties of the industrial hygienist fall in these three categories. It is important to realize the different skills an employee may need and to see into which domain they fall, that is, practical, communicative, or intellectual. Obviously it requires different educational approaches and time frames to produce changes in intellectual or communicative behaviors than it would to change a practical behavior.

The manager's objective is a change or improvement in behavior that will benefit the organization and the individual *and* that is measurable. To accomplish this, clear, concise educational objectives must be set for the employees.

The objectives must have certain characteristics if they are to be meaningful and effective (1). They must be logical, relevant, feasible, observable, and measurable. These are obvious desired characteristics. The challenge is to make them a reality.

Educational objectives derived from the needs assessment process should be put in writing and again discussed with the employee. It is important to obtain the *buy in* of the employees for the educational objectives. If they support and understand the plan, there will be fewer problems in implementation. Also the employee will have a clearer understanding of what will be expected in the future. When putting the objectives in writing, the objectives should be composed of both a clear description of the new tasks to be undertaken as well as the way in which attainment of the desired performance is to be reached. In short, state what will be expected and how one will measure to see if it has been accomplished.

Consider again the industrial hygienist who is working in a metal casting operation. The operation is changing and the industrial hygiene group is faced with implementation of a complex radiation protection program. The objective for the employee may read:

Establish radiation protection program by the end of third quarter of this fiscal year that meets or exceeds current OSHA standards for employees using X-ray thickness measuring devices.

The goal is relevant, logical, feasible, and so on. The employee can easily see what is expected of him or her and in what time frame. The missing piece is *how* does the employee get the training necessary to accomplish the objective and *what* form should the training take—didactic, on the job training, workshop?

4 PLANNING AND IMPLEMENTING A PROGRAM

The completion of the needs assessment is the first step in implementing an effective training and development program. Once the needs assessment is done and the objectives are clearly written, the manager should have, for each employee, a number of training and development activities in order of priority *for that individual.*

If there were unlimited training funds available, we could stop here and schedule everyone into whatever training is needed. The reality is that budgets are limited and the amount of time available for training and development activities is also limited. Recognizing these limitations, another level of prioritization must take place, one that ranks the training and development activities according to the potential benefits. Using the example of the industrial hygienist working in a metal casting plant again, we find that the employee indicates a desire to be put on a management track with a goal to be in a manager's role in 5 years. Simultaneously one finds out that a new process is being brought into the plant within the next 6–9 months. The new process will require implementation of a rigorous radiation safety program, and it has been determined that the skill which will be needed does not currently exist in the organization. Although this is a simplistic example, it does illustrate the conflict that often arises, that is, short-term needs versus long-term career development. It may be possible to accomplish both objectives by appointing the industrial hygienist as the radiation safety officer, send him or her to training, and make implementation of the radiation safety program part of his or her career development for being a manager. It is up to the manager to determine the best solution.

Once a list of training activities has been prepared and prioritized, the training must be identified, budgeted, scheduled, completed, and evaluated.

Many types of training are available and should be considered. Training ranges from on the job training to classroom didactic education. No one type of training is appropriate for all situations. Table 16.1 focuses on the types of training available, the advantages and disadvantages, and describe those situations where the training should provide maximum benefit.

As Section 3, educational objectives will fall into one of three areas: practical, communicative, or intellectual.

The training required to give an employee the skill needed to accurately measure the levels of xylene in the breathing zone of a painter is different

Table 16.1. Identification of Training Resources (1)

Type of Training	Disadvantages	Advantages
Lectures	Passive	Time savings
	Lack of problem solving	Presence of teacher
Practical work and field work	High transport cost	Active situation
	Poor standardization	Closer contact with reality
	Requires careful planning	Realistic evaluation possible
Programmed learning	No group dynamics	Self-paced
	Requires special teaching skills	Mass teaching
Models/simulations	Model situations not like real thing	Provides concept of reality
	Models situations are often expensive to set up	Allows examination of multiple scenarios
	Not good for large groups	

than the training required to evaluate the resulting number in terms of what it will mean to the long-term health of the painter. The first case involves a practical skill; the second involves an intellectual skill.

To assess which type of training would be best in a given situation, perform a crude classification of the desired skill into the three categories previously listed. If the skill is of a practical nature, logic would dictate that some field work be included in the training plan that will permit the industrial hygienist to actually perform the sampling operation. If the resulting skill is either in the communicative or intellectual domain, then the training program will need to include combinations of simulated conditions, lectures, and discussions with a practical portion toward the end. In this case one is trying to impart a skill that requires certain knowledge, not currently present, and have the industrial hygienist apply the new skill to new problems. This is significantly different from the first situation where the newly acquired skill belongs to the practical domain. As one can see, the intellectual and especially the communicative skills are more difficult to teach and will require more time and effort to improve. If the skills one desires the industrial hygienist to have or develop are in the communicative domain, the training should include work with groups—some role playing. These communicative skills are the most difficult to change. A variety of approaches may need to be attempted before significant change occurs.

Industrial hygienists today need to have a combination of skills from the practical, communicative, and intellectual domains.

They deal, extensively, with measuring devices that are delicate and complex; they often are faced with employees concerned about their health; and lastly they are asked by managers, physicians, and so on to form an opinion, based on what they have seen, heard, and measured, as to the safety of an operation.

As one can see, the skills needed for an industrial hygienist to be considered competent come from all the domains. This must be kept in mind at all times when planning the training and career development of the industrial hygienist. If skills from any of the domains are not developed, then the industrial hygienist will probably not be considered competent by the organization's management, the employees, or peer industrial hygienists.

5 EVALUATING PROGRAM EFFECTIVENESS

Evaluation is the most difficult part of any education/career development program. There is a distinction between knowledge, competence, and performance. Knowledge can be tested through written tests. Performance is viewed in retrospect and competence lies somewhere between (4). This concept was originally intended to cover physicians; however, it seems to apply equally well to the field of industrial hygiene. We also can test the knowledge of prospective industrial hygienists through written examination. This is currently done by the American Board of Industrial Hygiene. Part of the requirements necessary to sit for this exam are 5 years of applicable experience. In the view of this author this requirement is a recognition of the fact that knowledge alone will not make a good industrial hygienist; there must be a performance factor. Performance plus knowledge demonstrate competence. This same type of analysis can be applied to the work setting. For example, an industrial hygienist is determined to need development in the field of radiation protection due to anticipated process changes. The knowledge can be obtained through a variety of classroom, on the job training, and short course work. The performance, that is, the implementation of an effective radiation protection program, involves much more than just rote memorization of formulas and facts. The competence of the industrial hygienist will depend on how well he or she integrates the knowledge gained into the situation at hand. In short, one can be an incompetent yet knowledgeable industrial hygienist if there is no performance.

In the work setting, the best measure of the competence of an industrial hygienist is performance not knowledge. Knowledge is useful and necessary, but the application and integration of the knowledge is much more meaningful. Therefore, the setting for the evaluation of the benefits of a particular training/career development program must be evaluated in the field, that is, a workplace setting. A written test at the end of a didactic training course is not sufficient to determine the value of the training. Application in the workplace is the key.

6 CONCLUSION

To make the material in this chapter more useful, a series of steps has been identified that provide a feedback loop for designing, implementing, and modifying a training/career development program. The key point, feedback, is essential to the success of the program (5). Another important point in the evaluation phase is the most difficult. It is relatively easy to determine what type of training will benefit an employee. It is very difficult to determine if the training had any beneficial effect on the employee or the organization.

The following will help determine effect of training:

1. Perform a needs assessment for the individual as well as for the institution.
2. Prioritize the needs to satisfy the needs of the individual and the institution.
3. Establish clear training/career development objectives that are accepted by both the employee and the manager.
4. Establish clear performance criteria by which the employee will be measured after completion of the training/career development.

5. Evaluate the performance of the employee to the agreed-upon criteria.
6. Assess whether there was a gain in performance.
7. Make modifications to the training/career development program based on the results of the evaluation.
8. Measure performance to goals. If performance to goal does not improve after the training resources were allocated, change the program and evaluate the effect of the change. It is a continual process that if conducted in an organized manner should produce more competent industrial hygienists.

REFERENCES

1. World Health Organization, *Educational Handbook for the Health Professional,* Geneva: World Health Organization, 1981.
2. C. W. Ford, *Clinical Education for the Allied Health Professions,* Saint Louis, MO.: C. V. Mosby, 1978.
3. C. J. Bland, *Faculty Development Through Workshops,* Springfield, IL: Charles C. Thomas Publishers, 1980.
4. J. R. Senior, Toward the Measurement of Competence in Medicine, *Report of Computer Based Examination Project sponsored by the National Board of Medicine Examiner and the American Board of Internal Medicine,* Philadelphia: Wadsworth, 1976.
5. I. J. Bates and A. E. Winder, *Introduction to Health Education,* Palo Alto, CA: Mayfield Publishing, 1984.
6. B. Shimberg, "What is Competence? How Can it be Assessed?" in *Power and Conflict in Continuing Professional Education* M. R. Stern, (ed.), Belmont, CA: Wadsworth, 1983.

CHAPTER SEVENTEEN

Consultants and Their Use

Donald R. McFee and Gary N. Crawford

1 INTRODUCTION

This chapter discusses the many reasons for and provides the reader with information on the what, why, when, who, where, and the how of working with consultants. A consultant is defined herein as a professional, independent from the client, who charges a fee for services. He or she may be an individual or a member of a firm.

2 WHY USE A CONSULTANT?

There are a number of reasons why employers turn to consultants to satisfy their needs. There has always been a need for special independent consultant services. It is well-established common practice for physicians, attorneys, accountants, and engineers to function as consultants.

More recently, there has been a management trend that emerged strongly from the recession of the 1980s. This was to trim staff positions. Foreign competition along with other economic pressures gave rise to the phrase "keep your staff positions lean and mean." Health, safety, and environmental staff functions felt the pressures of budget and staffing cuts. At the same time, business was also feeling pressure to do more about matters relating to industrial health and the environment. A liability insurance crisis, the proliferation of lawsuits pertaining to health issues, criminal prosecution of managers for health and safety negligence in the workplace, and new Occupational Safety and Health Administration (OSHA) regulations all created a demand for health, safety, and environmental services. At the same time, top management was calling for staffing cuts.

Getting the job done in the most cost-effective manner is what counts. This has forced top management to look at staffing in a new, more creative light. The use of consultants has become an increasingly popular alternative to a fully staffed department.

2.1 Cost-Effectiveness

Consultants used appropriately are cost effective. This is true even though fees may range up to several times an individual's salary. These fees include overhead factors similar to those of staff employees in an organization. The annual cost of an employee far exceeds annual salary. For example, payroll taxes, insurance, and fringe benefits might typically run 40 to 50 percent of an individual's salary. Then there is the cost of office space, furniture, and a pro-rata share of such things as heat, light, and janitorial services. Most technical specialists require at least some degree of secretarial support such as typing, filing, obtaining reference materials. There is also the need for a certain amount of scientific equipment such as sampling pumps, meters, and other forms of evaluation instrumentation. It would not be unusual to expect that a well-equipped technologist would require a dollar amount of equipment equal to a minimum of one or more year's salary. Then, of course, instrumentation needs to be periodically calibrated and repaired and replaced due to both wear and tear and obsolescence. Expendable elements such as battery packs and chemical cells used in many types of instruments are rather costly to replace.

Total all of these expenses and salary to determine an annualized cost for an in-house staff member. This is important for comparing consultant cost versus staff cost. Next, determine what that cost is on a productive hour basis, that is, how many actual hours of productive time does the staff member spend working on your company's problem? First start by subtracting hours on vacation, sick leave, holidays, jury duty, attending company meetings, attending professional conferences, training sessions, and other such time away from productive direct problem solving. Take into account that it is difficult for someone to use the remaining hours 100 percent effectively. There may be gaps in scheduling when processes shut down because of a strike or simply because of inefficient planning. This results in lost productive time.

Now that one has all of the costs and a fair estimate of the number of productive hours that can be expected from staff personnel, one may divide the cost by the number of productive hours expected to obtain an hourly rate that can then be compared to the cost of an outside consultant. Many organizations who have gone through this cost analysis have rapidly come to the conclusion that keeping a lean staff is better. The use of consultants is the more cost-effective alternative. This may not be true for all organizations however. The cost analysis should be performed frequently to assure that whichever alternative is selected and used is the most cost-effective one for the organization.

A deciding factor in the cost-effectiveness analysis is often the determination of whether the organization's needs are continuous or intermittent. Is the person's workload more intermittent in nature? It could swing the balance more toward the use of consultants since there is no cost for downtime in contrast to using organizational full-time staff to fulfill the function. If a consultant makes good economic sense for an organization, it will also gain the benefit of not having to go through emotional layoffs and costly outplacement services each time economic pressure requires a reduction in force.

2.2 Specialized Knowledge

Many consultants have specialized knowledge and experience on a particular situation that has unexpectedly developed. The consultant's specialized capabilities frequently exceed that of existing staff as well as those in the job market readily available for hiring. The consultant will not necessarily be any more knowledgeable about the industry involved but will have key information to resolve a specific situation or problem.

Also, specialized sampling or testing equipment may be needed to address a specific problem. A consultant firm that has specialized experience in a given area may already have the necessary sampling and testing equipment. This can be brought to bear on the problem along with the necessary knowledge.

For example, an organization might install new equipment that has a radio frequency exposure potential. Rather than buying special radio frequency measuring instrumentation and hiring a new staff member to operate it, or even sending off an existing staff member to a short course to learn more about radio frequency for a one-time application, a prudent manager will recognize that a consultant with prior experience in radio frequency measurements and who has the necessary instrumentation will present the optimum way of handling the potential problem. Similar examples could be cited for any number of other specialized situations such as noise, indoor air pollution, and microbiological organism exposures.

2.3 Objectivity

We have already dealt with objectivity to some degree in the preceding discussion. However, the objectivity advantage a consultant can offer is probably one of the most important and is worthy of more detailed discussion.

Emotional issues frequently develop in both large and small organizations. Group dynamics in the workplace can make both trivial and serious matters into big headaches for management. Frequently, management contributes to this seriousness by not knowing what they are dealing with and agreeing there is a problem. Management is subject to the same dynamics as the line employee. For example, a cyanide poisoning case reported in a newspaper article caused near panic in another company. Employees applying a diisocyanate varnish associated cyanide with diisocyanate and became fearful that their lives were being threatened by touching or working with this coating. Management reassurances only provoked distrust and further labor unrest. A consultant was called in to run tests and to explain the difference to supervisors and employees.

Most organizations that have existed for any length of time could probably compile an extensive list of emotional issues that have arisen in the workplace. Those related to worker health–safety issues can usually be handled more effectively by an outside consultant who is perceived and accepted by the employees and unions as being more objective. Where labor–management problems are persistent, regular use of consultants in place of company staff is an alternative worthy of serious consideration.

Frequently, individuals and groups use health and safety issues for their own purpose and political gain. Changes in production equipment, materials, methods, or supervisory personnel are responded to in a political manner. A common allegation is that the new materials or procedures or process may be unhealthy or unsafe. There may be allegations that a change imposed by management is aimed at increasing production and profits at the expense of employee health and safety. Such responses may not be contrived. The employee's natural aversion to change and a move away from their comfort zone can stimulate genuine fear that, although unfounded, is sincere and potentially disruptive when coupled with political skepticism.

In this instance the outside consultant should be perceived by employees to be more objective and more likely to give an honest appraisal of the health–safety issue involved.

Along similar lines, there are many labor–management issues that can be addressed more effectively by an experienced, independent consultant. There seems to be an inherent distrust of management by labor and vice versa.

The OSHA Hazard Communication Standard along with greater publicity on occupational-health-related issues has greatly raised the level of worker awareness. Some union contracts in recent years have contained clauses requiring an independent outside consultant, technically acceptable to both management and labor, to be called in at management's expense when labor believes there is a potential hazard to workers. Many times both the company and union have their own technical specialists on staff but need the third-party objectivity.

Accident investigations both with and without fatalities are instances where the objectivity of the outside consultant is extremely important. The most diligent efforts of in-house staff may never be able to get to the true cause of an accident or a fatality despite excellent capabilities and hard work. The key ingredient missing in such circumstances is objectivity. The in-house expert may be blinded by familiarity. He or she may be too accustomed to the environment and circumstances to see through the sequence of events and hence the true cause. The in-house expert's efforts also may be hampered by employees who are reluctant to talk to management or staff in a completely open manner out of fear for their jobs or a reprimand. Important facts surrounding the cause of a serious accident or fatality may be covered up by employees. They may fear they will be thought negligent by management and in turn be blamed for the accident. The independent consultant can be given the opportunity to question individuals and to guarantee their anonymity.

Employees are often reluctant to criticize management for certain procedures, design flaws, or negligence for fear of becoming involved in a confrontation and eventual retribution. Again, the independent consultant can be given the opportunity of talking with employees on a confidential, anonymous basis. The consultant, thereby, is better able to get down to their most complete and honest accounting of what took place.

A most thorough and incisive accident/fatality investigation provides an organization its greatest opportunity to avoid repetition of the accident. Independent action helps the organization tremendously in defending itself in subsequent litigation.

2.4 Temporary Needs

Many organizations recognize the importance of industrial hygiene, health, safety, or environmental assistance, but don't have the need for such services on a regular continuing basis. In other instances there may be a need that can be satisfied with permanent staffing, however, peak demands arise that overwhelm a small staff or individual. Under these circumstances a consultant may be utilized to handle temporary staffing. For instance, there may be a new OSHA regulation that requires development of an organizational program and employee training. An example would be the OSHA Hazard Communication Standard, which created a substantial short-term need for technical expertise in preparation of material safety data sheets, internal programs, and employee training. This type of peak workload may easily overwhelm a small staff. It can represent an insurmountable obstacle for an organization with no health–safety staff.

The use of consultants for temporary staffing allows an organization to quickly react to one-time or infrequent needs and peak workloads. When the task is complete, costs stop.

Good management dictates staffing up only for the routine and bringing in temporary outside assistance for the special short-term needs.

2.5 Additional Resources

Many organizations maintain an adequate staff to handle predicted needs for their technology. However, the unpredictable or unexpected can occur and create turmoil in what was an adequately staffed and equipped department. Before purchasing expensive equipment and hastily attempting to hire additional staff, management should consider utilizing a consultant as an alternative.

3 WHEN ARE CONSULTANTS NEEDED?

The discussion so far has primarily dealt with why an organization might benefit from using a consultant. In this section we will assist the reader with guidance on the most appropriate times to bring an outside consultant into an organization.

3.1 Litigation

Regardless of whether an organization has a specific staff or not, when it comes to issues involving potential litigation, use of an outside consultant should be seriously considered. The consultant represents independent, third-party objectivity in the eyes of the court, to top management, and labor unions. A reputable, well-established consultant can convincingly demonstrate professionalism and objectivity that even your best in-house expert cannot do. This is regardless of his or her level of education, experience, or capability.

It is not just a matter of appearances that makes the outside consultant a more valuable, objective resource. It is almost unavoidable that in-house staff become accustomed to their company's way of doing things, processes, and policies. This will subconsciously limit their thinking no matter how hard they try to be objective. The outsider coming in can see things from a totally different frame of reference. This objectivity can be immeasurably important in establishing the facts that may eventually become a part of legal proceedings.

If the circumstance that prompted initial concern over potential litigation eventually does end up in court, the outside consultant can serve as an expert assistant or witness. He or she can help present facts to the judge or jury that might be inadmissible or less credible if introduced by an organization staff member. In all likelihood the consultant will have had prior experience in courtroom situations and testimony. The consultant should be better able to handle questioning and cross examination than a staff member who may be appearing in court for the first time.

One of the most important things a good consultant can do when potential litigation is involved is to help their client avoid litigation. Bringing in an outside consultant will demonstrate to workers or potential claimants that the organization is well intentioned and is demonstrating good faith in solving the problem or remedying the situation. No matter how diligent and capable internal staff may be on working on such problems, their activities may be suspect by the complaining parties. They may believe that staff members are the pawns of management and are only seeking to coverup rather than solve a problem. Although the consultant may be similarly accused, he or she has a better chance of defending such allegations. This is based on a long career of independence and objectivity needed to maintain a reputation and an independent practice.

Whenever citations by a regulatory agency or civil lawsuits may be involved, an independent consultant should be considered.

Some situations may involve regulatory agencies such as OSHA, EPA, or other federal, state, and local agencies having various jurisdictions covering health, safety, and the environment. Organizations can make their situations much worse with regulatory agencies by giving too much, too little, or the wrong information. Consultants accustomed to working with regulatory agencies should be knowledgeable in the government's regulatory and enforcement procedures and can guide the client in responding properly.

Too frequently, an organization's management and staff may be too emotionally involved with a situation to effectively deal with regulatory representatives. An example would be a fatality that is being investigated by OSHA. Management and staff may be so emotionally distraught that they cannot organize and present facts to OSHA in an effective manner. There are also instances where management may be so angered by a citation or inspection that they say or do things that are detrimental to their position. An experienced consultant can be a very effective buffer between management and the regulatory agency. The consultant can be a catalyst for bringing about a fair and speedy resolution to the problem with the least amount of expense, stress, and strain on the organization.

3.2 Audit Function

More and more companies are recognizing the value of treating health, safety, and environmental activities in a more businesslike manner. This means periodic audits the same as if it involved the company books or other business elements. (Also, see Chapter 14.)

Many organizations have weathered economic storms over the years and succeeded in maintaining a health, safety, and environmental staff position or group. Such organizations will, however, be likely to require documentation that these functions justify their existence and expenditures. This is where the audit function becomes essential. A staff manager may wish to retain a consultant to perform an audit of the department's functions. If there are weaknesses in a program or inefficiencies in spending, it is better to find it out oneself. One can take corrective action before management draws a similar conclusion and takes action of its own. Admittedly, it is hard to be objective about one's own performance or department's function. Conscientious people naturally believe that they are doing a good job and would not knowingly do otherwise. A knowledgeable consultant is in a much better position to review an individual or department's accomplishments, procedures, and spending to determine if it's appropriate to the organization's needs. There are some important questions to be asked. Is the function adequately staffed? Or, is it overstaffed? Is the funding for the function too much or too little? Are the most important issues being addressed adequately? Is recordkeeping adequate and appropriate?

In some instances top management may retain the consultant to audit the health, safety, or environmental department or function. This will help management to determine if it is getting its money's worth and whether even greater rewards could be achieved by increased staffing or funding. Also, new perspectives can evolve from an audit. Even well-run programs can get in a rut and miss new opportunities to achieve a greater reward for the organization. A knowledgeable consultant can usually spot these opportunities during an audit and provide management with a list of items or areas where additional or shifted emphasis should be profitable.

3.3 Program Start-up Assistance

One very appropriate time to use an outside consultant is when a new program involving health–safety or environmental issues is first developed or implemented. Many organizations have lost valuable time and created tremendous problems by launching new programs that were flawed, inadequate, ineffective, or simply poorly implemented. A consultant who has gone through such program implementations in the past can help an organization avoid many of the pitfalls that can plague a well-intentioned program.

For example, one organization decided to develop and implement a hazard communication program without any outside assistance or review. Their intentions were admirable; however, they overlooked some essential factors in developing the program. Even more tragically, they made significant errors in implementing it. The result was a very angry and upset workforce. Many were afraid to go back to their jobs. In this case, management erred by allowing the hazard communication program to be presented by individuals with inadequate backgrounds and who were not fully versed on health and safety, and who were not well prepared to train workers. The way the information was presented and the way the presenters responded to questions resulted in a chaotic situation. Workers were now fearful to handle or work with materials involved in their jobs. Some were threatening lawsuits for past, allegedly harmful, exposures and practically every ailment they had endured in recent years. This is a situation where an outside consultant could have better organized information and presented it in a manner that would have had positive benefits rather than negative.

Practically any new program related to health–safety or the environment that an organization anticipates implementing should be reviewed, or at least considered for review, by an independent consultant. It is probable that an experienced consultant has been involved with similar activities and other organizations in the past. As a result, the consultant is in a position to steer the client away from some of the pitfalls others have experienced and help to emphasize those factors that have proven to be particularly effective for others.

3.4 Persistent Work Backlog

Many times an organization will get behind in its duties. It can be for any number of reasons. However, if the backlog persists for an extended period of time, then it may be the appropriate time to bring in a consultant. The consultant can do one of two things. The first is to look at the workload and determine if everything one is doing should be done or if routines or rituals have been developed in the organization that no longer make sense. It is amazing how often an outside consultant can go into an organization and ask the question: "Why are you performing this certain function?" The answer is all too frequently: "Because that's the way we were doing it when I started here," or "We've always done it that way."

After the consultant has helped to determine the necessity of all the functions that have resulted in the work backlog, one may then reevaluate the backlog of essential items. One then will be in a position to determine how long it will take for existing in-house staff to get caught up. If the answer is "too long," then the consultant may bring his or her resources to bear on the problem and provide the manpower and equipment necessary to help catch up. One then will have a more manageable situation.

3.5 Top Management Does Not Understand

Casual conversations with health–safety or environmental professionals at social or professional gatherings frequently result in conversations where the in-house staff person will comment, "we should be doing this," or "we should be doing that," but "top management just doesn't understand." How frustrating.

When this happens it is usually for one of two reasons. Either the in-house professional does not know how to effectively communicate with top management in terms that management understands or top management chooses not to believe their in-house staff for various reasons. Problems develop when this type of communication breakdown happens, as it all too frequently does. Rather than the in-house staff going off disgruntled and discouraged and perhaps top management doing the same, this may be an opportune time to bring in a consultant who can act as a translator or go-between.

There are many instances where a consultant's similar recommendation to top management has been welcomed and accepted although previously rejected when put forth by the organization's in-house staff. Why does the consultant have success where the in-house staff has not? Again, it is usually for one of two reasons. The first is that a well-qualified consultant has learned how to communicate with top management and can explain issues in a manner that top management can better understand, relate to, and see benefits to the organization. In other instances, sometimes hearing the same thing from an outsider means more to top management than hearing it from its own staff.

3.6 Things Are Not Going Well

One clue as to when one might elect to bring in a consultant is when things just are not going well. There can be any number of different specifics involved. There may be high turnover in the in-house staff or high turnover in production personnel. High turnover in production operations can frequently be linked to environmental factors that knowingly, or unknowingly, stress the workers and cause them to leave their job. If the in-house staff is not recognizing these factors, perhaps the objectivity of an outside consultant can. Then, there is the matter of turnover of health, safety and environmental staff within an organization. The consultant might also be able to determine why that is happening. The consultant's broad range of experience within the field may help to identify program or administrative deficiencies that are resulting in the dissatisfaction of a company's professionals.

Another time an organization may wish to consider bringing in a consultant is when employee complaints seem to be excessive or particularly confounding. All too often people fall into the trap of treating symptoms rather than getting down to the root cause of a problem. When this happens in an organization, it is often necessary to call upon the objectivity of an outsider to identify the base cause.

3.7 Uncertainty and Indecisiveness Appear

There are times when one of the things that are not going well is the decision-making process. Choices or alternatives are not clear-cut, or at least, they do not seem to be. Differences of opinion may abound within the organization's health–safety staff or there may be difference of opinion among managers within an organization over health–safety and environmental issues.

When these types of conditions develop, it seems as if nothing is being accomplished and it probably is not. Days, weeks, months, or even years may pass by without important decisions and resulting actions being taken. Opportunities to reduce risks, improve working conditions, comply with governmental regulations, or other important program elements never seem to get accomplished because no one is able to make a decision as to exactly what needs to be done.

This is an excellent time to retain a qualified consultant. An independent can be given the assignment of evaluating circumstances and acting as a catalyst to break the logjam and get things moving again. One of the reasons a consultant can be effective in this type of situation is strictly a matter of timing. Often, indecisiveness in an organization is a matter of no one in the organization having the time to devote exclusively to a problem and to develop the detailed information needed to make good decisions. Decisions are much easier when a knowledgeable individual is given the time to develop and lay out all of the details involved in the decision-making process. A formal presentation of alternatives by a consultant along with supported recommendations may be all it takes to clear up uncertainty and to get decisions made.

3.8 Insurance Rates and Availability

Within overall business cycles, insurance pops up too frequently as one of the things that is not satisfactory. This can be dramatic increases in rates, cancellations, or reduced availability. Product liability insurance and workers' compensation insurance are two types that are typically experience rated or experience sensitive. Although overall insurance market trends may be outside the control of any individual organization, the degree of impact may well be controllable for an organization.

When an organization is experiencing insurance problems, there are positive actions that can be taken:

1. Retain a consultant.
2. Evaluate workers' compensation experience and health-related and environmental liability experience.

Exposure potential as well as past experience can also be an important factor influencing insurance rates. This may be particularly true for organizations that do not have demonstrated technical resources to control exposures. Underwriters may perceive this as having a negative impact on potential loss experience and adjust rates accordingly. Using a consultant and making this service known to the insurance underwriters may help an organization obtain more competitive insurance rates.

When rates are increasing due to actual loss experience, the consultant should be in a good position to objectively review loss histories, investigate circumstances, and recommend preventive methods. Another cost-reducing factor is control of claims after an incident has occurred. Too often organizations rely entirely on their insurance carrier to minimize claim costs. They fail to realize that there are often many ways that the organization can also help to reduce these costs. This is an area where a qualified consultant should be very effective.

3.9 Unsolved Problems

Any organization that has the feeling that things are not going well can probably identify one or more stubborn problems that have not been resolved and will not go away. These types of nagging problems often take a disproportionate amount of time away from other staff priorities or cause persistent aggravation among managers who do not have an in-house staff to turn to.

The nagging, unresolved problem is a prime candidate for attack by an outside consultant. It takes the "monkey-off-the-back" of staff or management and places a focused effort dedicated to solving the problem. We certainly are not suggesting that consultants are all powerful and can solve the unsolvable problems. On those they cannot resolve, the consultants' efforts should have resulted at least in a formalized report of findings with documentation that should be helpful to management in making ultimate decisions about the future of a troublesome operation.

3.10 Timing

Whenever a situation arises indicating the need for a consultant, it is usually wise to bring in the consultant as early as possible. This is especially true for situations involving potential litigation. This will allow the consultant time to gather facts, evidence, and data while the circumstances are still as current as possible. This will allow the development of the most comprehensive documentation possible, which could be very valuable in future litigation. It is important to remember that civil lawsuits may not be brought against an organization until months or even years after the incident in question. Then it may be years after that before the case ever goes to trial. If an organization waits too long to bring in technical assistance, the trail is cold. Witnesses are no longer available, processes or materials are long since gone, recollections of those involved are not as clear, and records and data may become lost or destroyed. Bringing the consultant in early will give your organization the best opportunity to document facts and provide help that will be most effective in protecting your interests.

4 WHOM SHOULD YOU RETAIN?

We have already discussed many of the reasons why a consultant can be important to an organization and when consultants may be needed. The next important question is who should be retained. Not all consultants or consulting organizations are the same. Each may have a different area of specialty, skills, and benefits that must be evaluated in order to make the right choice. The following sections should help you organize your search for the consultant or consulting organization that is right for your organization.

4.1 Objectives

The very first task is to put down in writing, as specifically as possible, what it is one wants to accomplish. Entering into the selection process with only a vague idea of what one wants accomplished may lead to selection of the wrong consultant. This may in turn lead to an unsatisfactory result. Remember, as with most other tasks, setting well-defined objectives first is essential. After that has been accomplished, the rest falls into place much more readily.

4.2 Needs

What are the true needs? Knowing these needs will help guide one toward the consultant who can best satisfy those needs. Look for an organization or individual who can demonstrate their ability to satisfy specific needs. This demonstration should be a combination of both credentials and a track record established in handling similar needs to the satisfaction of others. Look carefully at the consultant's academic and special training credentials pertinent to one's needs. Also, look for evidence that those implied skills have been utilized effectively in the past.

4.3 Credentials

A consultant's credentials should be appropriate to the needs of the client. Understanding the many different combinations of letters that follow a consultant's name will help the client select more appropriately. Remember, at the beginning of the section on whom to select, it was stated that the selection should be based on satisfying the client's needs. Some tasks may require a consultant with extensive credentials in order to develop results with maximum credibility, while other needs are more basic and only minimal credentials are necessary. For example, if the need is for development of information that is expected to be used in court proceedings and possibly expert witness testimony, one should be seeking a consultant with extensive, impeccable credentials. However, if the needs are more basic as in someone to conduct routine air monitoring, then someone with more basic credentials is all that is required.

Some of the more common initials that follow an individual's name are easily recognizable indicators of credentials. Persons outside of the profession may not understand the terminology that is in common current use.

The initials "CIH" following an individual's name indicates that the person is a Certified Industrial Hygienist. It also indicates the individual probably has at least a 4-year college degree in the sciences or engineering (there may be rare exceptions). It also means that this individual has at least 5 years' experience as a practicing industrial hygienist and has successfully completed 2 days of written examinations given by the American Board of Industrial Hygiene. The first day exam is called the Core Exam, which all Certified Industrial Hygienists must successfully complete. The second day of written examination will be different depending on the hygienist's field of practice. For those in general practice this would be the Comprehensive Practice Examination. Those industrial hygienists who are more specialized may elect to take the second day exam in a specialty area such as engineering aspects, air pollution aspects, chemical aspects, toxicological aspects, or radiological health.

After successful completion of these examinations, the individuals must maintain their certification by proving to the American Board of Industrial Hygiene every 6 years that they have earned adequate recertification points to maintain active certification. These activities include attendance at technical meetings, serving on technical committees, professional association membership, continuing education, authoring technical papers and publications, and similar professional activities. Those who do not acquire enough recertification points must retake the second day of examination to be recertified.

Another common set of letters is IHIT. This stands for Industrial Hygienist in Training. To achieve this designation, an individual must successfully complete the Core Examination offered by the American Board of Industrial Hygiene. Completing only the Core Examination does not qualify the individual as a Certified Industrial Hygienist. It indicates only that the individual has met certain basic criteria to be eligible to take the examination and has adequate technical knowledge to pass the Core Examination. This is somewhat analagous to the professional engineering licensing procedure that similarly offers a core examination to recent engineering graduates and furnishes the Engineer-in-Training (EIT) designation to those who successfully complete the examination.

The designations CIHT means Certified Industrial Hygiene Technologist. This is not to be confused with the Certified Industrial Hygienist described earlier. The CIHT does not have to have a 4-year college degree and does not take the same American Board of Industrial Hygiene examinations as does a CIH. The CIHT designation indicates an individual with technical training and experience who has successfully completed a special examination offered by the American Board of Industrial Hygiene.

The designations CIH, IHIT, and CIHT, are the primary credentials to look for in individuals in the industrial hygiene profession. Many industrial hygienists also have achieved professional credentials in affiliated areas such as Certified Safety Professional (CSP), Professional Engineer (PE), Certified Hazard Control Manager (CHCM), and others. These added credentials may be of value to the credibility of a task depending on the client's needs. These should be defined at the outset.

College degrees are another important credential in evaluating industrial hygiene consultants. Generally, a consultant should have at least a 4-year college degree in the sciences or engineering. In recent years, many universities have begun offering bachelor's level degrees in occupational safety and health. Many industrial hygiene consultants will possess master's degrees in industrial hygiene or public health. There are also industrial hygiene consultants available with doctorate degrees.

When selecting a consultant, professional certifications and professional experience may be better indicators of appropriate credentials than college degrees alone. Generally, the longer an individual has been practicing in a professional field, the less important the academic background. An exception to this would be in situations where the consultant would be expected to serve as an expert witness. In these cases, juries may find additional credibility in witnesses with advanced academic degrees.

4.4 Experience

Experienced consultants should be able to demonstrate specific experience in areas applicable to a given situation. This is typically accomplished by presenting case histories or project summaries of prior assignments of a similar nature. These should be free of specific identification of prior clients' identities unless the client has specifically given permission to use its name. Governmental projects are usually an exception to this rule since many government projects are a matter of public record. Once an assignment is completed, the report furnished is in the public domain.

Another manner in which a consultant may be able to demonstrate experience is through published articles and papers on relevant topics. Remember, experience in the concepts involved is usually much more important than experience in a specific industry or process. For example, a consultant who can demonstrate extensive successful experience in noise problems may be the best choice for a noise problem situation, even though the consultant may not have had specific experience with a particular industry or process. Conversely, a consultant who may have extensive experience in an industry or process, but little demonstrated experience specifically in noise is apt to be an inappropriate selection for working on noise control problems.

4.5   Reputation

A consultant's reputation is of paramount importance. The types of things that one should know about a consultant's reputation would be very similar to the types of things one would like to know about a prospective employee. The difference is that the consultant's reputation is usually more a matter of public knowledge than is an individual's seeking employment. In recent years, many former employers of individuals have become reluctant to furnish much information about former employees. Personnel departments usually treat an employee's employment history as a confidential matter. With consultants, it is usually just the opposite. If a consultant performs poorly, the client is usually willing to tell people about any dissatisfaction. Therefore, when considering consultants, it is wise to ask for references and to follow through with contacts to check on the consultant's reputation.

Recognition is another way of evaluating a consultant's reputation. How well is the consultant known within the profession? Has the consultant received awards or letters of commendation for past work? Is the consultant well respected among peers in their professional associations? Has the consultant served in elective office for a professional or trade association in the field? Has the consultant had papers published, presented papers, or been asked to speak before a professional or trade association? Getting answers to these types of questions will help one to evaluate a consultant's reputation.

When checking on references, try to establish what the consultant's track record has been on three key items of performance. The first is quality. Have past clients been satisfied with the accuracy and thoroughness of the consultant's performance? Ask open-ended questions and give the reference an opportunity to expound on how effective a job was performed.

The next is timeliness. One of the advantages of utilizing a consultant is to get a job done in a timely manner. Assuming that this is important, find out how well the consultant has done for others in meeting deadlines. If a reference is unfavorable about meeting deadlines, press further to try to determine if the consultant was slow in following through or if there were scheduling or cooperation problems outside of the consultant's control.

And third, did the consultant stay within the project budget? If a reference had retained the consultant on a time and expense basis with certain budget restrictions, it is important to determine how well the consultant's fee stayed within that budget. If the project was on a fixed fee basis, it is important to determine if the consultant completed all of the tasks called for within the assignment and whether or not the consultant requested additional funds to complete an assignment.

4.6 Philosophy

Determine the consultant's philosophical approach and openness to your own approach. Are you of the same mind? Your philosophies should be in agreement. Otherwise, there will be basic conflicts and a poor chance at best of mutually acceptable or successful arrangements.

4.7 Business Awareness

Another important factor in evaluating whom one should retain as a consultant is his or her awareness of important business considerations. One important indicator of this awareness is business economics. In interviewing the prospective consultant, ask questions to determine the level of understanding of important financial issues. The consultant will ultimately be asked, in most cases, to provide recommendations. One must be concerned with cost-effectiveness of actions taken by the organization, and so must the consultant. Recommendations that are too expensive in comparison to the anticipated benefits are of little value no matter how well founded from a strictly technical basis.

Where matters of cost are particularly important, try to select a consultant who can demonstrate practicality and a respect for one's financial resources. Look for evidence of past assignments where the consultant's recommended approach has helped to make a client more profitable.

Another important indicator of business awareness is sensitivity to matters of law and liability. Consultant and client alike must be aware that reports and records generated by the consultant's work become important business records that could be introduced as evidence in future legal proceedings. These may include citations from regulatory agencies such as OSHA or EPA. Documents may also become an important part of civil proceedings or even criminal proceedings if criminal negligence is claimed against an organization.

The consultant must demonstrate an understanding and a sensitivity to the client's liabilities. Reports produced by the consultant that contain emotional words and speculation may be very detrimental to the client in the future. For example, a simple word such as "exposure" has a very specific meaning to industrial hygienists but carries much more emotional connotations to a jury of laymen. Laymen are accustomed to thinking of the word "exposure" in terms of contagious diseases and fail to see the important distinctions of exposures to air contaminants and dose–response relationships. Other examples would be consultant reports that speculate about hazards in the workplace that might be later used by adversaries in an attempt to prove willful negligence against an organization.

A business-aware and client-sensitive consultant will produce reports and documents that are factual, not speculative, and free of emotional words that are likely to be misunderstood by a layman.

Ask prospective consultants to show examples of past work, with client names deleted, to see how information is presented, and how matters of client economics are handled.

4.8 Availability

The availability of a consultant is a factor of varying importance, again, depending on the client's developed statement of needs. If the needs include emergency response capability, then it is wise to look for a consulting organization with multiple qualified individuals. A one-person consulting company may not be able to handle emergency responses due to commitments to other clients, vacation, and personal illness. Emergency response requires redundancy of personnel and supporting equipment in order to adequately respond to a client's immediate needs.

Realistic timing of task requirements should be compared to the prospective consultant's available resources. Most successful and established consulting firms have a high percentage of their consultants and equipment committed to existing clients. They could not stay in business very long otherwise. Any major project requiring extensive commitments of the consultant's resources should be planned with adequate lead time or gradual phasing of effort to accommodate commitments. The client should compare realistic timing and manpower requirements with the consultant's available resources. Determine the commitment the consultant is able to make with respect to timing needs. The most highly qualified consulting organization may be of little value if its current obligations will not allow an adequate commitment of its resources within the required time constraints.

4.9 Selection

Thus far we have discussed why to retain a consultant, when one needs a consultant, and whom one should retain. Now comes the task of how to go about doing all of this. In the following pages we will provide some practical guidelines on how to set about this task. The guidelines offered may not cover all possibilities but should provide an adequate basis to get started.

Principal criteria for selection of a consultant include: credentials, philosophy, availability, and personal characteristics. The principal evidence of the consultant's capability then is the credentials bestowed by the consultant's peers. Usually these include academic standing and certification by the professional societies involved. Choose a consultant with credentials appropriate for the assignment. Even when the consultant has the appropriate credentials and experience, if this person does not fit in with an organization or has an opposite philosophical approach, then the relationship is apt to be a failure. Choose a consultant with whom one is comfortable and can equate with philosophically.

Availability is also a critical factor. Regardless of the individual or organization's capabilities, if they cannot address a situation within the necessary time scale, they are of little value. It is important then, that one examines the time scale and confirm these requirements. Then, choose a consultant who can meet it.

4.10   Interviewing

Whether one is considering only one consultant or a dozen, be sure to engage in extensive conversation prior to making a commitment. Ask questions about prior experience on similar projects. Ask what the proposed approach would be to one's needs, and by all means ask about availability and responsiveness. It was mentioned earlier that business awareness is an important factor, and conversations should be conducted to draw out the consultant's attitudes and approaches to business matters. Look at brochures, resumes, and examples of work that the prospective consultant can show. This helps demonstrate the quality and the experience that one can expect.

Some organizations have developed and utilized a numerical rating matrix to help in the interviewing and selection process. In this matrix, list key factors specific for the proposed project. These should include such criteria as credentials, philosophy, availability, experience, location, business awareness, size, and any other factors that are important. Then establish a scale of, for example, 1–5 (or 1–10, or 1–100), and award points to each competing consultant in each category in completing the interviewing process. The total points for each candidate can be used as a helpful deciding factor. One still will want to give consideration to intangibles and to a "gut" feeling about the consultant, whether it be a single individual or a firm.

4.11   Reference Checks

Most consulting firms that have been in existence for any length of time should be able to produce a list of names and telephone numbers of past clients who are willing to provide a reference on past work. This list should preferably contain at least one past client who has utilized the consultant for a project similar to the one presently under consideration. Take the time to make the calls. It may be very revealing or only reassuring, but always worth the time.

Prepare a list of questions in advance of items that one believes are particularly pertinent to the project and any concerns that may exist about the prospective consultant's abilities. Do not be shy about asking blunt questions. The interviewing process with the prospective consultant may have raised some doubts about a weakness or a capability. Be sure to ask references specifically about their experience with the consultant and those items of concern.

4.12 Proposal

It is preferable a written scope of work be put together. It should define as clearly as possible what will be expected of the consultant. Also state any special credentials, certifications, or experience the consultant is to possess in order to qualify for a project. In turn, ask the consultant to respond with a written proposal that sets forth their understanding of the project and how fees will be charged. Do not accept a proposal from a consultant that merely states that he or she will furnish all of the services as set forth in the scope of work. The consultant's proposal should convey a complete appreciation and understanding of the objectives and needs of the project.

4.13 Price versus Quality

Experienced managers recognize that the lowest price does not necessarily mean the best value. The same is true for consultants as it is for commercial products. Most of us at some time in our lives have purchased a cheap pair of shoes that we thought were a great bargain. Then, they hurt our feet or fell apart in a short time. The old saying, "You only get what you pay for" is true up to a point. For instance, is a $1000 wrist watch 10 times better than a $100 wrist watch? It depends on your needs. If one is trying to impress one's friends at the country club, then it certainly is. But, if one just wants to tell time, it probably is not.

Consider several proposals from competitive consulting firms. Then go back to the original statement of need and ask what is really to be accomplished and of what value is it to the organization? As a general rule, it is best to review each proposal and to rank the proposals by technical merit. This includes the philosophical approach, the credentials of the individuals involved, and the qualifications presented. Then, look at the fee proposal to see if it is in line with the perceived value of the project to the organization. If it is not, then move down the merit ranking until a proposal is reached with a fee that is commensurate to the perceived value. However, be sure to fully evaluate the impact of this service on the organization. The impact of health and safety has a far greater financial impact on an organization than is readily obvious to most managers.

5 WHERE TO FIND A CONSULTANT

5.1 Referrals

Health, safety, and environmental consultants belong in a general category of professionals who receive much of their business from referrals of past clients. This is much the same as how doctors, lawyers, and accountants receive new business. Traditionally, people have preferred to obtain professional services by the word-of-mouth recommendation of friends or professional associates. Few people will select a doctor or lawyer at random from the telephone book unless they have no alternative. It is much the same with consultants. One of the first steps is to ask business and professional associates if they have used consultants or know of consultants that they would recommend. When a positive response is obtained, be sure to ask specifics about the philosophy, credentials, and reputation of the consultant. Also ask about the quality, timeliness, and cost-effectiveness of the services rendered.

5.2 Directories

Directories can be a valuable source of leads to finding qualified consultants. These are normally the second choice organizations turn to when personal referrals prove to be nonproductive or if they fail to provide adequate numbers of recommendations for competitive comparison. The American Industrial Hygiene Association periodically publishes a directory of industrial hygiene consultants. This directory includes information about specialty areas in which the consultants claim special expertise or training. Many other organizations and publishing companies offer directories or listings of consultants. These are all very helpful in obtaining the names and phone numbers but really offer little else to the reader. Most listings do not constitute any type of an endorsement by the publishing organization of the firms listed. Nor does the publishing organization have the resources to investigate each consultant listed or vouch for the consultant's capabilities. Use directories to obtain lists of potential consultants. But, do not substitute this as a means of qualifying prospective consultants. One still must do the necessary homework.

5.3 Location: Proximity

In selecting a consultant, one may find that the consultant's office location and the location of the consulting staff may be of great or little importance depending on the type of project and the defined needs. For example, let us suppose that the need is for a consultant to spend a few hours at a time at a facility based on infrequent need and relatively short notice. A typical case might be air sampling or evaluation of a batch process that only operates a few times a year and is scheduled within only a few days or less of its operation. In this type of circumstance it might seem important to have a consultant who is located nearby who can reach the site on short notice at low cost. Close proximity would be important if this were a fundamental task that could be performed by any competent industrial hygienist. However, if this were a very complex situation with extremely expensive or important consequences, one may wish to obtain a national expert regardless of the distance or cost involved. The decision is really based on quality.

Projects that call for periodic scheduled visits may be adequately and cost effectively addressed by either local or remotely stationed consultants. Most consultant firms operating on a regional or national scope can plan scheduled trips in a cost-effective manner that minimizes the impact of distance from job site.

Projects that require an extended stay at the job site may also be cost-effectively handled by either local or remotely stationed consultants. Typically, an on-site study of any duration will have an adequate number of man-hours on site that when travel and living costs are added, the overall percentage for travel and living is not that significant. In such cases, other qualification factors would take precedence over travel and living related expenses, which will probably be less than 10 percent of the project cost.

How would the consultant travel to a facility for on-site work? How long will it take? And, how much will it cost? Travel time and expense is either a part of a consultant's overhead expense or may be directly allocated to a client's project. Finding out the answers to these questions may help evaluate competitive consultants with similar technical qualifications. It is not simply a matter of determining which consultant is physically located closest to the site. The combination of air travel, land travel, and travel time categories of expense should be added together to determine the true cost to a project. For example, a firm located near a major airport may be able to reach a job site more cost effectively than another consultant located much closer, but not having close access to major air traffic networks. It might be less costly in total time expense dollars for someone to fly from 1000 miles away to a job site than for someone else to drive to the job site from 250 miles away.

Some consultants are located in small remote towns where the cost of living and the cost of doing business is less than in major cities. In some instances, this may give that consultant a cost advantage if the assignment is also in that general area. However, if a remotely located consultant must travel a substantial distance to reach an airport and then change planes in a major city to reach a job site, then the cost advantage of low rural overhead will be lost.

Generally, the geographical location of a consultant is one of the less important factors. Travel-related costs usually end up being a relatively small percentage of the total project cost. One is probably better off paying less attention to this factor and focus the selection process more on other qualification criteria.

5.4 Local Customs

What are the implications of bringing in a consultant from outside a local geographic area of the work? There are pros and cons on this issue that vary tremendously with the locale and nature of the problem under study. In many cases, it makes no difference at all. But, for those cases where it might make a difference, let us examine some of the pro and con issues.

In one case, suppose that the need for a consultant is prompted by a emotional or a political issue at a local facility. How would labor and management at that facility relate to a local consultant versus an out-of-towner? This will have to be determined on a case by case basis. In some instances, the out-of-towner might be distrusted and believed not to be sensitive to local issues or customs. In other instances, it might be the opposite, where the out-of-towner might be viewed as being more objective and impartial. The out-of-towner might even be perceived as being more of an expert. There is an old saying that defines an expert as anyone with a briefcase more than 500 miles away from home. This has a lot of truth.

Local customs and local perceptions of out-of-town consultants may not be an important consideration in most instances. However, in other situations, they may be very important and are therefore worth at least some consideration when determining your needs.

6 APPLICATION: HOW TO USE CONSULTANT EFFECTIVELY

Now that a consultant has been selected, one must next take the steps necessary to make maximum use of this resource. In the following discussion, we will outline what the client must do to help make this relationship successful. Too often, clients feel that once they have selected a consultant, their job is done and that good results will automatically fall into place. This is not necessarily so. As with any effective working relationship, there must be effective two-way communication from beginning to end. The degree of success is directly proportional to how well the client and the consultant manage their relationship.

6.1 Setting Goals and Objectives

Goals and objectives must be mutually understood and set forth in writing, in detail, at the very beginning of any project. Even though goals and objectives may have been stated in the original scope of the work or in the consultant's proposal, they should be reviewed and refined prior to beginning work on the project. Goals and objectives should be as specific and measurable as possible. Those that are too general or vague make it difficult to determine when they have been reached. They can become a source of frustration and misunderstanding between the client and consultant.

6.2 Defining Scope of Work

The scope of work should be reviewed and refined prior to beginning work. This should be done even though the scope of work may have been set forth by the client in advance or by the consultant in a proposal. As with goals and objectives, the scope of work should clearly and simply define the specific tasks to be completed. It should be clear to both the consultant and the client exactly what will be done, how it will be done, and when it will be done. There should be no doubt in anyone's mind about how one can tell whether a task has been completed. Specific items such as the areas involved within a facility, processes, number of samples to be collected, number of training sessions, length of time of each session, and other such similar specifics should be put down in writing.

An example of a poor scope of work task would be ''train asbestos workers.'' A better scope of work item would be ''conduct 10 one-hour training sessions on health–safety aspects of working with asbestos for groups of 25 asbestos workers at each session.'' ''Identical training materials may be presented to each group.'' These are only parts of good task descriptions and there would be a good deal more definition covered in the overall scope of work for such a project, at least on that one particular item. It should be clear to both the consultant and the client exactly what is expected. Each would know without question when that particular task was completed since it is specific and measurable. Other tasks in the overall scope of work should be similarly specific. These include what is to be delivered.

6.3 Defining Deliverables

Most consulting assignments will involve a consultant providing a client with some type of tangible, deliverable product. What these items are should be set forth specifically in writing at the onset of the project. For example, if a written monthly report is expected, it should be so specified in writing. The format and the content of the monthly report should be made clear so the consultant knows what is expected of him or her. The client also knows what is expected. Similarly, if some type of formal written report is to be a deliverable, it likewise should be specified as to content and scope. Failure to specifically spell out, in detail, deliverables in advance can cause serious dissatisfaction.

6.4 Interim Progress Reports and Meetings

Any project that is expected to span over several weeks, months, or longer should specify interim progress reports and client consultant meetings. It is imperative the lines of communication be kept open between the consultant and client at all times. By specifying certain reports and meetings, it forces both parties to engage in formal communication about the project.

Meetings with all interested parties can be the most important part of the assignment. This is because it provides for a free exchange of information and ideas.

Meetings and reports need not be long and detailed, but they must communicate. The client needs to know what progress the consultant is making, what the interim findings are showing, what problems have been encountered, and what interim corrective measures the client may wish to take pending final outcome of the project. Surprises are for birthday parties, not consultants' reports. A good client–consultant relationship should result in reports and final conclusions that are mere formalities and formal documentation. The client should be well informed throughout the course of the consulting contract so that there are no surprises to deal with at the end.

6.5 Establishing Milestones and Target Dates

As with interim progress reports and meetings, any project should have preestablished milestones and completion dates. Milestones give both the client and the consultant an opportunity to measure progress and keep on track. It is admittedly difficult to accurately set many types of milestone target dates at the onset of a project. There may be a great many unknowns and variables that complicate setting these dates. Both client and consultant should recognize this but proceed anyway to set dates to the best of their abilities. It is recognized that they may be modified by mutual agreement during the course of the project. Once target dates are set, everyone has something to shoot for. If the date cannot be met due to unforeseen circumstances, it should be rescheduled to a more reasonable date, by mutual agreement between consultant and client. This helps to keep communications open and to keep projects from dragging on indefinitely. Too frequently, this happens when no one takes the initiative to set target dates. Target dates and milestones are necessary tools for controlling project costs as well. It is easy to get overly involved in certain aspects of a project and expend all one's budget of time and money before ever getting through the full scope of the project.

6.6 Clearing the Way

After all agreements have been reached and there is a clear understanding of the project, it is the client's responsibility to clear the way within the organization so the consultant can work successfully. Internal communications are vital. Throughout the course of the project, consultants will no doubt have contacts with many different managers, company officers, workers, and union officials.

Prior to project start-up, a formal notice should be sent to all affected parties informing all personnel of the activities to take place and the names of personnel involved.

Everyone the consultant is likely to contact should be informed in advance with at least some explanation of who the consultant is, what he or she is doing here, and why it is important. Without this type of communication, the consultant will often be viewed with suspicion, as may be the motives of

the organization. People's imaginations and speculation about what consultants are doing can run erroneously rampant.

The consultant will need cooperation to do the job. Part of the communication process should be to inform all those involved what type of information and cooperation the consultant should expect from everyone. If the
nature of the assignment involves interviewing employees on an anonymous
basis, then the organization should reassure all involved this is the case.
Similarly, if there is process information that the client should receive, everyone should know this, such that the consultant can get the needed information freely and expeditiously.

The project will run much more smoothly and efficiently if the client takes
certain steps to help facilitate field work. Planning ahead for those accom-
modations the consultant will need is important. Do not overlook items such
as desk space and a place to store or set up testing equipment. If ladders or
scaffolding are needed for the consultant to reach certain areas of a facility,
make sure these are arranged in advance.

Schedules need to be confirmed to assure any processes or operations
involved will indeed be in progress at the time the consultant is present. Too
frequently, consultants are frustrated and the job delayed because they arrive at a facility only to find that the process or operation to be studied is not
running or operating that day. This is a dreadful waste of time and money
and is easily avoidable. Likewise is the circumstance of a consultant arriving
at a facility only to find that he or she is not expected or there is no one
available to answer questions or show him or her around. A little common
sense and planning can make for a productive and successful working relationship. Everyone has to cooperate.

6.7 The End Result

One gets what one asks for. The deliverables, information, or material provided by a consultant should be no more complete and comprehensive than
what is professionally practical within the purpose, scope, and value of the
project. Observations, findings, results, and conclusions will be based on
conditions apparent at the time. Recommendations with alternates should be
expected to be appropriate with the project terms. It is usually intended
that the client management will assess and analyze recommendations and
deliverables in relation to the client's more intimate knowledge of objectives, resources, and activities. The consultant is, by the very nature of the
relationship, limited in this aspect. The client management needs to recognize this and make decisions accordingly. Only then can proper decisions be
made and appropriate cost-effective actions be implemented.

CHAPTER EIGHTEEN

Professional Working Relationship with Non-Occupational-Health Professionals

M. Chain Robbins

1 INTRODUCTION

Industrial hygiene functions interact with many professionals from disciplines other than occupational health. This chapter is an overview intended to assist the industrial hygiene manager in a manufacturing or service establishment, union, government, academia, trade association foundation, insurance carrier, or consulting organization. Even with the Occupational Safety and Health Association (OSHA) regulatory system in place and a new public awareness of workplace and community health hazards from hazardous substances, some plants are still at risk from life-threatening workplace conditions.

The industrial hygiene manager is a manager of career professionals whose everyday activities interact with many non-occupational-health professionals. Industrial hygienists occasionally may have difficulty in relating this area of knowledge and expertise to the performance of the entire organization. The output of information and ideas of the industrial hygiene program can be most effective only when it becomes the input to other people (1). This requires the users (non-occupational-health professionals) of industrial hygiene output to understand what is being said. In carrying out job-related activities, industrial hygienists use their own special scientific jargon of the profession in reporting results and defining action to be taken by the decision makers. It is then the job of the industrial hygiene manager to ensure that the industrial hygienists realize that these reports and recommendations cannot become effective unless they are understood by the non-occupational-health professionals. The manager is the channel through which the industrial hygienists can direct specific knowledge, work, and talents toward the needs of the larger organization for loss control and cost avoidance.

Many non-occupational-health professionals have little understanding or appreciation of the industrial hygiene profession's role in or contribution to the total loss control program and the prevention of occupational disease. For this reason, the industrial hygiene manager in either the public or private sector is in a unique position to develop an ongoing educational program that lays out to non-occupational-health professionals the consequences of failure to recognize or control occupational health hazards.

Furthermore, during the past decade, a significant change has taken place in the traditional (smokestack) industries in this country with a move toward high-tech and service-oriented industries. This change has also brought about changes in the industrial hygiene profession and the way it is perceived, not only in the prevention of occupational disease but also in many other aspects of the corporation, the unions, government agencies, and the public. The profession has been deeply involved, as it should be, in community right to know, responding to the determination of potential hazards in the high-tech industries and the more subtle aspects of indoor air quality.

Often in the past, the industrial hygienist found that interaction with the non-occupational-health professionals occurred through the safety, medical, or personnel offices where the perception of health hazard evaluation and control may not have been fully understood or acted upon. At least one safety management author (2) has not only ignored the important aspects of occupational health toward total loss control but also has ignored the interrelationships that must (and do) exist among the professionals from other disciplines with the safety and health professionals.

The industrial hygiene manager's relationships with the non-occupational-health professionals must first of all be credible. Any transfer of information and ideas must have a basis in fact supportable with appropriate technical backup, whether it be toxicology, air sampling data, risk analysis, recommended ventilation design, or process changes. Management policy and action flows from information provided from many staff groups. In today's environment in an increasingly litigious society and with public opinion often being shaped by outside forces, the industrial hygiene manager's influence is of growing importance.

Of all the non-occupational-health professionals with whom the industrial hygiene manager must interact, the most important individual (or group of individuals) is senior management. Without a commitment from senior management, both verbally and in writing (health and safety policy), the industrial hygiene function cannot fulfill the professional obligation of adequately providing for the prevention of occupational disease and more broadly to the public health.

The thoughtful industrial hygiene manager, without alarming management, can demonstrate the "good business" of corporate financial planning by including an appropriate level of industrial hygiene activity—whether it be in-house staff or outside consultation support. The industrial hygiene manager will do well to use any past in-house financial losses, including workers' compensation claims or tort actions, as evidence for maintaining or increasing the industrial hygiene level of effort. Lacking this kind of first-hand information, a considerable volume of case histories and case law is excellent support for corporate industrial hygiene efforts. Unlike the safety function, which can "add up" injuries and property losses, it may be more difficult, but not impossible, for the industrial hygiene manager to demonstrate disease prevention and cost avoidance.

If the company or organization does not have a written health and safety policy, it is incumbent on the industrial hygiene manager, in coordination with the safety manager, to prepare such a policy and explain its importance to senior management. The policy should express the corporate commitment to health and safety on the job, outline responsibility, accountability, authority, and the intention to comply with regulations and best practices that apply to workplace health and safety. It is especially important that the policy be *signed* by *senior* management and then communicated through all management levels in both line and staff organizations with instructions that it be further communicated to all employees.

Table 18.1 lists a number of functional areas of responsibility in which the non-occupational-health professionals rely on the industrial hygiene function to assist in discharging these responsibilities. Often the industrial hygiene function is considered a staff function, that is, medical, human resources, and so forth. Ideally, however, considering the importance of industrial hygiene in cost avoidance and the total loss control program, the industrial hygiene manager should report directly to senior management. Nevertheless, the industrial hygiene manager will find it necessary to regularly cross the lines between the company staff and line organizations and

Table 18.1.
Non-Occupational-Health
Professionals
Who Interact with Industrial
Hygiene Function

Human resources/industrial relations
Legal affairs
Environmental affairs
Finance
Engineering
  Product
  Facility
  Manufacturing
Insurance
Purchasing
Public affairs
Marketing and sales
Government
  Emergency services
  Regulatory
  Legislative
Manufacturing
Research
Management information systems
Training
  Employee
  Management development

outside of the company in the discharge of occupational health responsibilities. These relationships with the non-occupational-health professionals have a significant effect on the industrial hygiene manager's everyday activities and the ability to "strive for the goals of protecting employees' health, improving the work environment, and advancing the quality of the profession" (3).

Table 18.2 shows a listing of the non-occupational-health professionals with key words indicating principal areas of interaction with the industrial hygiene manager and inputs that the industrial hygiene function provides to those professionals.

One author (4) points out that the health and safety professional has the staff responsibility to assist line management in fulfilling its responsibility. This is true; however, the industrial hygiene function has responsibilities reaching far beyond serving the line organizations. Probably some of the most significant activities for the industrial hygiene manager are in providing meaningful support and data to the other staff organizations.

Table 18.2. Industrial Hygiene Relationships with Non-Occupational-Health Professionals

Professional Discipline	Relationship Area	Inputs from Industrial Hygiene
Human resources–industrial relations employment–personnel	Recruiting	Position descriptions, professional credentials required for industrial hygiene recruiting
	Employment	Risk areas versus medical restrictions
	Employee placement	Information on teratogen, mutagens, and requirements for employees of childbearing age
	EEO	Interpretations of employee exposure data
	Labor relations	Combustible gas and personal protective equipment training
	Fire protection/security	Disaster planning
		Risk assessment
	Safety	
Legal affairs	Corporate counsel	Risk and exposure data
	Workers' compensation	Employee exposure data
	Product liability	Toxicology, exposure data
	Tort litigation	Toxicology, exposure data, hazard communication
Finance	Budget	Risk assessment, staff and equipment requirements
Insurance	Loss control	Risk assessment
	Workers' compensation	Industrial hygiene staff credentials to control risks
Engineering	Facility	Ventilation, plant process layout requirements
		Indoor air quality
		New facility review
Engineering	Manufacturing	Process control requirements
		New process review

Table 18.2 (*continued*)

Professional Discipline	Relationship Area	Inputs from Industrial Hygiene
Environmental affairs	Process exhaust to atmosphere	Toxicology, air-monitoring data
	Perimeter monitoring	
	Risk assessment	Regulatory requirements
Purchasing	Equipment specifications	Specifications on industrial hygiene and personal protective equipment, subcontractor qualification
Public affairs	Media	Interpretation of toxicologic and monitoring data
	Public	
	Stockholders	Hazard communication
Marketing and sales	Customers	Interpretation of toxicologic and monitoring data
	Public	Hazard communication, material safety data
Government	Legislative	Proposed standards comments
	Regulatory	Monitoring data, risk analysis
	Emergency services	Hazard communication, material safety data
	(Community right-to-know)	
Manufacturing	Employee health	Hazard communication
	Work practices	Controls to prevent exposures
	Personal protection	

Research	New products and processes	Toxicologic data
		Hazard anticipation and communication
		Recommended controls
Management information systems	Recordkeeping	Monitoring data for record retention
	Statistical analysis	Medical record data
	Management presentations	Material safety data sheets
Training	Employee	Hazard communication
	Management development	Instructor participation

2 HUMAN RESOURCES–INDUSTRIAL RELATIONS

Of the non-occupational-health professionals, the human resources–industrial relations group is possibly the staff with whom the industrial hygiene manager has the most interaction. In some organizations, the industrial hygiene staff reports to the human resources–industrial relations executive. Therefore, the relationship obviously must be well defined and understood.

For the acquisition of professional staff, the industrial hygiene manager must provide the recruiting and employment staff with proper position definitions and the educational and experience requirements for industrial hygiene jobs to be filled. It is also important that the hierarchy of jobs in the industrial hygiene function be properly delineated in position descriptions.

Also, for those operations involving exposures to hazardous substances or harmful physical agents, the employment staff needs guidelines or requirements for preemployment physical examinations and information from the industrial hygiene manager on employee placement. This information comes from the industrial hygienist's knowledge of workplace exposures to hazardous substances and would include requirements (both legal and corporate) for information to be provided to the examining physician and proper placement of any new employees with existing medical conditions that might be affected by exposure. This information may in some cases be prepared in coordination with the company physician (or medical consultant). For example, the OSHA asbestos standards 29 CFR 1910.1001 and 1926.58 require that the examining physician (on update annual examinations) be provided with data on the employees asbestos exposure during the previous year and a description of the employees duties as related to asbestos exposure. The industrial hygiene manager should develop with the management information systems staff a system for recording, maintaining, and providing the employee exposure data and job duties to the examining physician.

Often it is necessary to develop employee training and information programs regarding teratogens, carcinogens, mutagens, and their effects on employees of both sexes. The industrial hygiene manager should be knowledgeable of the regulatory requirements and toxicologic information that are to be provided. This may require coordination with company equal employment opportunity (EEO) specialists and other labor relations staff.

In the relationship with the labor relations professionals, the industrial hygiene manager provides information on employee exposures and risks involved in many occupations in the organization. Unfortunately, there may be times when risk information is used by both management and labor in "bargaining" for a position during labor negotiations. The industrial hygiene manager may have the delicate task of treading this mine field, recognizing the responsibility for employees' health on the one hand and possible unrelated demands made by labor or management on the other. Each situation must be judged on a case-by-case basis, and the industrial hygiene manager has to examine his or her conscience to ensure that prevention of occupational disease is the central issue and not wage differentials or other non-occupational-health issues.

Fire protection and security professionals need the professional advice of the industrial hygiene professional in the proper use and interpretation of combustible gas measurement equipment. Also, they need a fundamental understanding of the nature of chemical compatibility and the handling of facility emergencies involving escaping vapors or gases resulting from explosions, fires, or other accidents involving hazardous substances. The industrial hygiene manager might volunteer the industrial hygiene staff professional expertise for training of fire protection and security personnel on the theory, operation, maintenance, and calibration of combustible gas detection equipment. Since these same emergency response personnel would use self-contained respiratory protection equipment, the industrial hygiene staff can assist in defining requirements for training, use, and maintenance of that equipment.

Development of contingency planning for emergencies is important for any facility that has hazardous chemical processes or hazardous waste operations. The industrial hygiene staff should be an integral part of that planning with both staff and line organization. Furthermore, plans should be made for both in-plant and perimeter monitoring in the event of an emergency involving toxic vapor releases. The industrial hygiene manager or a designee should be responsible for declaring plant areas safe for reentry based on monitoring data that has been obtained.

Although some might argue that the safety professional is also an occupational health professional, the degree of professionalism will depend on many factors related to the safety professional's education, training, and experience. Professional safety organizations and some educational institutions' curricula are making significant strides in training the safety professional in the fundamentals of industrial hygiene. The private and public sector industrial hygiene manager will do well to assist in this training and educational effort. The safety professionals are important elements in the loss control team, and the industrial hygiene function can utilize these personnel as eyes and ears in the occupational setting. In fact, the industrial hygienist can become the eyes and ears to the safety function in a total loss control program.

3 LEGAL AFFAIRS

The industrial hygiene manager and staff have significant interaction with a variety of legal professionals. These include in-house corporate attorneys, outside counsel, regulatory agency counsel, insurance, and workers' compensation or plaintiff attorneys.

Depending on the nature of the litigation or technical support required, the industrial hygiene manager must develop information specific for the needs of the attorneys requesting it. Often it will be necessary to "lead" the attorney through an explanation of what industrial hygiene is and how the industrial hygiene information can be used in support of occupational health litigation. Here again, the development and presentation of risk analysis, toxicologic, and air-monitoring data must be factual and in the best interest of employee health.

The industrial hygiene manager should familiarize in-house and workers' compensation attorneys with the meaning and limitations of air-monitoring data including interpretation of results, quality control measures for sampling, and statistical validity of environmental sampling. The familiarization will of course include interpretation of the permissible exposure level concept, toxicity of materials in question, and degree of actual hazard.

Occasionally, a regulatory agency will ask for personal air-sampling data on exposures that the agency may believe are health hazards. Here the industrial hygienist may be dealing with an attorney or (hopefully) another industrial hygiene professional. A face-to-face meeting should be arranged with agency personnel to explain the data, and a written explanation of the meaning and limitations of the results should be provided.

Sometimes the industrial hygiene staff is requested by product liability attorneys to provide information on potential health hazards from consumer use of hazardous materials, which may or may not simulate in-plant production exposures. The industrial hygiene manager needs to develop reliable data on in-plant exposure monitoring and, depending on the scenario involved, interpret the data and its toxicologic significance to the attorney. Data on exposures measured during consumer-simulated use would of course be even more meaningful.

On occasion, the industrial hygiene manager may become involved in tort litigation where an employee is seeking a judgment against an employer—or third party—alleging harm due to chemical exposures or failure to be informed of the hazardous nature of workplace chemicals. The industrial hygiene professional's responsibility here is to conduct a thorough investigation into all of the allegations, including employee interviews, reviewing training records where appropriate, and monitoring results and analytical reports of monitoring data. If the employer will not permit full exercise of the professional obligation, then the industrial hygiene manager must determine a course of action with the tort lawyers that either permits this or withdraw as a professional consultant.

4 FINANCE

The financial professionals may at times appear to be the most difficult to approach with respect to the industrial hygiene function. Generally, these professionals will be seeking budget information on program requirements. If the budget process is through the human resources function, that executive may be the individual whose support is necessary for obtaining industrial hygiene equipment and staff. On the other hand, if the industrial hygiene group stands alone in reporting to top management, then direct interaction with the financial professional (executive) may be necessary.

The financial professional is probably the one professional who has the least understanding of the industrial hygiene (occupational health) function and, therefore, needs the most information. Regulatory actions (inspections and penalties) and criminal court decisions resulting from failures to control health hazards may need to be displayed to financial executives (and other management professionals) to understand the extent and scope of the industrial hygiene function in loss control.

5 PURCHASING

The purchasing organization is an important function with whom the industrial hygiene manager interacts. The purchase of reliable high-quality industrial hygiene equipment is necessary to ensure a quality industrial hygiene program. The purchase of safety equipment such as respiratory and personal protective equipment of high quality is an important function of this organization.

The industrial hygiene manager should provide specifications to the purchasing organization for air-sampling and physical hazard measurement equipment, for respiratory protective equipment, and other personal protective equipment for use against health hazards. Ideally, both purchase specifications and performance requirements should be provided. In the event this is not accomplished, then the industrial hygiene manager should establish a policy for approval before purchase of any sampling equipment or health hazard protective equipment. This is particularly true if the purchasing agent does not perceive the importance of buying specified equipment and buys only from the lowest bidder.

The purchasing department may be an excellent source of information on materials coming into the plant that may have dangerous properties and must have special handling. The industrial hygiene manager should make utmost use of this resource through close liaison with the purchasing department.

The purchasing organization often controls the employment of subcontractors. Guidance on subcontractor health and safety performance requirements before the contracts are signed should be provided to the purchasing professionals.

6 INSURANCE

The insurance professionals, whether they are purchasing corporation workers' compensation and general liability insurance or underwriting an industrial hygiene consulting firm, are an important interactive function for the industrial hygiene manager. The manager should provide risk assessment information on processes, facilities, and employees to the insurance professionals. Also, importantly, the manager should provide the insurance organization with details on credentials of the industrial hygiene staff. This information is important to the insurance underwriters in judging the corporation's ability to control risks.

7 ENGINEERING

Facility engineering in many companies has a responsibility for planning and layout of plant facilities and process operations. The industrial hygiene manager has a responsibility to provide ventilation design specifications, either directly or by reference. Also, processes and hazardous materials need to be identified and the required control measures spelled out to avoid any costly retrofits. An area that is sometimes overlooked is preventive maintenance requirements to ensure ventilation systems and processes continue to operate as designed.

Manufacturing engineering is often responsible for design of production processes and their integration into the manufacturing facility. Close industrial hygiene coordination with these professionals on process operations and proper design for health protection will (as with facility engineers) often avoid the need for costly changes after installation. Regulatory requirements affecting employee health related to the processes should be provided at an early stage in manufacturing process development or anticipated changes.

8 PUBLIC AFFAIRS

The public affairs professional explains to the public, stockholders, media, or government agencies the company position on corporate events involving hazardous substances or harmful physical agents. These events could be plant chemical process leaks, explosions, public use of distributed products, or transportation or disposal accidents involving hazardous substances. Generally, the public affairs professional is not technically oriented and for that reason it is important for the industrial hygiene manager to provide in-depth support on those occasions when hazardous substances are involved. There should be an understanding with the public affairs office that the industrial hygiene manager will be consulted before public release of information on employee or public exposures to hazardous substances either in the course of normal plant operations or resulting from an accident. The industrial hygiene manager must ensure that the communicated information is accurate and truthful to assure credibility with the public and government.

The legislative affairs professional is involved in providing positions (corporate or union) to legislative staffs at local and national levels on pending legislation and rulemaking proceedings. The industrial hygiene manager should provide the legislative affairs office with appropriate occupational health analysis of proposed legislation and rulemaking, the impact on employee health, and the company's (or union's) responsibility if the legislation becomes effective.

9 MARKETING AND SALES

The marketing and sales professionals need the benefit of industrial hygiene expertise when sales of company products (or services) involve hazardous substances. The industrial hygiene manager should develop a program to "educate" marketing and sales staffs on potential hazards with the use of company products or services. The implementation of the OSHA Hazard Communication Standard 29 CFR 1910.1200 has brought a new dimension to the industrial hygiene function. The industrial hygiene manager must provide hazard communication information not only to the in-plant organizations but also to marketing and sales staffs to assist these professionals in understanding the requirements of the standard on shipped products, especially the development of material safety data sheets (MSDS).

10 GOVERNMENT

Numerous state and local government public safety services, including fire departments, emergency medical teams, police, and hazardous material teams, are turning to the industrial hygiene professionals for assistance. State and community right-to-know laws are now mandating that employers provide to these public service agencies hazardous substance identification, location and quantities in storage, and use on company premises. In turn, these emergency service personnel need considerable information on detection, personal protection, reactivity, and compatibility for hazardous substances. The industrial hygiene manager needs to review requirements incumbent on the operations for which he or she has knowledge and provide the expertise and information to these public safety agencies.

The industrial hygienist will almost certainly be called upon to deal with regulatory agency professionals on inspections, opening, closing, and informal conferences, and possibly to testify before administrative law judges on contested citations. Some of these professionals may not be occupational health specialists, and the industrial hygienist is in the position of having to provide and explain information on worker exposures, plant processes, or company processes involving worker exposures to hazardous substances.

The industrial hygiene manager should develop written procedures to which the industrial hygiene staff and company personnel must adhere in the course of regulatory interfaces (inspections) involving occupational health. This is important so that the regulatory contacts are controlled and only one person or organization speaks for the company.

In dealing with members of legislative bodies and their staffs or local government officials, the issues for discussion should be clearly defined. These professionals are often looking for technical information on employee or public health. The industrial hygiene manager should assure that any data developed is credible and is used in a proper context and not for political purposes.

11 ENVIRONMENTAL AFFAIRS

The environmental affairs professional is responsible for ensuring establishment compliance with community air quality standards, permitting, and coordination with environmental regulatory agencies. Recently, the Environmental Protection Agency (EPA) has been granted broad authority by Congress to become more involved in occupational health matters. This brings the industrial hygiene professional into a close relationship with the environmental affairs function. The industrial hygiene manager should provide and interpret for the environmental specialist toxicologic data, the potential for exposures to hazardous substances (both in-plant and community), air-sampling methodology, and risk assessments where appropriate. An important interface is the area of plant process ventilation, stack sampling, and agreement on process controls that meet both employee health standards and the community air quality standards.

12 MANUFACTURING

Interactions with the manufacturing professionals involves all levels of management from first-line supervisors to a vice president. For those nonmanufacturing organizations (government, services, etc.), the line operating management is the counterpart of a manufacturing organization. The industrial hygiene function is in a continual relationship with these managers, providing guidance and data for health hazard controls. Generally, employee communications will be through the operating supervisors. As noted earlier, the translation of employee exposure monitoring results, their implications, and control requirements into meaningful information for management action is extremely important.

13 RESEARCH

The extent of the research function and its hazards will depend on the nature of the industry and the amount of basic or applied research conducted.

Research professionals on occasion may have attitudes that health and safety professionals are not important to research activities and may even resent attempts by the industrial hygiene professional to conduct risk analyses on research programs. For this reason, it is necessary for the industrial hygiene manager to develop information on risk analyses and controls required and the importance for the research facility to be in compliance with regulatory requirements and best practices to minimize potential losses. An organization's research function is highly visible to the public and the stockholders, and failures or losses reflect badly on the corporate image. Although highly educated research personnel will usually have knowledge of physical and chemical properties of many hazardous substances, they may not understand or appreciate the toxicology of or precautions necessary for hazardous materials used in the laboratory. The industrial hygiene function should become an integral part of the research department's planning and development activity to include industrial hygiene involvement in laboratory and process layout, ventilation design and maintenance, employee hazard communication training, hazardous waste management, and emergency procedures.

14 MANAGEMENT INFORMATION SYSTEMS

The management information systems (MIS) professional provides a vital service to the industrial hygiene function. The industrial hygiene manager must work closely with the MIS professionals to provide the appropriate inputs for the desired record collection and retention and statistical outputs for many purposes. These include, but are not limited to the following activities:

1. Recording and maintaining environmental sampling data and information associated with it, for example, equipment type, calibration data, flow rates, contaminant levels observed, employees' names, and plant location.
2. Integration of environmental sampling results observed and illness information into the employee medical records system.
3. Maintaining the exposure records to meet legal requirements and for ready accessibility to employees and regulatory agencies, for statistical studies, and so on.
4. Recording and maintaining material safety data sheets (MSDS) for ready access to employees and loss control professionals.

The industrial hygiene manager should insist that the management information system be both accurate and timely. Furthermore, there should be documented programming to ensure the longevity of an information data base (5). Standard note taking and the programming instruction should be understandable by any successive series of programmers. Fischoff and Freiberger's discussion (5) on data automation provides the industrial hygiene manager with excellent guidance on this subject.

Although data automation is necessary for the reasons noted above, it is also important for the industrial hygiene manager to access the data for management presentations at all levels and for predicting trends and focusing on areas of unusual risk.

15 TRAINING

Of the many non-occupational-health professionals with whom the industrial hygiene function interacts, the employee training professional is a very important one. It is through the training professional that hazard information (both company and regulatory requirements) is conveyed to employees and supervisors alike. The industrial hygiene manager should develop the hazard information that needs to be communicated and seek out the training professional to assist in preparing course outlines and assist the industrial hygiene function in training techniques to present the information.

Any management development program is not complete without the inclusion of a segment on loss control, including the importance of occupational health. The industrial hygiene manager should plan with the training professional an appropriate agenda for the management development program that addresses the consequences for failure to invoke a total loss control program. The agenda would also include cost benefits of the occupational health program and management's involvement in it.

REFERENCES

1. P. F. Drucker, *People and Performance: The Best of Peter Ducker on Management,* New York: Harper & Row, 1977.
2. D. Peterson, *Techniques of Safety Managers,* New York: McGraw-Hill, 1978.
3. *Code of Ethics for the Professional Practice of Industrial Hygiene,* Akron, OH: AIHA Board of Directors, 1981.
4. D. P. Bridge, *J. Am. Ind. Hyg. Assoc.* **40,** 255–263 (1979).
5. R. L. Fischoff and F. G. Freiberger, "Data Automation," in *Patty's Industrial Hygiene and Toxicology,* Vol. IIIA, New York: Wiley, 1985, p. 279.

CHAPTER NINETEEN

Recruiting

Howard J. Cohen

1   INTRODUCTION

If an organization's personnel is its most valuable resource, then recruiting those personnel is the lifeline of that organization. Industrial hygiene recruiting will vary depending on the type of position being filled and the organization. Generally, the types of positions are either in the laboratory analyzing samples or in the field sampling, evaluating, and recommending controls. These positions can be as a staff member, a manager, or a technician. Other areas may include working in product safety groups, safety, or environmental organizations. Clearly, the type of position to be filled will influence the recruiting process. The type of organization recruiting may also influence the recruiting process. Government organizations and some private corporations may make a great effort to hire a candidate from within their existing structure. Corporate staffs that are well established may know exactly the type of candidate they are looking for, while a company hiring its first industrial hygienist may have no idea of what is needed. In reading this chapter, keep in mind that several of the ideas or steps may need to be modified or eliminated to suit particular needs.

The purpose of recruiting is always to fill a position either newly created or vacated by the promotion or departure of an employee. The skills for most industrial hygiene positions will be highly specialized. The need for highly developed skills will be dependent on whether the opening is for an entry-level or senior position. It is also important, when hiring, to determine whether the individual will be expected to advance or whether the position is stationary.

1.1   Recruiting Procedures

Recruiting involves the following steps:

Searching for Candidates.
The more candidates the better, and there are never too many. It is better to say sorry many times then to have no one to fill a position.

Identifying Position Requirements.
A number of steps must be taken to establish the skills, education, and responsibility of the position. These requirements will determine the salary range.

Initial Screening.
Applicants must have their qualifications compared to the position requirements. This step identifies candidates who meet the minimum requirements of the job and who may warrant an interview.

Conducting a Comprehensive Interview.
It takes a well-planned and efficient interview to evaluate a candidate and to allow the candidate to evaluate the organization to which she or he is applying for work.

Candidate Evaluation.
This includes reviewing an applicant's abilities, personal characteristics, work history, education, and references to determine whom to hire. This process often involves the input of many individuals in the organization.

Selection and Offer.
Hopefully this concludes the process and results in a successful hiring. Otherwise, the recruiting process must start all over.

1.2 Recruiting Costs

Any organization attempts to be efficient and reduce its costs. This same principle applies to recruiting, and it is worth reviewing these costs. There are direct costs, which include advertising, administrative work, relocation, and training a new recruit. These obvious costs can be planned and budgeted. The indirect costs are the result of bad recruiting and include a low quality of work produced, reduction in productivity, a disruption of the organization, and, ultimately, a repeat of all the direct costs. It should be remembered that good people are hard to get. This is because the search involves looking for a person with very specialized skills and the right personality. Also, good companies do not easily give up good employees.

2 EQUAL EMPLOYMENT OPPORTUNITY REQUIREMENTS

There are a variety of laws, regulations, and federal guidelines designed to ensure equal employment opportunity (EEO) for all persons regardless of race, color, religion, ethnic origin, sex, or age. Substantial financial penalties exist for noncompliance with these laws. This section reviews basic requirements and how they affect the recruiting process.

2.1 Applicable Regulations

EEO Act of 1972.
This act affects all private employers with more than 15 employees, all educational institutions, state and local governments, labor unions with more than 15 employees, and joint labor and management committees. The act establishes a commission to investigate discrimination charges and attempts to reconcile differences. It also enables individuals to sue an employer for back pay, damage, and legal fees. There are guidelines published by the federal government to assist employers in maintaining compliance with the act.

Executive Orders 11246 and 11375 and Revised Orders 4 and 14.
These orders affect all contractors or subcontractors who have federal contracts in excess of $50,000 or who employ more than 50 persons.

These orders prohibit job discrimination and require the development of an Affirmative Action Plan (AAP). AAPs set specific goals and timetables for the employer to reach that goal. AAPs are designed to increase employment for all levels of minorities and women in order to remedy past discrimination. AAPs are audited by the government on a regular basis. The penalty for not complying with these orders may include the cancellation of an organization's government contact.

Equal Pay Act of 1963.

This act requires that equal pay be given to men and women who perform similar work. The Department of Labor has responsibility for enforcing this act. Employers who are found to be in violation of this act are required to make substantial back payment awards to the affected employees.

Age Discrimination Act of 1967.

This act prohibits the discrimination of individuals who are over age 40. The Department of Labor has responsibility for enforcing this act.

Rehabilitation Act of 1973.

This act affects companies with federal contracts in excess of $50,000 or who have more than 50 employees. The act requires the employer to take affirmative action to employ and advance qualified individuals with disabilities. The employer must take reasonable steps to accommodate employees or applicants with physical or mental limitations. An organization is exempt if it can demonstrate that the accommodations would impose undue financial hardship in the conduct of its business.

2.2 Relationship of EEO Regulations to Recruiting

The purpose of these regulations is to allow all groups in the labor force an equal opportunity to compete for jobs at all levels, unless a business necessity dictates otherwise. The burden of proof is on the employer to show why it is not in compliance. Company labor statistics are used to evaluate compliance with EEO regulations. Good intentions mean very little if the end result of the effort is not good employment practices. The EEO regulations require the following:

Job specifications must not require excessive or unnecessary qualifications. This includes excess education or unnecessary experience requirements.

An extra effort and expense must be made to seek out and recruit minorities.

The organization must develop and keep accurate records to document the date of an application, the applicant's name, sex, minority group, the position being applied for, the final disposition of the applicant (hired or rejected), and the recruiting source.

Most large organizations have written policies to assure compliance with its goals. The personnel department is usually responsible for enforcing compliance with these policies. Since industrial hygiene positions often require specialized technical skills, standard recruiting efforts to obtain minorities may not be fruitful. This does not exempt the industrial hygiene group and places even more responsibility on the recordkeeping of its applicants to demonstrate that job discrimination is not condoned.

3 SPECIFYING THE POSITION

The most basic requirement in recruiting is to define the job that is to be filled. If it is a new position, a thorough analysis of the job requirements will be necessary. When filling a job that previously existed, it is often still worthwhile to determine if the requirements should be modified.

3.1 Job Analysis

Analyze the requirements of the job and list its specifications. Several items similar to all jobs should be reviewed:

- Define the activities of the job. This may be analyzing samples in a laboratory, performing industrial hygiene surveys, preparing material safety data sheets, consulting clients, testifying on the company's behalf on lawsuits, or working to reduce the liability of products the company sells.
- Determine the responsibilities of the position. This may include supervising technicians or other professionals. Consider the individual's position within the organization. This will have a substantial bearing on the salary range for the position.
- List the specialized skills required in this position. This may include ability to calibrate or repair pumps, operate intricate analytical instrumentation, or have a thorough knowledge of Occupational Health and Safety Administration (OSHA) health standards. Additional expertise in ventilation, personal protective equipment, or noise abatement may be needed.
- Carefully evaluate the educational requirements for the job. A high school diploma may be adequate for some technician positions, while most may require a baccalaureate degree in biology or chemistry. A master's degree is usually required if the position requires formal course work in industrial hygiene. It may also be appropriate to list a number of specialized courses needed, including ventilation control, noise monitoring and abatement, and toxicology. Do not add more educational requirements than the job requires. This would be in violation of EEO regulations and also might result in hiring an individual who is not adequately challenged by the position.

- Determine what certifications are required for the position. This may include certification in comprehensive practice of industrial hygiene, industrial hygiene chemistry, toxicology, or safety. It may be important to have technicians who are certified as a safety and health technologist. Often an applicant may not be required to be certified, but it may be desirable to have the individual qualified to sit for the examination. This is especially important when the next step in their advancement requires certification.

- Evaluate how much overnight travel is needed to perform the job. Typically, more than 35–40 percent travel may be difficult for an individual with family obligations. Therefore, the amount of travel may need to be shared by another employee. There are some applicants who might not object to a great deal of travel. Nevertheless, it is important to know the travel requirements and to present them to applicants accurately. Otherwise, a well-qualified new employee may leave or a serious morale problem may arise.

- Good oral communication is required of many jobs that involve interfacing with employees, management, researchers, and customers. Some applicants might be well suited for communicating with company employees but not management. Lack of such skills might be fine for a technician but terrible for a manager. Some industrial hygiene chemistry jobs may not require the oral communication skills needed by a consultant.

- Determine what type of written communication skills are required. Skills will vary depending on whether the job requires filling out industrial hygiene sampling sheets or making recommendations for controlling exposures in a plant. The skills required will also vary depending on whether reports are prepared for internal use or for customers or regulatory agencies. The knowledge of certain computer software programs may also be a requirement for some jobs.

The job analysis must result in some determination of the net worth of the job in relation to other jobs within the company and to similar positions outside the company. The position must have a salary range that allows top candidates to be competitively recruited and at the same time does not cause problems with the salaries of current employees. This is often a very difficult task, especially in times of high inflation or when there is a surplus of jobs and scarcity of good candidates. It is not unusual to find that a new college recruit with a master's degree in industrial hygiene and no experience is demanding a salary similar to an industrial hygienist hired 3 or 4 years ago with the same qualifications. Salary differences will also exist depending on the cost of living for the geographic location and the type of industry.

3.2 Job Description

The next step is to write a job description. This typically is kept and approved by the personnel department. Prospective employees should be shown a copy of the job description. There should be separate job descriptions for all levels of jobs such as industrial hygienist, senior industrial hygienist, manager of industrial hygiene, and director of industrial hygiene. Salary ranges for all these positions should be established. Several items should be added to the job description from the job specifications:

The responsibility and authority for the position. The employee may be required to represent the company to customers, conduct exit interviews with plant managers, or halt production if an imminent health hazard exists. The job description may include authority to purchase equipment, sign expense reports, or hire other employees.

The degree of independent judgment and initiative required. The job may involve adherence to rigid protocols for sampling or analyzing samples. It may also require developing new analytical methods or solving complex exposure problems.

The level of supervision required. Technician level and some laboratory and industrial hygiene positions may be supervised most of the time. Positions that require travel, representing the company at regulatory meetings, or serving as the sole industrial hygienist at a facility will require the applicant to work well with very little supervision.

The potential for job advancement. An applicant is often hired with the thought of replacing another employee, often a supervisor, who is expected to retire or be promoted in the near to immediate future. This applicant will need to have the skills to perform the work of the supervisor. There are also positions available that have little or no opportunity for job advancement. This is often the case for positions at the manager or director level.

3.3 Job Specifications

The critical items of the job description should be summarized in order to advertise the position effectively. A distinction should be made between the minimum skills and education required and skills that would enhance the desirability of a candidate. The job requirements specified in an advertisement should include: the duration and type of work experience, level of education, certification(s), specialized skills, and a salary range. Indicate the specific job title and whether it is an entry-or senior-level position. Standard phrases such as ''good oral and written communication skills required'' add very little to the job specification.

4 RECRUITING

The goal of recruiting is to attract as many qualified candidates for the job opening as possible. Recruiting is tied to the economy: when economic times are good, it is difficult to recruit candidates; when the economy is bad, it is easy to recruit. Again, it should be mentioned that good candidates are hard to recruit because

Employers do not let good employees go.

The current regulatory pressures are increasing the need for industrial hygienists.

Only a limited pool of qualified applicants exists. There are only 3000–4000 certified industrial hygienists. Perhaps only 10 percent of that number are actively in the job market. A large number of those individuals may not find the salary being offered attractive or desire to move to the geographic area of the job. If additional specialized skills are required, even fewer applicants are available.

4.1 Fundamentals of Recruiting

- A large number of applicants should be sought for any position. Statistically, the more applicants available, the better the probability of filling the position. There is no such thing as too many applicants, although there often is the problem of too many unqualified applicants.
- Do not compromise on the requirements for the position. There are often pressures to fill a position in an unrealistic time frame due to budgets, new contracts, or regulatory requirements. However, hiring the wrong candidate will usually be worse than hiring no candidate.
- Most companies consider recruiting programs to be ongoing, even when the number of job openings are few. This is clearly not the case for industrial hygiene programs, where the opportunity to hire is very sporadic because of the small number of industrial hygiene personnel in most organizations. Several steps can be taken to make recruiting easier. These include developing ties at universities with respected industrial hygiene programs, being active in professional committee work to increase the number of industrial hygiene contacts, and attending major industrial hygiene conferences on a regular basis to maintain contacts with fellow professionals.
- Good recruiting should be creative, imaginative, and innovative. A recruiter is a combination of a marketing specialist and salesperson.

4.2 Recruiting Sources

4.2.1 Referrals. Recommendations and referrals can often be obtained from colleagues. Speak to persons who recently filled a position. They may have candidates whom they chose not to hire but who would be well qualified for a different type of job. There may also be individuals interested in transferring to a different geographic area and cannot do so with their current employer.

4.2.2 *Professional Associations*

- The American Industrial Hygiene Association (AIHA) runs an ongoing employment service. For a relatively small fee, the AIHA will send resumes of candidates who are actively looking for jobs. The AIHA screens candidates and sends out only those resumes that meet the requirements of the job specification. If no candidate is suitable from their initial inventory of resumes, the AIHA will continue to send resumes as they become available until advised otherwise. There is a small additional fee charged if a candidate is hired as a result of their service. The advantage of this service is that you can receive information on prospective candidates within 3 to 4 weeks and begin your recruiting quickly.
- The American Industrial Hygiene Conference offers a free employment service each year at the annual meeting. There are several ways to learn about candidates seeking industrial hygiene positions. Candidates are allowed to post a resume, and these are grouped together based on the number of years experience in the field. Information on applicants can be summarized, and they can be contacted after the conference. Employers are also given an opportunity to post a copy of their position, and these are also organized by the number of years of experience being required. Employers who post jobs can either indicate an individual to contact after the conference, a local contact for meeting during the conference, or can take advantage of free rooms offered by the employment service for interviewing applicants. The latter is accomplished by indicating times that a representative of the employer is available for interviewing candidates. A sign-up sheet is then filled out by candidates who desire an interview. Interviews are often limited to 30 minutes.

The advantage of using the employment service is that advertising and screening of applicants can be done free of charge. The disadvantages are that it is only available at the conference, which usually occurs in late May or early June. This may not coincide with the time frame needed to fill a position. The other disadvantage is that a substantial percentage of unqualified candidates may choose to have an interview if a sign-up sheet is used, since the interviewing is at the discretion of the candidate and not the employer.

- Advertising in the *American Industrial Hygiene Association Journal* or *Journal of Applied Industrial Hygiene* will communicate a job opening to nearly every professional engaged in industrial hygiene. The disadvantage of this type of recruiting is that there is typically a delay of 2–4 months to get an announcement printed in a journal issue.
- Local sections of the American Industrial Hygiene Association also provide a good opportunity to communicate the availability of a posi-

tion. This can be done by word of mouth or sometimes through an employment service offered by the local section, usually free of charge.

- Mailing labels can be purchased from several professional associations. This is usually not a cost-effective approach since thousands of mailings will be required and only a small percentage of those receiving a mailing will be interested in the position. This approach may make sense for very large organizations that have numerous openings to fill.

4.2.3 Employment Agencies. Employment agencies charge a large fee for their service, typically around 10 percent of the candidates annual salary. The fee is paid by the employer, but only when a candidate has been hired. The problem with using employment services is that few of them are familiar with the industrial hygiene profession. If an employment service is retained to find candidates, be convinced that the counselor assigned is thoroughly knowledgeable about the field and the requirements of the job. To avoid wasting a lot of time screening unqualified applicants, indicate that the resumes of only 5–10 candidates will be reviewed. This will force the counselor to screen applicants carefully. Also, indicate the time frame that the counselor has to work with. This will give the assignment some priority, but do not set an unrealistic time frame that will prohibit the counselor from doing an adequate search. The use of an employment service is best for organizations that have no industrial hygiene personnel, or when the opening involves the top position in the organization. Otherwise, it may be just as efficient to conduct a search without an employment agency's assistance.

4.2.4 Newspaper Advertising. Newspapers can be an effective media of advertising for industrial hygiene positions. The advantage of this approach is that it is quick, and you can get results in a week or two. When recruiting professional-level positions, use newspapers that are widely circulated through the nation, such as the *Wall Street Journal,* or *New York Times.* If the position is a technician-level job, for which the company may not be willing to relocate an individual, the use of local newspapers is preferred. There are some basic rules for advertising in newspapers.

It is usually better to advertise with a company name and logo, since some individuals will not respond to an unidentified box number.

Describe the job in detail, including location, education requirements, job skills necessary, travel requirements (if applicable), job title, and salary range.

Indicate that interested candidates should send resumes to the personnel department. This department can screen out those applicants who clearly do not meet the minimum requirements of the position. If quicker results are desired, allow applicants the option of contacting a representative of the personnel department by telephone.

4.2.5 College Recruiting. Recruiting applicants who are in the process of graduating is common practice for filling entry-level positions. The chief problem with college recruiting is that a job opening must be known well in advance or you must be willing to wait many months to fill the position. When searching for industrial hygienists from graduate school, recruiting must begin in the winter months to ensure a good selection of candidates. Job offers are common by late winter or early spring, 2 months prior to graduation. To advertise a job opening at a university, write to the department head of a program and ask to have the position posted. Candidates interested in the position can then send a resume. A better approach is to ask the department chairperson if personal interviews could be arranged. This allows a large number of potential applicants to be efficiently screened.

Successful recruiting at a university involves making an effort to learn about the curriculum, its professors, and the quality of its students. All graduation. To advertise a job opening at a university, write to the department head of a program and ask to have the position posted. Candidates interested in the position can then send a resume. A better approach is to ask the department chairperson if personal interviews could be arranged. This allows a large number of potential applicants to be efficiently screened.

4.3   Internal Recruiting

Many companies and government agencies have programs that advertise for jobs among their own employees. Sometimes this approach must be taken before any other recruiting methods are used. This has become especially prevalent when companies trim their workforce and prefer to avoid laying off an employee if these skills can be used in a different job. The advantages of internal recruiting are that the applicant knows the company, personnel structure, and methods of operation. Another advantage is that a great deal of information concerning the employee's past performance and ability to perform well alongside others can be easily obtained. The disadvantages are that the employee may not have the skills necessary to perform the job. Often there are significant pressures to transfer such an employee, and this should be avoided except for technician-level positions. Another disadvantage is that the current employee is usually making far more money than his or her skills are worth when transferred to an industrial hygiene position. Also, training costs will be similar to those needed for entry-level positions. New employees who come from other companies often bring novel ideas for solving problems. These ideas are usually not available with transferred employees. In general, recruiting applicants from within an organization works well when promoting plant positions to the corporate or division level or when seeking a supervisor or manager. Otherwise, this approach will seldom work for professional-level positions and will slow the recruiting process.

5   SCREENING APPLICANTS

Prior to interviewing candidates, it is essential to screen the applicants. This is done to compare the qualifications of the applicant with the requirements of the job specification. Screening eliminates time and money wasted conducting interviews with unqualified candidates. It also allows applicants who are not going to receive consideration for the position to be promptly notified, so that they can consider other positions.

5.1   Screening Methods

5.1.1 The Resume. Reviewing the candidate's resume will quickly reveal educational accomplishments, certifications, and work history. These can be compared to the job specification and a determination made whether the candidate is qualified, under qualified, or overqualified.

5.1.2 The Application Form. Application forms are often not used for professional positions, but they are better than resumes in eliciting information quickly. A typical application form is shown in Figure 19.1. The following are advantages of using application forms:

> The forms require an applicant to list all jobs in chronological sequence. An erratic job history may be revealed better than in a resume, where an applicant may choose not to list jobs of short duration.
>
> Gaps in working, where the applicant has been unemployed, will also be revealed.
>
> A history of an applicant's salary will be revealed in an application form. A steady rise in salary is usually indicative of good performance with increasing responsibility. A salary increase that reflects only the effects of inflation may be indicative of a marginal employee.
>
> The reasons for leaving past jobs may indicate problems with job satisfaction or personality conflicts with supervisors.
>
> Any disability or health problem that would prohibit the applicant performing the job would also be stated.

5.1.3 Telephone Screening. Telephone screening is used after applicants have had their resumes and job applications reviewed. Applicants are usually called at home after business hours to avoid disturbing their work and allowing them to keep their search confidential. The conversation could include the following elements:

AN EQUAL OPPORTUNITY EMPLOYER M/F/H/V **EMPLOYMENT APPLICATION** (Please Print or Type)

PERSONAL

NAME	(LAST, FIRST, MIDDLE)		SOCIAL SECURITY NO.
ADDRESS NUMBER STREET	CITY	STATE ZIP CODE	TELEPHONE NO.

HAVE YOU EVER BEEN EMPLOYED BY OLIN OR ANY OF ITS SUBSIDIARIES, GROUPS OR PREDECESSOR COMPANIES?
☐ YES ☐ NO

IF YES GIVE DATES, POSITIONS AND NAMES IF DIFFERENT FROM ABOVE:

ARE YOU A U.S. CITIZEN? IF NOT, WHAT IS YOUR VISA TYPE AND NUMBER.
☐ YES ☐ NO

REFERRED TO OLIN BY:
☐ EMPLOYEE ☐ AGENCY ☐ ADVERTISEMENT ☐ COLLEGE/SCHOOL
☐ WALK-IN ☐ OTHER (Explain)

HAVE YOU EVER BEEN CONVICTED OF ANY LAW VIOLATION OTHER THAN MINOR TRAFFIC VIOLATIONS?
☐ YES ☐ NO

IF YES, PLEASE GIVE DETAILS

POSITION APPLIED FOR:

EDUCATION

SCHOOL NAME AND LOCATION	DATES	DID YOU GRADUATE?	DEGREE	MAJOR COURSES OF STUDY
HIGH SCHOOL	FROM TO	☐ YES ☐ NO YEAR		
COLLEGE	FROM TO	☐ YES ☐ NO YEAR		
POST GRADUATE	FROM TO	☐ YES ☐ NO YEAR		
OTHER	FROM TO	☐ YES ☐ NO YEAR		

EMPLOYMENT HISTORY

(PLEASE LIST ALL EMPLOYMENT STARTING WITH MOST RECENT ONE — ACCOUNT FOR ALL PERIODS INCLUDING UNEMPLOYMENT AND MILITARY SERVICE — USE ADDITIONAL SHEET IF NECESSARY)

EMPLOYER/JOB TITLE	EMPLOYMENT DATES & SALARY	MAJOR DUTIES/SUPERVISOR'S NAME	REASON FOR LEAVING
NAME & ADDRESS	FROM TO / STARTING SALARY	MAJOR DUTIES	REASON FOR LEAVING
JOB TITLE	LAST SALARY	SUPERVISOR'S NAME/TITLE	
NAME & ADDRESS	FROM TO / STARTING SALARY	MAJOR DUTIES	REASON FOR LEAVING
JOB TITLE	LAST SALARY	SUPERVISOR'S NAME/TITLE	
NAME & ADDRESS	FROM TO / STARTING SALARY	MAJOR DUTIES	REASON FOR LEAVING
JOB TITLE	LAST SALARY	SUPERVISOR'S NAME/TITLE	
NAME & ADDRESS	FROM TO / STARTING SALARY	MAJOR DUTIES	REASON FOR LEAVING
JOB TITLE	LAST SALARY	SUPERVISOR'S NAME/TITLE	
NAME & ADDRESS	FROM TO / STARTING SALARY	MAJOR DUTIES	REASON FOR LEAVING
JOB TITLE	LAST SALARY	SUPERVISOR'S NAME/TITLE	

OC 1300 REV 9/86

Figure 19.1. Example of employment application. (Reproduced with permission of Olin Corp.)

333

Several brief opening remarks, including who is calling and the purpose of the conversation.

A description of the job in some detail, including the company and its organization, the reporting scheme of the job, and travel requirement (if any).

The type of personality characteristics and traits needed to perform the job.

The geographic location of the job. A description of housing costs and recreational activities available may be necessary if the applicant is unfamiliar with the area.

Review of the salary range for the position and major company compensations.

Allowing the applicant to discuss him or herself and interest in the position. This also allows for an initial determination of the applicant's personality.

If the applicant is interested in the position and appears to be a competitive candidate, discuss specific dates for an interview. The prospective employer will be expected to pay all costs for the interview and should arrange for airline tickets, if required, to be issued to the company and sent to the applicant. The candidate can be asked to pay for other expenses (e.g., mileage, hotel, and food) as they are incurred and to be reimbursed after the interview by filling out an expense report. The prospective employer should make all arrangements, including hotels and transportation for the applicant. Normally, this is done by the personnel department.

5.1.4 Visual Screening. Visual screening can be done and is preferred to a telephone conversation. A candidate can be asked to spend 30 to 60 minutes discussing the subjects described in telephone screening. The advantages are that the candidates' appearance and manner can be examined in addition to their personality. This method works well if the candidate lives within commuting distance from the interview. This is usually the case when recruiting from the local area but is seldom the situation when a professional-level position is being filled.

6   THE INTERVIEW

The interview is the most critical step in recruiting. If it is not done thoroughly, a candidate's capabilities may not be recognized and an opportunity to hire an excellent candidate is lost. Worse yet, when a candidate's shortcomings are not adequately identified an unqualified candidate is hired. The interview is also a two-way exchange of information, and the candidate must have an opportunity to evaluate a prospective employer. If the candidate is not satisfied, an opportunity is lost to hire the individual. If the candidate is not properly informed about the job, he or she may accept it and leave shortly after, re-creating a vacancy and causing disruption.

6.1 Preparation

The interviewer(s) must take time to prepare for the interview. All individuals who are expected to meet and interview the candidate must be available on the date of the interview. Often it is impossible to have everyone available to meet the applicant, but the critical interviewers should be available. These include the managers or directors of the department to which industrial hygiene reports. Also desirable are other employees in the department and managers of departments that interface closely with industrial hygiene, such as safety, medical, environmental affairs, and toxicology. Copies of the applicant's resume and job specifications should be given to each member of the interview team prior to the interview. The following should be reviewed:

6.1.1 Personal Background Information. Information concerning the applicant's interests and family are excellent areas to begin the interview and relax the candidate. The applicant's family (if any) and their willingness to relocate are important areas to explore. An ideal candidate is of little value if he or she will not consider the position because of a reluctance of the family to relocate.

6.1.2 Education. Review copies of the applicant's transcripts. Look for deficiencies or poor grades in subjects that are critical to good job performance. Any deficiencies should be discussed with the candidate during the interview.

6.1.3 Work Experience. Review the candidate's resume and application and look for areas where the candidate may have insufficient work experience. Any potential problems should be discussed during the interview to establish that the candidate is capable of successfully performing the required tasks of the position.

6.1.4 Gaps in Work Experience. All gaps in time when the candidate was out of work should be thoroughly explored. Employers look for hard-working employees, and periods of unemployment may represent times when the applicant did not aggressively seek work.

6.1.5 Reasons for Leaving Past Jobs. Review the candidate's reasons for leaving past jobs along with reasons for his or her current search. It is common to check the applicant's references to confirm reasons for leaving a job. However, it is usually inappropriate to contact a present employer at this stage since it may harm the employee's position and relationship with that supervisor.

6.1.6 Salary Requirements and Job Advancement. Review the salary range of the job specification and the candidate's current salary. It is almost always desirable to be able to offer a modest or substantial salary increase to a prospective candidate. The amount of salary increase will vary depending on the additional responsibilities of the prospective job, inflation rate, and job market, but will generally be in the 10 to 20 percent range. Also, be prepared to describe the potential for job advancement. This is especially critical for entry-level positions.

6.1.7 Housing Information. Literature should be available to give to candidates concerning housing costs and the advantages of living in the surrounding area. If adequate time after the interview can be allocated, have a local real estate agent or company relocation specialist talk to the candidate.

6.2   The Initial Meeting

It is important to put the applicant at ease during an interview. If an applicant has traveled the night before and is staying at a motel, offer to meet him or her for breakfast. This allows each party a chance to meet briefly and may help to make the interview more effective. Always be pleasant and cordial and indicate to the applicant an appreciation for his or her effort in making the meeting possible. Allow the applicant to talk about hobbies, interests, and family as a way of relaxing and "breaking the ice."

Determine the length of time for the interview and allow enough time during the meeting to cover all the important subjects. Typically, a half to full day is allocated when filling a professional-level position. If the applicant has plane reservations, there may be little flexibility in the interview schedule. If the applicant's travel arrangements are flexible (e.g., automobile), then the amount of time allocated for the interview may increase or decrease depending on the quality of the candidate.

6.3   Control of the Interview

It is important to allow the candidate to do most of the talking to learn more about him or her. However, the conversation must remain focused on critical issues to accomplish the goals of the interview in its allocated time. Often, the interviewer will ask open-ended and broad questions of the applicant to probe his or her background.

6.4   Content

- Review the candidate's work experience beginning with the most current position, including responsibilities, duties, accomplishments, likes and dislikes, and reasons for leaving the job. Ask the applicant how his or her work experience appears relevant to the requirements of the job opening.

- Starting with the applicant's most advanced degree, ask about those subjects he or she excelled in as well as the more difficult subjects. Ask the individual to describe achievements, awards, and honors while at school. It may be useful to determine how the education was paid for.
- Let the candidate describe overall strengths and weaknesses, career goals, plans to achieve goals, likes, and dislikes. Review what steps the applicant has taken for personal and profession improvement.
- Describe the job opening honestly and include information concerning responsibilities and duties, organizational structure, and travel (if any). Indicate the salary range for the position and where that salary fits within the company's pay structure. Describe the time typically required for merit or cost of living raises and indicate the promotional possibilities that may be realistically available.
- Give the applicant an opportunity to ask any questions regarding the job.

6.5 Sequential Interviewing

It is often desirable to allow a number of other individuals to interview the applicant, to assist in evaluating the best candidate. Typically, one or two hours is allotted for interviewing an applicant with the immediate supervisor. The other interviewers may take 30 to 60 minutes and may include department heads, heads of allied departments (e.g., industrial hygiene laboratory, toxicology, safety, environmental), and other employees with whom the candidate might work. Also, allow time for the candidate to meet with a representative of the personnel department to discuss the company's benefits and its salary structure.

6.6 Tour of Facilities

Allow enough time for the candidate to tour facilities, including manufacturing, research, library, computers, calibration, and field equipment.

6.7 Termination of Interview

When the interview has been completed, the applicant should once again be thanked for meeting with everyone. The candidate should be informed on the procedure used for filling the position. If the applicant has impressed everyone during the interview, determine the applicant's reaction to the position and a reasonable time frame when he or she could begin work. Indicate to all candidates when they can expect to be notified regarding the position. Sometimes when interviewing four or five candidates, it can take 2 to 4 weeks to schedule all the interviews. If this occurs, let the first applicants know when to expect notification regarding the position.

7 EVALUATING THE APPLICANT

Evaluating applicants after the interview should be an objective process. All interviewers should fill out a brief written rating of each candidate. A typical rating form is shown in Figure 19.2. Each interviewer should list the candidate's assets and liabilities and decide whether an applicant should be hired. When evaluating applicants, remember that a perfect candidate is not likely to be found, and the purpose is to determine those applicants that have a reasonably good chance of succeeding at the job.

7.1 Work History

- Determine whether the candidate's previous work experiences have built a solid foundation of skills for those required in the job specification.
- The candidate should have likes and dislikes compatible with the responsibilities of the job. The position should also have enough opportunity for growth to meet the candidate's objectives. This is often a problem as there is not a great deal of growth potential for industrial hygienists in many organizations.
- The new job should have responsibilities that satisfy the applicant's reasons for leaving or wanting to leave his or her current position.
- The current and future salary level of the position should meet the candidate's financial expectations.

7.2 Applicant's Abilities

- The most important attribute of a candidate is intelligence. This should come out during an interview by examining an applicant's alertness, ability to follow a train of thought, draw inferences, and conclusions. Candidates should have good judgment, common sense, and be able to solve problems.
- Determine the candidate's ability to prioritize responses in an interview. The applicant should answer questions systematically and logically.
- Consider how well the applicant's communication skills are developed. The applicant's ability to sell him or herself is a reflection of how well he or she can sell an industrial hygiene program to management.

INTERVIEW EVALUATION

Candidate's Name	Interviewer's Name/Title
Title of Position/JIS Number	Group/Location/Department of Position
Exploratory? Please check ☐	Date of Interview

Job Related Qualifications (Refer to Core Activity Description)

1. _____

_____

2. _____

_____

3. _____

Job Related Accomplishments

1. _____

_____

2. _____

_____

3. _____

_____

Interviewer Recommendations

☐ Hire   ☐ Do Not Hire   ☐ Hold

State Objective Reasons for Recommendation

1. _____

_____

2. _____

_____

3. _____

_____

4. _____

Return to _____   Interviewer
Signature _____

Within 48 Hours

Figure 19.2. Example of interview evaluation form. (Reproduced with permission of Olin Corp.)

339

7.3   Personal Skills

- Maturity is often considered the most important personal characteristic of an employee. Maturity includes an individual's self-discipline, goal orientation, ability to form realistic goals, and good judgment. When evaluating why a candidate left a previous job, be satisfied that it was for a logical and justifiable reason.
- The candidate should impress an interviewer with his or her motivation. Candidates should have aspirations and have taken reasonable steps toward their completion. They should demonstrate a history of improving their skills and striving for success.
- Evaluate the candidate's overall attitude during the interview, including alertness, ability to project him or herself, and flexibility.
- The candidate should be assertive, self-confident, and competitive.
- Determine the candidate's interpersonal skills. These include traits such as poise, warmth, cooperation, diplomacy, tact, sensitivity, and ability to be a team player.
- The candidate should show initiative, be a self-starter, imaginative, and resourceful.

7.4   Character Traits

- Evaluate the candidate's stability and ability to deal with stress and pressure. Look at a candidate's length of stay at previous jobs.
- Determine a candidate's work ethic. Review any awards and recognition, periods of unemployment or inactivity, and ability to identify well with previous employees.
- Judge the confidence of the applicant's ability to work independently, adapt to new situations, and solve problems.
- Consider the leadership qualities of a candidate, ability to motivate others, and grow in the organization. Examine the offices the applicant has held in other organizations as an indication of leadership potential.

7.5   Education

An applicant's educational credentials are often an indication of intelligence and motivation. The importance of evaluating a candidate's education decreases as work history increases. It is most useful for a recent graduate with no work history and less useful for a candidate that has been out of school for many years. Obtain an official copy of the candidate's transcript from college as proof of the completion of their degree. Look at how well the candidate performed, and the number of courses taken relevant to the job specification. If the degree is in industrial hygiene or a related field, determine the school's reputation in this specific area.

A student's extracurricular activities are often an indication of their ability to interact with others. Determine how the applicant paid for his or her education. This may be an indication of work ethic or academic abilities.

7.6   Rating the Applicants

Rate all candidates objectively. Avoid hiring under- or overqualified candidates. Determine which of the candidates are acceptable and which are not. If the prescreening methods used were successful, almost all the candidates interviewed should be acceptable. List the preferential order of hiring the candidates.

8   CONTACTING REFERENCES

An applicant's references should always be contacted prior to a job offer, to verify information given by the applicant and to obtain information that may have been withheld by the candidate.

8.1   When to Contact References

Some individuals believe that references should be contacted prior to an interview and that the information obtained be used in determining whether to offer a candidate an interview and in the evaluation process. This is a reasonable approach for applicants currently out of work or about to be laid off and should there be questions about the applicant that require answers prior to an interview. However, for the majority of applicants who are currenty employed, the correct time to contact references is after the interview and evaluation process, and only if the applicant is among the top candidates for the position. The reasons for this are:

The current employer is usually the most important reference. Often a supervisor may not be aware that an employee is interviewing for other jobs. If the applicant chooses not to leave his or her job, this information could interfere with the employee–supervisor relationship, hurt chances for a promotion, or lead to dismissal. The applicant seldom desires that the supervisor be contacted unless a job offer is imminent.

Contacting previous employers may still create a problem if the candidate's current supervisor becomes aware of this information. In a small field such as industrial hygiene, this is entirely possible.

Contacting references is unnecessary unless it assists in the decision-making process. If an applicant is not one of the top prospects for the position, references are unlikely to result in a job being offered.

8.2   Whom to Contact

The applicant's supervisor is always the best reference. The most recent supervisor, unless the job was held for a very short time, is the most important reference. Previous supervisors for industrial hygiene positions are also good references. However, supervisors for nonindustrial hygiene positions are of limited value and cannot comment on specific technical skills but only on personality characteristics.

Personal references such as the clergy, a colleague, or friend are usually worthless, since they probably will not present an objective opinion of the candidate's skills and traits. These individuals often are not in a position to judge whether the candidate's skills are appropriate for the job.

It may be useful to discuss the candidate with individuals not listed as references. This may be with previous colleagues or individuals who served on professional committees with the candidate. If this is done, it should be kept confidential, as would interviews with any other reference.

8.3   Telephone Interviews

Usually interviewing references over the telephone is the only reasonable approach. Sending forms by mail is time consuming and will delay the selection process. Interviewing in person is seldom realistic, unless the applicant's reference is in close geographic proximity.

When contacting a reference, be prepared with written questions. Explain who you are and the purpose of the phone call. Indicate that the interview will be brief and to the point. Express an appreciation for sharing knowledge of the candidate. Indicate a desire to confirm the following information given by the applicant: employment dates, nature of the job and responsibilities, and salary history. Ask the individual to discuss the following:

> An overall opinion of the candidate.
> Comparison of performance with others in the same job.
> Job progress.
> Why candidate is leaving (or left).
> Would rehiring the candidate at a later time be considered.
> What are the candidate's strengths and weaknesses.
> How did the candidate interact with others.
> Dependability.
> Attendance.
> Ability and potential to assume responsibility.
> Personal difficulties that interfered with work.
> Anything else of significance.

When the conversation is finished, express thanks and indicate that the conversation will be kept strictly confidential.

8.4 Evaluating References

Some references are critical of everyone and some are quick to heap praise. Consider the tone and attitude of the reference. The reference is not being used as the ultimate evaluation of the candidate, but rather to confirm present information and to uncover additional information. Use several references when possible to obtain information about the candidate.

8.5 Difficulties

It is not unusual to have a supervisor state that company policy prohibits discussing information concerning previous employees. When this happens, the person contacted should be told that if such information is not available, this might result in the applicant not being given consideration for the job. Indicate that the information you obtain will be kept confidential and will not go into the applicant's personnel file, should the applicant be hired. If problems persist, indicate the desire to contact the appropriate supervisor to discuss this problem.

Often the applicant may be hesitant to have a current supervisor contacted. Again, indicate that a position cannot be offered without having information verified by the supervisor.

9 HIRING A NEW EMPLOYEE

It is typical that a job offer will be made by telephone to the candidate. This can be done by a member of the personnel department or the supervisor. The offer should include the position title, salary, and any fringe benefits discussed during the interview. If the applicant agrees to accept the position, a starting date should be set. Typically, a candidate may want several days or a week to discuss the offer with the family. The prospective employer should indicate the necessity of a commitment by a certain date, usually within a week, to be fair to the other candidates. If the applicant refuses the position, the position should be offered to the next best candidate. If all of the applicants considered acceptable refuse the job, then it should be reviewed to determine if the salary is too low, there is a lack of job advancement, or the qualifications required do not realistically meet the job specification. In any case, the entire process must begin again.

If the job is accepted over the telephone by a candidate, it should be followed up with a formal letter to the individual. The prospective employee should also be asked to reply in writing accepting the position. The starting date should be clear to both supervisor and new employee. The personnel department should then contact the new employee and discuss moving arrangements, house hunting trips, benefits, and so on. The prospective employer may have to arrange for a physical to be taken by the applicant as a condition of employment.

Those candidates who were not selected for the job should be sent a letter promptly thanking them for their interest in the position and indicating that other candidates had qualifications better suited to the job. Rejected candidates should not be given any details about why they were rejected. Those candidates that were interviewed should be contacted by telephone and appreciation expressed for their interest and efforts. These candidates should be told that they had excellent qualifications, but that a more suitable candidate who more closely matched the job specifications was selected. Again, these applicants should not be specifically told why they were not chosen.

The entire process for recruiting and hiring an employee should be reviewed for ways to improve the process. If the salary range was not competitive, explore ways to work with the personnel department to improve it. If there was not enough evidence of job advancement, explore ways to create new positions. This, however, can be difficult or impossible in a small organization. The recruiting process should be examined if there were too few applicants.

Finally, everyone who assisted in the interviewing process should be thanked and informed as to the results of the job search.

GENERAL REFERENCES

E. S. Stanton, *Successful Personnel Recruiting and Selection,* New York: AMA-COM, 1980.

R. A. Fear, *The Evaluation Interview,* New York: McGraw-Hill, 1984.

Your organization's personnel department should be contacted for further references on this topic.

CHAPTER TWENTY

Salaries and Grades

G. H. Andersen

1 INTRODUCTION

Compensation paid to industrial hygienists in today's marketplace reflects their rapidly changing role in industry. Mainly an advisor to management in former years, the industrial hygienist currently has a more enhanced position, greater visibility in the workplace, and a responsibility to convince management that a safe and healthy working environment is essential to the well-being of the employee as well as to the smooth operation of an industrial plant and the profitability of the corporation.

There is also the need to keep management apprised of federal, state, and local laws and regulations that apply to health and safety in the workplace and in the community. Consequently, government regulations are making the job of the industrial hygienist more one of interacting with government officials in order to satisfy the demands imposed by such laws as the right-to-know regulations and the Superfund Amendments and Reauthorization Act (SARA). These laws require that there be coordination and integration of emergency plans with state and local governments or committees set up by them.

In order to find the most qualified people to meet these requirements, the profession must be made sufficiently rewarding, financially as well as professionally. Therefore, it is in the employer's as well as the employee's best interest to develop an attractive and competitive compensation package.

2 COMPENSATION PROGRAM

A comprehensive compensation program is developed in order to pay workers an equitable and competitive salary. To be effective, the compensation program should be based on the type and quality of work performed as compared to employees doing similar work in the same company and in other companies in the same geographical area.

2.1 Job Description

The primary document on which compensation is based is the job description or statement of duties. If written properly, it will form the cornerstone upon which the job may be evaluated. It need not be lengthy or cover every facet of the job but should state simply how this job differs from all other jobs in the company. Thus, a comparison can be made between the job described in the statement of duties and similar jobs within and without the company.

The position described in the next section is for an entry-level industrial hygienist and details the basic duties of the job. This job description could be used in a small (>200) or medium (>500) plant employing only one industrial hygienist. It might also apply to a junior position in a larger plant employing several industrial hygienists who are closely supervised by a senior person (Also, see Chapters 3, 12, and 19.)

The job descriptions for Industrial Hygienist II and III outline requirements for more advanced positions that entail more years of experience and the ability to interact on a professional level with and advise more senior people in the company, up to and including higher level management. Subsequently, experience in supervision, budgeting, and the ability to interact with senior management becomes essential.

2.1.1 Industrial Hygienist I. Performs basic industrial hygiene assignments and provides routine advice and assistance to supervisors. Identifies and monitors occupational health hazards in the workplace in accordance with established procedures. Ensures compliance with company and regulatory requirements. Conducts routine industrial hygiene surveys for noise and air contaminants. Recommends corrective action, where necessary.

This position is considered the entering professional level with the individual progressively developing professional maturity, judgment, and experience.

Minimum job specifications would be a bachelor's degree in chemistry, chemical engineering, or related science (the emphasis might be chemistry or biology, as appropriate) with 0–3 years experience.

2.1.2 Industrial Hygienist II. Exercises judgment and utilizes knowledge of industrial hygiene techniques. Plans and performs professional industrial hygiene activities and provides advice to management. Implements programs to recognize, evaluate, and control actual or potential occupational health hazards and diseases in a plant, laboratory, or similar work environment in accordance with corporate and regulatory agency guidelines. Works with limited supervision.

Develops monitoring programs for employees exposed to contaminants and toxic agents and determines corrective procedures. Participates in educational meetings to instruct employees on protective measures to be taken and matters pertaining to occupational health and accident prevention. Investigates, evaluates, and monitors adequacy of ventilation systems, lighting, and other factors that may affect an employee's health, comfort, or efficiency and coordinates implementation of corrective measures. Prepares reports, including observations, and makes recommendations for control and correction of hazards. When appropriate, accompanies Occupational Safety and Health Agency (OSHA) inspectors to assure that scientifically appropriate measurements are taken that accurately reflect employee exposures.

Minimum job specifications would be a master's degree, industrial hygiene preferred or related discipline, plus up to 2 years directly related industrial hygiene, or equivalent, training and experience. Certification by the American Board of Industrial Hygiene highly desirable. Good knowledge of applicable industrial hygiene regulations as issued by regulatory agencies.

2.1.3 Industrial Hygienist III. Performs advanced professional industrial hygiene activities requiring the exercise of independent judgment and discretion and utilizes broad knowledge of industrial hygiene principles. Participates in training and developing entry-level industrial hygienists. Plans, conducts, evaluates, and supervises occupational health control programs to assure compliance with company and regulatory requirements. Reviews engineering designs for all new or changed facilities to assure maintenance of satisfactory occupational health conditions. Develops industrial hygiene programs and procedures. Prepares and submits reports required by regulatory agencies. Remains fully informed of new and pending legislation in the industrial hygiene field as well as up-to-date information on newly recognized hazards. Provides professional advice to management, as required. Investigates complaints and develops and recommends corrective action. May represent company in trade associations.

Minimum job specifications would be a master's degree, industrial hygiene preferred, plus 4–6 years directly related industrial hygiene experience or equivalent education and work experience. Certification by the American Board of Industrial Hygiene highly desirable. Broad knowledge of chemical or related processes, related equipment and facilities, as well as knowledge of applicable industrial hygiene regulations issued by regulatory agencies.

The basic job descriptions may be too specific for other industrial, governmental, or consulting operations that have little or no chemical exposure. The author has presented these as examples and not generalizations for all potential job descriptions in this field.

2.1.4 Consulting. Consultant salaries may vary greatly since consulting firms consider the potential for business development and the ability to work well with clients to be of paramount importance. Salary and grade then is dependent on these intangibles as well as years of experience and education. In addition, certifications and registrations are important because they lend credence to documents and reports.

2.1.5 Regulatory Agencies. Qualifications and grades in government agencies, such as OSHA or state or local health departments, are usually set by law. Salaries and grades progress with the length of service. Certain grades require a qualifying examination prior to appointment or advancement.

2.1.6 Management Positions. The requirements for management positions in most companies are similar to those for Industrial Hygienist III with the addition of some or all of the following:

Policy making
Department trends/planning
Staffing
Development of standard operating procedures
Assurance systems policy and procedure
Assurance systems professional (continuing education)
Contracting for and evaluation of outside services
Integration and divestiture of businesses
Decontamination procedures

2.1.7 Dual-Discipline Management Positions. Managers may be called on to supervise more than one discipline such as health and safety, occupational health and product safety, or environmental services. In many cases, at a high management level, superior supervisory skills and ability to communicate well with other managers are as important as being technically proficient in the discipline or disciplines.

3 GRADES

Grades (Table 20.1) and salaries (Table 20.2) vary widely by employer, geographical location, and level of responsibility. Government agencies and some companies use a numeric system, with salary progression indicated by a rising sequence of numbers. Some systems indicate a higher salary grade by a descending sequence of numbers. Some companies use letters. No matter what the system, the job applicant would be wise to gain some understanding of the potential employer's system so that misunderstandings are avoided.

4 SALARIES

The midpoint of each salary grade is that point at which an employee should be when the job requirements of that grade are completely met. Barring

Table 20.1. Average Grade by Title and Industry

Title	Grade[a]
Industrial Hygienist I	
Government	1
Industrial	1,2
Consulting	1,2
Industrial hygienist II	
Government	2
Industrial	4
Consulting	4
Industrial hygienist III	
Government	4,5
Industrial	6
Consulting	5–8
Industrial hygiene manager	
Large plant (7500)	7
Division	8
Company	9
Industrial hygiene director	10
Dual-discipline director	10+

[a] Arbitrary numbering system by author.

Table 20.2. Monthly Salary Ranges

Salary Grade[a]	Minimum	Midpoint	Maximum
1	$1,800	$2,350	$2,800
2	2,000	2,650	3,200
3	2,300	3,000	3,600
4	2,600	3,400	4,000
5	2,900	3,800	4,500
6	3,300	4,250	5,100
7	3,700	4,800	5,700
8	4,100	5,400	6,500
9	4,700	6,100	7,300
10	5,250	6,800	8,200
11	5,900	7,700	9,200
12	6,650	8,600	10,400

[a] Arbitrary numbering system by author.

promotion to the next grade, this employee may progress toward the maximum salary of that grade. In the author's opinion, reaching maximum salary for a grade should not be an employee's goal since a promotion should occur prior to that event (Also, see Chapters 3, 12, and 19.)

4.1 Merit Increases

Performance level, position in salary range, salaries of other employees in the same department, and date of last increase are taken into consideration in determining merit increases. National economics have a major effect on increases. It should be kept in mind that merit increases are earned and should not be considered a routine event.

4.1.1 Merit Increase Timing. Merit increases are normally given annually, but as an employee reaches and exceeds the midpoint of the salary range, the time between increases may be extended and the amount lowered.

4.1.2 Promotion Increases. It is customary to raise an employee's salary to a point near the midpoint of the next grade on promotion. There is usually a maximum promotional raise that might be as low as 10 percent or as high as 25 percent.

4.1.3 Nonsalary Remuneration. Many companies have bonus plans for employees in a senior management or executive category. These bonus plans may consist of stock options or stock options and cash. This type of remuneration is usually calculated as a percentage of the annual salary, the percentage being based on grade.

5   CONCLUSION

It seems reasonable to assume that those new to the field of industrial hygiene will wonder what the job market is like. Thus, an attempt has been made in this chapter to set down facts and figures that will help to answer that question.

However, it must be reiterated that earnings depend on many factors, including one's experience, ability, the firm for which one works, and the section of the country where one lives. Statistics alone can never adequately portray the large differences in earnings of workers in a particular occupation.

In addition, as opposed to a salary survey, the data presented here, compiled during 1986, are a measure of salary and grade linked to a job description and not to a particular individual.

ACKNOWLEDGMENTS

The author wishes to acknowledge the assistance of Myma Andersen and Lorraine T. Daigle.

CHAPTER TWENTY-ONE

Budgeting

Joseph L. Holtshouser

1 WHAT IS BUDGETING?

Broadly speaking, the functions that managers perform for their organizations are planning, organizing, directing, and controlling. The document that helps bring all of these activities into perspective is the department budget.

But the terms "budget" and "budgeting" do not mean the same things to all people. Previously, the budget was understood to mean the overall plan. Now one hears the terms "sales budget," "expense budget," and "capital budget." For a common understanding of terms, a working definition is in order.

In this chapter, a budget is the written end product of a manager's attempt to tell the organization, in financial terms, what goals and objectives will be

353

accomplished during the period covered by the budget. The act of preparing the budget, with all the attendant planning and goal setting, is called budgeting.

A budget provides a number of services for the manager. It helps to organize and direct the department's efforts; it monitors the department's progress toward reaching its goals; and it provides the manager with a barometer for controlling department expenditures.

Budgeting should not be confused with accounting, however. The former term is concerned with the future, whereas the latter deals with the past. Even so, past performance can be measured by comparing prior budgets with actual past results, thus providing another yardstick for management evaluation.

Managers rely on budgets to assist in allocating resources, to predict future performance, to control current activities, to detect early signals of departure from plans, to detect opportunities or threats to performance, and to serve as learning devices.

A variety of budgeting techniques are available. The literature is replete with procedures, opinions, types, and preferences. However, a manager of the industrial hygiene function, within an organization, will probably be working with a budgeting system already set in place by the organization management. Rarely will the manager have an opportunity to implement a new budgeting procedure. Of course the manager always has the opportunity to use other techniques for the development of a budget proposal, so long as the form is accepted by the organization.

There are two broad classes of budgets: operating budgets and capital budgets.

This chapter will present three types of operating budgets: traditional budgets, program budgets, and zero-based budgets. Just these three are presented because they are the most widely used. The term, operating is used to describe budgets that aid in operating or managing a department.

Capital budgets describe a financial plan to upper management to spend capital or cash for a specific project that will return an anticipated flow of future benefits to the organization. The time frame is usually longer than a year. This is in contrast to an operating investment, which is an expenditure of cash for a particular project, generally taking place within a year's period.

Budgeting procedures will also be presented with respect to the two broad categories, operating and capital budgets.

1.1 Traditional Budgeting

Traditional budgeting is budgeting in its simplest form. It begins with an examination of the current year's budget and follows three basic steps.

First, the current year's budget is brought forward to begin the budget cycle for next year. In other words, the current year's budget is adopted as the base for the next year's budget.

Second, any increments for salary increases or adjustments for inflation are added, as well as increases in the cost of purchased materials or services.

Third, the cost of any new programs or projects planned for the coming year is added. The result of this effort may look like Table 21.1. This is a typical budget description for an administrative department, such as industrial hygiene.

Note that the expense categories are expressed in such general activity terms as travel or communications. And the incremental changes are shown at the end of the table, for review by the budget committee or upper management.

These general activities are generated from more specific line budget items that explain in what cost classifications the expenses will occur. Table 21.2 indicates the origins of expense for the category "Miscellaneous." Monitoring of the line expense items requires a good deal of attention from the manager to control expenses within budget limits.

The traditional type of budgeting approach is very easy to follow, but it can raise major questions of affordability if all organization departments practice it. It assumes, from the very beginning, that (1) all activities in the current year are essential to achieving next year's goals and objectives, (2) that these activities are more important than the new programs planned for next year, (3) that current activities are being performed now in the most cost-efficient manner, and (4) that these activities will continue to be performed in the most cost-efficient manner.

If these assumptions are not true, then the result will be a grossly inflated budget. Even though many industrial hygiene programs are based on requirements of federal or state laws, upper management will continue to insist that such compliance programs be cost effective.

Traditional budgeting, when left unchecked, fosters the birth of inflated budgets throughout the organization. When there is recognition by top man-

Table 21.1. Typical Budget Description: Industrial Hygiene Department

| | | 1986 | | | 1987 Budget | |
	1985 Actual	Budget	Estimate	1987 Budget	versus 1986 Estimate (%)	versus 1986 Budget (%)
Compensation	$300,366	$335,468	$331,328	$342,931	3.5	2.2
Travel	36,437	45,550	45,350	48,450	6.8	6.4
Communi- cations	8,324	11,713	7,081	11,813	66.8	0.9
Miscellaneous	150,690	184,080	176,575	209,384	18.6	13.7
Fringe	59,065	68,280	65,429	71,907	9.9	5.3
Other	58,824	51,260	52,247	51,245	−1.9	0.0
Total	$613,706	$696,351	$678,010	$735,730	8.5	5.7

Table 21.2. Miscellaneous Expense Category: Department Miscellaneous
Expense

Type of Expense	1987 Budget	1986 Estimate Expense	1986 Budget
Operating materials and supplies	$ 17,000	$ 16,200	$ 17,000
Moving expense	23,000	15,600	23,000
Office equipment repair	200	125	200
Art and visual aids	1,800	1,650	1,500
Licenses and permits	1,000	750	800
Office equipment not capitalized	300	300	50
Rental supplies, copy machine	845	280	300
Laboratory analysis expense	64,000	36,500	40,000
Expendable sampling supplies	15,000	12,570	13,000
Books, publications, etc.	1,544	1,100	1,430
Conference expense	500	400	500
Dues, association memberships	795	780	750
Computer expense	50,000	46,500	40,500
Hiring expense	2,300	2,500	2,000
Postage	150	135	150
Miscellaneous unclassified expense	200	160	200
Consultants	15,000	11,500	12,000
Stationery supplies	750	525	700
Training programs	15,000	29,000	30,000
Subtotal Miscellaneous Expense	$209,384	$176,575	$184,080

agement that the master budget will have to be trimmed, this insistence on cost-effectiveness is demonstrated by across-the-board cuts. The group that does the trimming, such as the budget committee, usually lacks the knowledge of what the resources are for or why the spending is important. And the industrial hygiene budget gets chopped right along with all the others.

Smart managers are unlikely to be caught twice with budget cuts that affect their programs. The result is a form of game in the organization where budgets are inflated on purpose, knowing they will be cut to a level that was required initially. Responsible managers, who made appropriate submissions, are penalized by the inevitable cuts. The cycle continues unless upper management changes the budgeting policies or procedures.

The culprit responsible for this cycle is not the traditional budgeting method. Rather, it is the frequency of its use that leads to problems. For the first-time budget of a group or department and for periodic refreshing of aged budgets, other methods are more suitable.

1.2   Program Budgeting

Program budgeting does not have a standardized definition due to its encompassing nature. It is not just a system and process, but also a technique. By application, it ties together strategic planning and long-range planning with conventional budgeting analysis. The desired end result is the effective assignment of resources to achieve short- and long-range objectives of the organization.

Program budgeting is really a consolidation of the Program, Planning, and Budgeting (PPB) system developed in the early 1960s in the Office of Systems Analysis of the Defense Department. It was also broadly applied to the U.S. space program.

Essentially, program budgeting transforms the annual routine of preparing a budget into a conscious effort to appraise and formulate an organization's goals via the long-range view. Program budgeting organizes spending by programs instead of by functions, as traditional budgets do. Spending is classified by "outputs tied to objectives rather than by inputs tied to functions."

The programs described by the budget are extended into the future so that the full resource requirements and expenses are displayed. This way, management knows how long a specific program will last and what it will cost.

Determining how long a program will last implies an effort at strategic planning. Ideally, the industrial hygiene manager should describe what the program will look like in the next 5–10 years and include a realistic statement of how it will be accomplished. This statement should accompany the budget proposal and detail the department's mission, its objectives, and major resources needed to attain the objectives.

The department mission statement serves as a basis for detailed planning and goal setting. This may be called long-range planning as distinguished from strategic planning, but the distinction is not critical. In either case, the desired end result is a specific description of the department's goals.

As a part of this budgeting process, all programs are subjected to a rigorous cost-effective analysis. The fallout of this analysis determines whether program expenditures are increased or if resources required to deliver a program are decreased. Cost-effective analysis can, for example, determine the most efficient choice between initiating a personal protective equipment program or the installation of engineering controls wherever a choice is present.

The primary thrust of program budgeting is toward planning, not budgeting. Although, when properly implemented, an operating budget is a natural result. An example of an operating program budget is displayed in Table 21.3. Note, however, that each element of the program budget would consist of activity subelements, as depicted in Table 21.1.

This form of budget presentation might not be accepted for final approval, but submitted with the approved budget form, it fills the knowledge gap

Table 21.3. Program Budget: Industrial Hygiene Department

	1985 Actual	1986 Budget	1986 Estimate	1987 Budget	1987 Budget versus 1986 Estimate (%)	1987 Budget versus 1986 Budget (%)
Surveys	$ 67,508	$ 79,599	$ 77,581	$ 80,930	4.3	1.7
Training	85,920	94,489	99,921	103,002	3.1	9.0
Consulting	159,563	181,051	186,283	191,291	2.7	5.7
Data analysis	55,233	72,672	56,021	66,216	18.2	−8.9
New program development	116,604	125,307	120,822	139,788	15.7	11.6
Plant auditing	128,878	143,233	137,382	154,503	12.5	7.9
Total	$613,706	$696,351	$678,010	$735,730	8.5	5.7

missing in the budget committee's analysis. They know not only how much will be spent but why.

Program budgeting clearly emphasizes the purposes and objectives of the department, whereas the traditional method simply details the means used. Program budgeting also makes a better framework for decision making and specific resource allocation. However, even in the light of these facts, there is a better budgeting technique that is more helpful in dealing with operations, performance, and efficiency.

1.3 Zero-Based Budgeting

The zero-based budgeting system was first named by Peter Pyhrr in an article published in the November/December 1970 issue of the *Harvard Business Review*. Pyhrr, then working for Texas Instruments, was invited by the governor of Georgia, Jimmy Carter, to join his staff and install the system there. The system worked very well in Georgia, and Carter introduced it to the federal government during his tenure as president.

Basically, zero-based budgeting (ZBB) is

> an operating, planning, and budgeting process which requires each manager to justify his entire budget request in detail from scratch, and shifts the burden of proof to each manager to justify why he should spend any money at all (1).

The concept of ZBB is implemented in four steps:

1. Objectives are formulated.
2. Decision packages are determined.
3. Decision packages are evaluated by analysis.
4. Decision packages are ranked in order of importance.

The formulation of objectives has been discussed elsewhere and needs no embellishment here. However, the criteria for evaluating performance is determined at this stage along with the setting of goals. And in a very real sense, the adage "what gets measured, gets done" applies directly to selecting the performance criteria. It is widely believed that if a goal cannot be measured, then it is not appropriate and should not be selected.

Decision packages are those individual program elements that are described in Table 21.3. ZBB packages are output oriented (improved training, increased plant audits) rather than input oriented by function (safety, industrial hygiene). They should stand on their own merits, and the elimination of any one should not severely affect the others.

If the decision package has a measurable benefit, then it becomes a candidate for cost–benefit analysis. By tying costs to benefits, ZBB addresses the issues of "what are we getting for this expenditure?" and "are there better ways to obtain the results we want?" This is not to say that intangible benefits are not important. Certainly efforts that are "legally mandated," "state of the art," or that promote "better human relations" require refinements of the ZBB process. But this procedure puts the cost for these issues in proper perspective so that alternative actions can be examined on an equal basis.

The ranking of decision packages is critical to the ZBB objective for better resource allocation. Once all programs are ranked in the order of their importance, packages are approved and funded on the basis of their affordability for the period. When the cuts have to be made, or programs postponed for a later time, the decisions are based on the intelligent assessment of current program needs rather than mindless chops, slices, or wholesale deletions.

ZBB tells what is really going on in an organization, why it is being done, if there are better ways to obtain the same or better results, and which activities are really important.

The critics of ZBB have argued that it is too costly an exercise to repeat annually as a standard budgetary practice. There is merit to this contention and some firms only perform the ritual on a 3- or 5-year periodic basis. During the other periods, traditional budgeting methods are employed. But for the infant industrial hygiene program, ZBB can provide an excellent foundation to justify the manager's efforts.

A simplified summary of these three budgeting techniques could describe each in this way: Traditional budgeting tells management what is being spent and where; program budgeting tells what is being spent, where, and why; zero-based budgeting tells what is being spent, where, why, and what the most important expenditures are.

2 BUDGET PROCEDURES

For organizations with fiscal years coinciding with the calendar year, budgeting usually gets underway in September. The cycle begins with the sales or revenue forecast for the coming year. Staff department budgets, such as industrial hygiene, are submitted in October or November for review and approval. The veteran manager is familiar with this process and has all the necessary information to complete the task. But the new manager, with a first-time budget, needs a few basic items of information to begin properly.

First, the manager must have a clearly defined organization guide that indicates individual cost centers and departments that match the organization. The guide might also state who is responsible for making what budgets. Accounting can help provide this information.

Next, accounting should also provide a chart of accounts that details where costs are charged and specifies the accounting codes that label the accounts. Account codes define cost centers for operating companies, groups, divisions, and departments. The chart of accounts allows the manager to track and control expenditures based on descriptions that are appropriate for the department.

With these accounting tools in hand, the manager begins the three phases of budgeting, namely, preplanning, preparation, and control.

2.1 Preplanning Phase

A good place to start is the analysis of any previous experience of the department in budgeting. Last year's budget and goal statements will show the emphasis placed on particular programs. Determining whether the hygiene program is preventative or reactionary in design is important.

In the absence of a previous budget or goal statement, one should determine the state of the organization's finances. Decide what type of hygiene program the organization can afford. Then form the department's objectives and goals for the first year in considerable detail, followed by a summary of the objectives for the next 4 years. Whether or not planning is done over a 5-year period, it is necessary to follow this preplanning procedure, at least annually, to lay a firm foundation for preparing the budget for the next year.

2.2 Preparation Phase

The manager must determine the costs or expenses necessary to carry out the goals of the department for each program, element by element. The hygiene training program, for example, would have expenses for travel, salaries, supplies, and communications that would support the training objectives for the year.

All expenses would then be consolidated into a budget summary in a form identical to that normally used when reporting financial results to management. The final work product looks like the figures in the monthly financial report, except that the numbers represent projections for the next year instead of actual results for a completed period.

This document is then submitted to the budget committee for their approval. Adjustments may be made at the recommendation of the committee. But if the proper support documentation is included with the budget submission, the chances of the budget remaining intact are much better. If approved, the document becomes the operating budget for the department.

2.3 Control Phase

Basically, this involves the preparation of periodic reports comparing performance with the budget. The accounting department usually prepares the reports. Variances from the budget are highlighted and may require explanations from time to time. Occasionally, expenses are charged to the wrong account codes and corrections must be made. These corrections are important for monitoring the true cost of programs and for guiding the budgeting of expenses for the next year.

During the course of the operating year, the manager may face several decisions about the budget. If department operation shadows the budget, then no action is necessary. But if conditions change, then the manager must alter the plan of operations to fit the budget or alter the budget to fit the new plan of operations.

In the former case, no change in the budget is necessary and approvals apply only to goal changes. But in the latter case, a new budget would require the same preparation process as described previously.

3 CAPITAL BUDGETING AND INVESTMENT ANALYSIS

For discussion purposes, assume that the industrial hygiene laboratory wants to purchase a computer for integrating and controlling all of its automated analysis equipment. The laboratory manager obtains estimates on the costs for hardware, software, installation, training for lab personnel, and site preparation. The manager must also take into account the need for future personnel in the lab to handle anticipated growth in sample analysis.

The manager knows that justification for the budget will require an estimate of benefits versus costs over the life of the project, and so prepares a cash flow table. An example appears in Table 21.4. The manager determines that the organization's tax rate is 35 percent and that the computer will have a useful life of 5 years.

The manager wants the organization to commit funds now in order to receive some desired return in the future. This is an investment and the document that describes it is called a capital budget. The capital budget allows management to evaluate a proposal and make a decision to spend money. The decisions fall into two broad categories for consideration: preference decisions and screening decisions.

Table 21.4. Cash Flow Estimates

Additional Cash Revenues	Year 1	Year 2	Year 3	Year 4	Year 5
Additional samples	200	250	350	500	700
Productivity savings	$15,000	$18,000	$20,000	$26,000	$28,000
Lower outside lab cost	12,000	15,000	20,000	25,000	30,000
Total savings	$27,000	$33,000	$40,000	$51,000	$58,000
Additional costs					
Personnel (salary + fringe)	$0	$0	$0	$27,000	$30,000
Supplies	1,200	1,400	1,400	1,700	1,900
Maintenance	250	400	500	500	700
Software updates	200	400	550	600	800
Income tax (35%)	4,743	10,780	13,143	7,420	8,610
Total costs	$ 6,393	$12,980	$15,593	$37,220	$42,010
Net cash flow	$20,608	$20,020	$24,408	$13,780	$15,990

Investment Costs		Depreciation			
Hardware	$35,000	Assume 5-year life			
Software	16,000	$11,800			
Installation	2,000				
Training	4,000				
Site preparation	2,000				
Total cost	$59,000				

Preference decisions relate to selecting a course of action from among several available choices. Screening decisions are related to whether a project meets a preset standard of acceptance. In this example, the screening decision will be made using several investment analysis tools. The preset standard against which the project will be judged is the cost of capital to the organization.

The cost of capital is the objective by which all investment opportunities are monitored. Although there is no concrete agreement as to how the cost of capital is calculated, it is the most important criteria that profit management uses to judge its performance.

Most investment proposals are financed from debt or equity, that is, either money is borrowed or equity is sold. The cost to borrow money (interest) or the funds raised from the sale of equity (stock) make up the cost of capital. The lab manager's proposal will be judged against the ability of the organization to earn a return on the investment that is greater than the cost of paying for it.

Five techniques will be used to evaluate the proposal described in Table 21.4. These commonly used capital budgeting techniques are well documented in the accounting literature:

1. Payback method
2. Initial investment rate of return method
3. Accounting or average rate of return method
4. Net present value method
5. Time-adjusted rate of return method

3.1 Payback Method

Also known as payout, this is the simplest investment method and is the most widely used. It determines the number of years for the earnings of an investment to pay back the initial capital outlay. Table 21.5 shows the procedure for using this technique to determine how long it will take for the lab computer to repay the $59,000 needed to purchase it.

This method is popular because the sooner an investment pays for itself, the sooner management can reinvest the capital and earn more money. The problem with using this method alone is that it does not consider the time value of money.

Money invested can earn interest, that is, money to be paid for the use of money. The concepts of money compounding and discounting are important terms that involve interest. These terms are the reverse of each other and can be defined by asking these questions:

> *Compounding.* If P dollars are invested today at interest rate i, what amount of A dollars will accumulate in n years?
>
> *Discounting.* How many P dollars should one invest today at interest rate i to receive a given amount of A dollars at the end of n years?

The payback method ignores these concepts and deals with one point: The longer money is tied up in an investment, the less utility it has for the investor. For this reason, the payback calculation is an important screening tool. If the payback is less than the standard set by the organization, then the project is acceptable.

Table 21.5. Payback Method: Number of Years To Recover Investment

	Cash Flow	Years
Investment	$59,000	
Less: Cash flow Year 1	20,608	1.00
Year 2	20,020	1.00
Needed in Year 3	18,372/$24,408	0.75
Total payback period		2.75

Table 21.6. Initial-Investment Rate-of-Return Method (IIRR)

Additional Cash Revenues	Year 1	Investment	Tax Rate (TR)
Productivity savings	$15,000	$59,000	35%
Lower outside lab cost	12,000		
Total savings (TS)	$27,000		
Depreciation/year	$11,800		$IIRR = \dfrac{NSAT}{Investment}$

NSAT = (TR) × (TS) + Dep/yr

NSAT = (0.35) × ($27,000) + $11,800 $IIRR = \dfrac{\$21,250}{\$59,000} = 36\%$
     = $21,250

NSAT = Net Savings After Tax $PB = \dfrac{\$59,000}{21,250} = 2.78$

  PB = Payback Period (years)

3.2   Initial-Investment Rate-of-Return Method (IIRR)

This technique, displayed in Table 21.6, also disregards the time value of money and tends to create a bias in favor of investments that yield a return in the first year. It is mostly used by organizations that are cash poor and must focus on short-term results.

The IIRR method takes into account the effects that taxes and depreciation have on the investment, an important point ignored with the standard payback calculation. However, it does not address operating cash flows that give information about the return over the life of the investment.

If the IIRR is greater than the cost of capital to the organization, then the project is acceptable. Notice that the reciprocal of the IIRR is another form of the payback calculation that does not use cash flows.

3.3   Accounting or Average Rate-of-Return Method (ARR)

This method measures the use of capital over the whole life of the investment. As displayed in Table 21.7, ARR also takes into account the effect of depreciation and income taxes throughout the period.

The main argument against this method deals with its focus on accounting net income and the lack of attention to the discounting of future cash flows. It tends to create a bias in favor of investments that yield the bulk of their cash flows in later years.

Were it not for the addition of personnel in the fourth year of the example, the amount of net income would be increased as well as the calculated rate of return. Even so, the amount of cash flows is overstated, lacking the discounting effect of money over time, and the amount of the return is inflated as well. However, if the calculated return is greater than the organization's cost of capital, then the project is acceptable.

Table 21.7. Accounting or Average Rate-of-Return Method (ARR)

	Cash Flow	−	Depreciation	=	Net Income
Year 1	$20,608		$11,800		$ 8,808
Year 2	20,020		11,800		8,220
Year 3	24,408		11,800		12,608
Year 4	13,780		11,800		1,980
Year 5	15,990		11,800		4,190
	$94,805		$59,000		$35,805

$$\text{Average Rate of Return} = \frac{\text{Average net income}}{\text{Average investment}} = \frac{\$35,805/5}{\$59,000/5}$$

$$\text{ARR} = \frac{\$7,161}{\$11,800} = 60.69\%$$

3.4 Net-Present-Value Method (NPV)

As shown in Table 21.8, NPV, is one of two methods that consider discounted cash flows. Essentially, NPV is the difference between the discounted cash inflows and the discounted cash outflows.

The first step for using this technique is to determine the difference between the cash flowing into the project (revenues or savings) and the cash flowing out (initial investment and operating costs) over the life of the investment.

Next, the net cash flow is then discounted at a given rate, usually the cost of capital, to determine the present values of that money. The sum of the present values is compared to the initial cost of the investment to determine

Table 21.8. Net-Present-Value Method (NPV)

	Cash Flow	×	Present Value Factors[a]	=	Present Value of Future Cash Flow
Year 1	$20,608		0.91		$18,735
Year 2	20,020		0.83		$16,545
Year 3	24,408		0.75		$18,338
Year 4	13,780		0.68		$9,412
Year 5	15,990		0.62		$9,929
Total present value of future cash flows					$72,959
Total investment required					59,000
Net present value (positive)					$13,959

[a] Factors calculated from NPV tables at $n = 5$, $i = 10\%$

which is greater. If the present values are greater than the initial cost (NPV is positive), then the project is acceptable.

Notice that depreciation is not deducted from future cash flows. Depreciation is important for computing net income for financial statement purposes, but it is not relevant for cash flows. Discounted cash flow methods automatically provide for return of the original investment, thus making the depreciation deduction unnecessary.

In the example of Table 21.8, the NPV is indeed positive. But the future cash flows show a far greater return than the 10 percent cost of capital. A much higher rate of return must be in the offering. And to determine the exact rate of return, a more precise calculation is necessary.

3.5 Time-Adjusted Rate-of-Return Method (TARR)

Time-adjusted rate of return, in Table 21.9, is the second method that considers discounted cash flows. TARR is the true interest yield predicted by an investment over its useful life. It is also frequently referred to as the internal rate of return (IRR).

> It can be computed by finding that discount rate which will equate the present value of the investment (cash outflows) required by a project, with the present value of the returns (cash inflows) that the project promises. In other words, the time adjusted rate of return is that discount rate which will cause the net present value of a project to be equal to zero (2).

The TARR calculated in Table 21.9 was obtained using a personal computer and a spreadsheet software program. However, the same result can be computed on a small business calculator. If future cash flows are even, that is, the same in each period, then the calculations are performed easily. If the

Table 21.9. Time-Adjusted Rate-of-Return (TARR) or Internal Rate-of-Return (IRR) Method

	Cash Flow	×	Present Value Factors at 19.4%	=	Present Value of Future Cash Flow
Year 1	$20,608		0.84		$17,260
Year 2	20,020		0.70		$14,043
Year 3	24,408		0.59		$14,339
Year 4	13,780		0.49		$6,780
Year 5	15,990		0.41		$6,589
Total present value of future cash flows					$59,011
Total Investment required					59,000
Net present value (positive)					$11

Therefore: actual rate of return is slightly more than 19.4%

cash flows are uneven, then a trial-and-error process is necessary to arrive at an NPV equal to zero.

In either case, if the TARR is compared to the organization's cost of capital and found to be greater, then the project is acceptable.

When working with discounted cash flows, there are two major assumptions that must be dealt with. The first is that all of the cash flows must occur at the end of a period. Even though this is rarely the case, this assumption helps to simplify calculations.

Second, all cash flows generated by an investment project are immediately reinvested in another project that will yield a rate of return as large as the first project. Unless these terms are met, the return computed for the first project will not be accurate.

4 CAPITAL BUDGET PROCEDURES

A request to spend capital must be a document that clearly describes, in a logical fashion, the project being recommended. It must include all the key factors in the proposal, both pro and con. It must be as realistic as possible and should not contain any dressing up statements that try to hide evidence of a marginal investment.

Most organizations have a systematic procedure in place for preparing and submitting capital budget proposals. The following steps are suggested as a guide in this process.

First, define in concise terms what the project is intended to accomplish. State the overall time frame for the budget and what the funds will specifically provide.

Second, gather all the cost data from the supplier(s) and state the initial costs, and any future costs, that will occur due to requirements of the project.

Third, determine the financial benefits of the project over its life time. Describe in detail what additional revenues will be received or what cost savings will occur.

Fourth, present alternative actions that could be taken and why this project was chosen. Remember that "to do nothing" is also an alternative course of action that should be addressed.

Finally, present the financial data justifying the project, with all the calculations used to evaluate the investment. Submit the proposal and be prepared to defend it. Table 21.10 provides some appropriate guidelines that can prove useful in the preparation of a capital budget request (3, p. 365).

5 SUMMARY AND RECOMMENDATIONS

The operating budgets discussed in this chapter were presented because of their utility and popularity. When used under the appropriate circumstances,

Table 21.10. Guidelines for Preparing a Request

1. Consider the knowledge of the reader
2. Make the story complete
3. Put the story in proper prospective
4. Analyze the alternatives
5. Identify and evaluate all the risks
6. Provide estimates on a comparative basis
7. Evaluate the financial projections
8. Avoid defending a project as absolutely necessary
9. Limit the length of the proposal
10. Be specific

all of these techniques can yield a budget that will help the manager perform the planning, directing, and controlling activities required.

For the first-time manager, however, the zero-based budgeting concept is recommended. Providing a firm financial basis for the industrial hygiene program is very important. After the initial budget has been devised using this procedure, the traditional budgeting concept can be employed for the routine submissions of the next 3–5 years. Thereafter, and on a periodic basis, the program budgeting technique should be the management tool.

Capital budgets require much time and effort if successful submissions are expected. The financial evaluation techniques presented have varying degrees of popularity in business. Table 21.11 indicates the results of a survey conducted on the effectiveness of capital budgeting techniques in practice (4).

The selection of a specific method depends on the technique preferred by the organization and the availability of financial data connected with the project. The critical element in the process is to obtain reliable cash flow estimates.

Usually, the shorter the payback period, the higher the accounting rate of return; the higher the return on initial investment, the higher the net present value; and the higher the time-adjusted rate of return, the more desirable the project. The recommended procedure most often cited, given the availability of the necessary financial data, is to use all of the methods presented.

Table 21.11. Capital Budgeting Techniques Employed by Sample of U.S. Corporations

Technique Used	Number	Percentage
Payback period	164	58
Time-adjusted rate of return	172	61
Net present value	94	33
Rate of return on initial investment	95	33
Rate of return on average investment	78	27
Total companies surveyed	284	

REFERENCES

1. L. M. Cheek, *Zero-Base Budgeting Comes of Age: What It Is and What It Takes To Make It Work,* New York: AMACOM, 1977, pp. 10, 12.

2. R. H. Garrison, *Managerial Accounting: Concepts for Planning, Control, Decision Making,* Dallas: Business Publications, 1979, p. 536.

3. S. S. Singhvi, "The Capital Investment Budgeting Process," in H. W. Allen Sweeney and R. Rachlin (eds.), *The Handbook of Budgeting,* New York: Wiley, 1981, pp. 345, 365.

4. G. H. Petry, Effective Use of Capital Budgeting Tools, *Business Horizons,* October, 58 (1975).

GENERAL REFERENCES

Bogen, J. I., *Financial Handbook,* 4th ed., New York: Wiley, 1964.

Brealey, R., and S. Myers, *Principles of Corporate Finance,* 2nd ed. New York: McGraw-Hill, 1984.

Byrd, D. B., and S. D. Byrd, Deciding to Purchase a Computer: A Capital Budgeting Decision, *National Public Accountant,* May, 18–23 (1986).

Hitch, C. J., Program Budgeting, *Datamation,* September (1967).

Iwaskow, W. B., "Program Budgeting: Planning, Programming, Budgeting," in H. W. Allen Sweeney and R. Rachlin (Eds), *The Handbook of Budgeting,* New York: Wiley, 1981, p. 696.

Jacoby, J. A., Successful Budgeting of the Industrial Hygiene Program, paper given at the American Industrial Hygiene Conference, Detroit, May, 1984.

Jones, R. L., and H. G. Trentin, "Budgeting: Key to Planning and Control," *American Management Association,* rev. ed., Saranac Lake, NY: American Management Association, 1971.

Matthews, L. M., *Practical Operating Budgeting,* New York: McGraw-Hill, 1977.

McMichael, J. H., and C. A. Polsky, "How to Prepare and Utilize Budgets as a Managerial Decision-making Tool," *J. K. Lasser's Business Management Handbook,* 3rd ed., New York: McGraw-Hill, 1968.

Rege, U. P., Planned Incremental Package Evaluation System, *Financial Accountability & Management,* Spring, 25–34 (1986).

Schwarz, H. W., "Budgeting and the Managerial Process," in H. W. Allen Sweeney and R. Rachlin (eds.), *The Handbook of Budgeting,* New York: Wiley, 1981, p. 1.

Singhvi, S. S., "The Capital Expenditure Evaluation Methods," in H. W. Allen Sweeney and R. Rachlin, (eds.), *The Handbook of Budgeting,* New York: Wiley, 1981, p. 373.

Torgerson, P. A., and I. T. Weinstock, *Management: An Integrated Approach,* Englewood Cliffs, NJ: Prentice-Hall, 1972.

Welsch, G. A., *Budgeting: Profit Planning and Control,* 4th ed., Prentice-Hall, Englewood Cliffs, NJ, 1976.

Index